Chasing I
Losing a Child

Jan Andersen

From the moment that we are conceived, death is chasing us. Some of us gamble with our lives by engaging in dangerous pursuits as though we are inviting death to come and grab us, but whilst most of us will keep running from it until it catches us, some chase it, knowing that when they have caught it, their misery will cease.

Jan Andersen

Perfect Publishers Ltd

Copyright © Jan Andersen 2009

All rights reserved. No part of this publication may be reproduced, stored in a retrieval system or transmitted in any form or by any means, electronic, mechanical, audio, visual or otherwise, without prior written permission of the copyright owner. Nor can it be circulated in any form of binding or cover other than that in which it is published and without similar conditions including this condition being imposed on the subsequent purchaser.

Second edition, November 2011

ISBN 978-1-905399-44-4

Cover design by Duncan Bamford
http://www.insightillustration.co.uk

Cover photography by Mike Horton
mike.propergander@googlemail.com

Design conceived by Jan Andersen
http://www.creativecopywriter.org

Proofread by Debora Pellegrin
debpellegrin@yahoo.com

PERFECT PUBLISHERS LTD
23 Maitland Avenue
Cambridge
CB4 1TA
England
http://www.perfectpublishers.co.uk

The Book Cover Explained

From the moment I began writing this book in November 2002, I also began thinking about the book cover. I thought of many images, but none seemed quite right. Then, one day, as I was walking through an interactive museum of science, I noticed a large white hand that had been painted on the floor. In that instant, I saw the front cover of the book. The hand was so symbolic to suicide, because when someone ends his life, he dies by his own hand. The hand on the cover is actually that of my daughter Anneliese.

The autumn leaves signify the end of one's current life and the season in which I lost my son. Although the image of the apparently lifeless hand amongst the leaves may appear disturbing to some, it was important that the cover evoked some of the shock that accompanies the loss of a child to suicide.

The Book Title Explained

The meaning of the title, Chasing Death, is twofold. The title first came to me when I was thinking about all the misguided souls who end up using heroin. One of the methods used is called "chasing the dragon" whereby users inhale the heroin vapours after it has been heated and placed on a piece of foil. It occurred to me that what users are actually doing is chasing death. The second meaning, also described on the title page, refers to the way in which the suicidal pursue death rather than avoid it.

Dedication

To Kristian,
Always in our hearts and our minds. Your soul lives on and continues to help others.
With so much love and gratitude,
Mum
xxxx

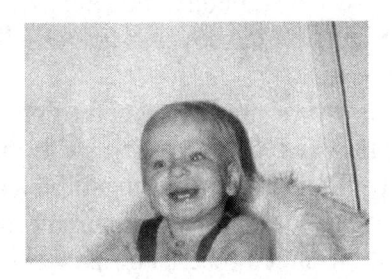

"Such a happy lad"

Acknowledgements

I would like to extend my deepest gratitude to all those bereaved families who were brave enough to open up their hearts and share their personal and poignant stories with me. I hope that, in some small way, this has been a cathartic experience.

I thank my partner, children and close friends for their unfailing support and understanding in the aftermath of Kristian's suicide. In particular, I would like to thank my partner's eldest sister Jo and my dear friend Rae, who did not hesitate in dropping everything to come to the hospital to be with me on 1 November 2002. Many thanks also to my friend and neighbour Kerry, who took charge of Lauren on that tragic day. I am also grateful to all those newfound friends around the world with whom I have connected through shared tragedy.

Thanks go to Sue Scott (was Neill), the nurse who supported me on the day of Kristian's passing and Deborah Rees, both of whom very kindly contributed to Chapter Nineteen, Professional Views.

I would like to thank all the medical staff who did their best to try and save Kristian's life and the police officer, Brian Sansum, who broke the tragic news and dealt with the case thereafter. I appreciate your sensitivity and diplomacy in a situation that must have been terribly difficult for everyone concerned.

Many thanks to Mike Horton, the photographer who was responsible for the striking images on the book cover.

I thank Kristian's girlfriend Millie and all of Kristian's dear friends who accepted him for the person he was; all his friends from his childhood and all those who knew him in his latter years.

To my spiritual sister, Angela, who very kindly wrote the Foreword for this book and proofread the book for the first time; I am so grateful for our connection and the fact that we linked up at exactly the right time. Although you never knew Kristian on the physical plane, I know that you have come to know him in the spiritual world.

To my dear friend Deborah, I thank you for all the laughs that we share on a regular basis via our email communication and for your skill in proofreading the final copy of this book.

Thank you to my publisher and friend, Shahida, with whom it has always been an absolute joy to work.

Finally, I thank my Spiritual Guides, Angels and Ascended Masters whose advice and timing has always been accurate, even when I have questioned it. Patience truly is a virtue.

About the Author

Jan Andersen has been a professional freelance writer, copywriter, author and editor since 1999, before which she had pursued a marketing and PR career spanning 21 years, between giving birth to four children.

She has participated in numerous national and international radio and TV programmes as a result of her websites and written work.

Jan has an impressive portfolio of skills, which includes writing lesson plans, dissertations, research papers, presentations, marketing material and commercial copy for a broad spectrum of industries. She also edits, formats and proofreads books and film scripts for other authors. Jan's follow-up book, Kristian's Heaven, channels words of comfort from the spirit world in order to answer some of the questions that plague the minds of suicide survivors.

Jan also owns and runs several websites single-handedly, all of which she also designed, including the world's premier resource for older mothers, Mothers Over 40 (http://www.mothersover40.com), Child Suicide (http://www.childsuicide.org), a supportive resource for families who have lost a child to suicide and Jan Andersen Writing Services (http://www.creativecopywriter.org), which is Jan's personal business site.

Jan lives in the UK with her partner and their daughter Lauren Erica.

Disclaimer

All personal events contained within this book are true. However, some names have been changed or omitted.

The names of many of the people mentioned in this book have been changed upon request to protect their identities, namely those families who have been kind enough and brave enough to share their heartrending personal stories with the author. Some circumstances have also been changed or omitted for the same reason.

The author does not take responsibility for the opinions expressed by anyone else in this book, but is committed to protecting the privacy of those mentioned within the book.

The author does not take legal responsibility if anyone mentioned within the book voluntarily chooses to reveal their identity, or if any other individuals choose to reveal the identity of anyone mentioned herein to the media or otherwise. Indeed, if anyone recognises themselves from the actions described within this book, then that in itself is an admission of culpability.

In addition, any outside source, whether an individual or media source, takes full responsibility for the accuracy, timeliness and nature of anything said or published following the publication of this book. Neither the author of this book, or the publisher take responsibility for anything said, claimed or published by a third party following the publication of this book.

No material from this book may be copied, reproduced, republished, uploaded, posted, transmitted, quoted, or distributed in any way without the express permission of the author of this book.

Foreword

by Angela

What an honour to write the foreword to something of such magnitude, and yet how does one find the words? As you read this book, you will likely understand the feeling that I have of wanting to dispense with words and search for a more meaningful vehicle through which to convey thoughts and feelings.

Fate intertwined the worlds of myself and Jan at a perfect moment and I recognised a soul sister, a connection that transcends our physical world; a connection through which I am truly blessed to be able to meet with both the energies of Jan and Kristian.

I will not add my comments about the book, as I believe it shall speak very differently to each soul who reads it. Suffice to say, it stands as an embodiment of love that needs no introduction.

It is the future pathways of which I can underscore a solid feeling that so many souls will be thrown some hope and some light by the work of Jan and her beautiful son, Kristian. Together, they are and will continue to be angels, working for others so that their paths may be a little easier to bear: Jan in this world and Kristian so close by her side in the next.

To those who flounder like me when faced with the desire to show support, but do not know how in such devastating circumstances, I can only offer the advice to open your heart. Our energetic links to each other, our brothers and sisters on earth and beyond, offer much untapped knowledge - a divine and instinctive soul knowing of what to do - and power. And the greatest power of all, is the power of love.

Words from the other side:

To Mum,
In strength, you feel my hand on your shoulder,
In sadness, you feel what might have been,
In joy, you feel my love surround you,
In despair, I know you wish I was there.

In the past, you remember with fondness and pain,
In the present, you live with me again.
Though I may not be able to kiss your cheek,
I blow them into your heart through the air that you breathe.

Every second I love you and will you to smile
As you remember our lives together for a while.
In the future I shall walk forever by your side
As we climb the mountains and push back the tide.

- Kristian Mikhail Andersen

Another candle lit my world the day I found you, Jan.

With love,
Angela
http://angelajanegrace.com

Table of Contents

Chapter	Title	Page No
Disclaimer		viii
Foreword	by Angela	ix
Introduction		xiii
Chapter 1	Kristian's Story	1
Chapter 2	The Shock, The Disbelief, The Horror	53
Chapter 3	Rewriting the Script	85
Chapter 4	Trapped in a Storm of Agonising Emotions	105
	Listen and Learn – A song for Kristian by Carsten	132
Chapter 5	Wearing a Mask	133
Chapter 6	Resisting or Craving Physical Contact	147
Chapter 7	Grieving in Your Own Way and Your Own Time	155
	What Size is Grief? Andrea Corrie	177
Chapter 8	Referring to Your Child as "The Body"	181
Chapter 9	The Day of the Funeral and After	187
Chapter 10	The Family's Grief	215
Chapter 11	Bizarre Thoughts, Actions and Secrets	243

Chapter 12	Memory Triggers: Sights, Sounds, Smells and Possessions	259
Chapter 13	The Inquest	273
Chapter 14	Handling Insensitivity from Others	285
Chapter 15	Firsts of Everything	319
Chapter 16	The Domino Effect: Is Suicide Contagious?	335
Chapter 17	Refocusing Your Energies on the Living	345
Chapter 18	Dispelling Suicide Myths	359
Chapter 19	Professional Views	373
Chapter 20	Life After Death	381
Chapter 21	Coping Strategies	397
Chapter 22	The Years Ahead	411
Chapter 23	Inspirational Thoughts	441
Chapter 24	Recommended Books and Resources	449
	Conclusion	455
	My Brother Kristian by Lauren Erica	456
	A Million Miles Away by Lauren Erica	457
	The White Dove Project	459

Introduction

Give sorrow words. Grief has need to speak, lest whisper the o'er fraught heart and bid it break.

William Shakespeare (Macbeth)

The moment that I learned of my 20-year-old son Kristian's suicide, the foundations of my life and all that I had regarded as stable crumbled into a million irreparable pieces. In that instant, I realised that the only guarantee in life is death of the physical body. The line separating this life and the next is so fragile that any one of us could slip over at any time. Eventually we all step across that line. The physical body and how we look after it is important, because it is a vehicle for the soul in its journey on earth.

Research shows that not only does the grief of parents last longer, but is more intense than any other. The intensity is further increased if the death was sudden, but even more so, death by suicide places overwhelming and terminal anguish on the surviving parents. If the death was totally unexpected, with no previous "signs" that may have been evident in someone suffering from a mental or physical illness, the grieving process becomes more complex and distressing, as the surviving families desperately struggle to understand the loss.

Far from being an act of cowardice, ending your life to alleviate your misery takes a huge amount of courage. People who have never felt suicidal themselves cannot possibly judge those who have. Some people may brand suicide victims as selfish and yet there is no doubt that many of them take their own lives as an act of selflessness, believing that they are relieving others of the burden of caring for someone who is terminally depressed, or worrying about someone who has seemingly insurmountable problems.

Looking back to a period in my life when I was suffering from deep depression, I felt as though I was trapped at the top of a burning skyscraper, with every floor below me ablaze and every possible escape route blocked off. There were two choices; either I could jump to my death out of the window, or I could remain where I was and be consumed by noxious fumes and flames. In my tortured mind there was no way out. My only chance would be for someone to rescue me. At the time, I was trapped in a very unhappy marriage and I felt that I was not in control of my own destiny. I could end my life, or remain where I was and be destroyed by ongoing mental abuse. I was waiting for someone to rescue me, even though I knew that this went against all my spiritual learnings and beliefs, for I had to want to help myself.

Thankfully, I found the courage I needed to break away and carry on. My marriage ended and hope reappeared on the immediate horizon. I realised then that most people find reasons for not doing things and say, "I can't, because..." instead of "I can and I will". Maybe I was not in control of the challenges that presented themselves, but I was certainly in control of how I dealt with them. However, I realised that my depression was circumstantial, not clinical, so I was able to take action to remedy the situation. Not everyone feels able to do that.

Someone told me that suicide is the abandonment of all hope. No one truly wants to die, unless they can see no alternative to ending their pain. When all other options appear to have been exhausted, suicide emerges as the only escape from the misery.

When my son died, I wanted to die. I was caught in an undercurrent of frightening and unbearably painful grief, the enormity of which is impossible to describe in the limited words that exist in the English language. I was thrown violently around, in danger of being sucked under and drowning.

I am confined to repeatedly using words such as excruciating, crucifying, crushing, overwhelming, torment, anguish, devastating, horrifying, shattering, shock, disbelief and so on. There is a need for a new set of words to be created to describe the depths of emotions that cannot adequately be conveyed using words that currently exist. Undoubtedly, if such words existed, they would inevitably be misused; the equivalent to people calling a normal headache a migraine, or saying they have the flu when it is just a common cold.

As time moved on, I desperately searched for something to grab hold of to lift me from the vortex and provide temporary relief. I would briefly catch my breath before the smallest trigger would force me to release my grip and allow the whirlpool to drag me mercilessly back in.

The whirlpool soon changed to a fast-moving river that carried me along the grieving journey. At more frequent intervals, I was able to reach out and grasp a lifeline that would partially pull me from the raging torrent and allow me to achieve something positive. When the river swelled, I was in danger of totally submitting to the violent flow, but instead of allowing myself to be hauled back in, I would find another safety line to regain control.

Very shortly after Kristian's death, I began seeking online support groups and forums for bereaved families. I needed to communicate with others who had lost a child in such a tragic manner. I searched persistently for information and research on depression and suicide. I bought and read many books.

What I discovered was that the stigma and lack of understanding surrounding suicide confined many grieving families to a world of silent, relentless torture. The fear of harsh judgement and cruel comments based on ignorance and lack of education imprisoned bereaved families within a cramped cell of inescapable emotional trauma.

The most effective form of counselling that they could find was through reading about and talking to other people who had endured the same tragic loss. Those who did not feel ready to share their feelings publicly, or even on a one-to-one basis, needed a resource that could be visited anonymously, or read and digested in their own time. My greatest comfort came from both reading personal experiences of others who had lost a child to suicide and communicating with bereaved parents, grandparents and siblings.

Most of the grief recovery books I read were remote and academic. There were a couple of excellent books, but nevertheless there was still a huge gap in the market for more sensitive and realistic resources for suicide grievers.

I have always believed that something positive has to emerge from every tragedy and I certainly did not want my son to have died in vain. The legacy left by Kristian's suicide was one of love, compassion and a desire to help others. I felt an insatiable urge to offer support to other bereaved families, to raise awareness of depression and suicide and to do whatever I possibly could to help prevent the same tragedy striking someone else. Every time I read about yet another suicide, my heart breaks for those families.

The best way to honour my son would be to do my best to help the thousands and possibly millions of young troubled people around the world who were still alive and in desperate need of support and understanding, not unfair judgement and ostracism. I thought of all those people as being my own family. I knew that they had their own paths to tread and their own lessons to learn, but whilst I could not learn their lessons for them, I could help them to help themselves by providing the words of comfort and the resources that they needed.

Within a couple of months of Kristian's cruel departure from this world, I established the Child Suicide website. It was a site that I felt had to be an all-encompassing resource for bereaved families, young people seeking help and parents seeking help for their children. It would also be an informative resource for people who were acquainted with someone who had been bereaved by suicide, helping them to respond more effectively to a griever's sorrow. It would be a place where families could honour and remember their children, grandchildren and siblings by enabling them to share photos, mementoes, poems and stories and to link to any personal pages that had been created as a tribute to their loved ones.

Within a few weeks, the website was attracting thousands of visitors from around the world. The response was overwhelming and it felt as though a central meeting room had been created for the members of a secret club. Until this point, no one realised that there were so many members. It made a mockery of official suicide statistics and revealed a phenomenon that was reaching epidemic proportions.

I began writing this book very shortly after the tragedy. It was important to be able to write truly from the heart as and when I was experiencing the full force of the emotions. It would have been easy to complete the book within a few months, but I knew that I also had to be in the position of being able to write from the perspective of a bereaved parent several years down the grieving road. The book would be of no help to anyone if I could not relay coping strategies that allowed me to carry on living, which may also encourage others to channel their grief in constructive ways. Therefore, it took six and a half years to finally complete this book.

I consulted my spiritual guides and archangels many times as I was writing, in particular when I was conveying Kristian's story in Chapter One. I agonised over several of the incidents that I relayed, considering the controversy they might cause, or disapproval from those about whom I was writing. There were occasions where I removed some of these parts, but then my guides and my own conscience informed me that I would be doing Kristian a disservice if I did not mention them, for they were pivotal to his story and the way that he felt about himself. Without mentioning them, his story would not be complete. It is my duty to tell Kristian's story, not to seek justice for all those who inflicted misery upon my son, but to give a complete picture.

I do not regret a single thing that I have written, for it is the truth. I cannot lie and conceal, because this would go against my spiritual beliefs and my own conscience. Above all, it is for my son that I have been open and honest.

Many of the situations that Kristian encountered and experiences that he endured tested his character and fortitude. It was important to include these experiences to provide true examples of Kristian as a person, rather than simply use my words as a doting mother; words that one would expect any mother would use when describing a beloved child. To me, evidence and anecdotes are important, because they allow the reader to judge for themselves and form their own picture, rather than allowing me to create the vision that I would like them to see. It may also help others who can relate these experiences to their own situation and know that they and their children are not the only ones who have suffered in this way. It may not remove the pain, but it offers some sort of relief in knowing that there are others who have also trodden this challenging path.

My son had his flaws, as we all do. I have not put him on a pedestal just because he is no longer with us on the earth plane. He was a normal person with an extraordinary capacity to love and forgive and that is how I hope all who knew him will remember him.

Chapter One

Kristian's Story

I want my son to be judged by the person that he was, not the way in which he died.

Jan Andersen

His hand was pale, with a youthful plumpness and soft, dimpled knuckles like a baby's and yet he was 20-years-old; my "special little boy" as I had always referred to him as a toddler. As I slipped my hand into his and stroked his flawless, satiny skin, his fingers seemed to curl around mine in a reciprocal gesture of affection. I pleaded with him to open his eyes and speak to me, to tell me that it was all some sick joke, devised as a test of my love for him, but he didn't respond.

Apart from his head and left arm, the rest of his body was covered neatly in a blue, latticed hospital blanket, identical to the one in which the midwife had swaddled him on the day he was born. This time, however, he was motionless. He was lying on his back with his eyes closed, concealing the striking emerald irises that were always emphasised by enviably long, dark lashes curling over his eyelids. His full and slightly parted lips looked as though they had been airbrushed with pale blue powder, as did his cute little ears, which still had the same characteristic kink in the top as they had when he was a tiny baby. His nail beds were also blue and his neck was flushed purple, which alarmed me, but about which I asked no questions. I presumed that this was due to cyanosis, caused by lack of oxygen in his blood. At that point, however, questions like that seemed pointless.

His short, neat hair looked as though it had recently been tinted dark red and my fingers glided through it with ease as I stroked his crown repeatedly. Why, Kristian, my darling little boy, why?

He looked more peaceful than I had ever seen him, but I desperately wanted him to wake up. I spoke to him softly through my sobs, telling him how sorry I was, how much I loved him and asking over and over again, "Why?"

I tormented myself with memories of moments when intense frustration had provoked me to shout at him and tell him that if he didn't buck up his ideas, he would have no chance in life. How I wished I had been more tolerant. I thought about the many times when I had succumbed to his pleas against my better judgement. How I wish I'd been less lenient. How I wished I'd done so many things that I thought could wait because I had assumed there would "always be tomorrow". However, most of what I did, I did because I loved him, not because I didn't care. Like most parents, I wanted him to lead a good, honest life, based on moral values.

With all due respect to Kristian's biological father, he rejected me almost from the time that I announced my pregnancy, although in no way do I blame him, or feel resentful for his initial reaction and subsequent attitude towards me. Whether this rejection was based upon fear, or because it would impact his personal and social life, I did not know. All I recall is the shock on his face and the dramatic change in his behaviour towards me from the moment I told him the news. He tried in vain to make me agree to an abortion. This I refused; a decision that resulted in having to travel alone on the nine-month long path towards Kristian's birth. His father appeared again briefly in my life when I was around six months' pregnant and told me how he admired me for my strength and determination to proceed with my pregnancy alone.

When I first announced my pregnancy to my mother, she said, "Of course, you'll have to have an abortion." This was not an option for me. Earlier that year, I had endured a traumatic rape and had become pregnant as a result, just a few months after returning from Sweden to my parents' home. Not only had my plan been to return to Stockholm, but I could not even comprehend the notion of raising a baby conceived via rape, so the pregnancy was terminated without a second thought, a decision that has plagued me with tremendous guilt and distress ever since. I always believed that I would be punished for my "crime" and my initial thoughts were that I would either discover that I couldn't have any more children, or that I would lose a child.

I desperately wanted my baby, whatever the personal consequences. He would be cared for and loved and raised to the absolute best of my ability. Almost from the moment of conception, I knew that I was carrying a boy and always referred to my baby as "he".

I can hear people asking what on earth I was thinking, becoming pregnant so soon after my previous experience, but the truth is that I wanted a baby, not just to assuage my guilt for the previous termination, but because prior to conceiving, my son's father had also expressed his desire to become a dad. In my mind, it was a joint decision and it was only after the pregnancy was confirmed that his attitude changed.

When I informed my mother that I was going to keep my baby, she told me that I would not be able to live at home and asked what I thought I was going to do. I told her that, if necessary, I would move into a mother and baby home. Her prime concern, I felt, was what other people would think, having been socially conditioned to believe that image and status were of prime importance, rather than my wellbeing and that of my baby.

A grandchild born to her unmarried daughter did not fit neatly into the perfect social image, so in her mind, the solution was simple and would spare any awkward questions asked by others.

"I felt so embarrassed having to tell people that I had an unmarried daughter who was expecting a baby," she told me one morning after she'd attended one of my father's business functions the evening before. She wanted to be able to tell people that she had a successful daughter pursuing a high-flying career, because she felt that would have been a better reflection on the family.

Through all this, my father remained silent, whilst my mother constantly reminded me that there was no way my father would tolerate a screaming baby in the house. In fact, when she eventually told him that I was pregnant, his response was, "I'm not really surprised."

For the next three months, I endured severe sickness, exacerbated by the stress of the rejection and emotional isolation that I felt. During the fourth month of pregnancy, I travelled down to stay with an old friend who had been my soul mate during my first year at college, before his family moved to another part of the country. Time spent with my friend and his family was always so therapeutic, not least because they were all very spiritual and there was such a tranquil ambience in their home.

Nevertheless, I still harboured a deep sense of emotional turbulence. How would I cope with a baby on my own? How would I provide for him? Would he be healthy? What would I do if something were to go wrong? How would I meet people? How could I enter into another relationship? Who would be prepared to accept me with a child? Was I being selfish bringing a child into the world without a father?

My spiritual side tried to offer reassurance by telling me that Kristian had chosen to incarnate through me as his mother and that I should not let my conscious fears control my thoughts. It was as though I was having an internal battle with myself and my higher self.

On the day that I left my friend's house, I could not bear the thought of leaving my secure, spiritual shell and returning home to silent hostility and verbal disapproval, so I decided to buy a train ticket to visit my paternal grandmother.

What started out as a few more days' respite with a relative whom I regarded as one of my best friends, extended into a five-week stay as the result of a frightening experience that occurred one morning when I visited the bathroom. I noticed that I had lost some blood; not much, but enough to frighten me. I went downstairs immediately, shaking and crying, to tell my gran. She laid a blanket over me on the sofa and called the doctor. "You know," she said, "I reckon you're going to lose this baby". Little did I realise then that I would lose him, but not until over twenty years later.

My baby seemed unperturbed by the drama and clung to his internal incubator, continuing to be nurtured and protected from the outside world until 10 days past his due date. I experienced two more minor bleeds, which were later diagnosed as a symptom of a cervical erosion, a common occurrence in pregnancy that was apparently nothing to worry about.

When my mother heard of the first scare, she telephoned my gran to say that she had arranged for me to attend antenatal classes when I returned home. I remember saying to my gran, "But she doesn't want me to have this baby." My gran, in her ever-consoling manner, assured me that my mum would never throw me out and that she seemed to be preparing for the arrival of her first grandchild.

When I finally returned home, I felt emotionally isolated in a world where it appeared to me as though all pregnant women were being fussed over and protected by loving husbands and partners. On many occasions, I would lay on the bed in the spare room that would become my baby's bedroom, stroking my belly and talking to my son, telling him how special he was and how much I loved him. In the next room, I could hear my brother telling his fiancée how much he loved her. Rivulets of tears would roll from the outer corners of my eyes and trickle into my ears and hair. I felt so alone. There were just the two of us, silently bonding. I felt overwhelming adoration for my baby and even though I could not see him, his vigorous kicks and the curve of my belly were a sign of the special new life being nourished within me.

During my sixth month of pregnancy, I bumped into an acquaintance of my son's father whilst on a shopping trip. When she enquired about my purchases and asked me whether I'd bought anything nice for myself, I remember telling her that I had only bought clothes and accessories for my baby, since I felt guilty spending money on myself. This lady already had teenage children and her advice to me was, "Spoil yourself now, because your kids won't appreciate what you sacrificed for them until they're adults with families of their own." I never realised then that my son would make the greatest sacrifice of all; his own life.

During the same month, Kristian's father telephoned me and asked me to meet him. He admitted that whilst my pregnancy had been a shock initially, he now felt differently about the situation and would like to meet up. I had already adjusted to the idea of raising my son single-handedly and had moved away from that uncertain, vulnerable place where I could have fallen so easily back into the arms of someone who could never offer me the stability I was seeking.

However, I would still have preferred to be part of a couple than on my own, but although it was easy to allow my hormones to let my head take control, my heart told me that I was better off alone than in an unsatisfactory relationship.

How could I ever entertain a long-term relationship with someone who had wanted me to kill our child? I knew that he had come into my life for a reason and I hoped that over the period we had been together, I had in some way taught him something or helped him, because I felt that my soul purpose in this incarnation on the earth plane was to teach, not just to gain knowledge.

We met on a sub-zero, but beautiful December day when a layer of fresh snow blanketed the ground and covered roofs and trees like the most perfect cake icing. We rarely experienced snow that settled and it created a magical ambience. However, the snow concealed more sinister ice beneath, which forced me to cling reluctantly to Kristian's father's arm for support like a frail, elderly lady. I hated displaying any signs of vulnerability, which somehow tarnished the independent, confident disguise that I was desperate to exude.

He took me to a park café on the outskirts of a nearby town, a place with which I was unfamiliar. The café was like a magnified version of the summer house in the Sound of Music, although I was in no condition to start leaping around singing, "I am 16, going on 17". 16 or 17 stone maybe, or at least that's how I felt. It was beautiful and romantic, but the only element that was missing was a devoted father-to-be who felt truly passionately about the baby and me and who would nurture us tirelessly.

His attitude seemed to have changed, but I still had doubts about re-embarking on a relationship based on such rocky foundations. Did I really want to share my life and my baby's life with a man who had wanted to have his own child mercilessly ripped from its life support?

What would happen when the baby screamed all night and he realised that his responsibilities extended beyond ordering the next round in the pub?

Over a hot cappuccino in the "summer house", Kristian's father expressed his admiration at my strength and determination to go ahead with the pregnancy alone, despite the enormous pressure that he had placed upon me in the beginning. For a brief moment I felt proud, but then experienced great sadness for my son, knowing that he was going to begin his life without a doting father.

After that meeting, I had limited contact with Kristian's father. On occasions, I would visit him at his office, but we did not experience anything that could be remotely regarded as a relationship. Emotionally, it may have been more beneficial to me to have stayed away from him, but I was determined not to let him forget that he had a greater responsibility to honour. Whether or not he wanted to be part of our lives was irrelevant; he had helped to create a child and not only had to acknowledge this, but also had a duty to help support his son financially, if not emotionally. He had agreed to be present at the birth, but I wasn't convinced that he would turn up.

Kristian's expected date of delivery was Friday 12 March 1982. That day passed with no sign of an impending arrival, just the late emergence of wide, purple stretchmarks adorning my abdomen like an intricate railway system. These would be the legacy of the creation of my beautiful son, indelible scars that would remain for the rest of my life and serve as a reminder that he really had existed and brought so much pleasure in his short, but troubled life.

Several more days passed uneventfully and I was finally booked in for an induction on Monday 22 March 1982.

The evening before I was admitted, I laid out all of the adorable little clothes and booties that I had bought for my son. My heart ached for a tragedy that hadn't yet happened. I imagined the worst-case scenario. What if something went horribly wrong and I didn't bring my baby home with me?

I recalled what my gran had told me just a few months earlier when I was apprehensive about buying anything too soon. She relayed the story of a friend of hers who had lost two babies in the first few years of their lives. She said that the most painful thing to look at after their loss were the booties and shoes that they had previously worn. Shoes are more indicative of the life of an able-bodied child than any other item of clothing, because they show movement, with the scuffs and the way in which the sole has been worn down being individual to the child concerned.

I looked at the little booties and wept. What if my son never got to wear them in life? What if I never got to dress him or bathe him, or watch him grow into a little person who was an exclusive blend of his parents? My fears barely touched on the reality of losing a child. In that moment, my heart broke for all those parents who had suffered miscarriages, or experienced the loss of a child in any way. I prayed that my baby would live and become strong and healthy.

At 8.30 the following morning, my mother despatched me to the maternity unit of the hospital where I was scheduled to deliver my son. It wasn't the closest hospital, but allegedly had the best maternity facilities. The admissions' nurse told my mother that because it was my first baby, delivery probably wouldn't occur for at least 12 hours. Even in the early 80s, the outdated idea of shaving the pubic area and giving the expectant mother an enema still prevailed. I recall being given a dry shave by an abrupt nurse, before having a suppository inserted with the dexterity of a butcher and being issued with instructions on waiting as long as possible before using the bathroom.

The process was uncomfortable, unpleasant and unnecessary, but who was I to argue? A 22-year-old single, first-time mum knew nothing in the eyes of the medical staff, although the procedures implemented seemed to be of more convenience to the midwifery staff than the poor mother.

I waited about five minutes before going to the bathroom with severe stomach cramps. When I returned to my room on the first-stage labour ward, I was told that once I had had the [1]Pitocin drip inserted into my hand to trigger labour, I would not be able to move. I was also linked up to the foetal heart rate monitor and felt as though I was strapped to a bed in a torture chamber, rather than relaxing in an environment that was favourable to giving birth as painlessly as possible.

I was left alone for long periods of time, with absolutely no sign of Kristian's father arriving to offer me support. The contractions very quickly became unbearably painful and I was concerned about the red light that kept appearing on the monitor to indicate that there could be a problem with the baby's heart rate. However, when I summoned the nurse, she banged the top of the monitor with her fist and tried to offer reassurance by stating that the machines were always playing up. What reassurance was that? That only added to my anxiety and made me wonder how they determined whether it was the machine at fault, or the baby who was in distress. She didn't bother listening to the baby's heart using any other method, but did say that if the baby moved it could affect the behaviour of the monitor. My fretfulness heightened with each contraction and each warning light on the monitor.

Three and a half hours after I had been admitted, I was suffering unbearably painful contractions every couple of minutes. When I called the nurse and told her that I felt a desire to push, she said, "Don't be silly dear. This is your first baby. You'll be in labour for hours yet."

I insisted that I wasn't imagining the feeling and when she then bothered to check the distance between the contractions and established that I was already 10 centimetres' dilated, she agreed that it was time to rush me to the delivery suite.

All I could think about was the pain and how much I wanted to push my baby out, so I did not feel I was in the right state of mind to consider whether I minded having a team of student midwives witnessing the birth. I recall a throng of uniformed figures and anonymous faces watching the farce of my son's birth. First they laid me on my back and then my side, which was extremely uncomfortable. When I requested that I move into a sitting position, I was instructed to remain on my side because it was "easier" for them. I just hope that their insensitive and archaic attitude has changed since.

Kristian's father arrived in the delivery suite at the crucial point, just before his first-born son entered the world.

I remember screaming that I wanted to push. Firstly, I was given permission to push and then I was told to stop, but the overwhelming and uncontrollable urge forced me to continue pushing. I remember Kristian's father yelling as I dug my nails into his hand. It only seemed like a few minutes before my son emerged, blue and with the umbilical cord wrapped around his neck. When I enquired after his wellbeing, the snappy riposte was a non-too-reassuring, "I don't know yet!"

My beautiful, blond-haired son was fine and had resumed a healthy pink colour when he was placed in my arms. I couldn't believe he was mine. I couldn't believe that he was the bump that I had carried wearily and proudly around for so many months. He didn't cry; he simply gazed in virgin curiosity at the new world around him.

I knew then that he was going to be an inquisitive little lad, not even considering that his curiosity would lead him down sinister paths.

For the five days that I was in hospital, I laughed, cried and spent hours just staring in wonderment at the little life that I had nurtured within me.

I remember the first day at home and the inadequacy that I felt as a mother. I was responsible for keeping this little person alive; so helpless, so needy and so beautiful. Overwhelmed by a continuous stream of curious visitors, I retreated to my bedroom with my baby and sobbed. Every part of my body ached and I was completely exhausted.

I did regret not having a proud partner on the scene to support me during the first few months and yet I knew that my son would fare better being raised by one, loving parent than by two who clearly didn't have a future together. I did not have to contend with a conflict of ideas on how best to raise my son and wanted him to grow up with the same values that all good parents instil into their children. I wanted my son to be a kind, unselfish, compassionate and well-mannered little boy who would always respect others' feelings. I am grateful that I at least had the opportunity to do that for him and that when he exited this world he left an indelible impression on others, an impression that led people to describe him as having "a heart of gold".

As a baby, Kristian went everywhere with me, even when I was socialising, and it was not often that I called upon my parents to babysit. In fact, since it was a situation that I had created for myself, I did not feel it was fair to burden my parents too often, although I know that they enjoyed their grandson immensely.

He was such a beautiful baby and I would spend so much time just kissing his marshmallow cheeks that were softer than the down of a baby bird.

There were few sights as beautiful and peaceful than that when my son was sleeping; so angelic, so innocent and so unbelievably perfect that I desperately feared anyone ever hurting him. He was my special little boy.

In June 1983, when Kristian was 15-months-old, my parents moved a couple of hundred miles away to a small village and since I did not feel this would be the right environment in which to raise Kristian because of the lack of available facilities, my paternal grandmother suggested that I move down to live with her.

My gran absolutely adored Kristian and at the time that we lived with her, her entire life revolved around her great grandson. I remember secretly dreading the day that I knew would be inevitable; the day when I felt could no longer be a burden upon my ageing gran and would move forward to a new life.

I idolised my gran. As a child, whenever I felt unhappy or lonely, I would cry myself to sleep worrying about what I would do if anything ever happened to her. Nevertheless, I still thought she would live forever. Her patience was endless. She never tired of my demands. If I'd already had sweets, she would still buy me an ice cream, much to the disgust of my mother. She never shouted at me, even when I filled my Wellington boots with water and twisted a comb around in my grandad's hair so tightly that it had to be cut free. She would exercise discipline with an enviable calmness that so many parents would wish to emulate, but never seem able to achieve in quite the same way. She spoilt me with love and I always wished that I could have given back to her all that she gave to me.

My gran had lived a relatively impoverished existence, but she never complained. She was always helping other people and running voluntary errands, always putting others' needs before her own.

She fostered a stream of difficult teenagers and continued to love and nurture them, even when they stole from her or were emotionally abusive. Many of them went on to lead happy and productive lives.

My biological grandad died of cancer at the age of 42, several years before I was born. My gran then re-married and I always regarded my step grandad as my "real" grandad. After Grandad had a stroke, my gran wheeled him around in a heavy, cumbersome wheelchair for the last ten years of his life; up and down kerbs and steps, twisting and manoeuvring until she was hot and exhausted and yet she never grumbled. The only time I ever heard her raise her voice was when people used to talk above Grandad's head, as though he were deaf. "How is he today?" they would ask. "Well, why don't you ask him yourself?" she would retort.

When my grandad died, she said, "I would rather have pushed him around in that wheelchair for another ten years than not have him with me."

When I reached my teenage years, we would sit and laugh together as my gran recounted hilarious tales of my childhood antics. She would remind me about the times when I used to come in from the garden with an interesting assortment of wildlife in my pockets and, in particular, the longest, fattest worms I could find. We shared a similar sense of humour and would double up laughing at the same comedy sketches on TV, the same unfortunate incidents that we witnessed in public and a variety of other situations that we both found equally amusing.

I used to skip my French A-Level classes and Russian History classes at college to go and visit my gran and help her in the old folks' home where she used to work. She used to say to me that if ever she ended up as batty and incapacitated as the old ladies in her care, would I shoot her?

We would often laugh at situations like that, ones that would otherwise make you cry unless you could see the humorous side. It was this quality of being able to laugh in the face of adversity that Kristian was fortunate enough to inherit.

My gran never judged me, even when I was pregnant with Kristian. When she took me under her wing in 1983, it seemed as though history was repeating itself when Kristian took her back to the halcyon days of hearing childish shrieks of excited laughter in the garden that was like a small child's wonderland. When I was very young, her garden appeared large and inviting, with an overgrown gooseberry bush at the end from which I would tirelessly pluck fruit from its overladen branches. As I grew taller, the garden grew smaller, but it was still magical to me and I could see in my son's eyes that he was visiting the same fantasyland that his mother had enjoyed many years before.

Kristian raced through the Kingdom of Toddlers like the Tasmanian Devil, whizzing curiously from one activity to the next, busy fingers probing curiously at everything around him, rarely sitting still, except to learn and recite, word-for-word, the pages from his favourite storybook; Goldilocks and The Three Bears. Surpassing all other interests was his obsession with cars and the same Thomas the Tank Engine video, which had been watched so many times over that it eventually developed a pirate copy fuzziness. His ceaseless chatter would ring in the ears of visitors long after they had departed, all marvelling at how delightful and advanced he was for his age.

He was a small boy with big dreams and his zest for life showed so much promise for the future that I never had any doubts that he would go far. However, he loved to be loved and would warm to anyone who spoke to him, even those who clearly had the potential to lead him in the wrong direction.

I feared that his good nature and desire to be accepted would allow him to be easily led when he was older, something that sadly came to pass.

One of my most vivid memories of the time that we lived with my gran, was Kristian's attachment to a little wooden chair that had belonged to my father when he was small. My gran had kept it and it had subsequently been used by all the other little people who had passed through her house over the years. It had been painted and re-painted and received a few knocks and gouges along the way, but still it remained almost perfectly intact. When my gran died, my father took possession of it and it now stands in his dining room. The pain of looking at that empty chair that holds with it so many memories of my gran and my son is crippling, but that same chair elicits happy memories that can make me smile through my tears.

When Kristian was 20-months-old, I was offered a full-time job at a local museum as the membership and PR manager. My gran was happy to undertake the role of childminder and it somehow gave her a new focus. I was conscious of the mental and physical energy it would involve, but she was delighted and took every opportunity to show off her great grandson and smile proudly when people told her that she looked far too young to be a great grandmother.

At the museum, one of my colleagues was a dear gentleman called Len who had one son in his early twenties. Len would often give me a lift home from work and he was one of the most pleasant and amenable people I have ever had the privilege to know. He was the sort of person who would be deserving of enormous luck, but of course life doesn't always work like that.

A couple of years after I had left the museum, another ex-colleague wrote to me and informed me that Len's son had taken his own life. He had jumped off a station platform in front of a speeding train. I remember being horrified and thinking, "How on earth does a parent ever cope with losing a child to suicide? How could anyone ever continue to live after such a tragedy?" Little did I know then that I would discover the answers to those questions firsthand.

As a small child, Kristian continued to thrive and everyone would remark on his intelligence. I did not enter into any other relationships until, in June 1984, I met my now ex-husband at a wedding. Within a few weeks of dating the man who would steal seven years of my life, Kristian began calling him "Daddy", eager to be accepted, loved and needed by everyone.

Just over a month after meeting my ex, he proposed and I had no hesitation in accepting. In all honesty I did not love him in the way that you ought to love someone if you are considering making a lifelong commitment to them. However, I felt there was a reason for his presence in my life and I was seeking security for my son and a way to offer my gran respite, even though I knew that she loved our company and the new lease of life that had been granted to her through Kristian. It was a false security, however, because I had my reservations long before our wedding the following year. I felt I was providing Kristian with a secure foundation; two parents, two incomes and a home that we could call our own. It was only later that I realised what a false illusion this was. No amount of financial security can provide the same stability as the love of two parents who clearly love each other, no matter how little they have in the material sense.

The most important lesson that I learned through my own experiences is that staying in an unhappy union "for the sake of the children" is the worst thing you can do. Every relationship has its purpose, but every relationship has its timeline too.

My parents were unhappily married for 27 years before my father finally decided the time had come to leave. I remember feeling relieved, but I also remember thinking, "I wish they'd separated years ago." My memories of my childhood are not entirely happy ones. I clearly remember the terminally gloomy atmosphere in the house, the constant bickering between my parents and both of them forever belittling each other in front of my brother and me. I used to hope and pray that they would get divorced and I would rather have been raised by one loving parent than by two who were so busy fighting with each other and so wrapped up in their own misery that they never enjoyed quality time with us. I should have learned by their mistakes, but I had to make my own to truly learn the lesson.

The day that I left my gran, in March 1985, was one of the most wretched days of my life. It was the day that I took Kristian away from her; the day that I moved away to marry the man who would not only bring me so much heartache, but who would also bless me with two more beautiful children. I remember wanting to turn around and hold onto my gran forever. Maybe I knew then that I was making a mistake. I felt that I was taking away her little boy, the child who had brought new meaning to her life.

That night, as I lay in my new bed, I sobbed for hours. Although my husband-to-be was next to me, I felt so alone. I was overwhelmed by guilt. I had taken away my gran's life and I could feel her pain. It was for her that I was sobbing, not myself.

In April 1986, Kristian's sister Anneliese was born. Despite having been an only child for four years, Kristian displayed few signs of jealousy and accepted that his mother now had to divide her love and time between two children. His brother, Carsten, arrived just seventeen months later in September 1987, at which point I decided that my family was definitely complete.

At Christmas 1992, over seven years after we had married, I finally summoned the courage to divorce my husband. I travelled through the whole range of emotions including anger, sadness, panic and fear. I also worried about how my three children would cope. I went through a period of self-assessment, wondering what qualities I possessed and what I could do to regain some of the self-esteem that had been destroyed during my seven-year marriage. However, above all, I felt relief. The burden that I had carried around for seven long years had been removed the moment I told my ex-husband that I wanted a divorce. What those words gave me were hope, with a big "H". Hope for myself, hope for my children and hope for our future; a future that I never imagined would entail my eldest son's premature departure from this life.

As I stared unblinkingly as my son's beautiful but unresponsive face, his life flashed through my mind in chronological order, as though I were watching video footage of various incidents in each of his 20 short years. Gazing with wide and curious newborn eyes through a Perspex cot. His first smile, first words, first steps. The face of an angel beaming from the cute little suits that I couldn't resist buying him. The way in which his grandad was the only person able to pacify him, by laying him across his shoulder and rubbing his back, or by serenading him with calming organ music.

I recalled how he accompanied me everywhere I went; a single mother so proud of her beautiful little boy that she couldn't bear to leave him for too long.

His first day at nursery, first day at infant school, first day at junior school; groomed and despatched in new uniform and shoes polished to reflective perfection, together with verbal instructions on the importance of impeccable manners, concentration and intelligent conversation. He did impress the teachers with his banter, although it wasn't always delivered at the appropriate moments, as was indicated frequently on his school reports, which displayed comments like, "Would achieve more in class if he spent less time chatting."

Above all, his greatest and most enviable quality was his compassionate nature and his ability to forgive, no matter who had hurt him. He was fiercely protective of his younger sister and brother and, despite the usual sibling scraps at home, if anyone upset them outside the home, he would be the first to leap to their defence. Small children adored him and he would spend many hours entertaining the younger children in our street. Our door bell was rarely silent as a regular stream of small people would be asking him to come out; something that was always far more appealing to him than completing his school homework.

He would use his charm to his advantage whenever he had been chastised for some wrongdoing. If he had been sent to his bedroom as a punishment, he would give himself permission to come downstairs to hand me an endearing note or drawing, accompanied by the sweetest smile you could imagine. The note or drawing inevitably contained the words, "I love you". Some might call this devious, or playing on the emotions, but I sensed that it was to encourage reassurance that he was loved and accepted too.

Kristian had experienced so much rejection in his short life and when he was being scolded, he must have felt that even his own mother was pushing him away. I always made it clear to my children that I chastised them for wrongdoing because I cared deeply for them and wanted them to grow into respectable young people. I also always explained why they were not allowed to do certain things, which was incredibly important. How else would they have learned the difference between what society regarded as right and wrong? Respect begins at home.

Kristian's enviably caring nature manifested itself in an adult concern for those less fortunate than himself. He gave the last of his pocket money to a homeless beggar in town one day when he was a mere 9-years-old. "I feel so sorry for that poor man," he said, bringing tears of pride to my eyes. Always there was a deep sadness in Kristian's eyes that revealed itself more clearly in moments like this.

The years passed with frightening speed and all too quickly my firstborn was beginning secondary school. Almost overnight he turned from an active, intelligent and enthusiastic young lad into what some would regard as a typical slovenly teenager. He gained weight after years of looking undernourished and he developed a love of large portions of everything, but in particular family-sized packets of chocolaty treats. We would laugh about how we always returned from work to find his bottom poking out from the fridge, as he scouted the shelves for something appetising to devour before dinnertime. The weight gain seem to coincide with his general lack of attention to his schoolwork, which culminated in letters of concern from his teachers, all remarking at how bright he was, but how he wasn't achieving his full potential.

I have continually battled with the thought that maybe Kristian had inherited some mental anomaly from me, although I was not aware at that time of any genetic or behavioural disorders in our family. There was also never any indication that Kristian had a propensity towards death as a way out of his problems, however large and apparently insurmountable. However, those who understand suicide will realise that there aren't always signs and that often, those who succeed, are the ones who most effectively conceal their intentions.

At Christmas 1992, my ex-husband moved out and the children stayed with me. He saw them every Saturday initially, but once he was involved in a new relationship, they began staying on Friday nights too and for the entire weekend once a month. This arrangement was short-lived. Before long, my ex-husband seemed no longer willing to accept Kristian into his home. He had never officially adopted Kristian and I assumed that since he had no legal responsibility toward him, he decided also to relinquish any emotional responsibility.

On one occasion, Kristian decided to visit his stepdad of his own free will, but was turned away on the doorstep. I will never truly know the extent to which this hurt Kristian, but he never dwelled upon the rejection and just seemed to pass it off as one of life's cruel tests.

When Kristian was around 10-years-old, we were living close to a neighbour whom I can most tactfully describe as unsociable. We lived in a very respectable neighbourhood with lovely neighbours and it was dreadfully sad that just one person should tarnish the otherwise congenial atmosphere. She and her poor, henpecked husband had just one son who did not relate very well to any of the other children in the street.

I could see that this boy's mother was a major influencing factor in his conduct and appreciated that his antisocial behaviour could partly be attributed to the values (or lack of) that he had been taught. I felt sorry for him and wondered what impact his overbearing mother would have in his future life.

This neighbour had made it clear to everyone in the street with two or more children that she didn't believe that parents could possibly give their love to more than one child. I hope that our ex-neighbour never loses her only son. I am even more thankful now that I had four children. My three surviving children have been my salvation. They gave me a reason to live. Not all parents are that fortunate.

It was in Kristian's nature to coax out the agreeable traits behind the most unpleasant exterior of some people. Despite the fact that the aforementioned neighbour's son was not well liked amongst the other children in the area, my son would always entertain him. Nevertheless, regardless of my son's attempts to teach this boy the importance of give and take, of sharing and taking turns, this boy insisted on having his own way all the time. Consequently, whenever he ran home crying to his mum because something had upset him, (which frankly wasn't difficult), his mother would storm out into the street and hurl abuse at any child who happened to be in the vicinity, my son included.

I ignored this neighbour's little outbursts, because I hated (and still do abhor) conflict and I also realised that this was not the sort of woman with whom you could engage in a reasonable conversation. Any such attempts would have been futile and would only have provided her with more fuel for malice. I also had an inbuilt desire to distance myself, where possible, from negative people.

However, I did not need to provide my neighbour with ammunition. This she generated in her own mind by spending her day peeping from behind net curtains, trying to live her life vicariously through the activities of the other neighbours.

Her husband Don confided to another neighbour one day that whenever they had moved to a new area, his wife Ellen very quickly alienated all the neighbours and then demanded that they move. This time he told her that since he liked the area and got on well with the neighbours, he was staying put. He also bemoaned the fact that he was banished to the spare room every night, because his wife insisted on allowing their son to sleep in their bed with her.

One day, shortly after I'd just grounded Kristian for a week for unacceptable behaviour, there was a knock at the door. I was greeted by an unfamiliar woman clutching a folder and proffering an identity badge, which I admit I didn't bother to read, because I assumed that she was a salesperson trying to promote a product that wouldn't interest me in the slightest.

"I'm from the Social Services," she said, "May I come in a minute?"

I was confused. Social Services? What reason would they have to visit? We didn't have a disabled person in the house, nor did we have any need for support from them. Maybe they had made a mistake, or were just conducting a survey.

"We've had a complaint," the social worker said. I was stunned. I felt sick. She confirmed my details and checked the names and ages of my children. I was still baffled.

"Apparently, you grounded your son Kristian for a week?"

"And?" I asked. "Is that a crime?"

"No, of course not," said the social worker, "but we are obliged to follow up every call that we receive, even if we believe it has been made by a malicious neighbour."

Everything instantly became clear. Although, the social worker was unable to reveal the identity of the caller, she said that if the person concerned was in agreement, they could write to me with his or her details. My suspicions were confirmed. I received a letter a short while later naming my neighbour as the complainant.

The only allegation was that my son had been grounded for a week. There was no implication that he had been physically abused, yet my neighbour obviously believed that it was a crime to ground a child. Judging by her son's behaviour, I don't believe she condoned any sort of discipline.

I was assured that there was no cause for concern, that the social worker was satisfied that the call had been made out of malice and that no record would be made of the visit.

This was not the only call that my neighbour made to the Social Services. Not long afterwards, a different social worker appeared on my doorstep, this time to question me about allegedly leaving my children in the house on their own whilst I went out. Thankfully, I had a wonderful childminder who was prepared to substantiate the fact that my children were never left unattended.

The social worker made reference to the first report, when Kristian had been grounded, which made me realise how I had been duped by the first social worker into believing that no details of the previous visit had been logged. I was horrified and began to feel very angry. What had been the purpose in lying to me? Was this to lull me into a false sense of security, so that they could try and "catch me out"?

I explained the situation with the neighbour to the social worker and even though she was aware that this same person had made similar calls about other people, I was given third degree interrogation. What were the names and ages of my other children? What was my marital status? Which school did they attend?

The social worker when on to ask the name of our family doctor, what I do for a living, what my husband did for a living and whether I had relationship problems. I half-expected her to ask me how many times a week I had sex and in which position. Were these questions necessary by law, or was she just trying to feel better about her own life by attempting to drag skeletons out of my closet?

Without requesting my permission and without giving any justification for doing so, she then told me that she had to check over my youngest son Carsten, who was with me at the time, whilst Kristian and his sister were at school. At this point, I was not aware of any law concerning the examination of children and believed this to be a standard part of the visit. I did not object, because I knew that I had nothing to hide.

She stripped my son naked and was evidently checking his body for bruises or other signs of abuse. My son, who was only four-years-old at the time, was most embarrassed by this and kept trying to resist by hanging onto the bottom of his T-shirt and then the waistband of his trousers as the social worker tugged viciously at them. She didn't tell me what she was looking for, but did question me about a bruise on his knee. She then said that when children are beaten, they often have bruises on the soft tissues rather than the bony areas, so dismissed the bruised knee as being caused by an accidental fall or knock. Why was she telling me this? There had been no allegation that my child had been beaten. When I then questioned her, she told me that it was routine procedure to check a child if a call had been made, in whatever capacity. I have since discovered that this is totally unethical and I could have taken legal action, since what the social worker did to my son constituted abuse.

Naturally, she found nothing else of a suspicious nature and was happy to leave shortly afterwards. However, I did inform her that I would like details of the person who had made the false allegations, so that I could consider prosecuting. Again, I discovered that it was this same neighbour.

I decided that I would not give my neighbour the satisfaction of believing that she had caused me any inconvenience. Instead, I felt flattered that she obviously must have envied me in some way and I found myself feeling nothing but pity for someone who obviously harboured a lot of bitterness towards others who led more productive lives. I did, however, feel angry with the disrespectful treatment by the Social Services, who had obviously adopted a "guilty until proven innocent" policy. I wrote a letter of complaint, but not surprisingly I received no reply.

A couple of years later, this neighbour's son was cycling up and down the road on his bike. Kristian was sat on the kerb with a group of friends chatting and not really associating with this boy, who was clearly enjoying his own company. At the time I was stood in the kitchen having a cup of tea with a couple of girlfriends. A car turned into our stretch of the cul-de-sac, so the neighbour's son aimed his bike at the kerb some distance from where my son and his friends were sitting. The front tyre of his bike collided with the kerb, creating a catapult effect, sending this boy over the handlebars. My son leapt to his feet and ran to pick him up, but before he reached him, he had run into his mum screaming, leaving the buckled bike in a heap on the side of the road. The other children present looked on and raised their eyes to heaven, clearly familiar with this boy's typical reaction to every "mishap".

The boy had barely set foot over his threshold, when this raging bull of a neighbour stormed out of her house and down the road towards Kristian. She screamed, "I'm going to b***** kill you", before grabbing Kristian by the throat and hitting him around the back of the head. This was the breaking point for me.

I telephoned the child intake team at the Social Services. This was clearly abuse that I and several others, including my two friends, had witnessed. I was told by the duty social worker that it was not their responsibility to deal with such matters and that I would need to call the police. Why then is it deemed acceptable for a social worker to come out on hearsay when a call comes from a malicious neighbour who has no evidence, yet when abuse of a child is actually witnessed, it is suddenly no longer the responsibility of the Social Services?

After this incident, Kristian came inside and sat on the sofa with tears of anguish and fear brimming in his eyes saying, "I feel awful. I really don't want to go outside again. I'm frightened of even walking down the road." My heart broke for my son. How unjust life seemed. Why were the good-hearted victimised? I consoled myself with the belief that what you give out returns to you manifold and that every deed you perform will return to you in one way or another. The universal law of karma.

Thankfully, the above situation was resolved. The police were called, my neighbour was cautioned and as a result she ended up moving shortly afterwards. A few months later, I discovered that she'd already fallen out with all of her new neighbours and had no doubt made a few more calls to the Social Services with more false allegations.

It has become apparent to me that some Social Service departments are only interested in dealing with cases that they know are probably not genuine causes for concern. This makes their lives easier after all.

I feel dreadfully sorry for all those compassionate people who decide to embark on social work as a career, believing that they are being employed within a caring profession. Little do they realise that bureaucracy and perhaps appalling management by the hierarchy within individual councils will prevent them from carrying out their work in an ethical and sensitive manner.

When Kristian was 15 and we voluntarily went to the Social Services to seek help for him, they weren't particularly interested. Even though they tried to assure us that his behaviour was "normal", they still used our request for help as an excuse to pry into our private lives and ask highly personal and irrelevant questions. They used our answers and domestic situation (divorced mother in new relationship) to try and act as amateur psychologists, whilst still telling us that Kristian was a regular teenager.

My "normal" son is now lying in a grave in a local cemetery. His "normal" life is over. My "normal" life is over. Nothing in my family's life will ever be "normal" again. I hope that the local Social Services' department is happy. One less person to worry about, I presume. In my opinion they lead people to believe that they offer support, when in reality they try and act as second-rate police and psychologists with only a real interest in alleged abuse cases. Their inability to distinguish between normal adolescent behaviour and mental illness means that my family have now been left to recover some of the pieces of our shattered lives; lives that were all but destroyed when Kristian ended his life.

It will come as no surprise to many that our then local Social Service department was graded as one of the worst departments in the country over several successive years.

On 1 November 1993, my beloved grandmother died. It was discovered that she had undiagnosed Ischaemic Heart Disease, caused by diabetes that again had only been diagnosed a couple of years previously. On the night that she died, I was asleep in bed when I was awoken by a loud, urgent banging on my back door. The sound was frightening and immediately jolted me to full consciousness. My curiosity overcame my fear and I went downstairs to investigate, believing that there must have been some sort of emergency for someone to be banging with such ferocity so late at night. However, when I answered the door, no one was there.

I returned to bed, feeling somewhat disturbed and a little unsettled at being the only adult in the house. Nevertheless, I fell into a sleep of vivid dreams. The most disquieting dream that I had was of being a guest at the funeral of a middle-aged man, whom in life I did not know. As I filed past the open coffin I was instructed to kiss this gentleman on the forehead, but I protested saying, "That's not him. He's not there."

At 6am the following morning, I was awoken by the sound of the phone ringing. I instinctively knew that it was bad news. I have always associated late and early phone calls with bad news, although of course, it can sometimes be news of a happy event. In this case, however, my fears were confirmed. When I answered the phone, my uncle (with whom my gran had lived for the past few months of her life) calmly told me that my beloved gran had died. He had found her on the floor in the morning, but it appeared that she had probably died the night before.

Although distraught, I managed to tell my uncle about my experience the night before. He said, "She was almost certainly coming to say goodbye to you."

When I then told him about my dream, he said, "Well, that's exactly what your gran said at your grandad's funeral. When she was asked to kiss him she said, 'That's not him. He's not there.'"

This experience simply reinforced my lifelong beliefs in the afterlife and the fact that those on the other side attempt to communicate with us regularly. It's what many people would term as intuition or "gut feeling" and why so many people believe that you should be guided by this rather than your intellect and the logical side of your mind. It is the intellectual side that often leads us astray and causes us to make bad decisions.

In 1996, at the age of 14, Kristian won a competition to spend Christmas in the Antarctic, a trip that few would achieve in their lifetime. Part of the competition involved writing an essay and everyone was impressed at his achievement, which rekindled hopes of an improvement in his academic studies and a focus for his future. The trip was organised by explorer David Hempleman-Adams in conjunction with the local paper and achieved much media coverage. During the journey, Kristian had the privilege of meeting and being photographed with another legend of exploration, Sir Ranulph Fiennes.

So enthralled was Kristian by this chance of a lifetime trip that when he had finished his education, he planned to join Adventure Network International (ANI), the only company in the world offering flights into the Antarctic interior.

Immediately prior to Kristian winning this trip, I also began a new relationship with my current partner whom I had met at work. Whilst Kristian and the other children very much liked and accepted him, there was suddenly another male authority figure around who, before long, would also attempt to exercise control over their behaviour and actions.

Initially, my partner was keen to make a good impression and for a while it worked. My children sang his praises to my ex-husband and his wife and, despite the inherent difficulties that come with divorce, such as issues with bitter ex-partners, life in general was very harmonious. I was happy because I was in a stable relationship with a wonderfully caring partner and, consequently, my children were happier too, not least because they were now part of what society regarded as a "normal" family with two parents.

My partner and I had to meet on common ground regarding discipline and whilst I had always been reasonably strict with my children, suddenly this new man, who wasn't their biological dad, began to enforce law and order in their domain.

To aggravate the situation further, the following year some other individuals regularly entered Kristian's life. Although we welcomed them with open arms, this was not gratefully received. They were sly, manipulative and dishonest and seemed to lack any degree of social conscience.

I did not believe that any lame excuses should be made for the sociopathic behaviour of these other individuals, who were certainly not underprivileged in any way. I had known many people who had endured the most abusive childhoods and yet grew up to be loving, caring people who used their experiences constructively. I had always enjoyed reading human interest stories of triumph over adversity. I wanted to give copies of these stories to all those self-obsessed people in the world who spent their lives blaming others for their circumstances - and to all the parents who made feeble excuses for their children's appalling behaviour.

As a child myself, I had been kicked, punched, hit around the head and occasionally beaten with a wooden spoon, which once snapped in half. I tolerated my parents addressing my brother as "Super Son", whilst I was just plain old "Jan". However, I did not regard myself as having had an abusive childhood. I recognised when I had done something that didn't meet with my parents' approval and ensured thereafter that I then complied with their expectations.

I felt totally responsible for the rejection that Kristian had received throughout his life. Although Kristian never admitted it whilst he was living at home, I subconsciously sensed the deep distress that he felt. Kristian should have had a father to whom he could aspire, someone who could fuel his desire to be successful and work hard at building a rewarding life. It broke my heart to think about the secret pain that my son must be harbouring, but he always hid beneath a cheerful exterior and there was never any outward display or acknowledgement of bitterness. He was never resentful and always found it within his heart to love others and to overlook their shortcomings, because all he ever wanted in life was to be loved and accepted.

The situation was not helped by these insensitive outsiders referring to Kristian as "Lard", because he was slightly tubby. Although he laughed this off in front of them, in private he would cry. He never fought back. He told me that he did not wish to lower himself to the same cruel and uncaring level. I remember him saying to me that at some point they would be teased by others, either about their weight or some other physical disadvantage they possessed, but Kristian was not heartless enough to be the one to do this, even though they had caused him such great distress.

There were so many situations where Kristian was made the scapegoat and again he never felt confident enough to defend himself. I remember the sly, self-satisfied smirks from the true culprits as Kristian was chastised for crimes of which he was not guilty. Even though I had personally witnessed many of these incidents and clearly knew who the culprits were, the perpetrators were always given the benefit of the doubt and my evidence was completely ignored. However, I will not elaborate, since dwelling too much on these past incidents does not serve the higher good.

I foolishly put up with this situation, believing that these things are sent to try us and that it was a spiritual test of endurance; that there was a divine reason why I had to face this. In hindsight, I wish that I had spoken out earlier and insisted that these individuals cease to associate with us until they had learned to treat people with respect and to exercise honesty.

Several people asked me how I managed to tolerate the situation and called me a "Saint". However, I did not view myself as a Saint, but more of a "mug" or idiot for not standing up to those who made the decisions without my consent.

With regard to Kristian, his distress was relayed to me by many other people who knew him and on many occasions. I did feel great anger and irritation towards those who had hurt him and yet, above all, I berated myself for not doing something more about the incidents that I did know about and also felt frustrated for not having been informed about the incidents that I had no knowledge of at the time they occurred. However, from experience I had learned that whenever I voiced my disapproval to the legal guardians of any of these individuals, I was interrupted and shouted down.

I think I learned that speaking out was pointless, but this was not healthy, since it caused the negative feelings to fester inside of me and manifest in unsightly and uncomfortable skin eruptions. I felt that I had a purpose to fulfil and that in the future, if the time was right and it was meant to be, then I would walk away from the situation, having achieved everything that I possibly could.

People come into our lives for a reason, a season or a lifetime. Not all are meant to stay. When a relationship has served its purpose, whatever that purpose may be, we have to move on, or let go. Many people hold onto relationships that drain them of their spiritual, mental and physical energy because of obligation and guilt. These relationships do not serve the higher good, so we have to learn to remove this self-imposed ball and chain and release ourselves from the thought processes that keep us tied to negative relationships with parents, children, blood relatives, friends and colleagues. I have learned that blood is definitely not thicker than water.

I clearly remember the point when things started going horribly wrong and Kristian began exhibiting behaviour that was beyond the realms of normal teenage conduct. Without any valid reason, he neglected his current circle of friends and began associating with a group of people about whom I knew very little; "friends" whom he never seemed willing to bring home with him. To this day, I still do not know how he was introduced to that alien community and who initially lured him into a dark world so different to the one in which he had been raised. I do believe that he was looking for an escape from the current misery in which he was living.

At the age of 15, his rebelliousness and intense dislike of abiding by rules and regulations culminated in periods of being grounded, a punishment that ultimately proved useless unless we had confined him to his room in shackles, which of course we could never do.

Between the dark periods of intense teenage stroppiness, secrecy and displays of fierce independence, his charm and open affection shone vibrantly and won the hearts of all those with whom he interacted in those brighter moments. He cried easily and never tried to hide his sensitivity behind that all-so-familiar macho exterior like so many other young lads. I regarded these open displays of emotion as a sign of strength, not weakness.

At the beginning of 1998, Kristian missed five weeks of school before the teachers informed us of his absence. I did feel greatly disappointed that the school had left it for so long before contacting us and made a mental note not to send my other children there. Kristian had been leaving home in his school uniform each morning, but didn't bother to catch the school bus, unbeknownst to us. We discovered that he had been walking straight across to the houses of one or other of his new circle of friends. Despite grounding him for this, he "ran away" to a friend's house and ended up staying there for a few days, despite our fruitless attempts at encouraging him to return home. We knew that the novelty would soon wear off and so decided to let him return of his own accord.

After disappearing on a few more occasions and following some unwelcome and largely unhelpful involvement with the Social Services, as mentioned previously, Kristian moved into a complex of warden-controlled flats shortly before his sixteenth birthday. My partner invented his own name for the social workers, based on his visual analysis of the type of person we encountered within the local council, but of course, this cannot be repeated here because it does not apply to everyone who embarks on such a career. Maybe we were just unfortunate to have dealings with a minority of inefficient busy bodies on a power trip with nothing but their blinkered text books as a reference point.

The Social Services' staff spoke down to us in an irritatingly patronising tone and informed us that Kristian's behaviour was "normal teenage behaviour". Normal by their standards, yes, because they only dealt with those children whose behaviour wandered outside the realms of what most people would regard as normal. They preached to us about raging hormones, struggling to find an identity, wanting to be independent and dependant at the same time and being torn between childhood and adulthood. We understood all of this and yet what we could not convince them of was that Kristian's conduct extended way beyond this standard framework that they had learned about in the textbooks.

The flats where Kristian was housed were offered to homeless people, or those in similar situations to Kristian who did not feel that they could live with their parents. Shortly after he moved in, my dad telephoned me expressing concern about Kristian as a result of an awkward telephone conversation he had just had with him and said that something was evidently not right. Apparently, Kristian had been speaking very slowly, slurring his words, taking a while to respond to questions and not appearing particularly interested in communicating. My dad didn't feel that Kristian was drunk, but was concerned that he was possibly using drugs. Although I did not want to believe this, I did consider it as a possibility, because I could not be sure whose company he was keeping and with whom he was co-habiting.

However, despite questioning Kristian every time he visited us, he vehemently denied that he was dabbling with drugs, even though I noticed that he seemed to have lost his usual enthusiasm for life and his eyes were glazed, with a sleepy heavy-lidded appearance. His immediate explanation for this was extreme fatigue due to too many late nights.

Nevertheless, during each visit he would always ask at a random moment, "Can I have a hug mum?" As if he needed to ask. Hugs were so important to him.

He had always been such a fast, excited talker and yet everything that he did seemed to be in slow motion, except for the speed with which he walked. That never changed. His sister Anneliese was forever complaining that she couldn't keep up with him. Watching him walk anywhere was like watching a video on fast-forward. I wonder now whether he subconsciously knew that his life on earth would be short, hence he felt that he had to hurry everywhere to cram as much as possible into the 20 years that he had been allocated, although I had always believed previously that suicide is a choice and not pre-determined.

Very soon after Kristian had moved out, he lost his puppy fat and developed an enviably slim physique, which I attributed to the fact that he now had to live frugally and provide meals for himself. Whenever he visited me, his first question was always, "Can I make something to eat mum?" Each time he left, I would package up some food items for him, not being able to bear the thought of him going hungry. I didn't like giving him money, other than for his bus fare, because I couldn't be entirely sure how it was being spent and was always concerned that maybe it would be stolen by someone else. There was also no way that I was going to fund any sort of habit that involved tobacco, alcohol or other drugs.

Kristian signed up for a mechanics' course at college in September that year, but shortly after the course finished, he decided to take a year out to gain some work experience. Over the following year, his work plans never really reached fruition. Not only did he move from one period of unemployment to the next, barely staying in one job for more than a day or two, but he also moved around to several different abodes in town, never really giving a valid reason for moving on.

It was as though he never really felt settled anywhere. What was clear though was how well liked he was wherever he worked. I received a couple of phone calls from employers when he failed to turn up for work. The one thing that they all remarked upon was what a lovely lad he was and how conscientious he was, so they were surprised at his failure to appear without giving a reason.

In 1999, when I was expecting my fourth child, Kristian finally relocated to a complex where he seemed to be a lot more secure and happy. He took great pride in the appearance of his flat and cleaned up almost compulsively. He thanked me for the "housework training" that he had received when he was living at home, even though he had protested vociferously at the time for being expected to help out with household chores. Nevertheless, despite his apparent newfound sanctuary, I experienced this overwhelming sadness each time I waved goodbye to him and watched his then too thin figure scuttle back along the corridor to his room, where he had only his rows of cuddly toys for company.

As I drove away, I was always engulfed in an inexplicable feeling of sorrow that made me want to turn around and bring him back home with me. I wanted to protect him and help him to carve out an honest, happy and successful life. Unfortunately, the only person who would be able to do that would be Kristian himself. The knowledge that you can never really have control over your children's lives just intensifies the feelings of helplessness that parents so often feel, not least the parents of suicide victims.

On one occasion when Kristian visited us, he brought with him a friend and neighbour called Carl. He appeared to be a nice enough lad; polite, well-mannered and fairly articulate. However, there was something about him that didn't feel right, but I couldn't really explain the uneasy feelings I experienced. It was almost like feelings of pity.

He was one of those lads who looked as though he was carrying the weight of the world on his shoulders. I sensed loneliness and rejection. He talked to me about his young daughter whom he hardly ever saw and I remember feeling terribly sorry for him, almost as though there was no love in his life. My daughter Anneliese later told me that this was true and that his family had disowned him many years previously.

As Christmas 1999 approached, I asked Kristian what his arrangements were and whether he wanted to spend Christmas Day with us. He assured me that he'd been invited to a friend's house. I told him that we had been invited to my partner's eldest sister's house for Christmas Day and that he was welcome to come with us. I felt sure that he would call, should his plans change.

On Christmas Day, as we were tucking into a splendid feast laid on by my partner's sister, I had no knowledge that Kristian was sat alone in his flat crying because he thought that nobody wanted him. He did not admit this to me until the following Christmas when he did come across to spend the day with us. My heart bled and following his admission, I spent many hours crying, wracked with guilt and feeling his solitude and pain. How could he have ever thought that he wasn't wanted? But obviously he did and in retrospect I wonder how much of his self-pity and paranoia was attributed to his drug addiction. He was fully aware that he had gone awry and knew that we didn't agree with his conduct at times, but to Kristian our "tough love" may have been translated as not being accepted.

When Kristian made this admission to us at Christmas 2000, he had recently started dating his then 16-year-old girlfriend, Millie. He seemed so happy and told me how much he loved her and how he had never felt this way about anyone before.

It was so important to Kristian to feel loved, as it is with most of us, but feeling needed was something that was fundamental to his well-being, something that became painfully obvious after 1 November 2002.

He had such an enormous capacity to love and now that he was being loved in return by someone other than family members, I felt a great sense of hope that this was the motivation he needed to turn his life around.

After that Christmas in 2000, he telephoned me sounding rather distraught and saying that he had been asked to leave his flat. When I asked why, he told me that the social security had allegedly messed up regarding his housing benefit. Consequently, he owed three months' rent and had been given one week in which to find alternative accommodation. I questioned this, asking how the social security could make such a huge mistake and, if it was their mistake, why he should have to leave? I can't remember his exact reply, but in his usual manner, he didn't seem prepared to stand up for his rights. I suspect that this was just a poor excuse, but I knew that by questioning Kristian, I was not likely to be able to extract the full truth from him.

We told Kristian that he could move back home until he had found his own place and offered to help him seek accommodation. However, the conditions were that he had to find himself a job and pay rent. Amazingly, this spurred him on and within a matter of days he had begun work for a local self-employed builder, which seemed to work well for a while. He was up early every morning without fail and returned home each evening dirty and tired, but satisfied.

When I look back to that time, there were no signs that Kristian was taking any drug of any sort. He never acted suspiciously, nor did he ever disappear off out anywhere. If he was on heroin at the time, which according now to his girlfriend he was, I wonder whether he was in possession of the drug in our home.

My partner drove Kristian around to view various flats, before he eventually found a place that he liked and which was in a much nicer location, not far from the town centre. We lent him the money for the advance rent he was required to pay and asked him to pay us back in weekly instalments, which he did religiously for the first few weeks.

A couple of months later, he telephoned to say that he was moving to one of the most deprived areas of town. When I asked him why on earth he wanted to leave his nice flat to move to an area renowned for its high crime rate and drug problems, he became defensive. He said that he was moving in with his friend Carl, because he had the offer of living there rent-free. When I asked Kristian whether he had been paying his rent, he assured me that he had.

We subsequently discovered that he had lost his building job through unreliability. Some mornings when his boss went to pick him up, Kristian either didn't answer the door, or else claimed that he was ill. A couple of weeks later, I received a phone call from his landlord who said that Kristian had left without giving any notice and owing two weeks' rent. He also said that the video recorder that had been in the house was missing, but since another tenant had also left at the same time, he could not be sure who had removed the equipment. Kristian denied all knowledge.

The police turned up on our doorstep on a couple of occasions asking if we knew of Kristian's whereabouts. Apparently, he was wanted for a number of offences involving the driving of a vehicle without a licence and giving a false name to police.

It seemed pointless questioning Kristian about his actions, because he always passed off my interrogation with answers that gave me the impression that the incidents were of no consequence and that he had sorted the situation out.

Whenever I lectured Kristian on an issue, it would always be some time before he contacted me again. Like most children and teenagers, he did not like being reprimanded and if he had done something to which he knew I would object, it was easier for him to avoid me rather than having to lie when I questioned him. Nevertheless, whenever he wanted something - usually money - he would give me a call, which would always begin, "Alright mum?" He would then launch directly into the reason for his call. He wasn't one to engage in pleasant chit chat about life when he had an ulterior motive. Kristian was always forthright in his requests: "Alright mum? Have you got any spare money?"

For a while after his move to his friend's flat, I didn't hear from Kristian and had no easy way of contacting him. Then I received a shocking phone call from his girlfriend Millie's mother, who informed me that Kristian had been again convicted for driving a vehicle without a licence and was serving a short spell in prison. She then told me that Millie was three months' pregnant. My immediate reaction was one of sheer exasperation and I found myself apologising for my son's reckless behaviour, even though the creation of a baby is of course the responsibility of two people engaging in consenting sex.

I am ashamed to admit that at that point I felt like disowning my son, rather than viewing it, as I should have, as another of life's tests in continuing to love and accept people unconditionally. I felt as though he had totally shunned all the values that he had been taught and I felt that he was demonstrating a total lack of respect towards those who cared deeply about him. I felt let down, but I also felt like a failure as a parent.

Kristian eventually wrote to me from prison and said that he hadn't contacted me for a while, because he felt deeply embarrassed about what he had done and thought that I would be ashamed of him.

He said, "I remember you telling me years ago that if I didn't buck my ideas up I would end up in prison one day. Well, you were right mum and now I'm paying for it. I wish I'd listened to you at the time". My heart softened as I read the letter and I found myself writing a lengthy, compassionate letter in return, trying to offer him hope for a decent future and reassuring him that he was still young enough to be able to turn his life around.

Kristian was elated when his daughter Kayla was born in November 2001 and said that she was his motivation to get himself together and do something with his life. He said that he didn't want his daughter growing up thinking that she had a "bum" for a father. I believed that the arrival of Kayla would be the turning point in his life.

It wasn't to be. In January 2002, I received yet another phone call from Millie's mother, telling me that again Kristian had been sent to a young offenders' institution for a period of 6 months for being caught on five occasions for driving a vehicle without a licence and giving a false name to police. It didn't make sense to me. After everything that he had vowed following his daughter's birth, what could have persuaded him to make such poor and irresponsible choices again? I felt irritated and distressed, but above all I felt a deep sadness for Kristian. He was such a kind, loving young man and he had always had so much potential, but he was completely wasting the talents that he possessed. It was incredibly frustrating. I didn't feel that he should be locked up, but at the same time I felt he had some harsh lessons to learn and that he had to take responsibility for his reckless actions.

During Kristian's sentence, I had concrete proof for the first time that he had been taking drugs, although he never actually mentioned the "H" word to me in his letters of remorse. All he said to me was, "I'm on a drug-free wing. You must have guessed that I had a big drugs' problem before I came in here".

The remainder of the letter talked about his plans for the future, Millie, Kayla and contained a degree of self-deprecation. He told me to ask Anneliese and my dad to write to him. I think he knew that they would support him, irrespective of any wrongdoing that he had He needed reassurance that he was still loved and accepted.

After I had received the first apologetic and loving letter, I curbed my feelings of intense disappointment and wrote Kristian another long and encouraging letter. He accepted that he had been reckless and now he was paying for his crimes. He did not need anyone else lecturing him. He needed understanding, motivation, hope, self-esteem and, above all, love.

In June 2002, a female friend of Kristian's, an ex-nurse who used to live in a flat adjacent to Kristian's, reluctantly informed me that he had taken an unintentional overdose of heroin a year earlier and that his heart had stopped. She had to give him CPR and also had to telephone the hospital to ask permission to give him an extra dose of Narcan (Naloxone hydrochloride), which is a drug that is used to prevent the heroin (opioid) from attaching to opioid receptors in the brain, thereby treating the respiratory depression caused by an opioid overdose.

Anneliese, who was with me at the time of this confession, verified this story, but said that she hadn't told me because she didn't want me to worry. After his release from the young offenders' institution, Kristian confirmed that this was true, but said that he couldn't remember anything about the incident and was flippant about the episode as though it had been of little consequence. Even then, he never actually used the word "heroin" and it was only after his death that I had total confirmation of his previous addiction to the drug.

Nevertheless, the impact that this revelation had upon me was tremendous. I kept thinking, "What if he had died? What if no one in a medical capacity had been there to administer resuscitation?" Even more frighteningly, "What if he contracted some blood-borne infection" or "What if he accidentally overdosed again?" My intellect overrode my spiritual beliefs that everyone's time of death is decided before they are born and that if he was going to die, then he would die, irrespective of the circumstances or any attempts to save his life. However, I also believed that suicide was a choice to opt out of this life prematurely. Nevertheless, suicide never entered my mind as a route that Kristian would choose to take.

During Kristian's sentence, further letters from him clearly highlighted his resolve to sort his life out and build a secure foundation on which to raise his baby daughter. Upon his release, he then demonstrated this by immediately securing a temporary building job at the new local hospital, not realising then that he would be one of the last people to die at the "old" hospital before it was demolished.

The only time that Kristian mentioned the word "depressed" was four months before he died. He had just been released from the young offenders' institution after serving his six-month sentence. He telephoned me from the train station on the day of his release, 9 July 2002, and said, "I'm frightened mum. I feel depressed." When I asked him why, he replied, "I don't like being surrounded by people; it scares me."

My initial fears that he would re-embark on the road towards drug addiction as a coping mechanism were quickly forgotten as he enthused about his job, his girlfriend and his daughter. He also told me that he wanted to stay right away from all the people with whom he had been associating prior to his conviction.

I think he knew that it would so easy for him to succumb to offers of heroin and to quickly be drawn back into the lifestyle that so many of his associates were leading. Although he had good intentions, he knew how to say the right things at the right time. In his mind, however, he may have been paradoxically viewing heroin as a safety net. Kristian always sought comfort and for this reason I feared that he would seek the instant gratification that was derived from injecting heroin into his system. For so many heroin users, it becomes a crutch, a lifeline and supersedes everything else, most of all, rationality.

Interestingly, research shows strong links between substance abuse and suicide. Is it because the drug itself causes depression, or that the depression is caused by an inability to curb the addiction? Maybe the stigma of substance abuse prevents many users from seeking assistance, because they fear prejudice and ostracisation. Additionally, the stigma that surrounds it may deter those who are feeling depressed or suicidal from also seeking the help that they so desperately need. Sadly, many people believe that substance abuse and addiction are moral failings and that this is something that one is fully capable of controlling. However, many mental health professionals and those who have a more accurate understanding of addictive behaviour don't view drug abuse as a sign of weakness, but as a genuine disorder that requires professional assessment and treatment.

After Kristian's death, I learned that heroin overdose is particularly common amongst opiate users leaving prison or drug rehabilitation programmes prematurely, because they have a reduced tolerance to the drug. In Kristian's case, he was obviously aware of how much heroin he needed to administer to constitute an overdose in someone who had not used the drug for ten months.

In August 2002, one month after Kristian's release, I learned from Anneliese that he had recently been beaten unconscious with an iron bar by an alleged friend on the night of his girlfriend Millie's mum's birthday party. The accused, who was allegedly intoxicated, apparently threw a hammer at Kristian's head. Always the pacifist, never the aggressor, Kristian ran away from the assailant. A while later, as Kristian was walking alongside a main road, the same lad appeared from a side turning brandishing an iron bar. Kristian was subsequently beaten across the head and back until he was unconscious. He was taken to the local hospital and kept in overnight. He had sustained a fractured cheekbone and eye socket, a broken nose and a cut to his ear, which needed stitches. He also had bruising to his back. The police were encouraging him to press charges, but he declined. The lad whom he claimed had attacked him is a lovely young man, not known to be violent and there is some suggestion that maybe he was not the person responsible and that maybe Kristian and this lad made a pact to protect, for unknown reasons, the real attacker.

As further testimony to Kristian's forgiving nature, he was sharing biscuits with the alleged perpetrator the following day.

Anneliese told me about the incident the week after it had happened. Again, I began contemplating the worst-case scenarios. What if he had been beaten to death? What if he had sustained irreparable brain damage? What if he'd lost his sight or had been disfigured for life? What if someone had a vendetta against him? What if it happened again with far worse consequences? Little did I know then that "What if…" was a question that my family and I would ask innumerable times over the coming months and years and probably for a lifetime.

Approaching the end of September 2002 was the last time that I saw my son alive. He visited me with his daughter Kayla, who was just beginning to walk. He looked extremely well and showed absolutely no signs of being under the influence of drugs. He was a tremendously handsome young man with such huge potential that seemed to have been lying dormant for the previous six years.

This visit was just a few weeks after he had been attacked, so I was relieved to see that his face was back to normal, with the exception of a scar and some bruising where his ear had been stitched up. When I asked him why he hadn't told me about the attack, he said, "Mum, I didn't want you to worry."

These were some of the last words that my son would ever say to me.

In response I said to him, "Supposing something like this happens again and you don't tell me about it. Can you imagine how I'd feel if a policeman were to turn up on my doorstep and tell me that something awful had happened to you? I would always feel that I could have done something to help, had I known about it."

These were some of the last words that I would ever say to my son.

Five weeks later he ended his life.

The evening of Halloween 2002 was a relatively peaceful one, save the regular flow of trick 'n' treaters who knocked at our door in the hope of being offered sweets that I kept in a bowl by the front door in preparation. My partner was away at the time and was not due back until late the following evening.

I thought of Kristian several times that evening and was surrounded by a sense of great peace. For the first time in many nights, I slept soundly, as though I had been given a sedative. It would be the last time that I did.

That night I also experienced a vivid dream in which I was in my departed gran's house. She was have a major clear out and when I asked her what she was doing she said, "I'm making room for someone else." I believe she was preparing for Kristian's arrival. Little did I realise when I awoke that my life was about to be hurled off its tracks and plunged into a deep, menacing ravine from which I would be screaming for release. People would hear me, but no one could rescue me.

I gazed at my son's serene face as he lay on the hospital trolley and tortured myself with the thought that he felt that he wasn't wanted. Every day since 1 November 2002, I have been consumed by overpowering wretchedness and guilt when I focus on how my poor, dear son must have been suffering. A life that began on the threshold of a promising future ended with no hope remaining. The moment that my son's brain was hi-jacked by heroin and depression, he was bound on a course to self-destruction. I realised that drugs stole my son from me long before he died, even though at the time of his death he was not an addict.

My son would light up any room that he entered. He had such presence. He could never be ignored. Yet despite the light that emanated from him, he was obviously trapped within a darkness that was too dense for any flicker of external light to reach him.

Kristian was not perfect and has not been put on a saint-like pedestal just because he is no longer with us physically. How does one define perfection anyway? As with beauty, it is a perception that is in the eye of the observer. What is perfect to one person may not be to another. Personally, I find someone more perfect because of their flaws, as long as they are not flaws that hurt or destroy others. Imperfections are part of what shapes a person.

We are not all clones and for everyone to have the same traits and features would not be perfection. However, the death of the physical body does cause the surviving relatives and friends to reflect on all that was good about the person who has passed over, and to talk with fondness about all the quirks and characteristics that identified a person who was special to everyone for different reasons.

The line separating life and death seems so fragile and yet some people survive against all odds, clinging onto life with an enviable grip that defies all probability. However, when the inevitable time comes for all of us, some slip gently over the edge, whereas other like my son throw themselves over impulsively when the pressure to remain where they are becomes too great.

I never thought that I would survive the agony of losing my special little boy, but I did and I am. I knew that something positive had to emerge from such a tragedy and that by giving up on life myself, I would be giving up on my son. I did not want him to have died in vain. From the depths of my despair emerged a strength and determination to carry on and help others, to follow my son's example in demonstrating unconditional love, compassion and forgiveness, to help pull others from the same desperation that my son felt and to offer faith that whilst there is still life, there really is hope.

Although I am growing older each day and Kristian's birthdays will also come and go, he will be forever 20 years 7 months and 7 days old.

22 March 1982 – 1 November 2002; the day my world stopped spinning.

---

[1]Pitocin is a synthetic form of oxytocin, a natural hormone produced by a woman's body that causes uterine contractions.

Eternal Grief

©*Jan Andersen - 1 November 2007*

Come and visit me a while in this place that I call grief,
A place that is dense with guilt, sadness and unbearable pain,
A place where past images and harsh words crowd your mind,
Where things you should or shouldn't have said haunt you
And things you did or didn't do rip your heart apart.
Come stay with me a while and feel the suffocating remorse.
Remember the pain in the eyes of the persecuted,
The one who felt he had nowhere to turn in his hour of need,
The one who hated himself and felt that no one loved him,
The one who saw no other way to end his anguish.
Come and be with me in this place of self-reproach and torture,
A place of failure and helplessness, nostalgia and longing.
Come with me and look back at his compassion and forgiveness,
His concern for those less fortunate than himself.
Watch the bullies taunt him and see him cry alone,
Suffering silently to protect his family from his pain.
Watch him give his pocket money to the homeless man,
Or give his last sweet to his mum or friend.
Watch him strive to be loved and accepted by everyone
And feel the pain of rejection in his heart with each rebuff.
Watch him find comfort in a needle of death,
Watch him sink into total oblivion; a permanent solution
To the meaningless abyss that had become his life.
Come by my side and view the future that will never be,
A future void of his laughter, his hugs and his love,
A future where he'll never share his daughter's life,
A future for his daughter without a proud father by her side.
Come walk with me and struggle to hold this mask in place,
A mask that smiles and says, "Hey, I'm fine,"
Even when you are dying inside and want to scream,
"No, I'm not fine at all. Can you really handle the truth?"
Come sit with me a while in this place that I call grief
And try to tell me that time is a healer.
When you sit with me in this invisible place, you will know
That grief after a child's suicide is eternal.

Chapter Two

The Shock, the Disbelief, the Horror

Sticks and stones may break my bones, but words can hurt me more. Words have the power to change someone's life forever.

Jan Andersen

The police officer's solemn expression and the four words that he uttered at 12.30pm on Friday 1 November 2002 will torment me forever. "I'm afraid I've got some very bad news," he said. He didn't need to elaborate. That was the point at which my previous life slammed to a halt. I felt detached from my body, trapped in a vortex of total horror, disbelief and torture and catapulted into a nightmare from which I could not escape. I couldn't breathe. I couldn't feel my body. An avalanche of emotions suffocated me. All I could hear was a high-pitched whining in my head. Everything around me seemed hazy and unreal.

The only words that I managed to utter between hyperventilated breaths were, "Is he dead?"

"Yes," the police officer replied.

I heard someone cry out in horror and then dissolve into hysterical sobs. I was watching this distraught mother as an outsider, feeling physically disconnected from this horrific scene and yet still experiencing emotional and physical pain. My chest tightened. I thought I would have a heart attack. I hoped I would have a heart attack, because at that moment I could not possibly conceive how I could ever live with the constant pain and knowledge that my son had hated himself and his life so much that he had chosen self-inflicted death. I couldn't live with the guilt of having brought him into this awful world, despite all my beliefs about reincarnation and choosing our parents.

I couldn't believe that my precious son was dead. The guilt burned and eroded my heart like acid.

Within a few minutes of learning of my son's death, the hysterical sobbing had been replaced by silent tears that tracked my cheeks in continuous streams, dripping onto my clothes. I had switched onto autopilot, making phone calls, breaking the awful news to family and trying to contact my partner. Where was he when I needed him most? Still, never mind. As always, I would cope. The shock and disbelief were allowing me to function. Nothing felt real. I believed that the alarm clock would go off and that I would wake up from this nightmare.

My other son Carsten, then 15, took charge of Lauren, who was just approaching her third birthday. Although shocked and distressed himself, he had taken Lauren upstairs to remove her from this frightening scene of anguish. They remained there until the police officer approached my neighbour and asked her whether she was able to look after Lauren whilst he drove us to the hospital. At some point I remember agreeing to formally identify my son's body.

On the trip up to the hospital in the police car, I stared vacantly at the world outside that carried on without my permission. I stared blankly into other cars that passed by and wished that it was I sitting there, going home to a son who was still alive. I wished I was someone else. I watched some seagulls circling in flight overhead and thought of my son's free soul. I wondered where he was and what he was feeling. Was he watching the scene of grief now? Was he realising the true value of his life and the devastation his suicide had caused? Was he watching the emotional crucifixion of his mother, his siblings, his girlfriend, his family and his friends?

Despite my anguish, I was still conscious about not wanting the police officer to feel uncomfortable. I found that when I was concentrating on talking, it seemed to suppress the part of my brain that enabled me to feel such horrific depths of sorrow. When I talked, I couldn't cry. At one point, I remember asking him whether he had any children and whether he ever became accustomed to breaking tragic news to families. The answer to both questions was, "No."

I realised that all our lives are as fragile as an egg balanced on the edge of a precipice. At the time of my son's death, the egg that was my life toppled over and smashed into a million pieces, with only some of the parts being pieced back together over time. Some parts would be irreparable and never again would my life be whole.

The ghosts, goblins and demons of Halloween suddenly become terrifyingly real. The horror costumes that many children had been adorning the night before were no longer cute or amusing.

Initially, I could focus on nothing else other than the manner in which Kristian's life had ended. I had to grapple with the heartbreaking realisation that death was the most favourable option to him at the time, that killing himself was preferable to enduring whatever circumstances had caused him to slide down into the dark, slippery depths of the emotional pit. My conversations with family, friends and acquaintances revolved around the suicide. The emphasis was on the fact that Kristian had killed himself, not the person that he was, or the life that he had led. As his mother, I was supposed to protect him, but when he made the decision to end his life, I realised that I was unable to protect him from his own mind.

Any form of sudden death is always a shock, because it is not inevitable. Unlike death that results from a terminal illness, the surviving families are robbed of the opportunity of devoting the last weeks, days and hours of their loved one's life with them, telling them all the things that they ever wanted them to know, acknowledging their love for them, sharing fond memories and being able to give them that one last hug. Even the parents of children who still lived at home would undoubtedly have spent more quality time with them and said all the things that they would have wanted to say, had they known that their child was about to die.

Whilst all sudden death is indescribably painful and tragic, the suicide of a child is also accompanied by horrendously distressing and awkward questions, not just those that the surviving parents are asking themselves, but those that you can sense are also being asked by onlookers. Young people should be thinking about their futures, not about death. What possible circumstances, therefore, could cause someone with so much life still in front of them, to choose to stop the clock prematurely?

I was determined to be totally honest about Kristian's death. I refused to gloss over the details of his suicide, because in addition to dealing with the loss of my eldest child, I did not wish to carry around the burden of secrecy.

If you try to conceal the truth, it has a way of clawing its way to the surface and hitting you - and everyone else to whom you've lied - with brutal force. I have heard people talk about the stigma of suicide, but I believe that much of the stigma lies within the mind of the survivor. Because of the punitive nature of society, I imagined that I saw some people almost retreat in horror, embarrassment and pre-judgement, when I mentioned the "s" word, but they were probably just shocked at the news of his death. Even the most articulate of people can suddenly feel verbally clumsy when confronted with a bereaved person.

Most people made the appropriate sympathetic sounds as I relayed the story of what happened and how I felt, but I imagined them making harsh and unqualified judgements behind my back. They would go home and say to their families, "Well, of course, I always said she was too tough on him", or "She should have held him on a tighter reign", their opinions all contradicting each other, thereby placing a guilty verdict upon me whatever action I had taken and whatever choices I had made.

Family members of suicide victims often hide the truth from people if they are able to do so, since they may believe that it reflects badly on their relationship with the victim, or that suicide is equivalent to the crime of murder. They think about suicide bombers, or convicted murderers who have taken their own lives in prison as a way of escaping their sentences and fear their loved one being compared to such criminals. This unsympathetic and callous judgement would be too much to handle, so in addition to their deep loss, many suicide survivors have to endure the pain of isolation from a society that is largely ignorant about depression and suicidal behaviour.

Whilst I felt that people would be laying the blame at my feet, I was not prepared for the anger of some people toward Kristian, even those who did not know him that well. On one occasion, a close friend of mine telephoned me and said, "Geoff is so, so angry with Kristian. He's really livid". My friend had met her second husband, Geoff, after Kristian had left home and, as a result, he had never even met him. Our reciprocal visits only included my children who still lived at home, so Geoff was making a harsh judgement about someone about whom he knew nothing. I presumed that he also knew little about true depression and understood even less about the extreme despair that makes someone view death as his only option.

Unfortunately, it is not the deceased person who takes the brunt of the anger, but the grieving survivors. Yes, I can understand people feeling angry about the misery caused to the surviving families, but in expressing their feelings of rage, they are placing an additional burden on the bereaved at a time when they most need support, sympathy and kindness.

People need to understand the major difference between insane suicide bombers, (a better term would be homicide bombers), who feel it is honourable to blow themselves up along with dozens of innocent victims, and someone whose tortured mind tells them that to continue living as they are would be intolerable. To many, suicide is a dirty word.

It is not surprising, therefore, that some families try desperately to conceal the truth behind their child's death. Some may even convince themselves that it was not suicide, but that the death had either been staged to look like suicide, or else was a dreadful mistake. Maybe the victim had taken an unintentional overdose, or maybe someone had murdered them. Perhaps the true perpetrator had employed someone to forge the suicide notes, or else forced the victim to write them at knifepoint. Maybe the victim had been pushed over the edge of the building, or in front of the lorry.

Many survivors actually cling to the thought that the death was not suicide and the absence of a note can prolong this belief indefinitely. Some families may eventually reconcile themselves to the fact that their beloved child's exit from this life was intentional, whilst others will go to their own graves believing that what happened was a horrible mistake.

Even though Kristian left two suicide notes, not one single member of my family, nor any of his friends, believe that he intended to die. They all believe emphatically that he was expecting his girlfriend to return to her flat that night, but that he wrote the notes to add impact to his attention-seeking act. Even if this were true, Kristian must have felt distressed enough to make such a desperate plea for help. I don't believe that many people seriously want to die. They just want the circumstances that are making them feel so distressed and hopeless to be removed, but in the moment that they decide to end their lives, those obstacles seem interminable.

When we arrived at the hospital, I recall two of the team who had attempted to save my son's life coming into the relatives' room and speaking to me. Still feeling part of a surreal world, it was as though I were remotely viewing a scene from a television hospital drama. I remember the platitudes, the clichés ("We did everything we could, but..."), the medical terms in layman's language, details of his temperature and vital signs when he was discovered, how they attempted to warm him up slowly and how, despite their best efforts, they had been unable to save him. I remember the sympathetic faces, the comforting arms around my shoulders and the dense atmosphere of grief, failure and lost hope. I remember my son Carsten just sitting there staring into space with his mouth open and I remember my partner's eldest sister arriving to offer what support she possibly could.

I remember another police officer being present, a colleague of the officer who had broken the tragic news to me. I recall the obligatory and routine questions about Kristian and the apologies for burdening me with such apparent trivialities in the midst of such a devastating tragedy.

I recall one police officer leaving and returning to the room with a white bin liner containing my son's clothes and other personal belongings that had been on his person when he was found. I wanted to grab the bag and bury my face in the very last clothes that he had worn in life. I wanted to smell and feel him as he was in life, not death.

I was handed the gold ring that Kristian had been wearing, because that was the only item that didn't need to be detained for forensic purposes. Because of the nature in which he had died, they had to rule out foul play and I was informed that an inquest would be opened. Even his two suicide notes had to be kept and examined to determine whether they had been scrawled impulsively, or had been written in a well formed manner when he was in a rational frame of mind, suggesting that his intentions had clearly been thought out.

I clutched the ring tightly in my palm, feeling the vibrations of my son embedded in the gold, cloaked in his pain and hopelessness and wondering whether this was the only possession of his that I would ever hold again. Was this all that remained of my precious little boy? Much as I wanted to keep it, I felt that it was something that belonged to his girlfriend Millie. After all, she had been closer to him over the previous two years and I could never have denied her one of the few possessions that he had.

There were formalities and questions that temporarily took priority over the grieving and apologies from the police officer for intruding on our distress with such insensitive, but necessary, procedures. I dutifully responded to each question with a controlled calmness, knowing that once the realisation of what had happened had truly struck, I may not be so accommodating to such interrogation.

I asked to see the suicide notes. The police officer told me that if I didn't feel ready, I could wait and view them at a later date. How could there ever be a good time to view such notes? I wanted answers now. I couldn't possibly feel any more pain than I was already experiencing, or so I thought. The police officer held each note in front of me. Again, for forensic purposes, I was not allowed to touch them at that time, but was told that copies would be made for me if I so wished.

The first note was addressed to his girlfriend Millie and shall remain largely private. However, he spoke of his love for her and their daughter Kayla. The only words that I will share are those that said, "I will always be up there looking down on you both." The second note read as follows:

"To Whom It May Concern, I am not a *skag head who od'ed on drugs. This was just the easiest way to kill myself, so make sure it doesn't get printed in the paper, 'Junkie overdoses on heroin.' Tell my mum and my family I'm sorry, but I hated myself and my life and I just couldn't take it anymore." (*Skag head is a slang term used to describe a heroin addict.)

The words tore through me like a hail of bullets. I was engulfed in his anguish and his hopelessness for this life, but also felt his paradoxical comfort and sorrow in having finally found a release; a permanent solution to his misery, but one that would cause unspeakable distress to his family and friends. I wanted to touch the paper, to trace my fingers over the final words of my son, to have evidence of one of his very last actions in life.

"I hated myself and my life and I just couldn't take it anymore" are words that have haunted me ever since. The guilt that those words alone elicits is insurmountable and the responsibility that I feel for his self-condemnation will never wane.

When I was finally asked whether I was ready to go and identify my son, I was swamped by an unbearable fear at seeing my son dead. At the same time, I was overwhelmed by an intense desire to be with him; to see him, to touch him, to spend time with him and perhaps even convince myself that he was still alive, or more outrageously to discover that there had been some dreadful mistake and that the body that I was about to identify was not that of my son. I then felt guilty for wishing that it were someone else, because that would be like wishing the same tragedy and pain on another family. If it was happening to me, I thought, then maybe it meant that someone else's pain had been spared. More bizarrely, I thought that seeing him might offer me some comfort.

The police officer told me that although it would be distressing, I had to use the words, "This is my son, Kristian Andersen" when I identified him.

I barely recall the short walk from the relatives' room to the side room in the A&E department where my son lay. A few people accompanied me, including the two police officers and a nurse. I don't even recall whether there was a door to the room, or simply a curtain pulled across the entrance. I do remember the curtain or the door being pulled back and the first horrifying glimpse of my son laid on his back on the trolley bed, covered in a blue blanket, with just his arm and his head uncovered, revealing the blue hospital gown in which they had dressed him. He looked as though he was simply sleeping, but I could smell death.

These observations must have registered in my mind in a split second, because in the moment that I caught sight of Kristian, my knees buckled beneath me as though all feeling had been removed from them and they were unable to support me. I collapsed in a heap at the doorway crying, "My poor little boy; my poor little boy!" I recall strong arms on either side of me pulling me to my feet and the nurse fetching a chair for me to sit on by Kristian's side.

"It's ok, you can touch his hand", said the nurse. At that moment, I wanted my life to be taken from me. I remember thinking that I would never survive this. "I just want to die. I want to be with him," I sobbed over and over.

He looked so serene, so beautiful; my lovely little boy. There were no signs that he had suffered physically in any way. He was free at last. I wanted him to hear what I was saying, to know how I was feeling, to know how much he was loved and how much he would be missed.

Psychologists may try to tell us that we will more readily accept the reality of a loved one's death if we have seen the dead body, but I did not find this to be true. Even now, I cannot believe that my son is no longer alive.

For the briefest of moments, I thought there was hope. I could hear a bubbling sound coming from Kristian's nose, but in seeing the alarm on my face, the nurse said, "That's nothing to worry about. It's just air escaping from his body." I felt as though I was witnessing the final signs of life escaping from his body. The air that had once sustained him was being expelled from his body forever.

How can one ever be prepared to view their dead child? They can't. Even people who deal with death every day of their lives surely cannot deal with the sight of their own child's body with the same professional detachment, if one ever is able to completely detach emotionally from the loss of any life. I presume that once one stops feeling, then that is the time that perhaps a change of vocation should be considered. How can those in the caring professions possibly demonstrate that care if they don't allow themselves to feel?

Sue Scott (was Neill), the wonderful nurse who supported me during those first few hours certainly did feel. As I sat and stroked my son's baby soft hand, I found myself telling her about his life and my life and the events of the previous four years.

In turn she told me about her three children and how, with my permission, she would be going home that evening and telling them about the awful events of the day in the hope that she would be able to prevent the same tragedy from befalling them. She had tears in her eyes as she spoke and I could see the pain in her face as a mother witnessing and showing compassion for the agony of another mother.

Sue told me how you never got used to seeing a young person die. She told me about the fiancé she had lost to a motorcycle accident when they were both teenagers. Although that tragic event had occurred nearly a quarter of a century previously, she told me how she still grieved for him now, something that the rest of her family had difficulty comprehending.

In a matter of minutes, two women who had previously been strangers were sharing some of their deepest and most intimate thoughts and experiences, building a bond through the shared tragedy of the loss of a loved one.

At some point, I remember going through the official procedure for identifying Kristian and I recall being left alone with him for periods of time, but what I don't remember is for how long I sat with him.

Someone came and told me that Kristian's girlfriend Millie and her family were at the hospital in another relatives' room and asked me whether I wanted to go and sit with them. I didn't want to leave my son and yet I felt that I needed to comfort Millie. I told Kristian that I would see him later and was taken to a room that was heavy with the residual energies of so many bereaved families who had been there before us.

I was completely swamped by Millie's distress. As we huddled together on the small, worn sofa that had accommodated hundreds of grieving families before us, I felt as though I was in her body, feeling what she was feeling and thinking what she was thinking.

I gazed at Millie's back as she huddled over, her head on her knees, sobbing and screaming uncontrollably. I remember thinking that she was dressed for grief, in a black jumper. She seemed so frail and thin and emotionally destroyed. I worried that she might die too. I felt her pain, her guilt, the despair and the absolute hopelessness in knowing that it was too late; the longing to turn back the clock and change the fatal outcome. If only, if only, if only. An impenetrable fog of crushing grief and guilt engulfed the two women who were key in Kristian's life; the woman who had given birth to him and the young woman who had given birth to his daughter just under a year previously.

There were phone calls to the hospital from friends and family to whom the awful news had been relayed. My best friend Rae dropped everything and headed up to the hospital. My partner was rushing back from the North to be with me and my dad and stepmum were on their way down from their home nearly 300 miles away.

My partner's sister took Carsten home and Millie and her family went home, but not before inviting me to Kayla's first birthday party the following weekend; a celebration that her daddy should have attended.

I was left alone with my thoughts, my memories, my guilt and my grief in this barren, shabby and depressing room that smelled of stale cigarette smoke. All that I could recall seeing on one of the walls was a small mirror. I remember wondering why anyone would possibly care what they looked like in such a situation. How superficial. I did not care that my tears had washed away my makeup, or that damp foundation and mascara had dripped onto my pale pink top. I did not care about anything except that my son was dead.

There was an open door leading from the room out into a tiny high-fenced enclosure. The air was still and the rain fell vertically and relentlessly, like my tears. In my solitude, I stared out of the door into the darkening skies that were signalling the end to the day on which my son died and on which a huge part of me had died with him. The hopelessness gripped me like a vice. Was this how Kristian had felt the night before? I could hear vehicles arriving and leaving and visitors, patients and hospital staff chatting and laughing as they walked along the pavement on the other side of the fence. My life had frozen in time whilst theirs continued, oblivious to my torment. I wanted to stand outside and scream, "Don't you know that my son has just ended his life?"

My friend Rae arrived and then my partner arrived. There were more tears and condolences. The nurse, Sue, came and went at intervals, but soon came the pressure from all quarters for me to go home. I wanted to stay where I was, in limbo, for fear of moving forward in a life without my son. I did not want to leave Kristian at the hospital. I could not accept the thought of what was going to happen to him after we had left. Did everyone want me to leave for my sake, or did they sense the urgency from hospital staff to shove my son into a drawer in a mortuary freezer in a mechanical fashion, completely devoid of emotion?

My partner eventually coerced me into going home, against my will. There was nothing that I could do to save my son now. It was too tragically late and yet I wanted to be close to Kristian, to be able to spend as much time as possible with him before the final goodbyes. I went back into the room where my son had breathed his final breath to say goodnight to him. Tears dripped onto his face as I bent over to kiss him on the forehead and told him that I would be back in the morning, not realising then that this would not be permissible, because the coroner was not available at the weekend.

It occurred to me that my 16-year-old daughter Anneliese hadn't been told the life-shattering news. On the way home, we stopped off at the flat where she was temporarily residing with her boyfriend. Her living conditions and her choice of boyfriend were not something that we condoned, but short of employing physical force, the situation was out of our hands.

My partner fetched Anneliese and brought her silently to the car.

What's going on?" she kept repeating, "What's happened?" I could see the fear in her eyes. She told me afterwards that she thought that something had happened to Lauren.

All I managed to say to her was, "Kristian's dead." With that, she collapsed sobbing into my partner's arms.

In the first few weeks after the tragedy, I carried everyone else's grief in addition to my own and it was debilitating. I bore my parents' grief, my children's grief, Millie's grief and the grief of Kristian's closest friends. I wanted so much to be able to comfort everyone else, even though it was almost impossible for me to find solace myself. I accepted the fact that whilst I may never come to terms with Kristian's loss and I could never see the grief or guilt lifting, I could at least attempt to help others along their grieving path. I found myself offering comforting observations, assuring others that although Kristian was no longer suffering, he was still with us in spirit. I asked them to consider what his quality of life would have been like, had he never been able to sever his contact with heroin and the people who had helped dragged him down to the underworld of substance abuse. I told them that had he lived, maybe something far worse would have happened to him in the long-term.

I will always feel responsible for Kristian's suicide. I had always believed in "tough love", but now I wonder whether I was too strict. Of course, other family members assure me that I was more than fair and that I carried him for longer than most parents could reasonably be expected to do. However, I felt responsible for bringing him into this cruel world, responsible for making ill choices in my relationships and consequently making myself responsible for giving him the love and the discipline of two parents. As a result of the continual rejection he had experienced from the father figures in his life, I had to play the authoritarian role of a father and the nurturing role of a mother. I often wondered how he was affected by hearing schoolfriends chat about their dads and being able to share father-son interests.

I had often put myself in Kristian's position and actually felt a deep sense of dissatisfaction and a more distressing feeling of not belonging. Was this what he really felt, or was I just imagining how I would feel in the same situation? Could I have done more to improve his self-worth? It is always far easier for people to hand out criticism than praise, but unfortunately criticism seems to have a far more powerful effect on the mind. You might receive ten compliments and only one criticism and yet which will you remember and which will play most on your mind? If you are sensitive, inevitably the criticism will override everything else and batter your self-esteem.

Some parents only communicate with their children when they have a grievance, yet forget to commend them with equal fervour when they have achieved something praiseworthy. How sad that this world revolves around personal conflict and condemnation of others. It sells papers and attracts TV viewers in this world of rampant greed and commercialism. If someone can make a mint by preying on others' misfortune, then they don't hesitate to exploit this.

My son was not strong enough to survive in such a brutal, hateful world. It is not a sign of weakness. On the contrary, you need to have a lot of courage to sacrifice your own life. His altruistic nature may have caused him to forfeit his life to relieve, what he may have believed, was his burden on others.

Although members of my family and many of his friends did not truly believe that Kristian meant to end his life, in reading his two suicide notes, it seemed to me as though it was not a spur of the moment act, but something that he had perhaps been contemplating for some time.

Facing the truth was excruciating. Reading my son's desperate words in his two suicide notes was the worst torture imaginable. It could not compare to any guilt, despair or pain that I had previously experienced in my rollercoaster life. I wondered how any parent bereaved by suicide coped with facing the ordeal of a suicide note. I wondered how parents coped when their child didn't leave a note and they were left with so many more "Whys".

Sheila's grandson Jake was 17 when she found him hanging in his room the morning after there had been a family argument. She and the rest of the family have had difficulty believing that Jake was the sort of person to take his own life after what appeared to be a trivial argument. He was not an impulsive type of person and had not shown any signs of being depressed or different in any way. Because he did not leave a suicide note, Sheila is still clinging to the idea that what happened was a terrible accident; a sick joke that had gone horribly wrong.

"My grandson didn't leave a note, so I cannot even imagine how it would feel to read something like that. Personally, if Jake had meant to kill himself, I would rather he had left a note, because that would remove the doubt.

"I still want answers as to why my beautiful, funny and talented grandson is dead. Even if I didn't like the answers, at least the rest of his family and I would not be left wondering for the rest of our lives. If only we knew for sure, perhaps it would help us move forward. I feel as though I will always be trapped at the same point, always going over and over what happened in my mind and searching eternally for clues.

"A few days after Jake's death, my daughter told me that the policeman had referred to some sort of note and, for a brief moment, we thought that maybe some of our questions would be answered. At first, I couldn't understand how the police had custody of a note about which his family knew nothing. Surely they would have mentioned it to my daughter and son-in-law when they went through his room? However, it transpires that because Jake's parents were so distressed, the police did not wish to burden them with too many questions and any possible evidence they had discovered in his room at that time.

"It turned out that the note was an old letter written to his girlfriend after they'd had one of their many tiffs. Although it wasn't dated, he and this girl had separated several months before, so we knew that it wasn't a recent letter. Nevertheless, I asked if they could give me a copy of it. Maybe I was attempting to play amateur sleuth, but I remember scanning it over and over again, trying to search for some sort of signs that he may have been suffering from depression or thinking about suicide for some time, but there was nothing.

"The image of my grandson hanging in his bedroom is embossed on my mind. It is an image that beggars description and one that will never be erased. There are many days when the image appears with brutal clarity, whether my eyes are closed or open.

"Only those who have witnessed the same paralysing sight can ever fully comprehend the total horror of finding your grandchild murdered by their own hand. It still seems like some atrocious nightmare. Nothing seems real anymore and I keep hoping that maybe one day I will wake up and discover that it was all just some horrid, horrid dream. Realistically, I know that that is not going to happen and that relief will only come on the day that I die.

"Losing Jake has nearly killed me. It has nearly killed his family. It has certainly killed the many facets of my personality that comprised the "me" that people knew and loved before his death. His choice to end his life, whether rational or not, will hurt me until my dying day. The many questions that will never be answered contribute to our daily struggle. We may search the world over for the truth, even though everyone else wants us to accept what has happened and move on. And of course, those who are most insensitive to our needs are those who cannot even begin to comprehend what it is like to lose a child, grandchild or sibling, even before you add suicide to the equation. Maybe if they were to lose a child in the same way, they would understand our need to search for answers."

Leigha is 19 and lost her 23-year-old brother Shaun in December 2000. He was in his flat alone when he shot himself. Leigha has mixed feelings about the fact that her brother didn't leave a note.

"I have always felt somewhat relieved that Shaun didn't leave a note, because it means that his suicide was probably an impulsive act and that he didn't really mean to do it. If he had left a note, it would mean that he had planned it and that would make my family and I feel that we could have done something to save him. I would find the notion that he actually planned his suicide very hurtful and difficult to handle.

"If he shot himself in the heat of the moment, I can find comfort in knowing that he probably didn't really mean to end his life.

"There are some days, however, when I wish that he had left a note, because then we might have more understanding as to why he did what he did. Now, we'll always be left wondering.

"Whether a note is left or not, the result is still horrendous."

Those survivors who endure the horror of either witnessing the suicide, or discovering their child after they have committed the act are not spared the gruesome details. Nevertheless, those families who only hear about the suicide from a third party are often tormented by thoughts of how the scene looked. They visualise how their child looked based on limited information passed on by others. The police, medical staff and anyone who discovered the body may believe that they are sparing families further agony by withholding the full, gory minutiae, but the imagination has a cruel way of constructing the missing pieces and replaying the fabricated images unceasingly.

Even though I did not see Kristian until after the hospital staff had desperately tried and failed to save his life, my mind has continued to reconstruct the scene of his suicide based on information relayed to me by the police officer handling the case. I have replayed these assumed images so many times in my mind that it would be easy to believe that I had actually been present when the paramedics were attending to him. I wish I had been there. I wish I had been given the opportunity to have a few final, loving words.

Perhaps, even in the dark, impenetrable abyss of his unconscious state, his mother's words would have filtered through. Perhaps he would have left this life not feeling so wretched or lonely. Perhaps, for just a moment, he would have experienced some comfort in knowing that he was very much loved and wanted. Would he also have felt sorrow in realising that he would be leaving behind a deep void that would never be filled?

Unlike "rewriting the script" when a bereaved parent mentally changes what has happened to a more favourable outcome, one tries to imagine what actually did happen and creates images that relate to the facts provided by others.

In the very early days, the minds of every family member, whether openly admitted or not, are continually occupied by the same re-enactment of events. It is like a movie reel being repeated over and over and over again, as though one were strapped into a chair in a torture chamber and being forced to watch gruelling footage 24 hours a day. The thoughts not only plague the grieving throughout the day, but may invade their dreams at night. There appears to be no escape, save the occasional respite when one's mind is briefly occupied by something else. Even day-to-day mundane tasks, such as what to prepare for dinner or writing out cheques for bills can be an unusually welcome diversion, although at times even the easiest of tasks can become strenuous, mentally and physically, when grief has drained us of all our energy.

Do these thoughts, images and debilitating emotions rule one's life forever? Does it ever get better? Will one ever be able to experience joy again without feeling guilty? These are just a few of the many questions that I have heard so many bereaved families ask. For me, over eight years after the event at the time of this book's latest publication, the answer is no. I will never stop being tormented by what happened, what I didn't see and what I didn't do, but these thoughts no longer occupy every waking minute.

Some days are worse than others, but the gaps between the awful days when I feel as though I am drowning are becoming longer. I may have a spell of several days when grief, lethargy and depression make me want to retreat within a place of solitude and to go anywhere or do anything to escape the pain. On days like this, where possible, I try to take time out to just be. I give in to the grief rather than trying to fight it or escape it. There is no escaping it, so the best action to take is to acknowledge it, however painful or unbearable that might be.

In June 2001, Greta arrived home from work one evening to find her 18-year-old daughter Rikki hanging from a drainpipe in the back garden. The horrific vision of her swollen, blue face and haemorrhaged eyes still haunts her on a daily basis and she feels that she would rather not have witnessed the scene.

"I arrived home at around 6.30pm on a relatively warm, breezy June evening and wondered why the house was so silent. Rikki was usually in the kitchen beginning to make dinner. She was so good like that. Ever since I had separated from her dad, Rikki had assumed a supportive role, always taking care of her younger sister Sofia and helping around the house without being asked. I was always conscious that she was doing too much, particularly when she also had college to attend and homework assignments to complete. She was such a loving, caring, beautiful girl. She was also very sensitive, but always seemed to be happy, even when her life wasn't running smoothly.

"On this particular evening, Sofia had gone to a friend's house for tea and wasn't due home until an hour later. I called for Rikki, thinking that maybe she was in her bedroom, but there was no answer.

"It was only when I walked into the kitchen that I heard a rhythmic thud as though something heavy was pounding against the outside of the house. It was when I went out onto the veranda that I saw her. I still find it incredibly difficult to talk about this calmly. She was hanging by a bed sheet that was attached to the drainpipe running down the side of the house. She was a slim girl, but I still don't know now why her weight didn't pull the entire pipe from the wall.

"I remember screaming hysterically for help as I lifted Rikki up to try and release the pressure on her neck. I don't really know now why I expected someone to hear me, since we live in a small village some distance from any immediate neighbours. I knew that she was dead, but part of me still believed in miracles and I thought that I could still save her. I was still screaming and gasping hysterically as I ran into the kitchen to fetch a knife. My hands were shaking violently as I cut her down and attempted to resuscitate her, but I was later told that she had been there for at least three hours.

"I can't even remember the exact sequence of events that followed. I'm sure that many other parents can identify with the feeling that you are watching some ghastly horror movie. It didn't feel real. I remember people talking to me and comforting me, but I didn't hear what they were saying. I was in shock. I didn't want to be alive. I didn't think it was possible for someone to suffer so much emotional pain without dying. In fact, were it not for my other daughter Sofia, I can't honestly say that I'd still be here.

"I have so many flashbacks. I cannot walk onto the veranda without seeing Rikki hanging there. I am just so thankful that Sofia wasn't there to see it. I think that would have destroyed her. I have not even told her that I have shared this experience, because I would not want Sofia to discover the details by reading about them.

"If there comes a time when she wants to know, then I will tell her. For that reason, I have asked Jan to change our names and some of the details in order to protect her.

"I have spoken to many families who have lost someone close to suicide and although many of them have said that they have constantly imagined what the scene of the suicide looked like, not one of them said that they wished they had been there. I wish I'd been spared that additional agony, but I'm also glad that no one else had to be subjected to that grisly and shocking sight. I also know that if I hadn't been the one to find Rikki, I would always have believed that maybe if I had been there I could have saved her life."

The surviving families often want someone or something to blame for the suicide of a child. They feel that an external influence must be responsible for pushing their child over the edge, for making them feel that their life was worthless and for causing them to take the drastic decision to permanently end their misery. Blame is natural, because it's hard to accept the idea that the person who has died was totally responsible for the decision. They don't want to believe that their loved one consciously made the decision to leave them devastated.

Blame is often thrown back and forth between family members, or sometimes directed at outside influences such as school, work or social circumstances. Blame creates anger, which can have a detrimental effect on everyone who was involved with the child and can intensify grief. The focus is shifted towards the object of blame, rather than on mourning the loss of the child concerned.

Blame can also be turned inward on oneself. A surviving parent may chastise themselves for not noticing the signs that their child was unhappy or depressed, for not being in the right place at the right time, for not being able to save their child, or for believing that they said or did something that precipitated the suicide. If the last words that a family member had with the child were cross ones, they may feel that they were responsible for the suicide. If you blame yourself and also have blame attributed to you by others, the resulting mental torture is crucifying and is not conducive to any sort of healing.

Cheryl's son Adrian was 27 when he took his own life via carbon monoxide poisoning in January 2002. He drove out into the country, parked his car at the side of a farmer's track, connected a hosepipe to the exhaust and gassed himself. Adrian left behind a 23-year-old wife and two small children, aged 3 and 1 at the time of his death. Whilst Cheryl blames no one for her son's suicide, the rest of her family feel differently.

"My husband and a couple of other people feel that my son's wife was responsible for his suicide. I think that they are just trying to find someone to blame, because they cannot believe that he would have been that desperate to do that to his family. Did she drive him out to the country and force him to sit in his car whilst she connected a hosepipe to the exhaust and then locked him in the car? I wish they would see that he had many problems long before he even met his wife, even though he kept his feelings under wraps most of the time. His struggles were much greater than anyone realised and because it was in his nature to protect others, I'm sure he felt that he didn't wish to lumber anyone with his troubles.

"We are all looking for someone or something to blame, but if we start apportioning blame, we are not supporting each other and it only makes our grief more difficult to handle. Maybe it's the shock and the complete and utter disbelief that makes some people behave in this way, but it doesn't help anyone. If the entire family ends up divided, whom else do we have to lean on?

"I can't deny that I am thankful that my son is no longer in pain, but I just wish he had talked to someone, talked to me, before he made that fatal decision. He was such a kind, caring young man who hated to see others suffer and yet his suicide has caused more suffering to more people than he could ever imagine.

"On New Year's Eve 2001, he seemed so full of life and hope for the future. He talked enthusiastically about his plans for the New Year and his children, whom he adored. That is why I cannot understand why he decided to opt out of life just three weeks before his daughter's fourth birthday. How do we ever explain that to her, or to his son?

"Although I find it difficult to understand why he did what he did at that time, I don't feel angry with him for feeling so desperate that he could see no other way to escape his gloom. I just feel desperately sad that a life so full of hope and promise has been wasted and that two beautiful children have been left without a daddy.

"Although it's been some years now since Adrian left us, I still don't think that I or the rest of the family have moved past the shock and disbelief stage. I don't think that I ever will come to terms with what has happened. Suicide is such an awful way to die, because you know that the person has left this life in misery and desperation. Suicide is shocking, horrific and brutal. There is no other way to describe it."

Suzanne's older brother Tom was 27-years-old when he shot himself in the bedroom of his flat. Suzanne blames his fiancée Claire for his suicide.

"Tom's fiancée had recently told him that she'd been having an affair with someone else. Tom was devastated, but he did seem prepared to forgive her, mainly I think for the sake of their two-year-old daughter.

"He did have a high profile job with an insurance company and I accept that he was under a lot of pressure, but he worked long hours to provide for Claire and their daughter. They were a one-income family, so it was particularly important for my brother to succeed in his profession.

"When he discovered that Claire had been having an affair with one of his so-called friends, he was naturally distraught. I can't ever remember a time when I saw him cry like he did after he found out. He'd always been my big brother, the strong, protective one whom I idolised. He'd always been my shoulder to cry on when life was tough.

"Despite the fact that he was incredibly upset, I never for one moment believed that he was suicidal. He did seem prepared to give Claire another chance and was determined to keep the family unit together. I don't believe Claire was ever really sorry about what she did. I know that she used every excuse under the sun and blamed Tom for working long hours, even though he was clearly doing it for her. I think that she was more upset that she was caught out.

"Tom left a note for everyone, but it was evident that he had been drinking when he wrote it. His English was generally impeccable and he was always one for pulling everyone else up on their spelling and grammar. However, his note was littered with errors and his normally neat handwriting was all over the place, disjointed and inconsistent.

"He began by saying that he loved everyone and that he apologised in advance for any distress that he had caused. He said that he thought it was better for everyone this way and that he hoped that his daughter would forgive him when she was old enough to understand. He then said that he couldn't come to terms with what Claire had done, but he said that she shouldn't be blamed and that he had made this decision to end it all.

"He talked about demons in his head that kept taunting him and I did wonder whether he was mentally ill, although he had no history of mental problems and had seemed fine the last time I had spoken to him.

"He finished up the note by saying that he would always be by everyone's side, even though we couldn't see him and said that he felt he could better support us that way. I know that he had always had a strong belief in life after death, so maybe he truly believed that everyone would benefit from his death in that he would always be with us in spirit, if not in body.

"When Claire found him, the note was by his side splattered with blood. When the police arrived, she had already screwed up the note, but they took it away with them as 'evidence'. If they hadn't done that, I don't think the rest of the family would ever have known about the note.

"I think she was more upset by the thought of coping on her own with their daughter rather than for the loss of Tom. I blamed her for everything at the time and was beside myself with rage. I wanted to strangle Claire. I spent most of those early days thinking about ways that I could get revenge, even though I knew that nothing I did would change what had happened. It was easier to do that than to believe that suicide was Tom's choice.

"Even now I can't help feeling that Claire was responsible, but I have realised that I should be spending my time supporting the rest of the family and mourning my brother's loss rather than wasting energy on such negative and destructive emotions as anger and resentment."

The shock of suicide can send some people into a state of denial. The disbelief of what has occurred can quickly turn to a refusal to accept it. Some bereaved families may ignore what has happened so that they are more able to cope. It seems to be a far easier option than facing the truth. Those who stay in denial longer are often those who were not present at the suicide scene, or who did not, or were not able to see their loved one after they died.

Had I not seen Kristian just after he died and again at the chapel of rest following the post mortem, I am certain that I would have kidded myself that the tragedy had not occurred. I could have pretended that I had been misinformed and that he would eventually turn up on my doorstep safe and well. I could have fooled myself into believing that he was on an extended holiday, or even living in another country; anything to avoid having to acknowledge the truth.

Cheryl understands this pretence well. Her son Dylan was 28 and married with a young family when he took his own life in August 2001.

"What happened to Dylan seemed so unreal. I didn't want to believe what had occurred. It was all too shocking to comprehend. I didn't want to see him. I wanted to remember him as he was; an intelligent, sensitive young man who was devoted to his family. I remember being forced to see my father after he had died and that gruesome impression still sticks in my mind. He looked like a different person. It certainly wasn't the Pop that I knew lying there. I didn't want the same waxy, lifeless image of my son to haunt me for the rest of my life.

"For a long time, I was in complete denial. I think there was a time when I truly believed that it hadn't happened and that Dylan was alive and well somewhere. Even the funeral didn't seem real and I found that I couldn't even cry, even though I felt that's what I should do. I didn't want others to think that I was cold, but I couldn't even shed a single tear. I was totally numb and I even wondered how everyone around me managed to sob so easily. I saw the coffin, but in my mind there was someone else in that box, not Dylan. It was as though I was a spectator at someone else's funeral.

"I remember other people thinking I was being strong and telling me that it was ok to cry, but I couldn't admit to them how I really felt. I wanted to say to them, 'It's alright; Dylan didn't die. You don't need to be sad.' I could tell that they were worried and I felt as though they were watching me the whole time, waiting for me to suddenly break down.

"I am now finally accepting that he is not coming back and I do cry for him, but an element of denial still lingers. I think I would more believe it if he were to walk through my door now than accept that he took his own life. I have heard people discuss what type of death is the worst; murder, cancer, accident and so on, but in all other cases the death is out of the control of the person concerned. Suicide is a choice that is made by the victim and self-murder just seems so incomprehensible. It's a loss that leaves so much guilt in its wake. How do families ever come to terms with that?"

Whilst all death is tragic and heartbreaking, surviving relatives can obtain some small comfort when the death has been from natural causes. The situation was out of their hands and the person who was sick did not make the decision to terminate their life. Murder, accidents and other unnatural causes of death are also not chosen and have been brought about by unfortunate circumstances.

In the case of suicide, the person has made the choice, whether conscious or not, to remove themselves from this world and it completely shatters the souls of the surviving families. The presence of a suicide victim has been stolen from you without warning, not giving you the chance to help, offer words of love and comfort, or say final farewells.

The suicide of a child, grandchild or sibling can initially erase every bit of hope or happiness, even in the most positive person, and the hopelessness can invade every aspect of the surviving families' lives. For a long time after Kristian's suicide, I would experience phases of numbness when I didn't really care what happened to me. I was just biding my time until my own life ended and I even began to welcome old age, because I would be closer to seeing my son again. The numbness was interspersed with periods of enormous guilt about my surviving children and how I could possibly have such morose thoughts when they were alive and well and needed me. These more rational thoughts helped to keep me sane and made me realise that I still had a purpose in life.

Whilst we are still dealing with the enormous shock of a child's suicide, we are consumed by other overwhelming feelings and horrific thoughts. There is little respite from the colossal blanket of grief beneath which we appear to be permanently trapped. Families don't feel that they will survive the tragedy and some even pray that they will be taken too. Healing is not a concept that they can even begin to contemplate in the early stages and in fact even the thought of healing can exacerbate the guilt. How can one even begin to selfishly think of healing when one's child never found emotional healing except through death? However, wanting to heal is not selfish. Quite the opposite. One needs to be able to cope in order to give one's best to surviving family and friends.

In those first few harrowing days, my partner said to me, "Before you know it, it will be one month, then six months and then a year will have passed and you won't believe how quickly the time has gone because you will always remember it as though it happened yesterday." He was right, although at that moment in time I could not grasp the concept that I would never see my son alive again. Everything was too unbearable, too horrific and too unreal.

Although parents will never forget, the acceptance of what has happened grows very gradually and you realise that whilst you believed you would never live through the loss, you have and still are. Healing doesn't mean never experiencing pain; it means learning to live with the pain, learning to live without the physical presence of your child and learning to find some enjoyment again. There will be many, many tears along the way, but at some point there will also be laughter and pleasure in memories of your child, memories that will always survive, irrespective of the number of years that pass.

Chapter Three

Rewriting the Script

If only he knew that I would have listened and suffered through ALL his problems with him, rather than bury him.

EA Gay
Mom to William Wayne Cox
2 November 1987 – 10 November 2003
Loved Forever and a Day
http://www.freewebs.com/williamwaynecox/

 I cannot possibly calculate the number of times that I have mentally altered the events of the day that Kristian finally decided to end his life and the morning after, when he actually died. Unlike a fictional script that can be re-written many times over until a satisfactory conclusion is reached, what has already occurred in the real world cannot be modified.
 Any parent who has lost a child to suicide will torture themselves for many reasons; for not noticing the signs, for not having said or done whatever may have been required to prevent the awful tragedy, for not being in the right place at the right time, for saying or doing things that they feel may have precipitated events and for not saying or doing the many things that they would liked to have said and done, had they known that their child was about to die. They may look back and think that their child's depression, if it was obvious, was disproportionate to a need to end their life, thus making the parents feel even more inadequate for having trivialised their child's problems.

I have thought about Halloween night 2002 over and over again. Whilst I was handing out candy to the streams of cutely dressed trick 'n' treaters who knocked at my door, my son was planning to end his life. The one child who should have called, didn't. It was the school half-term break and my partner was away at the time. I was sat alone, whilst our young daughter Lauren slept upstairs. I have tried to visualise exactly what Kristian was doing as I sat awaiting the next ring on the doorbell and the next round of assorted candy proffered to eager little fingers, some grasping as much as they could hold and others meekly taking just one sweet.

As I was giving dozens of children a heavy dose of sugar, my son was injecting himself with an equally heavy dose of heroin.

Accompanying most of the children were bored and weary parents, constantly checking their watches and coaxing polite "thank you's" from their progeny.

The following afternoon, as I was alone on my island of grief at the hospital, I wanted to round up all those parents who had visited the night before to tell them to cherish every moment with their children, however dull and tiresome those moments may sometimes feel.

In all the alternative scenarios that I have visualised, the final scene has the same conclusion; Kristian's life is saved.

In one script he calls me and asks to come 'round for a chat and company. My words give him hope and comfort. In another script he patches things up with his girlfriend and they spend the evening together. In yet another rewrite, a saviour appears at the right time and says something that tugs at his conscience and prevents him from taking the lethal injection.

In the least attractive script, he still takes the overdose, but his girlfriend's neighbours who walked past him twice as he sat unconscious on the stairwell landing of the block of flats, call the ambulance that night and the medical staff successfully save his life.

In the alternative, worst-case scenario, even the following morning, when the neighbours see him for the third time, despite his severely hypothermic state, the bleeding into his heart and lungs and respiration rate of only three breaths per minute, the ambulance staff successfully revive him for long enough to allow the ambulance to rush to the hospital so that the doctors manage to take whatever action is necessary to save him.

In both of the latter scenarios, I rush to the ICU at the local hospital to be at the bedside of my son, who is poorly but nevertheless alive and with an excellent prognosis. I tell him how much I love him and ask him to promise me that if ever he feels low enough to want to take his own life that he call me. I tell him that however great the pain, the only time that hope is all lost is when someone dies. Even though he may believe that there is no hope left, there truly is because he is still alive. I tell him that he is surrounded by people who love him and need him. I reassure him that everything will be ok and that I will offer him all the support he needs to climb out of the deep, dark pit from which he thought there was no escape.

Of course, no matter how many times I rewrite the script, the movie has already been screened, the final scene acted out and the conclusion reached. My son is dead. His final breath heralded the end of his pain and the beginning of ours.

In some cases, rewriting the script can keep suicide grievers trapped in the denial stage.

Heather, an Independent Financial Adviser whose 22-year-old son Andrew had hung himself in his flat in October 1999, recreated events that she still partly believes might be true. She said, "When my ex-husband, Louis, telephoned me to break the tragic news of Andrew's suicide, I was immediately flung into a state of utter disbelief. In fact, I remember calmly replacing the receiver and returning to my meeting with a client in my home, acting as though nothing out of the ordinary had happened. I had convinced myself that my ex was playing some sort of sick joke on me, because that was his style.

"About twenty minutes after I had spoken to him, Louis burst through the door and asked me what the hell I was playing at. He screamed at me, 'Don't you realise our son is dead? What's the matter with you? I thought Andrew was your life!' When I saw his face, I knew that this was no prank and I became hysterical. He had identified Andrew's body, but I refused to go to the hospital to see him. I thought that by not seeing him, I could somehow convince myself that he was still alive.

" Later that same day, after a flow of various people, including the police, friends and family had come and gone, I re-entered the total denial phase and, to a certain extent, I've never really moved on from there. I had no desire to visit Andrew before the funeral, even though a few family members went along to say goodbye. I had convinced myself that one of them would call me to tell me that it wasn't Andrew's body they had seen, but they didn't. I then thought that maybe they were too polite to say that it didn't look like him, for fear of upsetting me.

"Andrew didn't leave a suicide note and all the time I avoided facing any evidence, I could carry on believing that he had gone on a trip somewhere and that one day he would telephone or walk through my door, as he always did whenever he needed something.

"In my mind, Andrew didn't hang himself. There were no noticeable signs that he had been depressed and he had no history of depression, although I understand that suicidal feelings can be one-off occurrences, brought about by extreme circumstances. In my version of events, Andrew came home that day, packed his bags and left on a long trip. I have imagined that he didn't tell me he was going, because he knew I would be upset. The body that my ex-husband identified was not Andrew's, neither was it Andrew's body in the coffin at the funeral.

"Everyone around me was offering sympathy and making the appropriate gestures and yet I almost felt like a fraud. My son hadn't died. I wanted to tell them that he would be away for a while, but that he would be coming back so they didn't need to feel sad for me. Even as I speak, I know that I sound completely irrational and I suppose that the logical part of my mind prevented me from revealing my thoughts to people. I was sure that they would think I had gone completely mad, but it was – and still is – my way of coping. By rewriting history, I can change the future. If Andrew didn't die, then I won't have to face a future without him, even though I have lived without him for several years now.

"I know that psychologists and grief counsellors would tell me that what I am doing is not healthy, but this is real life and this is how I feel I need to handle the situation. I can't go by the book and follow some 12-step plan. Nobody has lost my child and everyone is unique, so in a way I resent other people trying to tell me how I should feel, when I should feel it and how I should deal with it. If my way of surviving is by rewriting the script, as Jan says, then that is what I shall do."

I wouldn't have been as able to detect the signs of the depression and hopelessness that eventually led to Kristian's suicide as readily as those friends with whom he had shared the majority of the last four years of his life. He had not lived at home since the age of 16 and every time I saw him, no matter what misfortune had befallen him, he was always bright, cheerful and optimistic. In speaking to his girlfriend and other close friends, however, they all said the same. Although there were indications that not all was well in his mind, on the outside he presented his usual happy-go-lucky persona. Even in moments when he appeared to be quiet and reflective, a brief "Are you alright Kristian?" would immediately switch the light in his eyes back on and he would be the same jovial boy that everyone knew and loved; an exterior of cheerfulness concealing a core of melancholy. In the same way that we survivors feel compelled to wear a mask, my son hid behind a disguise of cheerfulness and optimism.

Those who associated closely with him during the final weeks of his life said that they now realise that some of the things that he did and said were subtle indicators of his intention. He was passionately attached to a white, padded Valentino jacket. Two weeks before his death, he had verbally offered this much valued possession to a friend saying, "You can have my white jacket."

On the morning of 31 October 2002, he visited the friend with whom he had lived rent-free for a period of time the previous year. He hugged his friend and said, "You've always been like a brother to me." Several people confirmed that the last time they had seen him he was talking in the past tense and making similar gestures of gratitude, each time beginning his communication with, "You've always been……"

If any of us had realised his intention, would we have been able to do anything to prevent it? Maybe not. But maybe we would have be able to say that we had tried, that we were able to remind him of how much he was loved and how much he would be missed if he were no longer with us. Maybe our guilt would have been lessened and maybe we would not be feeling, as we are now, that there was so much unfinished business.

When a child completes suicide, there is inevitably a sense of failure on the part of those who have been left behind, not least of all the parents. They will always reproach themselves for past words and actions, but no parent is perfect. Sometimes we do and say things that seem right at the time and sometimes, often when tired, stressed or irritable, we say and do things that we know aren't appropriate, yet our children do exactly the same.

In chastising our children and teaching them right from wrong, we are preparing them for life, not death. When you are engulfed in guilt about something that you said and did that you feel may have contributed to your child's death, think about some of the hurtful things that maybe your child has said and done in the past. No child is perfect either and had it been you who had died and not your child, he or she would now be enduring the same pain and guilt about certain hurtful words or actions they had bestowed upon you in the past.

Unfortunately, we cannot change the past. We falsely believe that being able to rewrite the script would prevent the tragedy, yet we would almost certainly find that whatever we said and did may not have altered the outcome and we would still believe that we had made the wrong decisions. One parent may be saying, "If only I'd been more lenient with him", whereas another may say, "If only I'd been tougher on her".

Sometimes there doesn't seem to be any right or wrong way, because when your child dies you will always believe that the path that you chose was the incorrect one.

It is a sad fact that society has a tendency to blame parents for all the failings of their children. When a child takes his or her own life, in addition to the intense grief, bereaved parents may have to contend with feelings of shame. They may believe that others are pointing the finger at them, in the belief that the child must have had an unbearable home life. The parents imagine that neighbours and acquaintances are whispering behind their backs and criticising their parenting skills. However, research has shown the families of children who kill themselves are generally no more dysfunctional than those of children who move on to lead happy and successful lives.

Unlike movies and screenplays, real life does not allow us to edit and rewrite. We have to make up the scenes as we go along without the benefit of hindsight. When we make choices, we do not often realise whether it is the right or wrong choice at the time. Only by viewing the consequences afterwards can we make that judgement. We can sometimes anticipate the possible effects, but we never know for sure at the time.

We cannot personally alter the physiology of someone's brain. We cannot control how someone perceives or reacts to your words and actions. Different people have varying abilities to cope with the stresses of life. What one person may consider as a minor inconvenience from which they move onwards in their life can seem like an insurmountable problem to someone else.

We can only attempt to do the best for our children when they are with us. Even if we were permanently handcuffed to our children, we would still be unable to control their thought processes and even if we were able to rewrite the script, we may still have no control over the ending.

Whatever the situation, some suicidal people feel that they have no control over their lives and have a reduced ability to cope with the pressures of relationships, family life, peer pressure and school or work-related issues. If we could turn back the clock, we could only offer help, advice and support in a limited capacity. We cannot live someone's life for them and we certainly cannot control their feelings.

The frightening fact is that many suicidal people appear to be functioning normally immediately prior to their death and do not always emit "warning" signals. This is sometimes done as a conscious effort to fool close friends and family into believing that everything is fine, thereby maximising their chances of success.

Anneliese spoke to Kristian from our house two days before his death. She said that he sounded like the same old Kristian and that she could detect no signs in his voice or their dialogue that suggested that all was not well in his mind. Although I usually pride myself on being highly attuned to others' feelings, even when they are trying to hide their true emotions, I too did not perceive from the conversation that took place that my son was about to end his life. Kristian did not have a history of depression, nor was he ever engulfed in a black mood. He always had an amazing ability to pick himself up and carry on with life, irrespective of the circumstances. His most outstanding qualities were his compassion and his ability to forgive others, no matter how much they had hurt him. He did not carry around a heavy burden of grudges and had a very large circle of friends, including a devoted girlfriend and a family who loved him. Of course, we would never know what demons plagued his mind.

Since his death, I discovered that for three years he had been regularly attending a local support group for drug users and their families, so he had at least acknowledged that he had a problem.

Rewriting the script again, I have visualised myself attending this group with him. Would the ending have been different had he had the courage to admit to me that he was using heroin and had I been able to support him through his addiction? Maybe courage is the wrong word to use, since he claimed that he kept things from me that he thought would worry me. He felt that he was protecting me through his secrecy, even though I would eventually find out about any major events in his life. Unfortunately, the most major event of all was his suicide.

Not only have I re-written the script for the time before his death, but even after. Although his funeral couldn't have been more perfect, I have since re-played that day over and over in my mind, imagining that I saw him there joining in the celebration of his life. Although I sensed his presence, I wanted to be able to see him. I wanted to see his face smiling at everyone and appreciating how many people had made the effort to attend, even his heroin user acquaintances, who clearly didn't have a great deal of money and probably lived their lives for their next fix. The attendance was overwhelming; a sea of strange faces from the other world in which he lived and died. I wanted to see the pride in Kristian's eyes, knowing that he had touched the lives of so many.

After the service, I was quickly ushered into the waiting limousine, which left swiftly before many of the anonymous, tear-tracked faces had left the church. I assumed that I would have the opportunity to speak to people and thank them for attending after the burial ceremony, which took place at a cemetery situated several miles from the church.

At the cemetery, the sunshine appeared for the only time that day and shone like a celestial angel on the mourning assemblage and the coffin as it was lowered into the cold, sodden ground, with rainwater cascading down the sides of the grave.

After the brief ceremony, my partner took my arm and led me away from the grave, even though I wanted to stand and gaze at my son's coffin and visualise his body for as long as possible. I remember wondering why there were so many leaves lying in the bottom of the grave when it had only been dug out the previous day.

After a brief word with the vicar, my partner again seemed keen to guide me back to the limousine and as I glanced back over my shoulder whilst painfully forcing myself to step forward, I could see the trail of nameless young mourners filing slowly past the grave and casting in individual flowers. I wanted to speak to those people. I wanted to communicate with anyone who had spent time with Kristian over the last few weeks of his life. I envied them. I also wanted to be the last person to see my son's coffin before the grave was filled in with the heavy, clay-based earth and yet I didn't say anything. I felt as though I was in one of those dreams where you open your mouth to say something, but nothing comes out, or you try to run with legs that are instantly paralysed.

My partner told me afterwards that he was concerned that the water pouring into the grave would upset me and so he wanted to move me away from the scene before I saw my son's coffin become cruelly submerged.

In my burial scene rewrite, I wait on the path to greet people as they leave the graveside, introducing myself to those whom I have never met and perhaps seeking some answers to the never ending questions that have been dancing menacingly around my tortured mind. I wanted them to know how grateful I was to them for their loyalty to Kristian. I wanted to know in what capacity they knew him and the state of his psyche the last time they interacted with him.

The difference with the above rewrites is that I will still potentially have the chance to speak to these people, because they are still alive. Where there's life, anything is possible. In death, everything is too late.

Margaret's eldest son, Karl, died in April 1999 at the age of 33 after jumping from the top floor of a multi-storey car park. She believes that she did everything that she could to help him and although she says that if she could turn the clock back, she would not do anything differently, she still feels that his death could have been avoided.

"Karl had been suffering from bipolar disorder for 17 years before he died. He tried his hardest to 'live' with the condition. He tried every medicine available, both conventional and alternative, together with counselling and psychiatric help, not to mention endless support from his family.

"At one point, he actually admitted himself to a hospital, which unfortunately just proved to him that although he wasn't ill enough to be sectioned within a medical institution, he also wasn't stable enough to live independently in society.

"Karl was sadly never able to hold down any sort of steady relationship, because none of the girls with whom he became involved could handle his illness. The relationships would always begin when Karl was going through one of his settled periods, although he was always honest with everyone he met. He would tell his girlfriends about his illness at the beginning of the relationship to give them the chance to walk away. Of course, they were all understanding and thought that they would be able to deal with it, not realising how emotionally and physically draining it would be.

"Some of them stayed the course longer than others, but eventually the relationship would break down. Sometimes he would leave them, but more often than not, they would leave because they could not cope with the inconsistency of his moods.

"Although I feel that his family had done everything they could to help him, I have often visualised how different things might have been had he found a truly caring girl who continued to support and love him through the most difficult times. I feel like contacting all of his ex-girlfriends and shouting at them, 'If you had truly loved and cared for him, you would never have left him and he might still be alive now.'

"It now makes me question whether anyone apart from a mother is capable of unconditional love, but I will never stop imagining how different the outcome might have been had he maintained a successful relationship.

"So many people have tried to tell me that it was his time and that whatever else had happened in his life, whatever anyone had or hadn't said or done, he would still have died. I'd like to believe that, because then maybe I would be more accepting of his loss, but I can't. I will always believe that things could have been so different. I will always be saying, 'If only' until I take my final breath."

Stephen's son Gary put a gun under his chin in March 1996 at the age of 21. Gary had been mentally ill for four years and even though Stephen feels that he and his wife were constantly by his side supporting him and nursing him through his illness, they still couldn't prevent him from taking his own life. He knows that many bereaved parents feel that if they had the opportunity to go back and rewrite history that the ending would have been happy.

Stephen thinks differently and hopes that telling his story will demonstrate that even when you believe you have done everything possible, the final scene may still be the same.

"Although Gary knew the seriousness of his illness, he refused to acknowledge it and it was a struggle to encourage him to take his medication. He felt that he didn't need to be 'pumped full of pills', despite being eventually ordered to take his medication and receive psychiatric help, or else be sectioned on a psychiatric wing.

"On three occasions, we were so desperate that we actually had him committed. He had been refusing point blank to take his medication and was threatening to kill himself. He told us after the first time of being committed that if we ever did that to him again, he would leave home and disown us. He never carried out the threat to leave, but of course that black cloud of fear loomed over us. We knew that he would not survive alone and although we believed that he relied too much upon us to ever leave, we constantly worried that he might actually kill himself.

"He was unable to hold down a job or a relationship as a result of his illness and much of the time he was as dependent on us as a small child. What I found really frustrating was that nobody could tell us why Gary had become ill and there is certainly no family history of depression or mental illness on either side of our family.

"In June 1995, when Gary's condition deteriorated further, I took early retirement to help my wife look after him. It was a true labour of love. There were ok days, good days, bad days and absolutely diabolical days. The worst days were those when I felt that life could not continue as it was and that we would have to commit Gary to an institution permanently. In those darkest moments, however, something would happen to lift the veil of hopelessness and make us cherish the fact that we still had Gary at home with us.

"The beginning of the end came when Gary accused us of trying to poison him. Instead of trying to force him to take his medication, my wife would crush his pills into his food and on this particular morning he had walked into the kitchen and seen her doing this. A terrible argument ensued, which culminated in Gary trying to strangle his mother. I don't know how far he would have gone had I not managed to pull him off, but as a result he was arrested and committed to a psychiatric hospital 20 miles away.

"The police who arrested Gary were very understanding and thankfully realised that the best place for him was not a police cell. They understood that he was very unwell and were very good in helping us to facilitate arrangements for his admittance to hospital.

"As soon as Gary had been arrested though, he was extremely remorseful. He remained in a psychiatric unit for five days and did not put a foot wrong for his entire stay. By the end of the fourth day, the doctors told us that Gary was mentally stable and was well enough to be discharged. When we went to collect him the following day, he seemed very subdued and didn't say a great deal, only that he was glad to be coming home and that he was sorry for what he had done to his mother.

"As soon as we arrived home, Gary took himself off to his room and just lay on his bed with his hands behind his head staring at the ceiling. We checked on him compulsively, sensing that something was terribly wrong and petrified of what he might do to himself. We did everything that we could to coax him from his room. We offered him the opportunity to go and do the things he used to enjoy before he became sick, although I admit that I refrained from suggesting activities where I thought there was the potential for him to self-harm, such as paragliding.

"We tried everything, but nothing could move him from his room, except the call of nature. He even refused to eat with us and so we took his meals to his room. Sometimes he ate them, but most of the time he just picked at his food and pushed it around his plate. After a couple of days of this, he then began making disturbing pictures with the food, like a coffin and unhappy, distorted faces.

"On the third day following his release from hospital, we telephoned his psychiatrist, but ended up having to leave a message with the receptionist. We called seven times before the psychiatrist eventually called back. It appears that the first few messages weren't passed on by the receptionist, which made me begin to question the efficiency of the mental health system. The psychiatrist told us that as long as Gary was eating and was in our house, there was little cause for worry. He told us that he was in the safest environment possible, but to call back if Gary left the house without us, or became violent again.

"Gary didn't really leave his room for the final month of his life and we barely left the house. My wife and I certainly didn't leave the house together, so that there was never any time when Gary was alone, except in his room. I also made sure that I removed my air rifle from the house and gave it to my sister to store. We locked away sharp knives and potentially harmful drugs and thought we had removed any object that could obviously be used for self-harm.

"By the end of the first week, it was clear that Gary was not improving and he seemed to be losing weight rapidly. I called the psychiatrist again and after much persuasion he agreed to come out and assess Gary, because we knew that we would not be able to get Gary to agree to go and see him.

"Gary was not stupid. He could be very clever and calculating and during his session with the psychiatrist, he gave all the right responses and convinced the psychiatrist that he was behaving perfectly rationally and just wanted time out. As a result, we were no further forward and the psychiatrist left feeling satisfied that there was no imminent risk.

"I had this constant nagging feeling that something more sinister was going on in Gary's mind. I even asked him whether he wanted to go back to hospital for a while to 'recover', but he said that he was never going back to one of those 'institutions full of crazy, incontinent people'. He said he wasn't sick. He said he didn't want to talk. He said he just needed time alone to sort out in his mind what he wanted to do with his life. He said he had thought about returning to college and learning a trade, which sounded positive, but I still felt this deep sense of uneasiness.

"On 8 March 1996, the final evening of his life, Gary actually came downstairs and shared the evening meal with us. For the first time, I felt a little more positive. Little did my wife and I realise that it would be his last meal. He actually helped his mother with the dishes and then watched about half an hour of TV with us before retiring to his room. About ten minutes later, we heard an alarming gunshot and sickening thud, which was the sound of Gary's body falling to the floor. It was all over.

"Our son had lulled us into a false sense of security. Through all the precautions that we took in removing dangerous implements from his reach, we failed to check his room, although this would have been virtually impossible since he only ever left it for trips to the bathroom. We still have no idea from where he obtained the gun that he used to kill himself. I could have found out, I suppose, but I don't know how I would have reacted to the person who supplied him with the weapon. Was it someone who knew about his mental illness?

He didn't have any income of his own with which to purchase a gun. There are some questions like these to which I don't think I even want to know the answers.

"I hope our story shows that even when you have the opportunity to do everything that you can to change the situation, sometimes it is just not possible. If I allowed myself to dwell too long on the situation, I would inevitably think of something else that we could possibly have done and yet my wife and I weren't the only decision makers. The person who had the greatest control was Gary. Without his consent, it was practically impossible to do anything.

"I have spoken to many families who are beating themselves up over thoughts of things that they now feel they should have said or done and that if they were given the opportunity to turn back time, their children might still be alive today. What I would say to them is that even if they had done things differently, they may still have lost their children. You see, you cannot always change the way that someone thinks and feels, especially when you are dealing with depression, which is an evil, overpowering disease that can completely take over someone's mind and personality."

We all believe that we should have done more to protect our children, siblings and grandchildren, guiding them or being there for them, no matter what they did or how old they were. Sadly, we are often helpless when they make their choices in life and all we can do is stand by and watch as their lives unfold around them and they struggle through it in their own way. They are often so naive, believing they know so much about life, yet they know so little, just as we did at their age. The frustration is having to stand and watch as they make their mistakes, despite what we try to tell them or the advice we try to offer, for in their naivety they also believe we know so little and just "don't understand".

As a result, the family unit is often the last place they will turn to for help or guidance, despite the fact that we are the only ones who truly care.

If we all lived our lives in fear of the unexpected, we would never do anything. We would be paranoid wrecks confined to our homes, unable to perform the most routine of daily functions. Most of us have busy, complicated lives and the best that we can do is to love as much as we can, show those close to us that we care and let them know that we are there for them if they need anything. Sometimes, we just have to rely on others to come to us. Even if we sense a problem, some people may be too proud to ask for help. If they value their independence, they may resent any intrusion and may wish to hold us at a distance. If we pry and persist, we may risk alienating them. The important thing is to let them know that our door is always open.

We can continue to torture ourselves to the degree where our negative thoughts, guilt and feelings of helplessness can suffocate us and prevent us from moving forward positively in our lives. Whilst rewriting the script will never return our children to us in this life, we can learn serious lessons from the tragedy and do our utmost to care for those around us who are still living and breathing, by extending arms of love.

Kristian asleep with his favourite bear, 1983

Chapter Four

Trapped in a Storm of Agonising Emotions

The ghastliness and torture of suicide affects everyone, even those who only knew the victim vaguely and yet no one seems to want to talk about it. People silently question the certainty of their own lives and those of their loved ones, because what was once unthinkable could potentially and horrifyingly become a reality.

    The suicide of one's child raises agonising questions, doubts and fears and creates emotions of an intensity that cannot fully be described in words that we know. When your child takes his or her own life, at the very least you feel as though your heart has been viciously torn from within your body in an unprovoked assault. You are totally consumed by the loss. You always feel a sense of blame and believe that there is something you could have done to save your child's life.
    The eternal question that is uppermost in most suicide grievers' minds is, "Why?" Nevertheless, it is one that can usually only be answered by the person who has died.
    Wondering why your love was not enough to save your child, the doubts that you feel others may have about your abilities as a parent and the fear that something may happen to any other children you have, will almost certainly generate powerful feelings of guilt and failure. However, even though you undoubtedly gave your child your best, in situations like this you will probably torture yourself with all the negative things you said and did, even though they may have been fuelled by frustration, anger or exasperation at the time. You may want to punish yourself by feeling the way that your child felt at the moment that he decided to end his life.

Most suicidal people do not truly want to die. They want their pain to end. Sometimes, they believe that suicide is the only way to escape their problems and sometimes it is a cry for help that goes horribly wrong.

Although the deceased child can never be replaced, some parents may instantly feel the desire to have another baby if the mother is still of reproductive age. Others may feel that they could not possibly contemplate the thought of having history repeat itself. Many people feel inadequate as parents and may question their ability to continue to raise any other children they may have. If the child you lost was your only child, you may be asking the question, "Am I still a parent?"

I still tell people that I have four children, but I also mention that my eldest son died. I refuse to deny Kristian's existence. He was a major part of my life for over twenty years and he still lives on in my heart and my memory. I raised four children and therefore I am still a mother of four.

Immediately after Kristian's death, I felt completely detached from my body. The shock and disbelief knocked me into a dreamlike state and I was sure that I was a spectator in one of my very worst nightmares. The difference was that I couldn't wake up to the real world, because this was cruel reality. I performed routine functions on autopilot, existing rather than living. There were many moments when I thought that the grief and guilt would kill me. Suddenly, all the threads and knots that had formed the tapestry of my life became unravelled, leaving a disorganised heap from which I could make no sense.

For the first few days, I couldn't eat and I couldn't sleep. Every morsel of food I placed in my mouth lodged at the back of my throat, as a river of guilt tears cascaded down my cheeks. Kristian would never eat again.

He had always loved his food and rather than celebrating his life by partaking in one of his favourite pastimes, I felt that enjoying food was an insult to his memory. I felt as though we were mocking him. I did not see eating as being intrinsic to survival, because at that time, I did not care whether I lived or died. I felt selfish continuing to nurture my own body, when I had not been able to keep my son alive. I couldn't understand how the rest of my family managed to eat with ease and clear their plates with gusto. I was trapped within an inescapable bubble of torment, whilst the rest of the world carried on around me, oblivious to my loss.

Even though I was emotionally shattered, sleep evaded me for the first few nights. I sobbed, screamed and howled like a wild animal caught in a poacher's trap, finding solace in nothing. In between open displays of unyielding anguish, I frantically searched for folders of Kristian's old schoolwork, as though anything that he had once created in life was the most valuable object on earth. In fact, anything that Kristian had made, touched or worn became priceless to me.

My partner admitted that I was scaring him. He was so afraid that I would have a breakdown, so even in the depths of my sorrow, I found myself protecting him and allaying his fears by containing my most intense emotions whilst in his presence. At times it was impossible and often the tears would spill out uncontrollably, but instead of yielding fully to my grief, I would sob silently. It made me feel as though I would implode, but I felt that there was only so much that others were capable of handling. Their inability to do or say anything to remove my pain rendered them helpless. I wanted them to understand that I didn't want my pain to be removed. The fact that I was feeling the pain was a sign that I loved and missed my son.

What I did want was for my son to be resurrected, returned, for his body to be restored to life, for him to come back to me. I battled constantly with the realisation that I was never going to see my son again in this life in the physical sense.

During the daytime, all my energy was expended trying to stay afloat, but in the dark of the night when some senses were dulled and others heightened, I was drowning in my grief. My sight was impaired, being replaced by disturbing pictures in my mind; harsh, torturous images of my son, cold and blue, teetering on the edge of death, waiting for his pain to end. The silence of the night was interrupted only by the occasional sound of fallen autumn leaves being teased along the ground by the wind. My ears were free to be assaulted by echoes of the past; my son's voice, the life-changing words uttered by the policeman, the gentle delivery of distressing words from the doctor who tried to save Kristian's life and my own unremitting wailing that left me gasping for air.

My partner's fears for my health prompted him to telephone the emergency doctor on call after my second night of sleeplessness. I knew that I was exhausted and I knew that I needed to sleep, but I didn't want to. I was afraid of sleeping and dreaming that life was the "normal" I had known just a few days earlier. It was like the night terror scenario in reverse. I was terrified that I would have pleasant dreams about Kristian and then awake to the nightmare of reality.

"You need to sleep", said my partner before leaving to pick up a prescription for one week's supply of Temazepam tablets. I was not fond of taking any sort of unnatural medication and the irony was that Temazepam is the drug that addicts take when heroin is not available. My partner was adamant, however, that I would only be taking the tablets for five days.

That night I finally fell into a deep sleep after a couple of hours of torturing myself with thoughts of my son's heartbreaking exit from this world. My dreams were filled with vivid images of Kristian, alive and well, so that when I awoke in the morning the brutal realisation of what had happened struck me violently and agonisingly. Once again, I would curl up into a ball and sob, scream and whine piercingly. I was certain that I would not survive this and yet I knew that I could not fail my other children. How would they cope if I were to die and yet how could I cope if I continued to live? I then thought of Kristian and how distraught he would be to see me suffering that way. Had the situation been reversed and had it been I who had died, I would never have wanted my children to suffer and would certainly not want them to grieve terminally. This thought, however, only gave me very brief respite from the feelings of wretchedness in the early days.

Accompanying the shock, disbelief and intense sadness were totally overpowering and excruciating feelings of guilt. In my mind, it was my fault that he had felt the need to end his life. If I hadn't believed in "tough love", if I hadn't pushed him away when he was behaving badly, if I had been more tolerant of his shortcomings, if I hadn't allowed other people to treat him harshly, if I had stood up for him more when he had been verbally battered by others, if I had allowed him to move back home when he asked me, if I had lent him money when he needed it and if I had told him more often how much I loved him, then maybe, just maybe, he would still be alive.

I had convinced myself that I didn't care what other people thought of Kristian's actions. All that mattered to me, I told myself, was that my son was dead, yet when I heard about someone passing judgement, it did matter.

I felt that I owed it to my son to defend him, not least because he was no longer able to defend himself and no one, except those who had been there, could possibly be qualified to criticise. Other people's condemnation of Kristian's actions just intensified the already complicated emotions that smothered me. How could they speak ill of the dead? How could they allow the manner in which he died negate all of his wonderful qualities and the person that he had been before the desperation drove him to end his misery? How could they be so insensitive to my grief? If I had been a more insensitive person myself, I would have turned around to these people and said, "There are plenty of judgements I could make about your life, but I wouldn't be so heartless."

How can anyone criticise the schoolchild who has been bullied to suicide? How can they judge a child who is not mature enough to deal with such emotional and physical torture? How can they think negatively of someone who was so afraid of retaliation and further bullying that they felt powerless to protect themselves? Throw the critics naked to the bottom of a 1,000 metre well, with slippery sides interspersed with razor blades, with no light and absolutely no way out. Then ask them what their options are? The longer they are in the well, the smaller the options become until there are only two remaining; waiting for death or chasing it. From the moment that we are conceived, death is chasing us. Some of us gamble with our lives by engaging in dangerous pursuits as though we are inviting death to come and grab us, but whilst most of us will keep running from it until it catches us, some chase it, knowing that when they have caught it, their misery will cease.

Four days after Kristian's death, a sinister, vicious anger emerged from the depths of my despair. I had never experienced such intense fury and it terrified me. I was alarmed by the power of my rage and even though I was experiencing the devastation caused by death, I felt that this emotional lack of control could lead me to harm someone. My vehemence was directed not toward Kristian, but toward anyone who had ever hurt Kristian, emotionally or physically, directly or indirectly, in any way. I felt furious with anyone who had battered his self-esteem by making cruel references to his weight, or by falsely blaming him for crimes that they had committed in order to avoid their own punishment.

I felt intensely irritated that my partner was not affected by Kristian's loss in the same way as I was, because he had never formed any sort of emotional bond with him. I spoke to another bereaved parent who was in a similar situation and she admitted that she had toyed with the idea that maybe her husband was secretly relieved that part of the burden of being involved in a stepfamily had been removed. She never voiced her feelings to her husband, because she anticipated an explosive reaction, which would only send her further into isolation.

Nevertheless, my partner was my mainstay and I cannot emphasise enough the unfailing love and support that he gave to me in those early days and since. Maybe his emotional detachment from Kristian was to my benefit. It enabled him to be strong for me, to catch me each time I was about to fall and to carry me when I was unable to sustain myself. Were it not for his love and understanding, I don't know how I would have survived.

My anger brought out the worst in me and completely stifled my normally forgiving nature. I despised the ex-neighbour whose actions had caused so much distress to Kristian years earlier; I wanted to take down the drug dealers who had preyed on my son's vulnerability and, above all, I wanted to inflict emotional suffering on anyone in his life who had rejected or bullied him. In fact, a male acquaintance of Kristian's very kindly provided me with the contact details of numerous drug dealers in the area, which I had great pleasure in passing onto the police. I would have no hesitation in doing this again in the future. I refuse to allow bullies to control my actions through fear. If everyone took a stand, it would be a step closer to eradicating the problem.

My moods were totally unpredictable and could change in an instant from this venomous anger to despair, guilt and disbelief in a matter of minutes. Tears of anger, tears of intense sadness, tears for Kristian's pain, tears of guilt, tears for everything that had been and everything that would never be; tears for the past, tears for a future without my son and tears for a future that my son would never have the opportunity to experience.

If Kristian had had more self-worth, then maybe he would have realised that he was a valid person, who deserved a decent life and maybe he wouldn't have chosen the slippery road downhill to drug addiction, hopelessness and suicide. I wanted to physically attack the person who had supplied Kristian with the heroin that he used to kill himself. I wanted to reproach anyone who had ever sold him heroin, or taken heroin with him. I wanted to know why they hadn't stopped him, even though the rational part of my mind told me that it had been his personal choice, as was his decision to kill himself. The rational part also told me that reason and truth dive out the window the moment someone begins injecting heroin.

Nevertheless, at that point I felt that if certain people hadn't made Kristian feel rejected and unworthy, if certain people hadn't encouraged him to use drugs and if certain people had made more of an effort to deny him drugs, then my naïve but beautiful, reckless but caring, impulsive but sensitive son might still be alive today.

Many parents, grandparents and siblings will want to apportion blame for their child, grandchild, brother or sister's death. Some may want revenge, whilst others will search for fruitless answers that they believe may help them to understand why the tragedy occurred.

What is most tragic, however, is that there doesn't always have to be a circumstantial reason for someone's depression. Depression is very misunderstood, as demonstrated by the standard response of, "What are you depressed about?" whenever someone admits that they are feeling unhappy. Someone might appear to have the most fabulous life; the ideal home, enough money, a full social life, a loving partner, a supportive family and all the other elements that many people believe should equate to happiness and yet they may still be depressed.

Depression is controlled by the neurotransmitter, Serotonin, a chemical released in the brain. Disturbances in the Serotonin system are associated with depression and suicidal behaviour. Again, however, there is no doubt that in many cases, depression and suicide are linked to circumstances and problems within someone's life that appear undefeatable and which can cause the surviving families to blame.

Bullying is one of the circumstantial causes of suicidal behaviour. Sadly, bullying in schools is not being adequately addressed. Many schools boast elaborate anti-bullying policies and yet few are backed up with positive action. I know this from personal experience.

We seem to live in a "namby pamby" society where people feel rendered powerless to do anything to tackle the bullies and it appears as though it is the victims of bullying who are the ones being punished. Teachers are afraid of parents, parents are afraid of other parents and both are afraid of children and emotional blackmail. Nevertheless, bullying is not a sign of power or strength; it's a sign of weakness.

Jennifer's 14-year-old daughter Amy killed herself in October 1997 after stealing some sleeping pills from her grandmother's bathroom cabinet. Amy had been bullied continually at school by a group of girls in her year, but despite many complaints to the school, the bullying continued. Jennifer said that the teachers put it down to "normal, girly bickering" and reassured her that whilst they might fall out one day, the next day everyone would be friends again. She knew that the situation was far more serious than this and just felt that the teachers were shirking their moral and professional responsibility.

Jennifer said, "I thought the situation had been dealt with, because Amy suddenly seemed happier and stopped crying about the girls who made her life a misery. I realise now that the bullying hadn't stopped at all, but Amy's apparent happiness lay in her decision to end the torture forever. When I asked her how things were at school, she said, 'Fine. Everything's sorted now.' I feel so wretched now, knowing that everything clearly wasn't fine. Why couldn't I see it? Why couldn't I see further than her reassuring smile?

"On the morning that we discovered her lifeless body after she'd failed to get up for school, the feelings of total despair, helplessness, shock, disbelief and grief were quickly overpowered by an anger such that I'd never felt before.

"The bullies and the school staff were totally to blame for Amy's death. I didn't buy into the argument that it is the suicidal person who makes the choice to end her life. If my daughter hadn't been bullied and if the school had taken steps to effectively deal with the problem, then my beautiful, loving daughter would still be with us. My daughter was not mature enough to be able to take a step back, look at the situation rationally and take charge of her reaction to the bullying, as some experts might suggest.

"One day in the future I might feel differently and will be able to view the situation in a more rational manner, even though it happened over a decade ago. Even now, I don't feel at all rational. How can I? My daughter was bullied and now she is dead. I still don't know now how I would react if I were ever to encounter any of the girls who bullied Amy. Some of them probably have children of their own by now.

"Although I would never wish this tragedy on anyone, I would like to ask those who might think that I am not being fair in my reckoning to come back in the future and tell me how they then feel if, heaven forbid, the same fate should befall one of their children. The most judgemental people are always those whose own experiences don't even come close to the trauma of those upon whom they are passing judgement."

When my intense anger had faded, I then experienced remorse for having felt so ill-disposed towards those with whom Kristian had shared the last few years of his life. How could I feel angry with anyone who had shown him love and friendship, in whatever capacity? Kristian would have perceived even those who had offered and used heroin with him as friends, because to him, anyone who passed time with him in whatever manner was his definition of acceptance.

The number of friends and acquaintances at his funeral was overwhelming, as indeed have been the wonderful tributes and gestures of affection that have adorned his grave ever since. It was apparent that he had earned the respect of a great number of people, even though in the moment that he decided to end his life he had felt very isolated in his sorrow. Some of those towards whom I had felt the most intense anger had made the effort to travel across town to his funeral. Many of those acquaintances did not have a great deal of money, so I was touched by their loyalty and deeply saddened also by their loss.

With each week and month that passed, the incredulity of what had happened subsided and was replaced by bitter reality. I realised that the initial shock had acted as a shield to some of the most intense emotions. It allowed a degree of pain to filter through, but also acted as the body's protective mechanism, preventing me from enduring more pain than could possibly be tolerated at any one time. It was like being weaned off of an analgesic when the disorder still existed, allowing me to absorb some of the truth and experience the full force of the pain.

By the six-month mark, I had descended into my own living hell, fully aware of what had happened and paralysed by an avalanche of asphyxiating emotions. The disbelief, however, never entirely leaves. Even now, when my mind has been distracted and my entire focus hasn't been on Kristian, or when I wake up in the morning, the awful truth will suddenly strike me with violent force. My son is dead. I then keep repeating over and over in my mind, "Kristian's dead, Kristian's dead, Kristian's dead." I still feel as though I am ensnared in a horrendous dream from which I will eventually wake.

I found that when the numbness and shock began to wear off, there was nothing to soften the pain, just the full force of cruel reality. When others expected me to be feeling better, I actually felt worse. They assumed that the pain had diminished and that I should be emerging from my cocoon of wretchedness, culpability and non-acceptance to assume their interpretation of "normal". I felt unable to really talk to those close to me about the depth of my pain, because I didn't wish to cause them any further discomfort.

Tammy is 28. Her younger sister, Ella was 21 when she overdosed on a combination of anti-depressants and paracetamol in July 2002.

Tammy says, "Sometimes my grief is so overpowering, it frightens me. Although Ella was my younger sister, I always sought her advice if I had a difficult decision to make or needed help with anything. She seemed so wise for her years and had experienced far more of life than I had at the same age. She had lived and worked abroad as a nanny and she had spent just over a year backpacking around Europe. Ella was my guidance counsellor as well as my best friend. I looked to her for direction rather than our parents, because I felt that not only could she relate more to me, but I knew that I could confide in her things about my life that I could never admit to our parents.

"There have been many times since her death when I have needed to talk to her so badly that I end up walking around in circles howling. If I really focused for too long on what I have lost, I would probably end up in a psychiatric unit. I am trying to take each second, minute and day at a time.

"The first few weeks now seem like a dream. The memories are blurred, but what I do remember is the feeling that I was totally losing my mind and that the pain would kill me.

"A stream of visitors arrived and left and the thing that I remember most of them saying was that old cliché, 'Time is a healer'. That was not a state that I could possibly visualise at the time and even now, many years on, I wonder whether I have healed at all. I think it's a fallacy that you heal. I will always have an open wound in my heart.

"About three months after Ella's death, I attended a bereavement group. However, I was the only one who had lost someone to suicide and I didn't feel as though anyone else there could totally relate to my experience. Several members of the group told me that there would come a time when the pain would lessen and I would be able to experience good feelings when I thought about Ella, but to me that was years away. At that time, and sometimes even now, I can't see further than the next hour, let alone the next year.

"Not a minute passes when thoughts of Ella don't occupy my mind, because she was such an essential part of my life, which has now been removed and will never be replaced, by anyone or anything. I have a lifetime of memories, of attachment, of friendship and of loving. I have wonderful memories, but in a sense, this makes it even more painful, because I will never have the opportunity to build new memories with my sister. All my memories now will be created without her in my life and that is unbearably painful. Each time I think about growing old without her, I pray that I will be taken early. Never seeing Ella again is a concept that I find impossible to get my head around.

"My parents seem to have coped better with her loss than I have, but then again you can never judge another person's grief by the way in which they are behaving. It's just that they seem to be getting on with their lives, doing normal, everyday things and only very occasionally talking about Ella to anyone, but maybe they find it too painful.

"I find it difficult just getting out of bed each day. All I want to do is to go back to a state of dreamless sleep to block out the pain."

Even when someone has been clinically diagnosed with a depressive disorder, or help has been sought by parents who are concerned about their child's mental wellbeing, the battle for acceptance from society and the fight for adequate mental health care can result in the same tragic outcome; the loss of a precious life.

Nils' son Oskar took his own life in a more unusual manner in Norway in February 2001 just after his 21st birthday. Nils tells Oskar's story.

"Oskar's mother, Trine, (my first wife), died of cancer in 1992 when Oskar was just 12 and his sister Lene was 8. Oskar seemed to undergo a dramatic personality change at that point. He had always been far easier to handle and much more compliant than Lene, who was very independent, hot-headed and opinionated. Despite only being eight-years-old when her mother died, she was the strong one and took over the motherly role, making sure everyone else was ok and even assuming household duties and undertaking responsibilities that you would never expect of someone so young. Oskar, on the other hand, regressed to being almost like a toddler. His behaviour became a social dysfunction and he seemed to lose all control over his emotions. He would experience the most intense rages, usually brought about by frustration or his inability to have his own way.

"Despite seeking medical help and visiting countless therapists and child psychiatrists, not one of them mentioned that Oskar could possibly be suffering from depression.

"We were given the standard textbook, 'grieving the loss of his mother, coping with the pre-adolescent surge of hormones, struggling to find his identity' types of prognosis. He was given sedative-type drugs to calm him down and was, at one point, diagnosed with the equivalent of what I believe is now known as ADHD, which I actually believe is just a name that some parents like to use as an excuse for their children's atrocious behaviour. Everyone likes to give elaborate names to everything these days. What happened to good old fashioned depression?

"Oskar was exceptionally bright and I know that his teachers attributed his behaviour to the boredom of finding the work too elementary and wanting to move ahead a lot more quickly than the others in his class. Oskar went from being a boy who was always popular, to a young teenager who found it difficult to interact with his peers in an amenable fashion. He did have a couple of close friends who obviously saw his better qualities, but it was more common for Oskar to drive people away because of his hypersensitivity.

"I never stopped trying to talk to Oskar, because I never wanted him to feel that he could not come to me if he really needed something. Most of the time he would just grunt at me and be largely unresponsive, just wanting to spend most of his time shut in his bedroom reading, doing homework or watching TV, but on a few occasions he did communicate some of his fears. It seemed that although he was content with his own company within the home environment, he did not feel comfortable going out anywhere on his own. He admitted that he did not like being in crowds or amongst strangers and that he needed to be with a friend if ever he ventured out anywhere.

"Although I desperately wanted to establish a rewarding relationship with someone, I found that I avoided commitment because I was afraid of how Oskar would react to someone whom he might regard as a replacement for his mother. Nevertheless, when I met Marit, my current wife, I instinctively felt that it was right and although I had warned her about the problems with Oskar, she did not seem worried by this.

"Amazingly, Oskar seemed to change for the better when Marit and I got married. She was one of the few people who managed to get him to open up, although he still avoided discussing his deepest feelings and would instead talk generally about his interests, such as politics and sport. I then thought that maybe the main problem had been that he needed a mother figure in his life. Having just a father isn't the same, however hard someone tries to assume the role of both parents.

"Despite his good relationship with Marit, Oskar seemed to have no direction in life. He became lazy at school and we were frequently contacted by his teachers about his lack of attention to his work. Again, we assumed that this was because he did not find the lessons challenging enough. It was a foregone conclusion in my mind that he would attend upper secondary education, but shortly after his 16th birthday in February 1996, he told us that he wanted to leave school and get a job. I was extremely disappointed and although I tried to question his reasons as to why he didn't wish to pursue further education, he would always reply simply, 'Because I don't want to.'

"He did leave school, but he never seemed to have much success with maintaining any sort of employment. He would drift from one dead-end job to another, remaining in some for a few hours and others for a few weeks, but he never seemed to enjoy anything.

"Some jobs he would leave voluntarily and some jobs he was asked to leave because of his attitude. The jobs that he left the most quickly were those that involved being around, or interacting with people or customers.

"On the relationship front, he was never short of attention from girls. He was your stereotypical tall, blond, rugged-looking Norwegian with the most piercing blue-green eyes that would melt anyone's heart. As a small child, he looked like a cherub. All that was missing were the wings. Potentially he had so much going for him in the looks and intelligence areas, but his attitude let him down. He wasn't unkind, but he never learned to control his rages.

"When Oskar was 18, he decided that he wanted to leave home and move in with a friend who lived on the outskirts of Oslo. I knew that I didn't have the power to stop him, but I also thought that maybe that was the best move for him. Perhaps he would mature and maybe learn the importance of respect, particularly if he had to share a house with someone who was more of an equal in terms of age and outlook.

"The arrangement seemed to be working well and Oskar actually made more of an effort to be affable than when he was living here, although he had always been courteous to Marit. He secured himself a job in a clothing store, which he said he enjoyed and although the wage wasn't impressive, it paid for his rent and basic living expenses. I admit that he didn't talk much about life in his bachelor pad and when questioned about his friend, he didn't seem too keen to talk about him.

"One day, out of the blue, he brought back a rather stern-looking young woman whom he introduced as his girlfriend. My first impressions of her were not good. I can't exactly say what I didn't like about her, but I instinctively felt that something wasn't right.

"It was at this first meeting that Oskar admitted that his friend had moved out of the flat and his girlfriend had moved in, but the full circumstances were never clear.

"After that, we rarely saw Oskar and Marit had threatened on many occasions to turn up at his flat unannounced. We heard a few odd stories from various acquaintances and rumours about how he was controlled by his girlfriend. Although I ought to have felt some sort of confidence in knowing that he had met his match and was finally in a relationship where he could no longer call the shots one hundred per cent of the time, I felt extremely uneasy.

"In the months leading up to Oskar's death, each time either Marit or I telephoned him, he did not seem keen to talk. He would always make some excuse that would mean the conversation had to be terminated. If his girlfriend ever answered the phone, she would always say that he wasn't home, but I now feel certain that much of the time he was there.

"It was his girlfriend who telephoned us to tell us that Oskar was dead. She sounded completely unemotional as she delivered the news. Two days before he killed himself he told her that he wanted to die but she just dismissed it. He told her again before he left her house, but she didn't tell anyone until it was too late. I just can't help feeling that she controlled him and made him feel trampled upon and worthless.

"Oskar was found in just his underpants lying on a car blanket in the snow at the edge of a field early one morning. A suicide note was found by his side. He had literally frozen to death.

"Marit was hysterical, whereas I was numb with shock, although not so numb that I couldn't feel any pain. I did want to scream and shout, but I felt as though I had to support Marit, even though she was not his biological mother.

"Marit loved Oskar as she would her own son and she felt a deep sense of failure as his stepmother. She even began blaming herself for his death. 'If only this, if only that', she kept repeating over and over and over again. It tore me apart to see her suffering and I don't even know now how we managed to survive those early days.

"Again, my daughter Lene, then 17, was tremendously supportive. She seemed to put her grief on the back burner and attended to all the practical needs of the family. I don't know how we would have coped without her. She is truly an angel on earth.

"In many ways, the pain and all the more unpleasant emotions that accompany grief seem to have intensified as time has passed. I don't know whether that is because in the beginning, my brain was protecting me by not allowing all the emotions to completely crush me simultaneously. Marit seems to be coping better now than I am, but she totally succumbed to her grief in the first few months, whereas I feel that I suppressed mine so that I didn't have to cope with more than I could tolerate.

"Frequently I am hit by horrendous reality checks that completely knock me off of my feet and it is Marit now who picks me up. In the beginning, it was Lene and I who were supporting Marit. Now when I look back, I wonder from where I drew the strength to help Lene arrange the funeral and sort out the legalities. I can hardly bear to visit Oskar's grave now, because of the pain of seeing his headstone and having to accept the awful truth. I still find it difficult to associate the words 'died' or 'death' with Oskar. I can't believe that his funeral actually happened. It is all like some awful distant dream."

With each month that passed following Kristian's suicide, I communicated with an alarming number of bereaved families from around the world, all of whom had lost a young family member to suicide. Some parents had lost their only child, others had witnessed the suicide, others had found their child, grandchild, brother or sister and others had learned of the tragedy from the police or another family member or friend. Although every situation was unique, the common bond they now share is that of losing a child to sudden, self-inflicted death. Hearing about all this appalling loss of life made me realise that my grief was no more than just one droplet in a colossal, tempestuous ocean.

Vanessa witnessed the suicide of her 16-year-old daughter Lindsay in April 2001. Vanessa had recently separated from her children's father after he had an affair with a work colleague. Vanessa's younger daughter, Kirsty, who was 12 at the time, did not seem adversely affected by the split, but Lindsay had always enjoyed a very close relationship with her father and felt betrayed by his conduct. Nevertheless, although Lindsay was very angry, Vanessa did not detect any signs of depression or unusual behaviour. Lindsay continued to do well at school and remained popular amongst her classmates. She led an active social life and did not appear to withdraw in any way.

Vanessa said that the family had never owned a gun prior to her husband leaving, but following the separation and a move to a different area, a neighbour suggested that she buy one to protect herself. There had been a lot of burglaries in the neigbourhood and there was a rumour circulating about violent gangs breaking and entering and threatening any residents who confronted them. Vanessa now wishes she had never listened to her neighbour's advice.

"If only I hadn't purchased that damned gun. If only I hadn't listened to my neighbour's advice. The problem was that we were new to the area, so I was open to help and advice from others who were familiar with the place. I thought I was doing my best to protect my daughters, but my actions have resulted in my daughter's death.

"If Lindsay had been holding a bottle of pills in her hand, or even a rope or a knife, there is the possibility that she might have been saved. Whether or not her decision was impulsive, I will never know. If only I had been given the chance to save her, maybe she would have been grateful that she was still alive. Maybe I could have helped her. Maybe I could have got her some help. Once you release that trigger, you don't usually get a second chance. When you put a bullet in your head, it is usually a final act.

"The night of 23 April 2001 is the most horrendously memorable date of my life. It even surpasses the day that Lindsay was born, because the feelings of the horror and anguish of watching her die will always be more intense than the joy that I felt when she entered this world, awful as that may sound.

"Lindsay had seemed a little quiet when she came home from school that afternoon. I remember asking her whether she had had a good day and she said, 'Not bad.' She ate dinner and engaged in the usual bickering with her younger sister, Kirsty. After the meal, she said that she was going upstairs to do her homework, which again was not unusual for Lindsay.

"It was around 6.30pm, after I had finished cleaning up, that I heard Kirsty yelling to me. She came tearing downstairs yelling that Lindsay had a gun and was threatening to shoot herself. I thought this must be some kind of very sick joke, but one that seemed totally out of character with Lindsay. I told Kirsty to stay downstairs and rushed upstairs to find Lindsay standing on the landing facing me with my gun pressed against her temple.

"I remember screaming at her in both fear and anger, asking her what she was playing at. I was horribly aware that the gun was loaded and will never forgive myself for not removing the bullets and keeping them locked away somewhere. I suppose I thought that that would defeat the object of owning one, should anyone ever try to break in and attack us.

"What I will never forget is the blank look on Lindsay's face before she pulled the trigger. The only words she said were, 'Let's see if he cares now' and I can only assume that she was referring to her father, because at that time I don't believe she had a boyfriend.

"I began viewing the images around me in slow motion as I realised that her grip on the gun was tightening and her forefinger was curled around the trigger, but even though I was only a few feet from her, I could not get to her in time. It was like some dramatic, breath-catching scene in suspense thriller. I remember my feet leaving the floor as I threw myself at her in a vain attempt to remove the gun from her grasp, but I was too late. I must have been in mid-air when the sound of the gunshot blasted in my ears as the bullet exploded in my beautiful daughter's head. I collided with Lindsay as she fell to the ground. I remember the blood. I remember the screams. I remember the total and absolute horror that I cannot even begin to describe accurately. I don't know who called the police. I don't remember the details of what happened afterwards. My most vivid memory is the image of my beautiful daughter with a hole in her head and all her bodily fluids creeping across the carpet.

"I wish I didn't remember any of it. I have suffered the most dreadful nightmares since the day Lindsay died. In some she is like the walking dead with blood flowing from her head, but she is laughing in my face. In others she is alive and well and then I wake to the real nightmare of realising that she is dead.

"One of the worst things in all this is not really knowing why she did it. Why weren't there any signs? Why was I so stupid that I couldn't see the signs? Why, oh why, did I ever buy that gun?

"It affected her father very badly and I know that even now he blames himself for her death. He even tried to encourage me to give the relationship another go, but I feel so bruised and battered that I cannot even conceive of attempting to have a relationship with anyone, least of all the man who caused us all so much pain in the months before Lindsay's suicide. If I am honest, I lay the blame ultimately at his feet too.

"I had to have the blood-soaked carpet ripped up the following day. The floorboards beneath had also absorbed the blood, but I just had to let others deal with the organisation of the cleaning process. Strangers came and went, uttering dutiful words of condolence as they set about removing all traces of my daughter's suicide from our landing.

"My parents and my in-laws came together and were extremely supportive, but nevertheless I found that I needed to confide in those who knew what I was going through, but who weren't personally connected to my situation. I could find little comfort from those I knew well, because I couldn't talk about Lindsay and my grief without being conscious of the fact that I was probably causing them more pain. This isn't all about me. There are so many other people involved; my family, my friends and Lindsay's friends.

"What I originally found immensely difficult about Lindsay's loss was that I was extremely sceptical about life after death, so I could find no comfort in believing that Lindsay was still with me, or that I would be with her again someday. My views have since changed.

"Religious quotes and articles offered little solace in the beginning. I've never followed any religion because I believe they are all a form of mind control invented by people who claim that God made up the rules. I now believe that a loving God would not impose any rules; he allows people to make their own choices and learn by their mistakes. I have also since had so much confirmation that Lindsay is still with me, not because I want to believe it, but because everything that has happened since those early days cannot simply be passed off as pure coincidence.

"Before Lindsay died, I used to enjoy watching crime dramas and movies, but I now find many of these grossly offensive. I cannot even switch on the TV now without seeing an image of someone being threatened at gunpoint, or else lying in a pool of blood.

"Kirsty has been amazing. She was devastated by her sister's death, but has somehow drawn this remarkable strength from somewhere and has been my life support. Sometimes we just hug each other and sob until there are no more tears left and then we find comfort in talking about the good times and laughing about some of the crazy things that Lindsay would do. I will guard her with my life.

Maybe we all really do have a time to die, but I am not a fatalist. I will always believe that some things should never have happened. Lindsay should never have died like that. First I had to learn to build a new life without my husband and now I have to learn to build a new life without Lindsay. It does make me paranoid about what will happen next, but it also makes me realise how important it is to treasure every minute of the day, because none of us can ever be certain what is going to happen next."

On the day that Kristian died, I kept thinking, "This time yesterday he was still alive". With each day that passed, I thought, "This time XX days ago, he was still alive. As more time passed, I thought, "This time last month", "This time last year" and so on. Maybe there will come a time when I will stop thinking like that, but even now, I cannot conceive that I ever will.

The grief following suicide is, unfortunately, not a storm that will blow over. It may calm after a while, but without warning can return with full intensity, knocking down your safety barrier and rendering you emotionally incapacitated.

I too have experienced the deep, isolated, dark and seemingly inescapable pit of depression. I know what it is like to be totally incapable of thinking about anything other than finding a way to end the pain. I would never have wanted anyone to suffer what I was enduring and I would never have considered that taking my life would have caused immense suffering. At that time I could not think rationally, in the same way that my son would never have consciously made the decision to end his life just over a week before his daughter's first birthday. He would never have wished this much pain on us.

As I battle to convert my pain into something positive, I weep for my son every day. My grief is like travelling along a country road lined with tall trees. The sunlight that filters through the gaps in the leaves and branches and makes me wince is like the pain. There are brief intervals of respite when the protective foliage is at its most dense, but without warning I am temporarily blinded again. Like the sharpness of the sun's rays, the pain seers through me. It finds me wherever I am attempting to hide.

"Live for today" is a cliché that we hear quoted constantly and yet how many of us abide by this? We always believe there will be a tomorrow, particularly for our children. Consequently, when we are robbed of someone prematurely, we experience tremendous regret for the things that we didn't do. "I wish…" precedes the infinite number of words and actions that we will no longer be able to deliver.

I know that my pain is a tribute to my son, a sign that I have vivid memories of him. He was not perfect and I do not want to have memories only of his best qualities. I want my many memories of him to condense into an accurate portrait of the personality that he was, an image that will be perfectly maintained until the day I die. I want to preserve his memory like a precious piece of artwork, a masterpiece that depicts this beautiful, clever, naïve, vulnerable, compassionate, impulsive, forgiving, cheerful, but deeply troubled boy; a sensitive, caring soul who was too gentle for this harsh world.

My life will always be divided into three distinct sections: the time before Kristian was born, the time before he died and the time after he died. In the future, my life may be further divided by other dramatic events, but at the moment it is separated into three unequal segments. Should I survive into old age, the section of my life without him will become the greatest and most painful segment, but his age will always remain the same. He will always be 20.

Listen and Learn
©Carsten Emil Bates, Kristian's brother

"A Song for my brother Kristian"

Never been to heaven before,
That's just one place I don't want to explore.
Kristian why didn't you let us know?
I know you had your reasons to go.
We just have to face it now
That you're out of our lives somehow.

We gave all we could give you
And you took all that we gave,
But you just fell away.
Why couldn't you stay?
We fall to our knees
And beg for your return.

You just could not see
The evil of the weed.
Too late for you now,
But we just have to listen,
Listen and learn,
Listen and learn.

Chapter Five

Wearing a Mask

Society is a masked ball, where everyone hides his real character, and reveals it by hiding.

Ralph Waldo Emerson

From the day after Kristian died when friends, neighbours and old acquaintances began calling and offering their condolences, I began wearing the mask of falseness; the mask that said, "I'm doing fine", "I'm coping well" and "Life goes on". The truth is that I wasn't doing fine, I wasn't coping well internally and my life, if no-one else's, had been frozen the moment I learned of my son's death. Everything that I did that may have been perceived as strength was performed in a detached, robot-like fashion. I quickly realised that so many were unable to cope with anything other than "fine". Some people would even answer the question for me before asking it, such as, "You're feeling ok, aren't you?" I felt like saying to them, "If you don't want to know the truth, don't ask". It seems that we, the bereaved, are the ones who are attempting to comfort others rather than the other way around.

On the occasions when my mask slipped and the pain was just too much to bear, I immediately sensed the immense discomfort and agitation of those present. I found myself apologising for breaking down in front of them, when what I really wanted to say was, "Look, this is the real me. The whole fabric of my world has been torn mercilessly apart. I'm far from ok. The agony of what my son must have been going through and the pain of losing him is consuming me. My son killed himself. How can I possibly be fine?"

I even protected those dear, close family members and friends who did allow me to be myself, by containing the full force of my grief in their presence. Yes, I would weep and I would talk about Kristian, but weeping was a gentler substitute for wailing and screaming in an alarming manner. Talking rationally about what had happened was a substitute for yelling, "WHY? Why didn't he call me? Why hadn't I noticed the signs? Why didn't I try to contact him more? Why hadn't I done and said things differently? Why couldn't I protect him? Why didn't I tell him I loved him more? Why? Why? Why?" I would struggle to keep the artificial smile glued to my face and contain the swelling ball of emotion in my chest and throat that threatened to burst out in a startling display of uncontrollable grief and anguish. Once suppressed, the ball would settle until a time when I was alone and could allow it to be fully released.

Standing in the supermarket queue, I would try to focus on anything but my son, but somehow every alternative focus would remind me of him; a small child demanding sweets, laughing teenagers walking past, a song being played over the tannoy, or even an item of shopping that the customer in front of me had placed on the conveyor belt. I tried to think of nothing, but in doing so must have appeared deranged, with wild staring eyes from which a fountain of tears threatened to erupt.

Barbara's, 22-year-old son Nick drove into a lake and drowned himself in May 1993 after battling with drug addiction for six years. A suicide note was later found in his room. Despite the utter devastation that Barbara felt, and still does feel, she began hiding behind a façade of wellbeing within a few weeks of his death.

"Very shortly after Nick's suicide, I stopped crying in front of my husband. My husband is not my children's father. My first husband and I had divorced when the children were fairly small and he emigrated with his new wife some years later. He has never once bothered to try and contact his children and I don't really have any idea where he is now. He doesn't even know that his son is dead. I remarried about five years after my divorce, but have nobody with whom to share the extreme loss as I would if I were still married to my dead son's father.

"My husband tried to be supportive and understanding at first, but now I don't think he has any comprehension of the ongoing pain. He lived through five years of emotional problems with Nick, as Nick was still living at home when he died. My husband urged me to throw Nick out, but how could I give up on my son? I couldn't even contemplate doing something like that.

"In the early days, I had to distance myself from my husband, because I was so afraid of breaking down in front of him. Because he had always viewed Nick as a pain and an immense strain on our emotional and physical resources, I secretly feel that he saw Nick's death as a welcome release from five years of stress and frustration. I have, of course, never said this to my husband, but even if it were true, I could empathise to a certain extent, because I know how much pressure Nick placed on our relationship. The difference is, of course, that Nick was my son and I loved him. Had he been someone else's child, I don't know whether I would have been so tolerant and I have to put myself in my husband's position in this respect.

"I have felt like an actress for the past eighteen years, where my life is the movie, because I don't feel as though I am permitted to play the part of myself. I don't feel as though my pain has eased, because I haven't allowed myself to grieve properly.

"I have cried every day since Nick died, but in the privacy of the bathroom or moments when my husband is not in the house; when I don't have an 'audience'. Even so, I have to quickly control myself, so that my husband cannot see that I have been crying. I know that others may think that this is unhealthy and that good relationships are based on being able to communicate your feelings to your partner, but I just don't feel that I can. My husband is a lovely man, but he has no tolerance of the shortcomings of others. He said that he hated what Nick was doing to me and I feel that he would feel angry with Nick for causing me all this pain, so I still think it is best to continue wearing this mask.

"I cannot lay the blame totally at my husband's feet, since so many people whom I regarded as true friends suddenly distanced themselves from me after Nick died. I remember phoning (whom I believed was) my closest friend about a month after Nick died, because I thought I would explode if I didn't talk to someone about him. Everything was fine until I began telling her how awful I was feeling. She quickly made excuses about having to go out and said she would call me back later. She never did. That experience taught me that so many people who call themselves your friends are only interested in being around when the weather is bright. It made me realise that I probably didn't have any genuine friends, because a true friend will still be there on the stormiest days.

"Rather than making me a stronger person, I feel that I am less able to cope with criticism and unkindness from others. My feelings are hurt a lot more easily and I have become a terminal worrier. Still no one would guess, because this mask seems to have become denser as the years have passed. I have, however, become more aware of others' feelings and even if someone has said something with which I do not agree, I tend not to say anything for fear of provoking an argument or upsetting them.

"I long for the day to come when I can say that I feel happy, but I don't believe that will happen. The only event that would create instant happiness would be if Nick walked through my door and told me that he was alive and well."

The reason why people avoid the subject of suicide is that it makes them question their own mortality and that of their loved ones. Our situation is a shocking reminder of the fragility of life and is something that they don't wish to confront. It raises questions that they don't want to think about. They may fear that thinking about it and pondering those questions will somehow precipitate the same awful tragedy in their own lives.

Suicide can take a physically fit and healthy person from this life in an instant. Suicide ends life abruptly, with no chance for recovery and no opportunity to spend some final loving moments with your child, telling them all the things you would want them to know, including how much you love them. People find it difficult to know how to comfort someone who has lost a child in such a desperately sad and catastrophic manner. It's easier for them not to have to deal with it and so, to avoid isolation, we survivors spare others this agony by presenting a false exterior of cheerfulness.

As time moves on and the distance between a child's suicide and the present grows, so do people's expectations of your grief. They expect you to have moved forward with your life to the extent where you no longer break down in tears at the mere mention of your child. They assume that you feel better, that the pain has lessened, that you have accepted what has happened and that you may even have "got over it".

Bereaved families will often increase the density of their mask as time passes in order to live up to these unrealistic expectations. They only remove the mask in private, or allow it to slip when they feel truly comfortable in someone's presence.

Richard's only son Marcus was 17 when he took his own life via carbon monoxide poisoning in December 1999. Richard's first wife died of ovarian cancer in 1995 and in 1998 Richard embarked on a new relationship with his current partner Alison.

"When Marcus took his own life, I had only been with my current partner Alison for just over a year. It was obviously a very difficult time for Alison because she hadn't really had the opportunity to get to know Marcus that well and, although she was sad for me, she didn't have the same emotional bond or the history. I wanted desperately to be able to pour out my feelings, but held back and constantly reassured her that I was ok and coping. Inside it was a different story. I felt as though I was dying a slow, painful death myself, as my wife had done four years previously.

"It was the second time in four years that I had experienced the most awful grief, but the feelings that overwhelmed me after Marcus' suicide were very different to those when my wife died. Whilst I still miss my wife dearly, I was not prepared for the intensity of grief and force of emotions that hit me when I lost Marcus. It has been a far more difficult situation to endure than when his mother died. My wife's illness was beyond anyone's control and although it was excruciating watching her waste away, her last few months were made as comfortable as possible and we were all prepared for the end. We were all able to exchange comforting words and express our love.

"When someone dies by suicide, you are robbed of that opportunity. It's unexpected, a complete shock and you are left not only with the grief, loss and sadness, but a host of unpleasant feelings that assault you concurrently. The mask that you wear to protect others from your grief has to be more solid because there's so much more to hide.

"There have been several times when the mask has slipped and I have broken down in front of Alison, but I regain my composure very quickly and readjust the mask, mainly to prevent her from feeling awkward. When someone is grieving so deeply, of course you want to be able to do something to ease their pain, but sometimes it is just not possible and so the onus is on the grieving person to put on this pretence that they are really ok.

"Over a decade on, I am still wearing the same mask. In some respects it is more tightly secured, because I have found that most people who have not experienced such trauma in their own lives believe that I should have stopped grieving. I want to be able to tell them how I really feel, but I don't think that they will understand. I would never wish them to experience what I have in order to understand, but I do wish that sometimes some of them would try and imagine how they might feel if they were to lose one of their children to suicide.

"It's not something that I will ever accept, or get over, or even come to terms with. I don't imagine that I will feel any differently in twenty or thirty years' time even. This mask is firmly in place and will only be removed when I am alone or in the company of someone else who has endured the same awful loss."

I have reached a point where I feel able to admit to people that I do wear a mask. I still tell people that I am fine, but I also tell them that the frontage of cheerfulness conceals the real emotions of immense sadness, anguish and guilt. I feel it important to let them know that this woman whom they perceive as "strong" and "coping admirably" is really not as resilient as they think she is. I want them to know that there is a part of me that they will rarely see and that grief is not something that diminishes like a temporary illness, but is a terminal condition that sufferers learn to live alongside. It is important for others to understand that many bereaved people wear a mask lest they encounter grief in their own lives. I would not want them to wonder why they are unable to handle their grief as well as they perceive others to have, or why they have difficulty keeping their mask pinned in place. It is a gruelling task and one that requires extreme concentration every minute that you are in the presence of others.

I still smile and exude joviality to make others feel comfortable in my presence, because of course moods are highly contagious and the last thing I want is for people to walk away from me feeling depressed. Why would I wish to pass my grief onto others? The masks that we wear, therefore, are for the benefit of others, not just ourselves. Masks are not confined to the bereaved. Everyone wears them. Every smile conceals a sorrow and it is a tribute to the resilience of human nature that we continue to cope with such adversities in our lives. The masks that we wear are dependent on the situation and with whom we are interacting. Sometimes these masks are a reflection of some true facet of our personality and sometimes they portray a false image; conveying an impression of the type of person we would like to be, or think that others would like us to be.

Our whole existence seems to revolve around other people and their opinions of us. How tragic it is that these opinions can trigger feelings of depression in some vulnerable people.

Tara's son Anthony hung himself in his closet in October 2004, just 17 days before his 13th birthday. Tara said that she felt she had to be strong for the sake of everyone else in the family and wears the mask of wellbeing on a daily basis because she is afraid to show people how she really feels.

"One of Anthony's older brothers found him. I tried to get him down. The other brother came in and cut him down. I saw the life leave his body. I lost my breath and a part of me died that day. I cannot even begin to explain the range of emotions I have felt and feel. My heart has died many, many times. I hold all of these feelings in because no one around me truly understands. Yes, my husband has lost a child also, but it is different. My sons have lost a brother, but it is different. I do not mean less important, just different. If they really knew how I felt I would be put in a padded cell.

"I have been the strong one through all of this and I am tired. I just want to cry. Above all, I want to cry for my son. I need to talk with other mothers. Anthony was an all consuming child. He had behavioural disorders and they suspected bipolar. From the time Anthony was born he demanded all of me, unlike my other three sons. And with his disorders I was his advocate in schools, with doctors and treatment. I fought for him or with him every day for almost 13 years. And then, in just a few minutes, he was gone.

"I feel so bottled up inside. Like other survivors, I wear many faces. I feel like I am in a catch 22 situation. Nobody really wants to see how much pain I am in and I am afraid to show them. If I were to show them, I would have to feel it. I have been pretty numb since it happened, because feeling the pain is too much. I go right back to that day, to that moment and die all over again. I have days when all I want to do is to sleep. My working theory is, if I sleep enough, enough time will have passed and it won't hurt so much. I must say it isn't working really. There are other days when I just want to scream and yell and throw anything that is within reach, but I don't, because I don't want to scare anyone. I don't want to do anything inappropriate because that would just be regarded as overdramatic. I don't wish to embarrass anyone, or myself.

"I have suffered from depression in the past. It took up a good portion of my life until I realised I didn't like feeling like that anymore and found a ray of light at the end of a very long tunnel. All those years wasted and drugged out on antidepressants. I refuse to go back there. It was such a dark place to be and it pains me to think that Anthony may have experienced that on any level.

"I am so tired of hearing 'I am so sorry; time will heal all wounds'. My favourite is 'I know how you feel' from people who have no clue because they have never lost a child. I just want to ask those people, 'Do you? Do you really know how I feel? Because if you do, then please share it with me because I don't!'

"One thing that troubles me deeply is that I don't know how to share what I am feeling with my husband. We share everything, no secrets and yet when it comes to this I just can't tell him. Even at the slightest sigh he asks me, 'Everything ok?' or 'What's wrong Honey?' And I say, 'Oh, nothing; I'm alright.'

"Sometimes I tell him that I've just had a bad day. Those are the days I feel like crying and can't quite do it. I get close though and sometimes even a few tears will fall, but then I stop myself. Then he comes into the room and I put on the 'I'll be alright face' and yet all I want to really do is curl up to him and sob.

"I have from the beginning of all this told my other sons that they don't have to stop talking about Anthony. About a month or two after his death, I realised my children had done just that. I sat them down and talked with them and asked them why they don't say his name or talk about him? Their united reply was simply, 'Because we don't want you to cry.' I explained to them that I would rather cry from hearing his name, or hearing a funny story about him, than to never hear it at all. After that, when they said Anthony's name in front of me or near me, they would look for my reaction and I would just look back with a nod and smile to let them know it was ok and that I was ok.

"Maybe I should talk with everyone and not limit myself to just mothers. Talking with other fathers and siblings may help me to understand their side of it too."

The wearing of a mask is also familiar to those who are depressed or suicidal. Sadly, it's also the reason why so many who could have been saved, aren't.

My son wore a mask. It was a mask that said, "Life is great. There's nothing I can't handle", even when it was clear that he had problems. He had worn the mask for so long that no one saw the real Kristian, the melancholy child who had experienced so much rejection from those to whom he had shown so much love. They only saw the happy lad who loved life and loved people, but because he was my son I was occasionally allowed a brief glimpse beneath that mask. It was a mask that could not conceal the sadness in his eyes and yet even when asked, he would not admit to that inner distress.

Would he have opened up had I persisted? I will never know the answer to that question this side of life.

The Game

©Heidi Gray

This game is no fun,
But it's something I play,
I put on the smile
And pretend to have a good day.
I can't let them know,
They would not understand,
They think this is real,
But it's only a game.
They say I look good,
They think I'm happy too.
If only they knew,
I am so blue.
There are kids and a job
And a big world outside,
So I have to pretend
And keep playing the game.

In memory of Heidi's boyfriend, Ed Wick
20 February 1956 to 29 November 2005

"He was and is still very special to me. I am having a lot of trouble getting through without him. He has more friends and family that care about him than he realised. I hope that your book helps people to understand how suicide and the loss of a loved one affects people that love and care about them. I think that is a good title, 'Wearing a Mask', because that is what it is like. You almost have to wear the mask and put on that fake smile just to keep others from worrying about you.

I say that I put my smile on in the morning just like my clothes and take it off when I get home. It may not be the best thing to do, but it's just something you have to do to go on.

"*The same pain and feelings are there now that were there on Nov 29th, but I have to take care of the kids and go to work and go grocery shopping, etc. and you can't always have everyone watching to see if you are going to cry. So sometimes it's just best to pretend you are alright and then have a good cry when you are alone.*"

Jan, with the first edition of Chasing Death "wearing the mask"

Chapter Six

Resisting or Craving Physical Contact

Grief and sadness knits two hearts in closer bonds than happiness ever can and common sufferings are far stronger than common joys.

Alphonse de Lamartine

When someone dies, the automatic reaction for a greeter is for them to put their arms around the bereaved person by way of offering their condolences and attempting to provide some small comfort. Some people may crave this contact, whereas others may resist it for many different reasons.

In the days and weeks following Kristian's passing, I found physical contact very difficult, whether it was from friends and family or intimacy with my partner. I felt like a fraud. It wasn't I who deserved such comfort. It was my son who had needed those caring arms around him in his final hour of need. Whenever I was hugged, my heart ached for my son. I was receiving the comfort that he had so desperately sought and yet I couldn't welcome it. I wanted to push everyone away. I wanted to experience the loneliness and desolation that he had felt. I wanted to be where he was. I wanted to turn back the clock and transfer his suffering onto me.

At the time of Kristian's suicide, my partner and I had been together for six years. He is 12 years my junior and I had often joked over those six years that if there ever came a time when I was no longer interested in intimate relations, I did not believe that he could survive without sexual contact.

I would playfully suggest that he would inevitably seek gratification elsewhere, something that he naturally denied vehemently. He always maintained that it was love that he could not live without and that sex was not important.

Of course, I always had my doubts, given that after even short periods of abstinence, he would make flippant comments about the lack of action. I therefore felt under pressure to perform, because I felt a greater need to satisfy my partner than to succumb to my own need for space and time to adjust to this new living hell into which I had been mercilessly thrown. I was afraid that the one person upon whom I was relying for support would reach the end of his own allocated timeframe for patience and understanding. I was afraid that he might fall into someone else's arms, someone who didn't have as much emotional baggage and someone who could satisfy his sexual appetite on demand.

I found it extremely difficult to combine grief with personal pleasure, since I experienced tremendous guilt at engaging in any activity that gave me enjoyment. I didn't feel that I even deserved to be alive, but I did deserve to suffer every minute of every day for what had happened to my son and in order to experience that suffering, I needed to be alive. I should have spoken to my partner about my feelings, but I didn't want him feel that I was rejecting him.

Each time we made love, I was engulfed in a tidal wave of overpowering sadness, guilt and despair. I would excuse myself to the bathroom afterwards and bawl my eyes out, or simply turn my back on him and sob myself silently to sleep. I began to wonder whether these feelings would be permanent, or whether I would eventually allow myself to experience physical pleasure without the painful guilt and negative emotions that accompanied it.

Conversely, some survivors feel a desperate need for physical contact with others, because this is how they derive comfort in their interminable loss and their need for a tactile relationship can override any guilt that they may be experiencing.

Richard is divorced and was granted custody of his three children, Aidan, Alexandra and Brandon in 1998. In January 2003, his eldest son Aidan, aged 18, took his own life using a firearm. Aidan was gay and had struggled to come to terms with his sexuality for fear of being shunned by others. Although Richard believes that he did everything he could to bolster Aidan's ego and help him to accept himself for the way he was, Richard still feels that he wasn't there for him as much as he should have been. As a single parent, he was working very long hours to support his family. However, after Aidan's suicide, he resigned from his job to work from home on a consultancy basis, enabling him to be there for his other two children, Alexandra aged 17 and Brandon aged 14.

Richard admits that he found the lack of social interaction that he had in the mainstream working environment extremely difficult and his isolation has limited the opportunity of meeting someone else.

"I would desperately like to build a special relationship with someone and have craved physical contact since losing Aidan. I'm not talking about sex here. What I really miss are hugs and even the occasional reassuring pat on the back. However, I am torn between my own needs and the guilt of wanting to be happy when I know how unhappy my son was.

"Is it healthy to embark on a relationship so soon after such a devastating tragedy? Would it be selfish of me to expect someone else to share my heavy emotional baggage and that of my other children?

"I wouldn't want to have a relationship with someone else purely for my own gratification, because it's essential that both parties are benefiting from the relationship and of course I would want my partner to be as happy and satisfied as I was.

"People have told me that I have a right to be happy, but then so did Aidan. I suppose that part of me feels that I want to share his pain and that experiencing any sort of physical or emotional pleasure would contradict this. However, I do have a longing for physical contact. If someone could just put their arms around me at least once a day, then I think that I would cope far better with what has happened."

The feelings of overpowering guilt that suffocated me each time I experienced any sort of physical contact have become easier to handle over time. I have become more accepting of my entitlement to some sort of physical and emotional fulfilment and I feel that I also have Kristian's endorsement, for he would never have wanted me to live a life of deprivation. Denying myself guilt-free pleasure is a burden that I placed upon myself as a form of punishment for not being able to help my son. I have still not reached the point where my conscience has freed me from all guilt at grasping periods of enjoyment, but I can now savour these moments without immediately wanting to retreat from physical contact and allowing myself only to be wrapped within a shroud of intense pain.

Laura was 19-years-old when her 24-year-old brother, Jack, took a fatal drugs' overdose after he discovered that his girlfriend had been unfaithful to him. Laura thought of Jack as her best friend and he was the one to whom she always turned whenever she had a problem.

Jack was an enviably loyal person and would have done anything for his family and his girlfriend. Discovering that she had betrayed him completely devastated him, especially since he had already mapped out a future with her and they had just purchased their first home together.

Laura says that after Jack died she became very promiscuous, actively seeking out sexual partners.

"I don't think it was necessarily because I wanted to compensate for the bear hugs that Jack used to give me constantly, but because I felt so angry with what his girlfriend had done to him. I could no longer see the point in being faithful to one person, because Jack's loyalty had destroyed his life. In an odd way, I felt as though I wanted to get my own back on his girlfriend by using people myself, which sounds quite ridiculous when I say it, because of course the people I sleep with aren't the culprits! However, I know that I will never be able to vent my feelings to his girlfriend directly, not because I don't want to, but because I have no idea where she is now. She didn't even turn up to his funeral, which I suppose is a good thing, because I'm afraid I wouldn't have been responsible for my actions.

"Someone suggested to me that maybe it was my way of having control over at least one situation in my life, because I had no control over what happened to Jack. I admit that I hadn't previously thought about it in this way, but I guess that there is an element of truth in that.

"Some years ago now, I did meet someone very special, which curtailed my rather indiscreet sexual activities. My partner is very supportive and understanding and provides me with all the physical contact that I need, but with the bonus of also giving me emotional fulfilment.

"I realise that no amount of physical contact will change what has happened, but it's my way of coping with the tragedy and anyone who has ever endured something as awful as suicide has to muddle though in the best way that they can, in whatever way suits them."

In general, many men need physical interaction as a way of coping with their grief, whilst women are more likely to want to avoid it. This can cause problems in relationships where parents have lost a child and are attempting to deal with their grief in very different ways. This is a crucial time when relationships can become stronger or fall apart.

Jayne and Victor's 28-year-old daughter Libby suffered from severe post-natal depression after the birth of her second child. Despite counselling, medication and support from her family and health visitor, Libby took her own life in February 2002 when her youngest daughter was eight-months-old. She also left behind a four-year-old son. Both of her children are now being raised by Jayne's son-in-law.

Jayne says that for a long time after Libby's death she retreated from any sort of physical and sexual contact with Victor, whereas Victor seemed to crave sex and was constantly making demands on Jayne to perform.

"I needed support from emotional understanding and being able to talk about what had happened, but Victor could only derive comfort from physical, non-verbal contact. It was an extremely difficult time in our marriage, not least because we were dealing with the worst tragedy that can ever happen to a parent.

"If Victor started making approaches for sex and I made it clear that I wasn't interested, he would turn his back on me and move to the other side of the bed.

"He took my reluctance for sexual contact as a sign that I was rejecting him, which of course was completely untrue. I actually needed him more than ever, but in the emotional sense, not physically. When he was in that state of rejection, I found it very difficult to attempt to communicate my feelings to him. There was so much tension between us that I just wanted to distance myself from the situation and felt as if the barrier between us was growing wider.

"I soon realised that if we didn't address the situation, we would end up separating, which was ridiculous, because before Libby's suicide our marriage had always been very solid. I found the right time to broach the subject and made Victor understand why I found physical contact difficult. I reassured him that I still loved him dearly and that my lack of libido wasn't a reflection on the state of our marriage. I told him that grief makes people react in very different ways and that my guilt over what had happened to Libby was preventing me from engaging in pursuits that were related to pleasure. Thankfully, he did understand and admitted that he was very relieved.

"Very shortly after that I did find myself able to begin enjoying a physical relationship with Victor again, although I admit that it has not been totally without guilt. I still cannot help thinking of Libby, but know that she would never have expected us to lead a life of self-denial just because she is no longer around."

After Kristian's suicide, my reluctance for physical contact was not just as a result of guilt, but because I was completely exhausted emotionally and physically. Grieving can drain one's energy and leave no room for other activities. All I wanted to do was sleep, but at the same time sleep evaded me, leading to further exhaustion, depression and lack of libido.

Re-establishing intimacy after such a tragedy is something that can be easy for men and extremely difficult for women, because many women often need to be feeling good about life in order to enjoy sex. It can take a long time after the tragedy to reach a point where sex is once again emotionally, mentally and physically satisfying, but it can and does happen and the loss of physical desire does not have to be terminal.

I found that I needed to redefine the word "intimacy" and explore being close to my partner without it resulting in sexual intercourse. It was far more important for me to be shown love and support through actions other than sexual contact, including hugs, hand holding and other gestures of affection. Intimacy could mean sharing a deep emotional bond, a great friendship, showing compassion and offering a listening ear to one's deepest thoughts.

Many relationships can fall apart following the loss of a child and differences in desire for physical contact can widen any existing rifts and exacerbate the grief. In some situations, one parent may be blaming the other for what happened and the resulting anger and bitterness may make physical contact impossible.

There is no one piece of advice that is applicable to everyone and telling a bereaved mother or father that it's ok to find pleasure in physical contact is not necessarily going to change the way that they feel. However, knowing that these feelings are perfectly normal may help bereaved parents to accept that resuming normal physical relations may take time, the length of which cannot be predetermined.

Chapter Seven

Grieving in Your Own Way and Your Own Time

Grief to me is like standing on the water's edge of the ocean and trying to stand strong against the waves, only to have them wash over you and knock you down. You have no control when or how often this happens!

Ginger

    To say that time heals all wounds is false and misleading. Grieving for a lost child lasts a lifetime, but you will arrive at a point in the future, at no pre-determined time, when painful thoughts of your child will not occupy every waking minute of your day and you will move forward to a place where sadness and joy can co-exist. However, other people may try to push you towards that place in their time, not yours. You don't want to be told that you will feel better in time, because when your child has just died, the "time" to which they are referring is apparently at some unforeseeable point in the future and you doubt that you will ever arrive there.
    Don't succumb to pressure from anyone else, because no one else can determine your best interests as well as you can. Others may want to press "fast forward" and skip the grieving scenes, not realising that most of us have a need to think, feel and mourn the loss of our children, however excruciating that might be. Not grieving for them would be almost like an insult to their memory, as though they could be discarded and forgotten like an old toy, an empty food packet, or a broken piece of furniture.

I wanted to move forward, but in another respect I wanted time to stand still, because each day that passed was another day further away from the time when Kristian had been alive. I wanted to feel better, but I wanted to experience intense sorrow. I felt guilty wanting to feel better. I wanted to feel pain and anguish, but I didn't. I wanted to experience the suffering that I believe Kristian experienced before he took his own life. Why did I deserve to feel better when my child hadn't? The grief was unbearable and during the period immediately after Kristian's death, I felt as though I would not survive the tragedy. I wanted to be with Kristian, but I didn't, because I had other children and family who needed me and I had seen and experienced the devastation that suicide causes.

In the very early days, I felt as though some people were trying to control my grieving process and telling me what I should feel and do and when, where and how, even though the majority of them were unqualified to hand out such advice.

There is no right or wrong way to grieve and everyone's grief is different, even those who have experienced a similar tragedy. No two people will ever grieve in the same way for the same duration. If everyone could understand that, then perhaps it would help others to be more responsive to the bereaved.

Since nobody else has lost your child, no one will ever know exactly how you feel. Even those within the same family can only loosely identify with your feelings, since they will all have had their own unique and special relationship with the deceased child. Their grief may be just as intense and there may be some similarities in their thoughts and feelings, but it can never be exactly the same as yours.

Grief cannot be compartmentalised and other people can't tell you how to grieve. Many people talk about the stages of grief as though you can work your way through some 10-step plan, but you can't. Wouldn't it be wonderful to think that you could deal with each stage that could then be ticked off the list as you move onto the next stage, like some educational course? You could say, "Well that's the Shock stage dealt with, now I can move onto Anger." Unfortunately, grief produces a haphazard pattern of emotions - like a dysfunctional kaleidoscope - that can come and go at any time; hours, days, months or even years after the event.

A few weeks after Kristian's death, an increasing number of people in my social circle were keen for me to move forward as quickly as possible on the grieving journey. I suspected that this was not just out of concern for me, but as a result of their own inability to cope with someone who wanted to continually cry and speak about their son who had died by suicide. Other people can feel embarrassed dealing with someone else's grief, even if they have experienced bereavement themselves. They feel uncomfortable by their helplessness to do anything to alleviate your pain. They want you to feel better to eradicate their ineptness at trying to cope with your grief. I felt like asking them, "Do you think there's specified time frame within which to grieve? Is it not acceptable to still feel crippled by my grief for longer than a few weeks?"

Nevertheless, as mentioned in previous chapters, I found myself protecting other people by telling them that I was ok and coping well, when inside I felt the farthest from fine I had ever felt. They didn't know about the times where the pain was so excruciating that I would shut myself away, curl up into a ball and sob and scream until my entire body ached, as though I had been beaten relentlessly.

The pressure within my chest and my head was so great, that it felt as though I would explode and I was convinced that the stress would trigger a heart attack or stroke. Rather than feeling as though I was releasing my grief, it seemed to be trapped within me, swirling around violently like a tornado of emotions, consuming me and threatening to spit me back out in a thousand pieces that couldn't be put back together again. I knew that if anybody witnessed me in those moments, it would be frightening.

I knew that if I sounded terminally depressed each time I answered the phone, people might stop calling at a time when I needed to communicate the most. Two weeks after Kristian's death, I began answering the phone in a bright, welcoming tone. A friend responded by saying, "Ooh, you sound chirpy. You must be feeling better." I wasn't feeling better. I felt as though my heart had been buried with Kristian and it was a struggle to look further than the next hour. It was my friend who apparently felt better, hearing me respond in the same manner that I had when Kristian was alive, thereby removing her discomfort at having to placate someone who might burst into tears at any moment.

Pretending to be coping well was exhausting. An overwhelming fatigue haunted me every day and by about 8pm every night I was ready to wander off to the comfort and security of my bed. I wasn't really sure whether I was reverting to childhood or descending into senility.

Adriana lost her only child Carly, aged 26, in 1995 after she had suffered for eight years from a mental illness. Carly was discovered hanging from a rafter in their garage one evening in November after Adriana and her husband Bill had returned from a day out.

Adriana says, "I have never stopped crying since the day Carly died. She was my baby and I will cry for her until the day I die. However, the days where I sob continually have become farther apart. There are still days when all I can do is to sit and weep all day, but if that's what I feel like doing, then that is what I will do. It's no good trying to put on a brave face and carry on. I need days like that when I can just let it out and forget everything else.

"I have read practically every recommended grief book I have been able to obtain over the past few years. Frankly, I am tired of reading about the 'phases' of grief that we are supposed to work through. It's been over fifteen years and there are some days when I feel particularly bad when I don't feel as though I have moved past the first stages. I was more than happy to contribute to this book, because it is the first book, I believe, that accurately portrays the real grief of a parent bereaved by suicide and covers topics that some people don't dare mention because it is too uncomfortable for them.

"I did used to wonder whether or not I was normal and whether there was something more I should be doing to help me to move forward. However, I realise that there isn't really any such thing as a set process or period for grieving. Not only does your grief depend on the person that you are, but very much upon the type of relationship that you had with the person who has died, how they died, how old they were and so many other issues and circumstances that are individual to each bereaved person.

"When Carly died, my life changed forever and for a long time I felt that my life was over. The only factor that prevented me from taking my own life was seeing how suicide destroys the lives of the surviving families. I also know that Carly would never have wanted me to do what she had done.

"I now accept that I will never be able to move forward to a place where I can live my life as though she never existed. Not only would that be an insult to her memory, but I also feel that it would be like saying that I had never really needed her in my life. I did need her and I still do, although my husband Bill cannot understand my way of thinking.

"Bill has dealt with his grief in a totally different manner. He won't cry – at least not in front of people – and he drinks to blank out the pain. He feels that he is dealing with the situation and can't understand why I dwell on Carly constantly and cannot just push her memory aside and get on with life. How can I? She was my life. She was my only child. I have no other children on whom to focus.

"I don't believe my husband is dealing with the situation. He may say he is handling his grief in his own way, but I don't think he has allowed himself to grieve at all. I do worry that he is going to have a breakdown at some point in the future, but I know that in the same way that I don't like other people telling me how I should grieve, I cannot tell my husband how to grieve. I don't think he wants to forget her; of course he doesn't want to forget her, but I think he just finds it too painful to think about her. He can't deal with the terrifying and torturous feelings that would consume him by thinking about how Carly killed herself, how we weren't there to prevent it from happening and how we are never going to see her, speak to her, listen to her infectious laugh or hug her again. If he allows himself to think, maybe he's afraid he will lose control. I can understand that.

"On my bad days, I often feel as though I will never cope with another minute, let alone another week, month or year, without my beautiful Carly. Grieving is my way of showing how much I loved and valued my daughter and I will grieve for the rest of my life, irrespective of what other people tell me I should or shouldn't do."

Other people's inability to handle grief in someone else manifests itself in inappropriate clichés, such as, "Time is a healer", "Life goes on", "Think about what you still have" or "I know exactly how you feel". Other people want you to look to the future, but that's not what a newly bereaved person wants to do. When your grief is still like an open wound, you cannot even contemplate a future without your child. You want to dwell on the past, because in the past your child was alive and by focusing on memories, you are keeping them alive. You cannot always think about what you still have because your entire focus is on what you have lost.

I remember my partner telling me that I had to "go out sometime and the sooner the better", after I admitted that I didn't feel I was ready to face the outside world. I knew that everywhere I went, every path I walked and every street down which we drove would remind me of Kristian. I was afraid of seeing other young lads of a similar age, which would serve as a cruel reminder that they were still alive, doing the things that Kristian used to do, whereas my son was not and never would be. I was afraid of seeing someone who looked like Kristian and then, imagining that everyone I knew had collectively decided to play a sadistic joke on me, discovering that he was, in fact, still alive. I even had visions of walking into the church on the day of his funeral and everyone, including Kristian, shouting, "Surprise!" before the host of one of those TV set-up shows appears with a large microphone and Cheshire Cat grin.

When Kristian first died, the initial focus of my grief was on the way in which he died. Not only did I have to deal with the thought of never seeing him again, but that in his despair and desperation, self-murder seemed like the only option.

My mind replays the same imaginary images over and over and over again. I have tried to imagine what he was feeling at the moment when he decided to inject himself. I have tried to visualise the scene, as though I am the audience in some harrowing movie. I have tried to picture him pushing the syringe into his vein and pumping the heroin directly into his bloodstream. I have attempted to capture the same image that his girlfriend's neighbours will have had, as they walked past him and left him there, assuming he was drunk. The most harrowing thought of all, is picturing him propped up in the corner of a cold, hard concrete landing all night, with his body temperature plunging rapidly to hypothermic level, when he should have been tucked up in a safe, warm bed.

It is this last thought that tortured me from the moment that I learned of Kristian's death and one that I verbally repeated over and over again to the flow of friends and family who passed through our house in the days immediately following the tragedy. When I mentioned that I couldn't stop thinking about Kristian sitting on a hard, freezing concrete landing all night slowly dying, my mother said to me, "You mustn't think about that", but I told her that I needed to think about it, because it was my way of facing my grief. In travelling through the grief that follows the tragic and seemingly senseless act of suicide, extreme pain can never be avoided. I needed to habitually relive past moments, even those events that I had not actually witnessed, but which I needed to imagine and recreate in my own mind.

On a few occasions, I have visited the block of flats where Kristian spent the last conscious moments of his life and have sat in the same dismal, uninviting corner of the third floor stairwell landing, gazing at the bleak, grey walls that will have served as a final reminder of the miserable world my son was about to leave. Was this the last, sinister image that Kristian had of life?

Were all the happy memories completely erased from his mind? Was his memory like the blank, concrete walls that he faced as the life drained from his body? Was he sacrificing his life because he felt that he no longer wanted to burden his family, his girlfriend and his daughter? In ending his life, the suffering for his family was far greater than a lifetime of trying to help him deal with his struggles.

On the day following Kristian's death, I was typing furiously, transferring my deepest and uncensored emotions onto the computer screen. When my partner asked, "Should you be doing that?" I replied, "It's something I need to do". He said, "Well, if it makes you feel better". Nothing would make me "feel better", but writing was – and still is – a coping mechanism. Writing is a form of release, which not only enables me to work through my grief, but also keeps Kristian's memory alive. Writing can be mentally distressing, but it is also therapeutic. Writing can trigger a happy or sad memory, a painful or pleasant emotion. I can write and cry. I can write and laugh. I never write and feel nothing.

My daughter Anneliese frequently writes letters to Kristian and places them on his grave. This is her way of preserving the precious bond that she had with her brother. She sits on his grave and talks to him, as do I. This is our comfort.

My grief has been like taking part in a ceaseless game of roulette, where I am the ball and the numbers are the full spectrum of emotions. The route cannot be predicted. One minute I stop in despair and the next I find myself in hope. Immediately afterwards, I am thrown into anger, then into guilt and back again to despair.

I found that as time moved on and others felt I had reached a point when I should have been feeling better, I actually felt worse.

To a certain degree, I had been protected from the worst pain by the initial shock, which threw me into a surreal state and made me believe that this wasn't really happening. It allowed me to cope, but it was not permanent. At around six months, the reality began to creep painfully in.

Fran, a single parent from Chester, talks about resuming normal life very shortly after the death of her 23-year-old son, Callum in October 1999.

"Callum had struggled with bipolar disorder for six years and one of the reasons that my ex-husband and I separated was because he could not cope with Callum's ongoing problems. I do not blame Callum for our breakup, but my ex-husband's inability to cope when life was less than perfect. Callum didn't choose to be mentally ill. What angers me most is how I nursed my ex-husband's ego when he was made redundant many years ago and then supported him when his mother died. What a shame his love wasn't unconditional where his son was concerned.

"When Callum finally ended his suffering by taking an overdose of antidepressants mixed with alcohol, the pain and anguish that swamped me immediately after his death rendered me incapable of doing anything except rocking backwards and forwards screaming out loud. However, about two weeks later, the immobilising grief changed radically to a feeling of relief that his battle was over. I shut down the part of my brain that allowed me to feel all the crippling emotions and in an almost obscene fashion, I resumed regular duties; working, cleaning, shopping, cooking and taking care of my other two children like an automaton. That was the only way I knew how to get through each day and perform all those functions that you need to in order to exist.

"I actually wasn't that interested in existing, but I knew that I had to carry on for everyone else's sake, because I didn't have a husband to lean on, no family close by to help out and suddenly my two daughters became even more precious to me.

"The people who knew what had happened must have either thought that I was incredibly thick-skinned, or that I was in denial and that once the truth had really sunk in, I would end up having a breakdown. To a certain extent, the latter is true, although I wouldn't exactly call it denial but a fear of allowing myself to absorb the reality of the tragedy. Although it is over a decade since Callum died, I still wake up some mornings and the reality of the situation strikes me like a bolt of lightning. That is the point at which I have to shut down the emotions and switch onto autopilot again, because I am afraid that if I don't, I will not be able to cope with the overwhelming grief of acknowledging that he is no longer with us.

"I am still sensitive to other people's sadness and cry easily during movies, but this is only because I feel that I have permission to cry then. Thinking about what happened to my beautiful Callum is just too much for my mind to accept. Maybe one day I will no longer be able to hide from the agony and I will have a breakdown, but right now not coping is not an option. I owe it to my other two children to do my best for them, because they are still alive and that means that there is hope for them.

"My daughters, who were 18 and 14 at the time of Callum's death, grieved very differently. Emma, who is now 24, was very, very angry. She cried, stamped and screamed, but her tears were not just tears of sadness but ones of intense anger towards Callum. She kept asking how he could do that to the people he loved and how he had ruined her life by ending his.

"Only recently has she been going through a guilt stage. Through her own pain and sadness, she has realised how awful Callum must have felt in the moment that he decided there was no hope left in his life. She feels guilty for feeling angry with him and she now feels angry with herself.

"Jade, who is 20, always looked up to Callum. He was like a hero to her. It was Jade whom I worried about the most, because she became withdrawn almost immediately. Her personality changed completely and she went from being an outgoing, happy child who giggled at almost everything to this quiet, introverted, melancholy girl who totally lost her zest for life. She frightened me and naturally the thought crossed my mind that maybe she was thinking about suicide. I spent a lot of time trying to talk to her, but she refused to open up. She would either assure me that she was fine, or tell me that she didn't want to talk about it.

"I consulted the doctor, bereavement counsellors and even a child psychiatrist and was told that whilst it was important to keep an eye on her, she was grieving in her own way. They told me that she probably felt badly let down by someone whom she had put on a pedestal, someone to whom she had previously aspired. Eventually, I managed to persuade her to see a counsellor and after a few sessions, her mood seemed to lift and I began to see traces of the old Jade slowly returning.

"I have heard others describe us as 'strong', but there are many, many times when neither I nor my daughters feel strong. Others only see what's on the surface. They can't see into our hearts and minds. They don't know about the thoughts that I have also had about taking my own life. They don't know that I am only carrying on because of my daughters. I have realised that being strong does not mean we have to carry on as if nothing is wrong, or never breaking down when the grief becomes unbearable.

"We are strong because we carry on despite these things, even though there will be times when it seems impossible to live with what has happened. It's at those times that we need help. Seeking help is not a sign of weakness, but a sign of strength, because we can acknowledge that we are not afraid to admit that we cannot always deal with situations and feelings alone.

"It's difficult not to let the overwhelming loss supersede all the happiness, but it is because Callum brought me so much joy in life that the sadness that his death has brought overwhelms the pleasure. I desperately want to feel that the joy that he brought me exceeds the sadness that he caused in that moment of madness when he took his own life. I know that this will take time - a long time - and, who knows, maybe even in thirty or forty years' time, I will still feel the same as I do now.

"The only thing that I can say with all honesty is that I have to do this in my own time, no matter what other people believe I should do. No one else can tell you how you should feel. No one else has ever experienced exactly the same tragedy. No one has lost my son. No one else is in a position to judge. People can empathise and understand to a certain extent, but everyone is different and absolutely no one can ever say that they know exactly how I feel, because they don't and they never will."

Bengt's 19-year-old grandson, Kaj, ended his life after hanging himself in September 2002. Bengt and his second wife, Marianne, became Kaj's legal guardians after Kaj's mother, Mia, died in 1997.

"When Kaj died, I felt that everyone I loved was being ruthlessly removed, one by one. First I lost my daughter to bowel cancer and then my grandson to suicide. Who would it be next?

"Although I am still grieving for my daughter and her passing wasn't made any easier just because we knew she was going to die, we at least were more prepared. We had the chance to talk and reminisce about good times and tell each other how much we cared. Cancer is a devastating illness, the way it eats away at someone and changes them into someone you no longer recognise physically, but the same could be said of depression in the way that it takes hold of someone's mind and can change them into someone you no longer recognise mentally. As with cancer, depression can be fatal.

"The difference with Mia was that there was nothing anyone could do to save her. It was nature taking its course. I didn't carry around the same guilt or responsibility as I have since we lost Kaj. When Kaj died, the grief was - and still is - so different and so much more complicated. All these other emotions such as extreme shock, disbelief, guilt, helplessness, hopelessness and even denial swamped me initially to the degree that I didn't feel as though I could go on living myself. Were it not for the love and support of my wife, Marianne and my surviving daughter, Lotta, I think I would probably be sectioned in some institution by now.

"I know that it is still very early days and that none of us can expect to resume anything remotely close to normal, but I know that this is something from which there is no recuperation. I look and feel like a very, very old man now, totally drained of emotional and physical energy and extremely weary of this hideous world.

"When Kaj first moved in with us, we could see that he was a very troubled young man, but we did not believe this to be unusual considering everything that he had been through. His mother had died, leaving him alone with a man who cared little for him and who was quick to shun any parental responsibility for him. He never knew his biological father, since he disappeared almost the moment that Mia announced her pregnancy.

"I feel responsible for Kaj's death and, oddly, accepting this has lifted some of the crushing weight from me. So many people have told me that if anyone should feel guilty or responsible it should be his stepfather who never accepted Kaj, even after he married Kaj's mother – my daughter. His stepfather was never physically abusive towards Kaj, but he never bothered to communicate with him except to reprimand him for the smallest misdemeanour. Kaj said that although he had lived in the same house as his stepdad for seven years, since the age of nine, he still felt like a complete stranger to him. Many times he told me that he could never remember a time when he had had a normal conversation with his stepdad, or when he had ever spoken to him in a congenial tone.

"After Kaj's mother died, his stepdad severed all contact with him. Rather than feeling upset, I think that Kaj was rather relieved, although I still sensed that this must have been incredibly hurtful to him and added to any feelings of rejection that he already harboured.

"Kaj was not a very open person verbally, but physically he was extremely affectionate and showed his appreciation through actions and gestures of kindness. He would always help out around the house and would never forget a birthday or anniversary. Hugs were also very important to him and he desperately wanted to be liked by everyone, even to the extent of allowing others to walk over him. I was concerned that others took advantage of his good nature, but it never seemed to bother him. The thought that maybe Kaj was hiding his unhappiness from us never occurred to me and I will always believe that had I known how desperate he felt, I could have done something to help him and he might still be with us now.

"Kaj was also very studious and did well at school. Very unusually, he left school at 16 to work at a sportswear store in Gothenburg. I was very disappointed, because he had so much potential, but at the same time I just wanted him to be happy. I know from experience that there's nothing worse than pushy parents – and in our case, grandparents – who steer their children into courses and professions that they would like to see their children do without giving any consideration to what their children want.

"Kaj appeared to love his job and everyone in the store loved him. He worked a lot harder than was necessary and always gave that little extra. I often think now that he felt he had to do more than everyone else in order to be liked. Although it was clear that everyone liked him, maybe he couldn't see it himself. He was popular with the customers, which is also how he met his girlfriend. She became a regular customer, although we used to laugh that the main reason why she kept returning to the store was to see Kaj.

"Before long he was promoted to assistant manager, his relationship with his girlfriend appeared to be going well and, although he occasionally experienced dark moods for no discernible reason because he never discussed his feelings, his life seemed to be on track.

"Looking back now, I think I must have missed something, even though I have replayed those last few weeks over and over in my mind. His girlfriend did mention to us on a couple of occasions that she could never read him and that sometimes when she sensed that he was in one of his moods, she would just leave him alone. Whenever she tried to question him, he would coldly tell her that he was fine. He was exactly the same with us. It seemed as though no one had the power to penetrate the barrier that he had erected around himself to prevent his emotions from escaping.

"Of course, I now believe that there must have been some way of reaching him and persuading him to open up. If we had known that he was feeling suicidal, we would have done absolutely everything in our power to help him. The strange thing was that after his mother died, he had a fear of death, so how could we possibly have known that he was thinking of ending his own life?

"I find it very difficult to talk about what happened on the day that Kaj passed away, because it is so horrific. It's like every nightmare you've ever experienced blended into one horrific and inescapable scene. The greatest gift in the world for me would be to be able to turn back time and save him, but of course that is not possible and that is what eats away at me.

"It doesn't matter how many times others tell me that I am in no way responsible; I have found it impossible to feel differently. I have realised that in order to move forward, I have to learn to live with that feeling of responsibility. Anyone who has assumed a parental role in a child's life will inevitably feel responsible. Only the most insensitive people can deny any feelings of responsibility. I was my grandson's legal guardian and it was my job to protect and look after him.

"There are times when I feel that I am going crazy and it can be terrifying, but the only way of controlling this is by shutting down and not thinking and not feeling. I honestly feel the only way to move forward in our lives and attempt any sort of healing is by experiencing our pain and grief to the fullest. I don't fight these feelings anymore, although in the beginning I felt as though I had to in order to live. Sometimes I will experience just one emotion – anger or guilt or sadness – but at other times, every emotion imaginable will descend upon me.

"Maybe I will reach a point where all the 'whys' don't matter anymore, but right now I will always feel that I could have made a difference if only I'd known what was going on in Kaj's mind. I suppose that because I feel responsible, if I accept the things I couldn't change it will seem as though I am shunning that responsibility.

"I am convinced that people look at me differently. Some people don't even bother asking how I am anymore, because I feel they don't want to know the true answer. Because they can't handle the truth, they feel more comfortable avoiding the question. To those who do ask, I will honestly say, 'Fine' if I am feeling fine and on not-so-good days, I will say, 'Not feeling too bright today, but it's kind of you to ask.' Other people avoid me altogether, which I do find hurtful and which just exacerbates my grief, but at least this tragedy has been a test of true friendship. Those who really cared have stuck by us and are happy for us to talk about Kaj. Of course, the conversations aren't all morose. We have reached a point where we can reminisce about the good times and celebrate his life.

"I refuse to live my life by someone else's agenda. I will not allow others to dictate to me how I should be feeling at any given time. I have spoken to many grieving parents and grandparents through various support groups who constantly pretend that they are ok when in fact they feel like hell. Why should we have to lie? If anything, being honest after such a tragedy helps us to identify our true friends and eliminates the worthless elements in our lives."

Alysha is 15. Her close friend, Kelly, hung herself in January 2007 after an argument with her parents. Alysha talks about the gross insensitivity and lack of support that she and her friends have endured from their school and a minority of classmates.

"Kelly was the one friend whom I could trust to keep a secret. When I needed someone to talk to in confidence, Kelly was always there for me. I had known her since we were in infant school and because I have limited memories of my life before the age of five, I cannot remember a time when she wasn't around. Since she died, I have felt as though I am stranded alone on a desert island, not wanting to be rescued by anyone except Kelly.

"My family has been great. My parents have allowed me to pour my heart out to them without being told that I should 'pull myself together' and move on with my life. I wish I could say the same for the school counsellors, who were brought in to talk to us. Just two months after Kelly died, I was told very sternly that I should be 'over it'. I was so cross that I said to the counsellor, 'I haven't just had flu you know. If I could get over this like a temporary illness, why are you here talking to me? I could have got better all by myself.'

"She seemed quite shocked, but then went on to tell me that I still had my whole life ahead of me and that I shouldn't let this loss affect my chances of having a successful life. When I then asked her whether she had lost anyone to suicide, she told me that she hadn't, but that that wasn't important. Her reaction was that counselling obviously wasn't for me and that she wasn't going to waste any more of my time or hers.

"I am sure that counselling works for some people, particularly those who would rather divulge their innermost thoughts and feelings to a stranger, but it was not for me. I have gained far more comfort from communicating with a couple of supportive friends, or from other bereaved families.

"I can understand that the teachers were concerned that we should not let the tragedy affect our schoolwork and our future prospects, but being so unsympathetic made us feel less able to concentrate on our work.

"Sitting in the same classes that we used to share with Kelly was so hard. There was an empty chair where she used to sit and there were so many memories all around me. I frequently ended up crying, but the teachers soon became impatient and felt that I was using it as an excuse to leave the class or not do the assigned work. The more impatient that they became with me, the worse it made me feel. I found that I got far better grades in the lessons where the teachers showed more compassion and understanding.

"One day, when I was sat outside a class, one of the less caring teachers walked past and said, 'Oh Alysha, you're not still crying over your friend are you?' I felt that people who spoke to me like that thought that there was something wrong with me, because I couldn't just pick myself up and get on with my life as though Kelly had never existed. How heartless would that be if I could? If it were that easy, then she couldn't have meant that much to me.

"This is the most difficult thing I have ever had to deal with and although I am still young, I cannot imagine ever experiencing anything that will come close to losing someone dear to suicide.

"Nobody should be told for how long they should be allowed to grieve, or in what way. I write letters to Kelly and I talk to her aloud when I am doing things that we used to enjoy together. I even ask her opinion when I am buying clothes and instinctively know whether she would have liked my choice or not. I am certain that she is still around giving me guidance and that gives me great comfort. Maybe some people think I'm mad, but I don't care. If it makes me feel better, then it can't be bad can it?

"I surround myself with happy photos of Kelly, so that I remember her for the wonderful person that she was, for the many times she made me laugh and for the fun times we had, not for the pain that she caused when she left us.

"I do feel guilty if I do something that gives me pleasure, but I know that Kelly would never have wanted her friends or family to be sad. I believe that she is happy now and I am happy for the good things that she brought into my life. I can smile through the sadness and I feel grateful that I was lucky enough to have such a special friend, even though it was for too short a time. Some people don't have a true friendship like that in their entire lifetime.

"Right now, I believe that my grief will always be with me, like the deep scar on my knee from an injury sustained when I was younger. Maybe I will focus on it less as time passes and will not think about Kelly every minute of the day, but it will still be there like the scar. The grief will lessen, but it has left a scar that will remain until my life is over and my own body has disintegrated."

There will always be books and articles that try to tell you about the phases of grief, as though at some point when you have passed through all these stages, the grief will end. This is a fallacy. You will always grieve the loss of your child and learning to live with the loss is not the same as "getting over it". People outside the grieving circle may feel that they are qualified to tell us when our grieving time should be "up". Sometimes this maybe because they are worried about us and feel that we are not moving forward in our lives and sometimes it could be that they are not able to cope with our grief. If they feel uncomfortable, then this is their problem, not ours. They should learn to deal with their discomfort rather than force us into an unhealthy situation of feeling unable to acknowledge our feelings openly. It is not fair that we should have to compensate for others' ineptness when we are already bearing the heavy burden of child loss.

How do you carry on living with such intense grief? Some coping strategies are provided in Chapter Twenty-One.

Grief cannot be quantified. It doesn't fit neatly into a pre-defined package of organised emotions experienced at set times. It will very often be a lifelong process, but should not prevent us from re-investing in life. Whilst we will always desperately miss our children, we can still love them in physical separation. Throughout our lives, we will experience our grief in different ways at different times. We should not allow others to dictate to us when and how we should grieve. Even if they have experienced a similar loss, it does not mean that their grief will be identical to ours. It is important not to compare your progress to that of other bereaved families, because there are so many criteria that can affect the way in which we grieve.

My grief is not isolated to specific times or days. It is always there, lurking beneath the surface, waiting to burst out when I least expect it.

Remember, do what you want to do when you want to do it. You don't need anyone else's permission to grieve, nor should you have to schedule times to grieve. This is your grief. You own it. You have the absolute right to handle it in your way.

What Size is Grief?

by Andrea Corrie

I've been thinking a great deal recently about the nature of grief and the way in which it changes with the passage of time. When James first passed, I can remember asking out loud where on earth I could put my grief. It was massive, all encompassing and dreadful in its intensity. I couldn't see how I could possibly assimilate something so enormous, so utterly life-changing, into my everyday existence. The greatest components in my grief were shock and bewilderment that such a thing could have happened. The oft repeated question 'Why?' as for all of us, remains unanswered.

A friend of mine, who is Swiss, uses an expression for extreme sadness that translates literally as 'carrying a stone on your heart'. Initially, that stone replaced my heart, and each beat and every breath felt as heavy as lead.

As the days passed, I began to visualise my grief as a huge rock, and my desire was for time to accelerate, to chip away at that rock, until it became a stone and, ultimately, I hoped, a pebble. But I have learned that this process cannot be rushed; it will take as long as it takes. There are no short cuts and no magic chisel to whittle away the layers.

Today, 15 months on from my loss, the rock is on its way to being a stone, still heavy on my heart but more manageable day by day. Of course, there are many obstacles that cause the rock to assume greater proportions again – birthdays, anniversaries, holidays – but each time one of these is faced, it is placed in 'yesterday' rather than 'tomorrow' and causes another little shower of stone chips to fall.

The presence of the rock has given me the capacity to feel greater compassion for others. I believe that the mutual exchange of empathy and support via The Compassionate Friends (TCF) increases my own ability to deal with my personal grief. As parents, we reach out and are reached out to in return. Collectively, we have strengths that the non-bereaved parent cannot begin to understand.

The future begins to look more attainable, more bearable. Ideally, it is a future where our children live on in our minds, ever present but not consuming us to the extent that we cannot function. Resilience, strength from our memories, human nature itself and the desire to behave in the way our children would wish, all push us forward, however reluctantly, step by step. We slowly emerge from the black heart of despair, blinking at the chinks of light that begin to warm our rocks of grief. I currently view my own rock as having changed its character, from being a flat, grey, heavy chunk of matter to a lighter, more porous and colourful piece of stone.

Years ago, whenever we visited the coast, here or abroad, my children and I would pick up a few stones that had been smoothed by the sea. These had to fulfil certain criteria; they had to be tactile, preferably sun warmed and the size needed to fit comfortably in your palm. We called them our 'thinking stones', and all took to using them the way some cultures use worry beads.

Today, I habitually carry one of these 'thinking stones' in my pocket. Every so often I clasp it in my hand, roll it around and warm it and it has gradually acquired the identity of my grief. I know that one day, in the future and however long it takes, this stone will represent the size of my grief.

It will fit into the palm of my hand and no longer be an insurmountable challenge. It will be smooth and curved without the jagged edges of early mourning. It will represent the softening of the harsh reality of what has to be faced on a daily basis. Its tiny mineral chips will reflect light instead of absorbing darkness.

This evolution is something I could not have envisaged at the outset, but it remains my daily quest to work as positively as I can through my loss and to come out the other side in something approaching calm acceptance for that which cannot be changed.

© 2006 Andrea Corrie, Addlestone, Surrey, UK
Mum to James
http://www.pbase.com/andreac/tribute_to_james

Chapter Eight

Referring to Your Child as "The Body"

There is no death, only a change of worlds.

Chief Seattle

    For twenty years, my son was a living, breathing child with a personality and feelings and yet the second that he died, he was referred to impersonally as "the body". Just a couple of hours after he died, I recall someone telling me that until the post mortem had been conducted, they wouldn't be able to release "the body" and that when I went to sit with him, I had to be careful not to disturb "the body". So that was it then. The instant that my son was pronounced dead, he was no longer the Kristian that we knew and loved. He was "the body".

    Whilst I acknowledge that Kristian's body was just a shell for his spirit and that when he died, "the body" was no longer the boy that I had known for 20 years, it still upset me to hear my son described like a nameless, inanimate and insignificant piece of meat. Maybe he no longer had feelings, but those he had left behind certainly did. It seemed as though respect for a person ended the moment they died.

    My son's body was how I identified him as the person that he was. Even the clothes that he wore on that body were an indication of his personality and a reminder of the son I had nurtured, loved, guided, scolded and with whom I had shared happy and sad times. I knew that when he died, his body ceased to function, his brain became inert and he was physically dead, but since I could not visualise his spirit, I had to focus on his body as being him.

We live in a physical world where the emphasis is on physical things to which we become attached. Kristian communicated with others through his physical body - his ears, eyes, mouth, hands and limbs, as we all do. After his death, his soul continued to have a connection to his physical body in the sense that I associated his soul with the speech, actions and expressions that emanated from his physical body. Therefore, referring to the child that I had loved dearly as "the body" was intensely painful and made it brutally clear that he would never walk through my door again.

We will often be told that it is "the person inside that counts" and yet, when we see someone for the first time, we judge them by their appearance, not their soul. It is a sad fact that society still judges people by their image, size and perceived attractiveness and yet that is often the basis by which we remember people. I can talk about the person that Kristian was; his sense of humour, his impulsiveness, his compassion and his naivety and yet even when I am describing his character, I am visualising his body; the way that he looked, the way that he dressed, the way that he moved, his facial expressions and his mannerisms. I cannot visualise his soul, only his body.

In the same way that I felt offended to hear my dead son referred to as "the body", other grieving parents may equally feel offended to hear someone continually refer to their dead child by name without using the word "body" as a suffix, thereby apparently refusing to acknowledge that he or she is no longer alive.

Karen, whose 23-year-old daughter took her own life in March 2001 said, "When the hospital staff told me that they would be moving Shannon to the morgue, I thought, 'What do you mean, they're moving Shannon to the morgue? Don't you mean Shannon's body? That's not my Shannon anymore; it's just an empty shell.'

"In my mind, the real Shannon – her soul – left her physical body the moment her heart stopped beating. The body that remained was just a temporary vehicle for her soul. However, I could not bring myself to say anything because everyone would have just assumed that I was out of my mind with grief. I know that they thought they were being sensitive, so I do not feel angry with them."

How each parent feels can depend on their own beliefs and perhaps their views on the afterlife. Whilst I have always believed in life after death and the fact that we all incarnate on the Earth plane to learn different lessons in each lifetime, the moment that Kristian died, I immediately questioned all my beliefs and however much I wanted to believe that Kristian had simply discarded his earthly body, it was still the body that I associated as being my son. It was the body to which I had given birth, the body I had watched grow and change, the warm, soft body I had hugged, kissed and tucked up into bed at night and the body from which tears of sadness had fallen and peals of laughter had emanated. It was the body that portrayed my son's soul.

Some people reading this might be thinking, "Well, at least you had a body to visit", because the violent nature of some suicides means that seeing their child is not possible and yet they too will probably have a visual image of their child when they are thinking and talking about them. Even those who have the opportunity of viewing their child at a chapel of rest may still choose not to do so, preferring to remember their child as they were in life. Not everyone wants the image of their dead child to haunt them forever.

In life, the body and the spirit are inextricably linked. We refer to someone as having a "kind face", or a "friendly smile", or a "mean expression", because our emotions and personality are expressed through our faces and our physical bodies.

When a child ends his or her own life away from the home environment and the parents are informed of the death by a third party, there is often a strong urge to see, touch or hold their child. Not only did they not have the chance to say goodbye, but they may have difficulty in accepting the reality of the death and wish to seek firsthand proof that their child is no longer alive. Our minds require evidence that our child's life has ended and the presence of their body provides this evidence, however painful it might be.

Connie, from Brisbane Australia, whose 16-year-old daughter April jumped from the sixth floor of a block of flats in October 1999 said, "Using the word 'body' without a name attached sounds so impersonal. When the police officer asked me whether I wanted to identify 'the body', I remember thinking, 'What body?' It was as though the body was totally detached from April, which I grant that many people might say is true if they believe in life after death. But April's body was how I identified her as a person. When you're walking along a street, you don't recognise someone's personality do you? You recognise them by their body; the way they look, dress, walk and move."

Whenever I visit my son's grave, I visualise him beneath the earth that has been continually adorned with flowers, candles and words of love. I am visualising the body that was my son, the body that encompassed everything that he was. We are constantly reminded that it is not exterior image that is important, but the personality beneath and yet all this changes when someone dies, as you realise the enormous significance of the body. For some people, the body is an obsession in life, but for me, the body became an obsession in death.

The loving bond and the memories that I have built up with my son over 20 years cannot be erased, even though he is now, apparently, "the body", a body that can no longer feel pain, sorrow, happiness or love, but which nevertheless has the power to elicit those feelings in others until the day they also die and become just "bodies".

Kristian's art and schoolwork compilation
by Mike Horton

Chapter Nine

The Day of the Funeral and After

Grief doesn't end after the funeral. It's just the beginning.

    Although thoughts of organising a funeral seem unbearable and only heighten the indescribable agony that you are already experiencing, this farewell ceremony is a personal tribute to the child that you nurtured and loved. Your child will only have one funeral, so you want everything to be as perfect as it can be, to celebrate your child's life and to be able to acknowledge the person that he or she was.
    I found the thought of organising a funeral not only unbearable, but repulsive, because of the obscenity of funeral directors manipulating the bereaved for extortionate sums of money.
    The phone call from the coroner informing us that the post mortem had been performed and giving us permission to go ahead and organise Kristian's funeral, propelled us another stage closer to his final farewell.
    How do you choose the organisation to bury your child? I had no idea. It's not like selecting a plumber or a builder or a landscape gardener. Where does one begin to ask questions when there is so much emotion attached to the process? I did not have the emotional strength to cope with this and so my partner did the research, made the phone calls and chose the funeral director.
    The day that we paid our first visit to the funeral parlour to choose Kristian's coffin and discuss arrangements, I picked up Kristian's girlfriend Millie and her cousin Amanda, who had been one of Kristian's closest friends. They had been such an important part of Kristian's life and I wanted them to be involved with every aspect of the arrangements.

It is all too easy for blood relatives to take over and be insensitive to the needs of those who were closest to the person who has passed over.

We then went to collect my partner from his office. As we were waiting in the car outside, one of my partner's work colleagues walked up to the car and said something along the lines of, "It's not worth buying an expensive coffin because, after all, it's only going to be burned."

I think I was too shocked by this insensitivity to say anything other than, "He's not being cremated. We're having him buried."

When we arrived at the funeral parlour, the owner of the firm ushered us into a small room leading off from the reception area. Against one wall near the door was a wooden bookcase containing files and catalogues of coffins and headstones. There were a couple of sofas and chairs and a small, central table upon which sat an obligatory box of tissues. I don't recall much else other than the smell of old roses and tea that permeated the air; the smell of embalming fluid, the smell of death.

It was a smell that my Uncle, a retired vicar, had described to me over the phone when he learned of Kristian's death. He told me that he had been walking through Hastings, Sussex with his wife when they were both engulfed by this same powerful smell. My Uncle told me that whenever this smell surrounded him, he knew that someone had died. In fact, the moment that he and his wife experienced this was the exact time of Kristian's death. One of his parishioner friends, who had also known Kristian, said that at that exact time she also sat down and spontaneously burst into tears, without knowing why.

The Funeral Director was a short, middle-aged man with greying hair and laughter lines etched into his face, which denoted much mirth. Did someone in such a grim profession find it easy to laugh, or was laughter a necessary survival tactic when dealing with such misery every day?

I was struck by how "normal" he appeared. I had always imagined funeral directors to be a weird, macabre bunch who had an unnatural obsession with dead bodies and looked like members of the Adams' family. How did they manage to cast off the vibes of bereaved families, detach themselves from the suffocating sadness and grief that they encountered each day and return to their own family life? Maybe the money they raked in enabled them to undergo expensive therapy. I had no idea, but pondering on these questions provided a temporary diversion from the gruelling task ahead.

We were handed a large, hard-backed book that advertised the available coffins no differently to any other item that one would choose from a catalogue. I again experienced that surreal feeling of detachment from my body. We were handed the catalogue to browse through alone and I could not get my head around the fact that we were there to decide how my son's body would be dealt with and the box in which he would be shut away forever.

I stared vacantly at the first page, not feeling mentally or emotionally prepared to pick out a box into which my son would be encased. It seemed so callous, so perfunctory and so final. Tears blurred my vision and dripped onto the laminated pages. Amanda passed me a tissue. I looked at Millie and passed her the book. In fact, she liked the idea of a white coffin, which mirrored my desires. White seemed to symbolise youth and the purity of childhood. Even though Kristian was 20, he was still a child; my child.

I recall the funeral director sitting opposite me with his open diary, prompting us to agree on a date for Kristian's funeral.

"This Friday?" he asked.

It was already Tuesday. Friday was far too soon. Everything was suddenly happening too quickly.

We agreed on Friday the following week instead, 22 November 2002. Born on 22nd of the month and buried on 22nd of the month.

Fridays would never be the same again. Kristian died on a Friday and was buried on a Friday; the end of the working week and the end of my son's life.

I remember the heartrending process of trying to select the clothes that Kristian would wear in his coffin. So few of his belongings had been returned to me, which somehow made the selection a little easier, because there was such a limited choice. Millie had given me a photograph of Kristian wearing, what he claimed to be, his favourite shirt. When I asked Millie where this shirt was, she said that she thought it had been ruined in the wash. I later discovered that she had destroyed it in retaliation following an argument. We all do impulsive things out of anger, but I could fully understand why she didn't have the courage or heart to tell me about it at the time.

Eventually, I chose a pair of stone jeans and a smart blue shirt that I had already washed and ironed after Anneliese had managed to retrieve them from his friend's flat following his suicide. I ironed them again meticulously, wanting my son to look as immaculate in death as he had in life. I don't recall the moment when I delivered his clothes to the funeral parlour. The emotional blur of those first few weeks has erased some of the finer details, but allowed others to remain with alarming and excruciating clarity.

Four days following the booking of Kristian's funeral, I received a telephone call informing me that he had been transferred to the chapel of rest in the funeral parlour and that we could go and see him. My partner was at work and I had no transport. I also had Lauren to think about. Was it appropriate for a child who had only just turned three to see her dead brother? Would it be traumatic for her? Was she too young to understand the concept of death?

I believed that without confirmation of her brother's death, she may assume that he would return one day, or think that perhaps Kristian had chosen to go away, or had stopped visiting her because he no longer loved her or that she had done something wrong. Whether right or wrong, I telephoned for a taxi to take us to Kristian.

The last time that I had been permitted to see Kristian was prior to the post mortem. I yearned to see him again and yet I was afraid that he would look different, that he had begun to decompose or, worse still, that the violation of his body during the post mortem would have somehow altered him beyond recognition. I had already trawled many websites for information on what happens during a post mortem and how a body is prepared for viewing, partly out of morbid curiosity and partly to prepare myself for what I might see. I knew that the process of embalming and preparing the body for viewing was to protect the living family and friends from the influences of death, to preserve the body as far as is possible in a state that is non-threatening and as familiar as possible to that of the person when he or she was alive.

The Funeral Director led us into the chapel of rest, which contained a row of small, curtained off sections into which the coffin containing a family's loved one would be placed for viewing. That same smell of death enveloped me; the smell of old roses and tea. I entered the same dream-like state that I experienced immediately following Kristian's death. Was this my body's way of protecting me from the overwhelming distress that I was anticipating, or was it simply that I could not process the fact that I was about to view my son in his coffin for the first time?

We walked to the end cubicle. I caught my breath as the Funeral Director pulled back the curtain to reveal my son lying so peacefully in his white, wooden box, dressed in the clothes I had lovingly prepared for him.

Although at an initial glance, he still looked like my little boy, there was no doubt that he had changed. The staff had done their best to dress him in a way that concealed (as far as was possible) the damage to his body caused during the post mortem.

His shirt was buttoned to the top, but his neck bulged obscenely over the collar and exceeded the width of his head. Although his lips were still so soft and his face was perfect, his neck was purple and swollen and foul-smelling fluid was seeping from the stitched incision around his neck onto the oyster-coloured satin cloth that lined his white coffin. His once-soft hands had turned pallid, waxy and wrinkled, almost as though he had taken a long bath and his body felt rigid and inhuman. At the back of his scalp there were crude stitches running up and over his head from ear-to-ear and his beautiful hair was matted together in stiff clumps around the slit. My beautiful son's body had been violated and treated like a slab of meat on a butcher's block, even though in life he had violated his own body with drugs. He suddenly seemed like an empty shell, unlike the first time I had seen him immediately after his death when air was still escaping from his body and he looked as though he was sleeping.

The first thing that Lauren said was, "Why is Kristian asleep in a big box?" Such innocence. She peered curiously into the coffin, oblivious to my internal torture and then began wandering around, searching for something interesting to occupy her inquisitive and agile little mind.

Over the following two days, a flow of bereaved friends and family visited Kristian to pay their last respects and lay tokens of affection beside him. Unwrapped Christmas presents, family photos, letters, poems, jewellery and soft toys surrounded him.

As every available gap around Kristian became filled with gifts, we shared a brief, lighthearted moment when we joked that on the day of his funeral, it would be impossible to close the lid of the coffin.

The rain lashing viciously against our bedroom window heralded the beginning of the cold, wet and emotionally crushing day on which we buried my son. I wasn't ready to say goodbye to him. I had already kissed him for the last time the day before, held his hand and tidied his hair, not realising that had I wanted, I could have visited him once more before the lid was finally placed on his coffin. This would possibly be the worst day of my life; the day that I would watch my beautiful son lowered into a hole in the ground and the moment that I would have to let go of him forever, along with the hopes, dreams and opportunities of creating future memories with him and the future life that he should have had. When the funeral was over, I thought that my life would finally cease.

Many people told me that the worst time is the time leading up to the funeral and that once the funeral is over I could seek closure. How could I ever seek closure when my son had chosen to end his life? I was not in a hurry for the funeral to take place. I wanted to keep Kristian's body with me for as long as possible. Although spiritually he was not in his physical body and physically his body was at the chapel of rest, I still felt that whilst he was above ground, I didn't have to let go. I could still see him, touch him, kiss him and talk to him "in person". I could still give him gifts and place other tokens of affection in his coffin. Until the funeral, he was safe and cared for and uppermost in the minds of those who loved him.

Parents of children who have killed themselves can never obtain closure on their deaths, because they will never really know for sure what their children were thinking in the moment when they decided to inject themselves, or swallow a bottle of tablets, or put a gun to their head, or leap in front of a train, or drive into a brick wall, or jump from a chair with a noose around their neck.

When a child takes his or her own life, not only do the survivors have to cope with the loss, but the trauma of organising a funeral raises a range of uncomfortable, painful and sometimes ethical questions. How much do you reveal about the circumstances of your child's death to the Funeral Director and the Vicar, Priest or Minister conducting the service? The sense of shame may cause some suicide grievers to conceal the details surrounding the death, particularly to casual friends, colleagues and acquaintances and may affect your decision about who to invite to the funeral, lest the truth be exposed.

Although the major recognised world religions treat death in different ways, they all view the funeral as an important part of the grieving process and a way to acknowledge the life of the person who has died, irrespective of the various rituals and traditions associated with each religion.

Although I decided upon a burial because I needed a real focus for my grief and could not bear the thought of his body being incinerated, I still found it unbearably painful to think of my son being shut in a box and buried in the cold, damp ground. It felt as though he was being discarded, pushed out of sight, because he no longer served any purpose and was symbolically forgotten. Nevertheless, I could not even entertain the thought of having him cremated. I have, and always have had, an extreme fear of fire. The thought of its ability to quickly and irreversibly change something from its recognised form into a pile of ash is, in my mind, horrific.

Since that time, however, I have realised that my son does still have a purpose and that he has achieved more in death than he did in his earth life. Were it not for his suicide, I would never have established the child suicide website, I would not have written this book, I would not have campaigned for suicide awareness and I would not be helping the people whom I attempt to help, whether they are other bereaved parents, or depressed youngsters. Ultimately, I believe that Kristian has helped to save the lives of others.

At 7am, my dad, stepmum and I were already in the kitchen preparing food for the wake in an emotionally detached way that allowed us to do everything that needed doing. My stepmum created a beautiful flower arrangement for my dad to drop off at the funeral parlour before 11am and I cleaned and tidied the house in preparation for the throng of visitors who would come and go before and after the funeral.

I had cried so much over the previous three weeks that I didn't believe I had anything left inside of me. I felt a sense of detachment as I had on the day of Kristian's death and performed necessary functions in a ritualistic fashion, not daring to ponder, even for a second, on the ceremony ahead. Again, I was propelled to the position of a bystander, remotely viewing this intimate scene of a grieving family preparing to say goodbye to a loved one. It wasn't real, it wasn't happening to me; I didn't want it to be happening to me. It was just a ghastly dream from which I would wake and breathe a huge sigh of relief, as I had done on so many occasions in the past when I had experienced a nightmare about losing one of my children.

In preparing for the funeral, my partner asked me whether he thought it was better for Kristian's coffin to be transported directly to the church from the funeral parlour on the day.

I found the personal detachment and insensitivity of such an arrangement to be unthinkable. I didn't wish to "meet" my son's coffin at the church. I wanted him to be able to come back home to his mum and family for the last time. I wanted his last journey to be from our house to his final resting place. I wanted him to return to the house where he had spent many years of his young life. I wanted him to know that he belonged here, that he was welcome here, despite everything that had happened in the time since he left home. Although my memory would enable me to hear his ghostly footsteps running around upstairs, or listen to echoes of his excited chatter from the past, for now I wanted the body that gave physical presence to his soul to be as close to home as possible, for the final time.

Family and close friends arrived at our house in a steady flow, each offering hugs and enquiries after each other's wellbeing and exchanging appropriate words of sympathy and understanding. Of all the platitudes offered, the one that they would never be able to use was, "Oh well, at least he had a good innings."

It felt as though our house had been cocooned in a black shroud, briefly uniting everyone in Kristian's life within a hub of shared grief. I remember laying out extra chairs around our living room to accommodate everyone, as though we were throwing a celebratory party. But that's exactly how it should have been; a celebration of Kristian's life, a celebration of the years of joy that we had with him and, now, a celebration of his release from pain and his journey to the other world.

I freely handed around cups of tea and coffee and glasses of wine, engaging in strained and forced conversation in an attempt to create a relaxing ambience prior to the heartbreaking event ahead. I took large gulps of red wine myself to try and steady my nerves and numb my pain as I compulsively watched the clock tick by, awaiting my son's final homecoming.

As I stood in the kitchen pouring a glass of white wine to serve to Millie's uncle who had just arrived, the black and imposing hearse invaded my peripheral vision. It crawled silently to a halt outside our house, followed by the limousine containing Millie and her dad.

I recall my partner swiftly removing the glass of red wine from my hand as panic overwhelmed me and I felt my knees begin to buckle beneath me. I don't remember moving from the kitchen, or how I got upstairs, but I do remember being in our bedroom and walking around in circles crying, "I can't do this, I can't do this," whilst my partner attempted to pacify me.

"You can do it," he said, "You have to."

The last time I saw my son alive, I watched him scuttle quickly down the road pushing his baby daughter in her pushchair. Today, he returned slowly in a white coffin.

When I opened the front door to the funeral director, he said, "Are you alright?"

"Not really," I wept.

I climbed into the limousine next to Millie, who was already sobbing. Others followed in their respective vehicles on the short, but slow journey up to the small church within the grounds of a beautiful country park, about 10 minutes' walk from our home. One of Kristian's favourite places to pass time was in a hidden dip within one of the wooded areas of this extensive park, a secluded area that he and his mates called their "den". Although not visible from any of the nearby paths, you could clearly hear disembodied voices and laughter emanating from the "den" if you happened to be walking by. I couldn't have wished for his funeral to take place in a better location. I could think of many beautiful places in the world, but this was a place that had been special to Kristian.

Rivers of friends from different directions pooled into the area surrounding the church gates, people I didn't recognise; sad, nameless young faces forming a sea of respect, sorrow and disbelief. My partner and I huddled tightly together beneath a large, black umbrella to shield ourselves from the relentless vertical rain that fell like a waterfall of tears on this tragic farewell scene. My partner's arms gripped me like a vice, as though to prevent me from feeling any physical or emotional pain. I watched the sodden autumn leaves fall silently from the myriad of surrounding trees that gave them life. I equated the falling leaves to my son's final breaths, symbolic of a life ebbing away and the trunks as the trees' souls, continuing to live on.

    I watched the funeral staff solemnly slide my son's coffin from the back of the hearse onto a trolley, so that it could be wheeled up the path into the small church. Again, I idly wondered whether they were able to completely detach themselves from the emotion of such proceedings; whether it was just a job to them, or whether they felt for each family at every funeral they attended. Did they go home at night and carry on as normal without a thought about their working day, or did they – as I would do – dwell on what had occurred, think about the families concerned and feel emotionally drained?

    Millie and I walked directly behind Kristian's coffin into the church, Millie with her hand on the head of the coffin repeatedly crying, "I'm sorry Kristian, I'm so sorry." I kept telling her that it wasn't her fault. We all felt guilty and we could all blame ourselves for what happened, but the reality was that no one person could be responsible for the tragic choice that Kristian made.

When we entered the church, I was surprised to see that some of my friends had already arrived in advance of the funeral cortège. Everyone stood as we entered the church and proceeded down the aisle to the front pews, accompanied to one of Kristian's favourite songs, "Angel" by Shaggy. I remember thanking people for coming as we walked past and felt so grateful for the loyalty and compassion of those who had made the effort to attend and pay their respects to such a beautiful young man.

Carsten, Anneliese, my partner, Millie, Millie's cousin Amanda and I sat in the front right-hand side pew as you faced the altar. The rest of the family sat in the pews behind. The vicar stood immediately in front of us, but I don't recall her words or the order of service. I remember glancing around the church and wondering whether Kristian was sat there with us watching his own funeral. I remember talking to him in my mind and asking him to comfort everyone. At that moment, I felt the lightest brush against my cheek, as though a hair was tickling my face and wondered whether his spirit energy had touched me, or whether the angels were comforting me.

After the service had commenced, we heard the church door open and the sound of several pairs of high heeled shoes tapping rhythmically across the stone floor and echoing from the church walls. Amanda looked over her shoulder and said that it was a group of girls. Millie didn't recognise them. There were so many girls in the church that day. I was amazed at Kristian's popularity with the opposite sex, but also felt a pang of sorrow for Millie. Not only had she lost her boyfriend and the father of her daughter, but for the first time she had some insight into the life that he led when he was not with her; his other friends and, more painfully, the other girls.

Part of the service that I do recall with clarity is the eloquence and feeling with which my friend Lorraine read out the poem that I had written for Kristian on the day that he passed over. It was maybe not the most academically outstanding piece of poetry, but was written directly from the heart at a time of immeasurable grief.

At the end of the service, when we were following Kristian's coffin out of the church, Westlife's version of "I Have a Dream" by ABBA was played. Kristian loved that song and the line, "I believe in angels" seemed so apt.

The one face I remember clearly and which broke my heart even more was that of a lad about Kristian's age. As we walked down the aisle towards the church entrance, I briefly glanced up and saw this lad sobbing loudly. I later learned that this was one of Kristian's best friends, who very tragically died in the same way two months later. His face will always haunt me and I weep every time I think of him.

As we climbed into the car to follow the hearse up to the cemetery, I looked around at the dispersing group of young people with tear-tracked faces comforting each other, people whose lives and hearts had been touched and broken by my special little boy.

The burial ceremony took place at the only cemetery in town that still had space for burials, which was about five miles from the church.

I visualised my son's final journey as a heartbreaking scene from a movie and in my head could hear the appropriate melancholy music being overplayed as the hearse crept slowly through the pouring rain towards the resting place of so many who had gone before Kristian and of those who would follow after him.

After we had arrived and were waiting to walk behind the pall bearers to my son's burial spot, other friends and family members who I had not seen at the church appeared around me.

Maybe I had been too distracted and distressed to even know exactly who was in the church. Most of the time my eyes had been transfixed upon my son's coffin. I had desperately wanted to go over and remove the lid so that I could gaze one last time at his beautiful face before it disappeared forever in the flesh.

It's amazing how one can find humour in the most dire and heartbreaking of situations. One of the pall bearers was an elderly gentleman with a stoop who was supporting Kristian's coffin at the rear left-hand side. Since the bearer to his right was also taller than he was, the coffin tilted to one side and I could not take my eyes off of it, or the rather unsteady gentleman, concerned that the imbalance would cause it to tumble to the ground. I could hear my son chuckling and imagined him and the angels offering their spiritual support. Later on, a couple of other people also commented about how they were terrified that the coffin was going to topple off the elderly gentleman's shoulder.

At the graveside, as Kristian's coffin was lowered into the sodden ground and the vicar recited the standard burial verse, I felt the urge to rip the lid off the casket and hug my son one last time. Instead, I stood there in numbness and disbelief as dead leaves were carried by the stream of dirty water that flowed across the waterlogged earth and cascaded into my son's grave. I remember worrying about his clothes and skin getting wet. I tried in vain to convince myself that it didn't matter because he couldn't feel any physical discomfort, but then thought how awful it was to stop treating a person's body with care, love and respect just because it was lifeless. To me it was no different to abusing a child's cherished teddy bear just because it was a piece of material, an inanimate object with no feeling. The fact was that anything that had endless amounts of love invested into it deserved to be preserved forever.

I recall my partner ushering me quickly away from the grave the moment the vicar had finished her recital. At that point, I felt too emotionally weak to object, even though by choice I would have remained with my son until everyone had left and the graveyard workers had finally hidden him from view, removed him from the life that carried on regardless, even though the world within me stood still. As mentioned previously in Chapter Three, he said afterwards that he thought I would be distressed by the sight of the water pouring into the grave and wanted to take me away as quickly as possible.

For the first time, I saw my best friend from school standing there with her husband. Again, I felt touched that they had travelled so far to be with us. It meant a lot to me. I walked amongst the crowd of friends, family and strangers and again thanked everyone for coming. Many people smiled, others hugged me and said nothing, some offered words of condolence and others wept. All the time, my partner was by my side with a steadying hand on my back, gradually steering me away from the grave in the direction of the waiting car.

Had my partner not been there, I would never have left. Not having the emotional, mental or physical energy to protest, I submissively allowed him to lead me back to the car. I did feel cheated of time with my son; time that I would never be able to get back and time that I would not be able to spend with him in the future. Yes, I could stand by his grave as many times as I wanted to in the gruelling days ahead, but this was the closest that I would ever get to his physical body again as it was in life, before it was earthed over.

As the car pulled slowly away, I turned my head around to have one last glance at my son's resting place and noticed a solitary figure gazing down into the grave. Kristian's biological father was looking down at his first born and his only son.

In an instant, I felt what he was feeling; remorse, pain, failure and, above all, tremendous guilt and sadness. My heart bled for him, even though some would say that I should not feel sorry for someone who had turned his back on his son for so many years. However, I did feel sorry for him, because I could feel his pain and, despite everything, I knew that he had a good heart. It was also because of him that I was blessed with having a beautiful young man in my life for twenty years.

In those very early days, I felt as though I was grieving more for other people's loss than for my own. Maybe it's because I had always been sensitive and could easily pick up on others' thoughts and feelings. It was the reason why, I believe, I would often feel depressed whenever I had returned from a trip to town. I felt like a magnet to negative energies and other people's sadness. In order to feel better, I had to psychically "unhook" from all those souls who had latched onto me.

Back at the house, people politely ate, drank and chatted sympathetically to me. Everything was still such a blur; just a nightmare created by my subconscious. I responded in a composed fashion, my mouth and brain disconnected from my emotions. I was afraid of feeling too deeply, of wondering how I would cope after the visitors had stopped calling. Would they assume that the funeral equated to that clichéd term of "closure" and that I could now move on with my life? If only they knew! I was terrified of being alone, of people not coming to see me, of being allowed to think too deeply and of becoming so overwhelmed by my grief that I would not be able to carry on. I was afraid of my own mind and memories, afraid of the immense power of thought.

What does the word "closure" mean anyway? Does it mean acceptance of what happened, the ending of a chapter in life, or finality for everyone else so that they can get on with their lives without feeling any further need to offer their condolences or support? To me, it's a grief "buzz word" that people use without really knowing what they mean by it.

Maybe everyone was all secretly relieved that my son was now buried, because it would finally release them from the burden of having to listen to me talk about topics that made them distinctly uncomfortable; Kristian, death and suicide.

The problem is, of course, that until someone has experienced a situation themselves, they don't really know how to react or what to say. Why would people know what to say in advance? After all, it's not something that you learn in school; "How to react when someone you know is bereaved by suicide." If it's not something that you think will affect you on a regular basis, you take little interest in it. Why waste your energy learning about something that you hope will never affect you?

I would never blame people for thinking and feeling the way they do, but I do feel a need to help people understand. I vowed on that day never to stop talking about my son and the issue of suicide, but to try to do so in a way that would not make other people feel uncomfortable.

After the last guest had left, I wandered aimlessly around the house thinking, "Now what?" Everything outside seemed cold, grey and depressing. My heart ached so intensely that in that moment I fully understood the expression "Dying of a broken heart." It seemed like a distinct possibility.

I wondered whether Kristian's grave had already been filled in. Did the cemetery staff wait until they were certain that there would be no late visitors to the graveside, or did they mercilessly move in with their shovels the moment the funeral cortège left the grounds? Did they view it as they would when digging out, or filling in, any other hole in the ground?

In the days that followed Kristian's funeral, I visited the cemetery every day and gazed at the pile of earth on top of his grave, not really believing (or wanting to believe) that my son was buried there. I placed candles, flowers, cards, toy cars and cuddly toys on the sodden earth and wept. The ball of pain that encompassed indescribable grief, guilt, self-blame and sadness was lodged firmly in my chest. It was not just an emotional, but a physical pain that I felt was spreading like a malignant growth, with no relief and no cure.

I felt guilty the first time that I was unable to get to the cemetery. I felt as though I was neglecting Kristian, even though I knew that he would understand my reasons for not going.

Henrietta's brother Graeme ended his life in September 2003, a year after the break-up of his marriage. His ex-wife moved 200 miles away with their two daughters, then aged 7 and 4, which made it very difficult for Graeme to have access. Henrietta said that it was Graeme's lack of contact with his children that she believes contributed to his depression. He told her that without his kids, he didn't feel that life was worth living. Although he wrote letters to them on a regular basis, they were always returned to him unopened. He believed that this was through his ex-wife's intervention and also believed that his children had no knowledge of the letters.

Henrietta said that Graeme was very popular, but rather than being comforted by the fact that the church was packed with people at his memorial service, she felt devastated that despite her brother being loved by so many, no one could help him. His life was ruled by someone who didn't care about him.

"Although it was moving to my parents that so many friends and colleagues came to support us and show their respect, it made me so terribly sad that there were so many people who cared about Graeme. If only he could have focused on all the good people in his life rather than his bitter ex-wife who didn't really care whether he lived or died.

"Despite all the guests at his service, the absence of his two daughters made it seem as though that part of his life had never existed and yet it was ultimately that part of his life that was the reason for his untimely death.

"I don't believe that his ex-wife would have put in an appearance even if she'd wanted to, because she knows that she would not have been welcome there. In fact, when my mother broke the news to her, she seemed more concerned about whether she would receive anything in the monetary sense. Thankfully, she was not entitled to anything, but there was some money that has been put into a trust for his daughters when they are older. My parents have control of that.

"There were many tributes read out by friends, family and colleagues during the service. The most heartrending of all was a piece written by his best friend, Colin. Colin made reference to Graeme's daughters and how he always spoke with such pride about them. Colin said that Graeme felt that they were his motivation for living and working hard. He mentioned how distraught Graeme was after his wife took his lifeline away from him. By this point, I think the entire congregation was in tears. At the same time, I felt this intense anger well up inside of me.

"I wanted to run out of the church and get straight on the phone to his ex and call her a murderer. I found it very difficult to focus on anything else for the rest of the day. I cannot even begin to describe the anger that I felt and, in that moment, I could understand how someone could kill. Is that what they call a crime of passion? My feelings scared me, so much so that I wondered how I would react if I were ever to see Graeme's ex-wife again. I can't even refer to her by name, such is my detestation.

"Until the day of the funeral, I was in that state of shock and disbelief, as I am certain most suicide survivors are. It was only during the service that the ghastly truth hit me and that's when the rage began to surge up inside. The difficult part was keeping my feelings to myself, because I did not wish to place any additional stress on my parents and I also knew that it was not an appropriate time to start venting my anger.

"In the days that followed Graeme's funeral, I felt dreadful. Friends stopped calling and carried on with their lives and yet I felt that I was in a time warp. I was so wrapped up in my grief and anger that I could not concentrate on anything else. I had compassionate leave from work, but at some point I would have to return. I felt that before I returned, I had some unfinished business to complete – and that was telling Graeme's ex-wife exactly how I felt.

"Three days after the funeral, I began composing a letter to his ex. In the first draft I wrote from the heart, making accusations and condemning her for her actions. I then wrote and rewrote, each time trying to remove as much of the anger and raw emotion as possible, but still in such a way that I hoped would penetrate her social conscience, if she had one. I also had to protect myself from any possible legal repercussions, knowing how vindictive she was.

"I kept the letter for three weeks before sending it, during which time I made many amendments. I told her that I did not expect, or want, a reply.

"I would not necessarily recommend this course of action to anyone else in a similar situation, but it did make me feel better. What I would recommend is writing your feelings down and then perhaps burning what you have written.

"I'd like to say that things get better after the funeral, but in some ways the days and weeks following the service are the most harrowing. In the beginning, you are in such a state of shock and are involved in all the arrangements that follow any death. You have people rallying around helping and comforting you and you do not have as much time to sit and think. Following the funeral, everything stops; your mind is no longer as occupied and as soon as you sit still, the grief closes in on you. There is no one there to hug you in the way that they did immediately after the tragedy and at times you feel so dreadfully alone.

"My advice to anyone going through the same trauma is to try and remain occupied, which of course is easier said than done. Although it is not healthy to block out your grief completely, it is equally unhealthy to allow your grief to consume you and control every minute of your waking day."

Elsa's son Cary was 19 when he hung himself in his bedroom in August 2003 following a short period of depression. Elsa says that Cary's funeral was the worst day of her life.

"I am certain that many people have said the same thing, but until Cary's funeral I suppose I had convinced myself that it hadn't really happened. I thought I would wake up at any moment and breathe an enormous sigh of relief.

"I wanted my son to have the best send off possible, so in spite of my distress, I ensured that I was involved in every aspect of his funeral arrangements. My husband, Cary's stepdad, was marvellous; he was my strength. Cary's biological father had died several years previously and I was strangely grateful that he never lived to endure the loss of his son.

"My friend wrote a poem for Cary, which I was adamant I wanted to read out, even though my husband and friend had offered to do it for me. It was the least I could do for my son. I managed to maintain my decorum throughout and did not break down, because I truly believe that Cary was there helping me. During the rest of the service, I sobbed.

"I suppose that reading the poem, which referred to Cary in the past tense, made me realise that he was gone. This was further backed up by the minister's speech, especially when he said that Cary was in a better place. I have to admit that that is an expression that irritates me. I know what is meant by it and I know that my son is no longer suffering, but to me there was no better place for him than at home with us. Using that expression felt like an insult to our parenting capabilities, as though the minister were pointing the finger and saying, "Cary's far better off on the other side than he was with you."

"After the service, we went out for a meal rather than having the standard wake with people hovering around feeling uncomfortable and not knowing how to react to you. The fact that we were all seated around a large table meant that people could chat to those sat next to them and not feel obliged to try and engage in awkward conversation with me.

"I have to admit that I am not fond of large gatherings, but this was a chance to toast Cary's life and to bring some enjoyment to an otherwise thoroughly miserable day. I can honestly say though, that it was the worst day of my life, very closely followed by all the days that followed.

"The following day, there was an eerie silence in the house. I felt abandoned. No one called to ask how we were and there was nothing left to do. In fairness to everyone, I suppose they thought they were being kind in leaving us alone to grieve in peace. Although I did not like being surrounded by crowds of people, I was equally afraid of being alone.

"I think I spent most of the day in Cary's bedroom; a room that held so many memories, including the horrific one of his suicide. I tried to focus on the good memories and to erase the image of him dead. I did not want to move anything in his room. I wanted it to remain as it had when he was last there, with all his possessions still containing his energies. I was afraid to throw anything away because that would be like discarding him and also removing anything physical that proved that he had existed. I lay on his bed and hugged one of his jumpers, not wanting to move from there – ever.

"It was only a few months ago that I finally mustered up the courage to make some small changes in Cary's room. I still dust it and clean it as though he were still with us. My husband feels that we have to move on and keeps trying to persuade me to clear out his room completely, but I'm just not ready. Maybe one day I will have the strength to do it, but right now I cannot possibly see a time when I will feel differently."

At the cemetery where Kristian was buried, we were advised to leave the ground to settle for at least six months before erecting a headstone. Although not wishing him to have a "nameless" grave, this time delay was a small relief, because it meant that we had time to secure more funds for a decent headstone. The truth is that money was no object in such circumstances and had it been possible to erect a headstone immediately, we would have done so, irrespective of cost. It did, however, mean that I had more time to choose exactly the right words for his epitaph, words that would sum up the person that he was as succinctly as possible.

Each day that I visited the cemetery, I noticed other recently bereaved families who had disregarded the six-month advisory warning and still erected headstones for their loved ones almost immediately following the burial. However, some years later, these prematurely erected headstones were amongst those that were being propped up with iron support bars where the ground had subsided.

It was actually one year and one month before Kristian's headstone was in place; a beautiful black granite stone with a hole cut out in the shape of a heart near the top of the stone in which stood a white dove. The inscription read:

Treasured memories of Kristian Mikhail Andersen
Fell asleep
1 November 2002
Loving Son, Grandson, Brother and Daddy
He had a Heart of Gold
xx

When I viewed the headstone in place for the first time, it was as though my son's life and everything that he was and stood for was condensed into his seven words of his epitaph, "He had a heart of Gold". And he did. Kristian was loved by so many, except himself. "I hate myself and my life" constantly echoes in my head. He won the hearts of so many and yet the love that was most important and the only love that could have kept him alive was his own self-love.

Kristian

It seems like only yesterday
I rocked you on my knee,
With dreams about the future and
What you were going to be.

You were so bright and happy
Such a precious little boy,
You gave your love to everyone
And filled our hearts with joy.

Strangers would admire you
And stop to say "Hello";
"He'll break a lot of hearts", they said,
"In twenty years or so".

But less than twenty years from then,
What they said came true,
As we were forced against our will
To say goodbye to you.

A life so short and unfulfilled,
With so much left to go;
"Why, oh why?" we ask ourselves,
When we all loved you so.

Life shows us many options,
But whichever path we take,
The destination's still the same,
Whatever choice we make.

So many questions flood our minds,
"What if, and Why and How?"
If we had done things differently,
Would you still be with us now?

I don't know what the lesson was
That you were sent here to learn,
But now your purpose is fulfilled
It's time for you to return.

When I hear the phone ring,
I expect to hear you say,
"Alright Mum? What're you doing?
Can I come 'round today?"

But you don't need to ask now,
You're with us every day;
Within our hearts, our minds, our souls,
Your memory will stay.

No fear, no pain or sorrow
Can touch you anymore,
But the love you've left behind
Will live with us forever more.

©Jan Andersen, 1 November 2002

Read out at Kristian's funeral on 22 November 2002 by
Lorraine Rodgers

Kristian, Anneliese and Carsten, 1990

Chapter Ten

The Family's Grief

Sorrow makes us all children again - destroys all differences of intellect. The wisest know nothing.

Ralph Waldo Emerson

When a child dies, everyone's attention and sympathy seems to be focused on the grieving parents and in particular the mother, but what about the forgotten grievers; the brothers, sisters, grandparents, aunts, uncles, cousins, nieces and nephews? Grandparents have the double burden of grieving for their grandchild and seeing their son or daughter suffer pain. Likewise, siblings may mask their own grief in order to protect their parents from further worry and suffering. In today's complicated family situations created by divorce and remarriage, there are often many more people involved, such as stepparents and stepchildren, all of whom may have had their own special relationship with the lost child.

When a parent loses one child, they may question their ability to nurture any other children they may have. Their shock and grief for their lost child may make them act in ways that they later regret, such as not including children in the processes and events following the death of a child. They may feel that their decisions are based upon their desire to protect their children from further distress, but then later realise that in doing so, they caused more sadness. They may isolate themselves from their surviving children, or else cling to them to the point of suffocation.

The life plan of most families does not include a course of action following the death of a child, because most of us never expect to face such situation. It's not something that a parent even wishes to consider. Losing a child maybe one of our greatest fears and yet many of us still somehow believe that it will not happen to us. Some parents may believe that in planning what they would do should such a tragedy occur might be tempting fate.

Surviving children have other struggles that can complicate their grief. The birth order changes in an instant. If the child who died was the eldest child, then the next child will suddenly become the eldest sibling and likewise with a middle or youngest child. What is most frightening is when a surviving child in becomes an only child as a result of their sibling's death. Whatever the situation, the dynamics of family life change forever.

If the child who died was the eldest, the younger siblings will have memories of that brother or sister always being in their lives. It may be impossible to contemplate the notion of that sibling never being around again. If the child who died was not the eldest, the older siblings may feel that they should have protected their brother or sister and that they could have done something to save them. Again, we return to those overpowering feelings of guilt, failure and blame, which although not healthy or productive, are entirely normal.

When parents lose their only child, they may regret their decision not to have any more children. Maybe it wasn't a conscious choice, but irrespective of the circumstances, the loss of an only child is a trauma that can only ever be understood by those who have experienced such a devastating loss.

When a sibling becomes an only child after the suicide of a brother or sister, this can put enormous pressure on the surviving child. The amount of pressure may depend on the relationship this child has with his or her parents and also the relationship that the deceased sibling had with the parents.

Naturally, the relationship that brothers or sisters had with their deceased sibling may have a significant impact on how they handle their grief. If, for example, they had had an argument prior to their sibling's suicide, they may endure excruciating guilt, believing that they were in some way responsible for what happened. If a parent senses that a surviving sibling may be shouldering the blame, it is important to reassure them by reminding them that everyone argues with those they love, but that we don't all go and end our lives because of one disagreement.

It is always difficult attempting to convince someone that they were not to blame, because of course one of the greatest legacies of suicide is tremendous guilt. However, by sharing your feelings with your other children and letting them know that everyone feels guilty, it may help to ease at least some of the burden from their shoulders.

In addition to their own personal grief, any surviving siblings will still be moving through their individual developmental stages, some more challenging than others. Sometimes it may be difficult to determine the difference between symptoms of grief and normal mental and psychological 'growing pains'.

My daughter Anneliese expressed the following thoughts about the loss of her brother.

"Although, my mum and grandparents grieve his loss, it is different to my grief. They have the childhood memories of Kristian. I have more recent memories of my brother as a best friend and confidante almost constantly over the final two years of his life.

"I did not always agree with some of the things that he did and the way that he lived his life at times and we occasionally had some terrible arguments, but I loved him. After all, how many brothers and sisters are there who don't fight at some time? If I hadn't have cared about him so much, then I wouldn't have bothered arguing with him and would have just let him get on with his life in his own way. I miss him terribly, but I also still feel angry with him for what he did."

Five months after Kristian died, my youngest son Carsten said to me, "Since Kristian died, I can only think of all the good times we had. I can't believe we had so much fun – all the videos we used to watch together and the things we used to laugh at, yet when he was alive I could only remember the fights and arguments."

I said to Carsten, "That's good that you can think about the nice memories. So what does that teach you?" He replied, "To appreciate people whilst they're alive."

I always worried that Anneliese may press the self-destruct button, as she always had in the past whenever she encountered any crisis in her life, however trivial. When she was 13, she had suffered from Anorexia after being bullied by a girl at school and then would self-harm by cutting her arms, albeit superficially. I worried constantly that I may lose her in the same way and, in November 2007, I lived with the real fear that I might end up burying another child. That situation has, thankfully, been resolved through my daughter's strength and determination against all odds.

Many people regard their home and family life as their haven of safety, security and comfort. When someone within that unit takes their own life, the foundations of that sanctuary no longer seem so secure. Part of it has been torn away, leaving the remaining part less stable for a while.

The tragedy can cause the part that remains to crumble, or it can cause the surviving family members to build stronger foundations to nurture and support those who continue to live.

Parental favouritism is an ugly topic and yet sadly it occurs. This places enormous stress on siblings in life and becomes even more of a burden when one child dies.

Imogen and Felicity were fraternal twins. Felicity always felt that her sister was the favoured twin, so when Imogen took her own life in August 2005 at the age of 17, Felicity felt that one of two things would happen; either her parents would despise her, or they would become more protective.

"Imogen was always a follower, rather than a leader. If my parents told her to jump, she would, just to please them. I was always more independent and argumentative. I would always challenge their decisions if I felt they were unreasonable, whereas Imogen would do as she was told even if she didn't agree with them. She would voice her true feelings to me, but would never dare question our parents' judgement. As a result, I can see why it would be easier to like Imogen.

"Imogen always placed enormous pressure on herself by trying to please everyone all the time. If she ever thought she had upset someone, she would worry endlessly about it. I was a lot tougher. I told her that some people were just paranoid and would always misinterpret what others said, even when no offence had been intended. Imogen could not be so objective though and I think she bore other people's pain.

"Despite her sensitivity, I never for one moment thought that she was depressed or suicidal, particularly since I believed that she told me everything that was going through her mind.

"Although we had completely different personalities, we were still extremely close. After all, twins usually are aren't they?

"I don't know whether there was any particular incident that made Imogen feel that life was no longer bearable, because all that she said in her suicide note was that she loved us all very much and that she was sorry.

"She took a bizarre concoction of pills that she must have found in our medicine cabinet. Imogen was always an early riser, so when she hadn't got up by 11am on the dreadful day that it happened, my mother went into her room to check that she was ok. My mother's hysterical scream will haunt me for the rest of my life. What happened after that is something that I cannot bear to describe. It was so horrific that I want to block out that moment of my life completely.

"Imogen didn't officially die until four hours after my mother discovered her. We all clung onto the tiniest glimmer of hope that she would survive, despite the hospital staff telling us that it was almost certainly too late.

"I don't know how my parents felt about me in those early days because of course they were trapped in their own pool of grief, unable to function properly or talk to anyone about what had happened. I felt as though I needed to be there to support them and yet I felt useless. Did they want me there? Did they realise that I had lost not only a sister, but a best friend? Did they care? Would they have preferred it if I had died rather than Imogen?

"I also had to deal with other friends and relatives and the way in which they responded. Their sympathy seemed to be directed solely at my parents. I remember some of them saying to me, 'Now you make sure you take good care of your parents' and 'How awful it must be to lose a child', without even acknowledging my grief, or contemplating how awful it must be to lose a sibling.

"In hindsight, I realise that I was probably quite close to a nervous breakdown. I didn't feel able to tell anyone about my feelings because everyone was viewing me as the one taking care of everyone else and I suppose I internalised my grief.

"After a few weeks had passed, my parents began to talk to me about Imogen. In fact, we began talking in a way that we had never spoken before. I had never really opened up to my parents emotionally, but I suppose that is because I felt that we were so different and I never really thought that they would understand my problems and concerns. However, I now realise that I never gave them a chance.

"If anything positive has occurred as a result of Imogen's suicide, it is that I feel much closer to my parents. This has been an enormous surprise to me. I truly believed that losing Imogen would drive a huge wedge between us, but it hasn't. I don't know whether they feel any guilt about favouring Imogen. Having said that, maybe I was imagining that they preferred her because to me she appeared to be the perfect daughter. I guess that they loved us to the same degree, but in different ways. We all have good and bad qualities. Imogen was certainly the perfect sister. The pain of losing her is unbearable. A part of me will always be missing."

When Brett's older brother Julian, 25, hung himself in March 2001, Brett became stifled by his parents' reluctance to allow him lead a normal life. They would no longer allow him out of their sight, fuelled by a fear that they would also lose their only surviving child. As the youngest child, Brett felt that his parents had always been more protective of him than of Julian.

"Julian was ten years older than I was, so I don't have memories of how he was treated when he was a young child. However, Julian used to tell me that he had far more freedom when he was my age than I have ever had. I don't know why this should be, although Julian always believed that my parents favoured me over him. He always thought that they worried more about something happening to me, so consequently didn't give me the same licence to do as I pleased.

"Julian lived life to the full and had the freedom to do so, whereas I had always felt as though I was at the end of a leash that my parents were controlling.

"Julian was very much into high-risk activities such as rock climbing, scuba diving and bungee jumping, so although I am sure that my parents worried about him having a fatal accident, I am certain that they never considered suicide as a risk factor. Julian was very volatile, but to our knowledge had never suffered from depression. Maybe he did, but hid it well. It goes without saying that he must have been terribly depressed to have killed himself. To this day, the reason for his suicide is a complete mystery. There was no note and no other evidence from those who were with him around the time it happened. He hung himself in the room of the lodge where he was staying whilst on a team-building exercise with some work colleagues. They were equally as shocked and said that there had been nothing strange or uncharacteristic about his behaviour.

"Understandably, my parents became paranoid about losing me, but their over protectiveness was suffocating. I was no longer allowed to go out with my mates and my mother would insist on driving me to and from school. It was terribly frustrating, but since we were all in the depths of grief, I did not feel in a position to say anything. I did not want to upset my parents further. They were not coping well with the tragedy, which is to be expected.

"I lost a brother, which was hard enough, but my parents had lost a son and had had ten more years of loving him than I did. Although I wanted my freedom, I also felt that I needed to be close to my parents to support them.

"I assumed that the situation would change when everyone was a little further down the grieving road, but I was wrong. My parents had become so used to me being around all the time that it was even more difficult for them to let me go.

"When I was 18, I achieved a place at university, which meant that I would have to move away. They were devastated and even talked about moving house to be closer to the university, so that I could still live at home.

"Eventually, I sat down with my parents and told them how I was feeling and how much the university place meant to me. I threw statistics at them and said that I was more likely to be killed or injured in the home than anywhere else. I tried to put everything into perspective, whilst letting them know that I did fully understand their fears. I asked them whether they would really want me to live with them for the rest of their lives and that if I needed to move out at some point, then I would need to be able to afford to do so. By going to university, I told them that I would be in a better position to attain a good job and live independently. I tried to avoid saying anything about feeling resentful in the future if I were denied the opportunity to further my education, because I knew how easily upset my parents became.

"The good news is that I did go to university and subsequently enrolled on a postgraduate degree course. My parents still live in the same town and I visit them as often as I can. Naturally, they still worry about me and my mother rings me at least three times a week. It is comforting to know that they care, but I don't think that I would have the freedom I have now if I had remained living close to them.

"I think they have just reached a state of acceptance, but I am sure that if I were to move back, I would feel the shackles tighten once more."

Mandy lost her younger sister Laura, 16, to suicide in March 2004. Although devastated by Laura's suicide, Mandy feels angry with her for placing the "only surviving child" burden upon her.

"Laura was bipolar, but I never really believed that she would take her own life. Although there was seven years' age difference between us, we were very close. Whenever Laura was going through an intensely low period, she would always talk to me. I did bring up the topic of suicide once, but she laughed and said that she would never consider doing that. I feel betrayed that she went ahead and did it and inflicted so much pain upon us.

"Although it has been three years, there are still many days when I find it impossible to get on with life. I just sit and sob and then I become angry and start shouting at her photo.

"The burden of becoming an only child is overwhelming. I do feel extremely angry with Laura for putting me in this position, because I can see what it has done to my parents. They want to smother me constantly and although I had already left home when Laura died, it still feels as though I am a dependent child. My parents often call 'round unexpectedly and if I am not available on my mobile, they go into panic mode. I even had the police on my doorstep once! I feel as though I have to give them an agenda of my weekly movements.

"I don't blame them for feeling like this; after all, I'm all they have left, but I feel like a tagged criminal at the best of times. I live on my own at present, but am planning to move in with my boyfriend soon, so hopefully my parents will feel a little more at ease knowing that someone else is there to watch out for me.

"When my parents ask me whether they can come over, or whether I would like to go across for dinner, I don't feel as though I can say 'no'. I also never feel able to pour out my feelings to them. It breaks my heart to see them suffering and I don't want them to hurt more by allowing them to see how much pain I am in.

"When someone is feeling suicidal, I don't think they realise the true impact that their death will have on the rest of the family. Do they ever consider how the structure of family life will change? It's not just the grief that is hard to bear, but everything else that changes as a result. There have been days when I have questioned whether life is really worth living myself, but then I look at what suicide has done to our family and know that I could never do the same thing, however dire the situation became. Had we not lost Laura, then I would not be aware of all this, so I cannot criticise those who do feel that there is no other way to escape their pain."

Deanna's younger brother Bradley was only fifteen when he hung himself in the garden of their home in 1999. Although Deanna has now left home, she feels that whenever she speaks to her parents and other members of her family, she is unable to talk about her feelings and her intense grief for her brother.

"When Bradley ended his life, all the attention seemed to be on my parents. Whilst I appreciate that the worst loss in the world for any parent to suffer must be that of a child, nobody seemed to appreciate that I was suffering too. People offered the usual well-worn condolences, but then I was left alone to 'get on with it', whilst everyone fussed around my parents.

"I also felt that I had to mask my feelings for fear of upsetting my parents further, but the truth is that I wanted to cry with them; I wanted to sob on someone's shoulders and I wanted someone to acknowledge that Bradley had been a special part of my life too. As his older sister, I also felt that I had failed him and that I should have been there for him when he was obviously so miserable. At the time, I was studying and admit that I didn't have much time for anything or anyone else.

"At times I feel worthless. Does anyone notice or even care that I was deeply hurt, or that I'm still hurting now, so many years on? I don't feel that my family has given me permission to grieve. Sometimes I believe that they don't notice and that I am the forgotten griever. Maybe because I automatically took on the responsibility of being the strong, dependable one, my parents have never realised the enormous burden that I have carried around since the tragedy.

"I hope that by sharing my feelings in this book, it will help other grieving parents to think twice about the way they deal with their surviving children after such a tragic loss."

Brothers and sisters often share secrets and aspects of their lives that they feel unable to share with their parents, particularly if they are close in age. When a sibling dies, any surviving brothers or sisters may feel that they have also lost a close friend and confidante.

Maya's brother, Lewis, was only eighteen months her junior. At the age of 21, he gassed himself in his car following the breakup of his relationship with his girlfriend of four years.

"Although Lewis and I were close in age, I always regarded him as my baby brother. He was my only brother and sibling, so there was always some kind of rivalry brewing. Nevertheless, we could confidently share secrets and know that we would never betray each other. I would have died defending my brother and vice versa.

"We were poles apart personality wise and yet we had a fantastic relationship. The 'opposites attract' saying certainly applied in our case. Lewis was outgoing, athletic, socially popular and far better at practical than academic subjects. Lewis would describe me as a 'boffin', because I always had my head in a book and took my academic studies seriously. I suppose that in contrast to Lewis, I would be regarded as socially inept. Whereas Lewis liked to be the centre of attention, I far preferred to blend in with the crowd and would rather go unnoticed. Not surprisingly, therefore, I achieved top grades in all of my subjects, whereas Lewis only excelled on the school playing field, in art and, of course, socially.

"I guess that together we achieved the ideal balance. I was his calming influence, his reality check and he reminded me that life isn't all about work and that you have to take time out to play. Despite our differences, Lewis was always there when I needed him and I hope that I was always there for him. However, that bothers me, because of course I wasn't there for him when he really needed me. If I had have been, maybe he would still be here today. People say to me, 'You weren't to know Maya' and 'You shouldn't feel guilty' and so on, but I feel that I should have known and I do feel guilty.

"I left home when I was 19 and Lewis left when he was 18, but we still spoke regularly and met up whenever we had time. He phoned me eight days before he took his life, which is why I beat myself up now for not noticing the signs.

"He did talk about the split with his girlfriend, but he was very matter-of-fact about it and didn't come across as being particularly devastated. I realise now that he was probably dying inside, but maybe he just didn't want to burden me with his problems, because he knew that I'd recently been through a difficult time myself emotionally. The one thing that he did say as we concluded the conversation was, 'I love you Sis. Never forget that'. Although we had always openly expressed our affection for one another, he had never before said, 'Never forget that'. Looking back now, I believe that he had already made the decision to end his life.

"If only I had known what he was feeling and what he intended to do. If only I could turn back the clock. Maybe I would have asked different questions. Maybe I would have asked him why he said, 'Never forget that'. Things always become clearer after the event.

"I know that we can't live our lives on 'If onlys', but I will always believe that I could have talked Lewis out of it if only I'd known his intentions at the time."

When the child who died had younger brothers and sisters, parents may dread the time when they reach the age at which their sibling's life ended. My eldest daughter Anneliese was 16 when Kristian died. I remember the concern I felt in April 2006 when she turned 20. I wondered how she was feeling about being - and passing - the final age of her brother. That year she became my longest surviving child.

As September 2007 approached, when my son Carsten would also turn 20, I again wondered whether he would consciously think that he had reached the age at which his brother had taken his life. How would he cope with that realisation? Would he question his own mortality? I hoped that the thought wouldn't even cross his mind.

Carla's eldest sister Paula took an overdose of antidepressants in August 2002. She was 26. Carla's grief intensified when she celebrated her own 26th birthday in February 2006.

"I was dreading my 26th birthday. I felt guilty that I would soon have lived longer than Paula and wondered whether, in some strange way, my parents would feel resentful towards me, because although we were treated the same, she was their firstborn. Some people may think that I'm being ridiculous even contemplating such a notion, yet grief can have a strange effect upon the mind and reasoning.

"When my birthday arrived, I didn't feel much like celebrating. How could I celebrate reaching the age at which my sister's life had ended? Instead of going out, or having a party, I decided to do something for Paula. She had always been incredibly fond of animals and was always concerned about the effects that the environment had upon wildlife. I therefore decided to make a donation to the World Wildlife Fund in her memory. Although it was a bitterly cold day, I spent it tidying her grave and sitting 'talking' to her. As I did so, a butterfly came and landed on my hand. How often do you see a butterfly in this part of the world in February? A sign that she is still around maybe? Some might call it a coincidence, but I like to believe in a more spiritual explanation. I felt a great sense of peace and comfort envelop me and went home feeling strangely uplifted."

Family relationships are no longer as straightforward as they used to be. With the increasing incidence of divorce, many families metamorphose into stepfamilies and often complicated situations that are not always easy to handle, even before tragedy strikes.

When a child within that extended unit dies, stepparents or stepsiblings may suddenly feel excluded from any arrangements or, worse, not have their own grief acknowledged simply because they are not biologically related to the deceased. Biological family members may feel that the stepparent or stepsibling cannot possibly comprehend the depth of their loss, or indeed be experiencing any grief of their own.

People outside the immediate family unit may forget to include the stepparents or stepsiblings on sympathy cards, or may fail to accept their grief as legitimate. The loss of a child may unite the biological parents in grief, irrespective of their previous relationship, whether amicable or not, making the stepparent feel insecure and isolated. They have to exercise tolerance and support their partner and any other children they may have, whilst trying to process their own grief, sometimes silently.

The biological parents may blame each other for what happened, placing further pressure on the stepparent to maintain an equilibrium and be a calming influence in the midst of turmoil.

When Joe's 22-year-old stepson Scott shot himself in January 2000, not only did he feel like a spare part that had no place within his wife's close-knit family, but his own grief nearly drove him to suicide himself. Joe had raised Scott from the age of three and could not have felt any more love for him had he been his biological son.

"My wife Joyce and I had always maintained a solid relationship because of our ability to talk to each other about absolutely anything. We had no secrets and if anything was troubling either of us, we knew that we could talk about it to each other in the knowledge that we would both listen and try to understand, even if we did not always agree. Yes, sometimes I would hear things that I would rather not have heard and yet Joyce was inevitably right.

"We always believed that bringing problems out into the open was the first step towards a solution. There is nothing worse than harbouring grudges and keeping one's feelings locked away.

"All that changed when Scott died. We had both experienced traumatic situations and bereavement in the past and yet nothing touched on the total shock and devastation of Scott's suicide.

"Almost from the moment that we received the agonising news, Joyce seemed to build an impenetrable wall around her and was unreceptive to anyone else's grief. Her family fussed around her, occasionally issuing me with instructions to perform some function or other. To everyone else it appeared as though I was an emotionless outsider, occasionally useful for undertaking necessary tasks.

"The pain was excruciating. I felt as though my heart had been torn out and I desperately needed to tell someone how I was feeling. On one occasion, I attempted to confide in Joyce's sister, who I felt would be sympathetic. However, when I began pouring my heart out to her, she said, 'If you think you're feeling bad, just imagine how Joyce must be feeling. She was his biological mother after all'. That comment knocked me back completely and although I am ashamed to admit it, I believe that it was at that point that I contemplated ending it all myself. At that time, I suppose it seemed like the only solution to my misery and was not something that could be 'cured' by taking a pill. For a while I understood how Scott must have been feeling; the loss of all hope and the desire for permanent alleviation of pain.

"I worried about what the grief might do to Joyce, probably more so than about what it might do to me. I continued supporting her after friends and family stopped calling by so regularly and yet I was still unable to share my own feelings with her. Not once did she ever ask me how I was feeling.

"The strain eventually took its toll when, two months after Scott's funeral, I suffered from a minor stroke and had a nervous breakdown. I spent a week in hospital and a further three weeks in a psychiatric unit. I won't divulge the full details, but it was extremely distressing and frightening.

"This was a serious wake-up call for Joyce. Not only had she lost her only son, but she had nearly lost her husband too. They say that everything happens for a reason and whilst I would never wish this experience on anyone, it did make Joyce realise how self-obsessed she'd been. She then went through a period of extreme guilt and could not apologise enough for having discarded my feelings. From that moment onwards, we decided to do something positive in memory of Scott. We began participating in challenge events to raise money for a mental health organisation and in 2004 I am proud to say that I completed my first marathon.

"Naturally, I cannot tell anyone else how to deal with their grief, but the advice that I would give to any other family who is enduring a similar bereavement is never to dismiss the feelings of other family members. Never assume that your grief is worse than someone else's. Any degree of grief should be acknowledged, even if you feel that it cannot possibly be as intense as yours. All grief is different, but all grief is important."

Danielle lost her younger stepsister Keira in April 2003. Despite having been a part of Keira's life since she was two-years-old, Danielle felt completely disregarded following Keira's suicide at the age of 18.

"My parents divorced when I was only 5-years-old. Within two years, my mum had remarried. My stepdad was a widow whose wife had died just after she gave birth to my stepsister Keira. As a result, he had not only raised Keira from birth, but also my older stepsister, Katie, who was eight-years-old at the time of her mother's death.

"When we all began living together, I was 7, Keira was 4 and Katie was 12. Although my memories of my young childhood are fairly clear, I still can't really remember a time when Keira wasn't in my life and I have always regarded her as my baby sister, not my stepsister. Although Katie was Keira's biological sister, she was never as close to Keira as I was. I presume that that is because she was older, had different interests and was allowed more freedom to do her own thing.

"I know that Keira suffered inner turmoil from knowing that her mother had died as a result of post partum complications and I believe that she shouldered the blame for what happened, even though it was just one of those rare and unfortunate incidents. Keira did mention on more than one occasion that if she hadn't been born, then her mother would still be alive. Of course, unlike Katie, she also never had the privilege of knowing her biological mother and this tore her apart.

"Keira was very sensitive to other people's trauma and sometimes it appeared as though she was carrying everyone's burden for them. She had already decided that she wanted to work with disadvantaged people, but I did worry that maybe she wouldn't be able to switch off from work at the end of each day and would end up becoming depressed. Sadly, that is exactly what happened.

"I was at university when the tragedy occurred. Although I hadn't lived at home for over two years, Keira and I spoke several times a week and we saw each other whenever we could.

"She phoned me the night before she died. The odd thing is that she sounded uncharacteristically jubilant, as though she had won the national lottery or something. In retrospect, I realise that she had found the ultimate solution to her misery. Before our conversation finished that night, she said to me, 'You've always been my best friend. I've always regarded you as my real sister. Thank you.' Not for a minute did I interpret this as a 'Goodbye' message. Maybe if she had sounded upset, then I would have read more into it.

"When Katie phoned me the following day to tell me that Keira had been found hanging in her bedroom, I became hysterical. There are no words to describe the shock and the grief. At that point, I didn't realise that things were about to get worse. I did not consider for one moment that my grief would be disregarded, just because I was Keira's stepsister.

"I travelled home immediately. I wept most of the way back on the train. I could feel other people staring at me, but I didn't care and I felt unable to control my emotions. One lady kindly comforted me. Quite bizarrely, when I told her what had happened, she told me that her own mother had died by suicide. Horrifying as that was, I found myself consoled by the fact that other apparently normal people leading normal lives had also experienced such an unspeakable tragedy.

"When I arrived home, I was expecting a communal outpouring of shared grief. However, I was greeted and hugged and then completely ignored. My mother cried all over me, attempting to seek comfort in my arms and my stepfather just sat there in silence without even acknowledging my presence. Did he resent the fact that it was his daughter who had died rather than me?

"Katie was being comforted by her biological grandmother and a handful of other miscellaneous relatives were huddled together in their respective groups. Where did I fit in? I might just as well have been invisible. That may sound selfish, but it seemed as though I was expected to be the strong one and that, as a stepsister, I was somehow emotionally detached from the tragedy. I couldn't have been closer to Keira had she been my biological sister. She was the only person that I can honestly say I trusted 100%. I shared secrets with her that no one else ever knew about – and never will.

"I so desperately wanted to be able to share my despair with someone and yet I didn't want to appear insensitive to my family's pain. I got the impression that friends and relatives believed that because my mother and stepfather had lost a child, their grief was worse than anything that anyone else could possibly be suffering. Had they all suddenly forgotten how close Keira and I had been? Did they think that because we weren't tied by blood that my grief should be minimised?

"They say that tragedy can either bring families together or drive them apart. In our case, I believe it has driven a wedge between us. My relationship with my parents and Katie has definitely been strained since Keira's suicide. I have often wondered whether my stepfather resents the fact that I am still alive. Does he believe that as Keira's confidante I could have done something to save her? Does my mother feel guilty entertaining me for fear of upsetting my stepfather? Does Katie wish that she had lost her stepsister rather than her biological sister? These are not questions that I have ever dared ask. Maybe it's not healthy to remain silent, but living away from home has made the situation easier to ignore. Maybe they all just need time to come to terms with what has happened – and maybe they never will.

"I miss Keira like nothing else on this earth. In the beginning, I allowed her death to erase all my aspirations and every bit of happiness I had. When we are engulfed in such hopelessness, it affects every aspect of our lives. It makes us feel that nothing we are doing has any point. I made plans and then cancelled them at the last minute and I lost so-called friends that I never should have had in my life in the first place.

"In the first year I felt so alone, because no one seemed concerned about my feelings and because of that, there was no one who could say anything even remotely comforting. I felt as though I was the one doing all of the comforting. I think that many people believed that because I appeared to be coping on the surface (out of duty, not choice), that I was ok. Of course, I was far from ok, but they didn't want to know that.

"I ended up joining an online support group and this has helped me more than anything. I have been able to connect with other stepsiblings in a similar situation and it really is comforting knowing that I can express my innermost thoughts and feelings without walking on eggshells. Having a support system is so important when you are feeling desperate and the pain is overwhelming. It is a route that I would recommend to anyone who feels isolated in their grief and unable to communicate with other family members or friends."

Although it is hard for parents to be strong when they too are overwhelmed by grief, it is important to reassure the surviving siblings that life will continue and that you will continue to love, support and help them. Above all, they need confirmation that what happened was nobody's fault. How you approach this very much depends upon the age of the surviving siblings. If a child is very young, it may be inappropriate to divulge the details of their sibling's death.

In the case of my youngest daughter Lauren, who was just approaching her third birthday when her brother died, I simply told her that Kristian had unfortunately taken something poisonous, which had caused him to die. In effect, this was true. Therein was a lesson to her not to touch, eat or drink anything she found without first asking me, especially if she wasn't sure what it was. Thereafter, she would occasionally say, "Kristian was very silly because he took some poison."

Lauren seemed to view Kristian's death as temporary. She was born with a naturally high level of spiritual awareness and accepted that his soul had only left the physical body that he had been given in this life. She talked about him being up amongst the stars and at the time of his passing did not cry for her brother. When she was 5, however, she began sobbing for him and at the age of seven, she would frequently cry herself to sleep at night saying how much she missed him and that although she knew he was still around in spirit, she missed being able to hug him.

Three months before her eighth birthday, Lauren repeatedly asked for the exact details of her brother's death. She has always possessed wisdom and understanding way beyond her years, so as a result of her persistence, I decided to tell her exactly what had happened. She processed the information remarkably well and in one respect it offered her some comfort in knowing that he was no longer suffering any emotional pain. It did not lessen her desire for him to be alive again, nor did it ease her pain of missing him, but it did help her to understand why he had died.

I believe that the natural instinct of any adult within the family unit is not to tell children that a sibling or relative died by suicide. The belief is that one is protecting the children from the truth because they are too young to understand.

Personally, I do not believe in lying to children. Eventually, they will uncover the truth and how can we teach our children to appreciate the virtues of being honest if we lie to them? The danger is that they may also discover what has happened through other people and may then feel a sense of betrayal and distrust towards their parents. They may wonder whether there is anything else about which their parents have lied.

Withholding the full details of a suicide when a child is too young to understand is an entirely different matter. This is acceptable up to a point, as long as the parents make it clear that when the child is old enough to understand, they will explain it properly to them. In the case of my daughter, she asked for these details.

When Faye's younger brother, Jude, took his own life in November 2004, Faye wasn't sure what to tell her children who were then aged 7 and 4.

"I knew that telling Chloe and Emilia was going to be extremely difficult. They both loved their uncle and he had loved them. If they knew that he had felt unhappy enough to kill himself, would they believe that they had in some way contributed to his sadness? Would it make them believe that if one is unhappy, there is no other solution than to end your life? These notions may sound far-fetched, but I believe that no feeling or worry is irrational when someone close to you has died by suicide.

"Initially, I decided to tell them that their Uncle Jude had suffered from an illness of the brain, which had caused him to die. In fact, Jude was bipolar and it was this that had contributed to his suicidal behaviour, so this wasn't exactly a lie. I was just being economical with the truth to protect my daughters from further distress and, I suppose, to prevent awkward questions, the answers to which I believed they would have difficulty understanding at their age.

"Nevertheless, I soon discovered that even this information was difficult for my 7-year-old Chloe to accept. She wanted to know why her Uncle Jude always looked well and happy whenever we saw him. She couldn't understand why someone who didn't look sick could suddenly die. I tried to explain to her that there are many different types of illness; physical illnesses that stop your body from working properly and make you look sick and illnesses of the mind that prevent your brain from working normally, but which don't make you look ill. I told her that her Uncle Jude had suffered from an illness of the mind.

"Chloe still didn't seem satisfied by my explanation and the questions continued. She asked how the illness of the mind could kill you if it wasn't one of those illnesses that stopped your body from working properly. As she understood it, he had died because his body *had* stopped working.

"Eventually, my husband and I decided to seek the support and advice of a grievance counsellor. She told us that it was best to be totally honest with Chloe, although she did agree that Emilia was too young at this stage to be able to handle the truth. However, Emilia had never asked any difficult questions, so this was not going to be a problem.

"One evening, after Emilia had gone to bed, we sat down with Chloe and explained that her Uncle Jude had suffered from a disease of the mind called bipolar, which meant that it affected the mind and made him do things that he could not control. Of course, we then had to tell her that one of the things that the illness made him do resulted in his death. She then asked exactly how he died. Suddenly, I felt like terminating the conversation, but I knew that Chloe would continue to ask the question until I gave her an honest answer.

"When I told her that he had jumped off of the top of a high building, she looked horrified and said, 'Oh, how horrible.' Then she was silent for some time, obviously trying to process that horrific information.

"Chloe has asked fewer questions since that time and although she was obviously disturbed by what happened, she seems more accepting of the tragedy because she now understands why her uncle died. She now talks about him fondly and says that he is watching over all of us.

"Emilia is now 7-years-old, but has never asked as many questions as Chloe, probably because she was so much younger at the time of the tragedy. However, if she does ask, then I will have no hesitation in being honest with her too.

"If we had lied to Chloe, or glossed over the truth, we know that eventually she would have discovered what really happened. We could have risked losing her trust if we had done that, so I don't regret our decision at all.

"I created a memory book of Jude, containing photos, special times, amusing stories, his likes and dislikes, his talents and all the other traits that made him the unique person that he was. If ever the children ask, I will get it out for them to look at. At least it means that they will never forget him."

It is clear that siblings and other relatives are often the forgotten grievers. As these experiences demonstrate, the attention is primarily centred on the biological parents and their grief tends to overshadow that of other family members.

Whilst it may be difficult for parents to focus on anything other than their own grief, it is important to try not to make any other children and family members feel excluded. Whilst I did not want my children to see me upset, I now believe that an open emotion policy can be beneficial.

If you permit yourself to cry in front of your children, this validates their own feelings of loss and demonstrates to them that it is permissible for them to cry too without feeling uncomfortable or ashamed. Encountering sad situations is an integral part of life, so helping children to cope with such situations when they are younger equips them with the emotional resources they will need when they have to face difficult times in their future lives.

It is also important to let them see you laugh and reminisce about the good times. My youngest daughter will always come to me and cry openly when the loss of her brother overwhelms her. However, as with my eldest daughter, we will also talk about Kristian with fondness and recollect special moments and amusing incidents.

There are many ways to encourage siblings to articulate their grief and, of course, everyone is different. What is right for one person may not be right for another. Everyone will react differently depending not only on personality type, but also the personal relationship that they had with the deceased family member and the state of that relationship at the time of the tragedy. Both of my daughters express their grief creatively, through writing and drawing, whereas my son Carsten conveys his deepest thoughts and feelings through songwriting.

Children will also view death differently depending upon their age, maturity, individual personality and what they have learned about it from other people. Young children may view it as a temporary condition; it is only when they are older that they realise that death is irreversible. Some children will understand this concept earlier than others. Only the parents of the children concerned will be able to establish when it is the right time to fully explain the details of what has happened.

Children's views of death will also be influenced by the people around them, so it is also important for parents not to frighten children. Death via suicide, for example, can never be explained as "natural", or "something that happens to everyone eventually".

What is most important is to reassure younger children that they were in no way responsible for what happened and, with older children, it is crucial to acknowledge their grief as valid and normal and to allow them time and space to grieve in their own way.

It is essential for parents to take care of any surviving children's physical needs as well as their emotional needs. Grief may prevent them from eating or sleeping properly, which of course is entirely natural, but not healthy. Paying attention to the basics of physical care will help children handle the process of grieving from a healthy position. If they are in poor physical health, this will affect their mental health and make the grieving process so much more difficult.

Although parents will be consumed by their own grief, focusing on their surviving children's needs will be a diversion and, at the very least, will help them to realise that there is a continued reason for living; to nurture those who are still here and help the entire family to find joy beyond tragedy.

When all else fails, it may be necessary to seek professional help from an organisation such as The Compassionate Friends (TCF). The beauty of TCF is that it only employs people who themselves have lost a child, so you know that you will always be communicating with someone who can empathise with your loss. It's not always easy asking for help, but everyone who is involved with TCF will recognise this and will help any individual or family affected by the death of a child, including unmarried partners, adoptive parents, step families and single parent families.

Chapter Eleven

Bizarre Thoughts, Actions and Secrets

Sometimes, when one person is missing, the whole world seems depopulated.

Alphonse de Lamartine

    Prior to Kristian's funeral, I still lived with the outrageous notion that perhaps the medical staff had made a mistake. Maybe he was in a cryogenic state and would be buried alive, despite knowing that a post-mortem would totally eliminate that possibility. How horrific it would be for him to awake to find himself encased in a freezing, confined space with no light. I visualised his desperate attempts at clawing his way from his coffin, of screaming helplessly to a deaf audience. These thoughts were too ghastly and shocking to reveal to anyone, but they haunted me inexorably.

    One day, about three months after Kristian had died, I was standing by his grave with my daughter Anneliese when I admitted to her, "You know, it may sound gruesome, but I've often thought about coming here at night time, digging Kristian up and taking him home with me." Instead of being horrified, Anneliese gasped and replied, "I've thought exactly the same thing. I even asked a friend if it would be illegal to dig him up. I've just wanted to take him home with me and look after him."

    I derived a strange comfort from this admission, knowing that I probably wasn't suffering from some post-traumatic psychotic disorder, even though these thoughts may not have been entirely healthy for either my daughter or me.

That same day, memories of one of the most heartbreaking periods of my life, when I was 12-years-old, descended upon me with such vivid brutality that those two phases of my life – then and now – merged into one phase when suddenly all the years between had not exactly been erased, but had been more like an extended dream. In the moment that I revealed my secret thoughts to my daughter, it felt as though I had experienced only pain in my life.

When I was 12-years-old, my mother drowned my pet mouse Geraldine. Geraldine had developed a large lump on her shoulder, which my mother told me was cancer and the only way that she could convince me that the poor animal should perish, was by telling me that cancer was contagious. With those shocking words, she disappeared.

I remember tearing out to the garage where Geraldine was housed, my hearting pounding with terror. The side door of the garage was ajar, just allowing me a glimpse of this inverted mouse, her legs scrabbling wildly and helplessly at thin air, with her tail firmly lodged between my mother's thumb and forefinger, dangling like a smelly sock. Immediately beneath this doomed, suspended creature stood an empty paint tin, filled to the brim with water.

"Go away!" my mother yelled at me.

I ran back to the house, sobbing hysterically. I couldn't breathe. I couldn't bear the agony. I turned and sprinted back to the garage, just in time to see my beloved Geraldine lying motionless at the bottom of the rust, fluid-filled pot. In the midst of my intense pain, I concluded that mice can't swim.

I thought I would grieve forever. I cried until I was convinced that I would die from dehydration. I wanted to die. I wanted to be with Geraldine. It seemed that everything I had ever loved had been torn mercilessly away from me.

When I awoke the next morning and realised that I was still very much alive, I resigned myself to the fact that I wasn't ready to join Geraldine, so I devised a plan to be closer to her. On Monday evenings, when my parents went off to their art club, I used to dig up the sodden, cardboard box in which she had been lovingly buried during a funeral ceremony conducted by my brother and me. My tears would drip onto her white, inert body. Her eyes, which had once been a deep, translucent pink, had turned opaque and white. I convinced myself that she was just sleeping. After a few weeks of Geraldine's continuous weight loss and decomposition, the truth finally dawned that she wasn't going to wake up. I think the smell finally persuaded me to call a halt to this regular Monday evening ritual.

It is these same thoughts, feelings and desires that have plagued my mind since Kristian's death. The loss of my pet mouse was as significant to me as a child as Kristian's death has been to me as an adult. My mouse brought me emotional comfort in a world in which I felt vulnerable and threatened.

The day after Kristian's suicide I began morbidly thinking about his funeral and began "asking" him what songs he would like played. I searched analytically through boxes of old CDs that had been stored in the attic, feeling that the least and the last thing that I could do for my son would be to give him a great send off. I wanted to find songs with lyrics that encompassed everything about my son, his life, his situation and how his family felt about him. Did such a song exist? When I look back now, I wonder how I ever managed to detach myself from the heavy cloak of grief that shrouded our home.

Six months after Kristian's death, I felt an intense desire to withdraw from life completely. I wanted to run away, to be invisible and live in an isolated cottage totally hidden from view in the middle of the country, with just trees, plants and wildlife as my companions.

Whereas contact with others had been so crucial in the beginning and I had experienced an overpowering fear of being alone, all I wanted now was to live a solitary existence. I still needed contact with close family and friends, but the thought of being in a crowd of strangers repulsed and terrified me.

I wanted to live my life amongst nature. I hated concrete. Urban environments seemed hostile and claustrophobic, in which I could never find peace of mind. I needed open spaces, fields, trees and flowers, with only the sound of birdsong, rustling leaves and the gentle current of water flowing down a brook.

I would flick through the property sections of newspapers trying to visualise my dream home. Each time we drove through the countryside, I would be scanning the area to gauge a feel for any remote properties nestling snugly within the landscape, far from any main road.

Of course, I would want to take Kristian with me. I began wondering whether by law, as his mother, I would have the right to request that his coffin be exhumed. As mentioned in Chapter Eight, despite all my spiritual beliefs, I am living in the material world and still need to be close to the physical frame to which I had given birth. It helps me to connect to my son, in the same way that some mediums use physical objects to connect to a spirit. I wanted Kristian to rest in beautiful, serene surroundings, where the ground beneath which he lay would not be trampled upon by strangers, nor violated by anyone who showed disrespect to cemetery graves.

Catherine's 17-year-old son Sam was killed by a train after someone apparently saw him jump from a bank onto the rail track just a few seconds before a train arrived at that point. Sam had no chance. By the time the driver had seen him, it was too late.

"I didn't want to accept the fact that what Sam did was intentional, because I feel so wretched not to have realised that he was so deeply troubled. He had always been such a secretive boy and never spoke much about his feelings, even when asked.

"When I finally had the courage to go through my son's room about four months after his death, I discovered a copy of Suicide and Attempted Suicide: Methods and Consequences by Geo Stone hidden at the bottom of one of his drawers. I never told my husband. In fact, I have never told anyone else about this, but I feel that it is important for parents to know that even when there aren't any obvious signs that their child is depressed, there could be other indications that they are possibly contemplating suicide.

"I wrapped the book in a carrier bag with other items of rubbish and disposed of it in a skip on a nearby trading estate. My husband has always believed that Sam's death was a huge mistake and that no son of his would ever be weak enough to allow his problems to control his life. He really couldn't handle the truth, so thankfully because Sam never left a suicide note, an open verdict was recorded. Because of that, my husband will always be able to convince himself that it was an accident. I don't know whether he is aware that he is deceiving himself, but I do think that this is the only way in which he knows how to handle it. If he knew about the book, I think that might destroy him.

"There were many other things that I have done secretly and many peculiar thoughts that have travelled through my mind that I could never admit to my husband. Not only do I feel that I have to protect him, but I know that if he knew how convinced I was that Sam's death was suicide, it would almost certainly create a huge rift between us and I don't know whether our relationship would survive.

"There have been many times since Sam's death when I have spoken to him and told him that I am not angry with him for taking his own life. I have even written him letters, which I would love to be able to leave on his grave, or in his room, but I always end up destroying them once I have finished writing them. I am so afraid of my husband discovering any of these little rituals that I perform in order to help me to cope."

Nicola's youngest son Dale was 19-years-old when he shot himself in February 1997. Immediately after his death and in a state of deep traumatisation, Nicola was obsessed with finding out everything she could. She left no stone unturned in her quest for answers and some reassurance that Dale's death could be attributed to anything but suicide. Dale was discovered in a wood by a couple out cycling. It was estimated that he'd been dead for about five days.

"I pestered the police and the coroner constantly. I requested copies of the autopsy report, the toxicology test results, the police report and the alleged suicide note that had been found in the back pocket of his jeans. I even asked to see photos that were taken at the scene, which sounds horrendous, but I suppose I was looking for some other reason - any reason other than suicide - for his death and suspected that maybe foul play was involved. I was trying to convince myself that he'd been murdered and that perhaps someone had forged the note. I needed to see it for myself to verify that it was his handwriting.

"Despite the fact that everything pointed to suicide, I still decided to conduct my own private investigation. I say 'private', because I told nobody about what I was doing, not even my husband. He was too distraught to do anything except sit in shocked silence, refusing to see or talk to anyone.

"I drove out to the spot where Dale had been found expecting to find some clues. I even took a camera, notepad, pencil and dictaphone with me to record my findings. How crazy is that?

"I purposely didn't tell anyone where I'd gone, because I knew that not only would they try to stop me, but would think that I had gone completely mad and would maybe inform the authorities and attempt to have me arrested or sectioned. I didn't even take any form of communication tool with me, such as my cell phone, because that way I wouldn't have to lie to anyone if they called me. I realise now how foolish that was, because there I was, going to a place where I believed my son could have been murdered and had I encountered difficulties, I would not have been able to contact anyone.

"When I arrived at the scene of the 'crime', I remember crawling around on my hands and knees sobbing and frantically searching for any clue as to what had happened. I suppose that part of me was hoping to find some sign that he had not been alone. I took a bag with me and some food storage containers in which I placed anything that I thought might be relevant; a broken coke bottle, a cigarette butt (Dale didn't smoke, so maybe it was from his assailant), a used tissue, plant matter and earth from the immediate area that I believed could be used for forensic tests.

"Not only was I searching for clues, but I wanted mementos, however distressing or gruesome. I wanted to tear up the earth and foliage where Dale's body had lain when he fell and preserve the findings. I have never mentioned that to anyone before, but from talking to other bereaved families, I now know that these kind of thoughts and emotions are not unusual and a perfectly normal reaction to a sudden death. I don't think that anything we think, feel or do is abnormal where the grieving process of a survivor of loss by suicide is concerned.

"Even now I don't feel that what I did was ridiculous. I owed it to my son to seek out the truth and demonstrate my love for him. What I find more ridiculous is how his flatmate didn't let anyone know that Dale hadn't been home for five days. I have since spoken to Dale's flatmate to ask him whether Dale was in any sort of trouble, or whether he had seemed depressed, but he told me that he did not notice any unusual behaviour and that the last time he had seen him, Dale had been his usual cheerful self. He said that Dale would often disappear off for a day or two at a time, or stay over at other friends' pads and not always say where he was going, or for how long, so he had no reason to suspect that anything was amiss.

"I don't know whether this makes me feel better or worse. Maybe Dale was depressed, but was hiding it well, or maybe his flatmate was just not a very perceptive person, or maybe something more sinister was involved. I guess that one of the painful tragedies of suicide is that the surviving families will never know all the answers. There will always be so many whys, what ifs and hows.

"Because a suicide note had been found that had been written, without doubt, in Dale's handwriting and very briefly stated that he had had enough of life, the police did not suspect any foul play and were satisfied that it was suicide, but I still have my doubts. In my mind the case will always be open. Dale was such a happy boy and had absolutely no history of depression. Something happened that we don't – and probably never will – know about. I know that if anyone had a hand in what happened that day, they would have to live with the guilt - or worry about being discovered - for the rest of their lives. We will certainly live with the tragedy uppermost in our minds and broken hearts for the rest of our days."

In the three days prior to Kristian's funeral when we had the privilege of visiting him at the funeral parlour's chapel of rest, I had some of my most macabre thoughts. I was longing to lift up his eyelids to see his eyes. I just wanted one more glance at my son's beautiful, expressive green eyes, the eyes that I had seen brim with tears so many times, even when he was a teenager. I didn't look, because I was afraid of what I might see. I wanted to remember his eyes as they were in life, not opaque and expressionless. Most of all, I was afraid of seeing sadness and despair.

By the third day, the day prior to Kristian's funeral, I began to detect a more nauseating smell. I wondered whether anyone else had noticed this, but was too afraid to ask at the time. I think I knew why, but didn't want confirmation from anyone else. I could only liken the odour to a joint of meat that had been immersed in a solvent and left out at room temperature for a few days. Some weeks later, Anneliese mentioned that when she had visited the chapel of rest with one of Kristian's friends, he had made a remark about the "horrible smell".

As mentioned in Chapter Nine, a stream of distraught friends flowed through the door of the funeral parlour to take one last glimpse of their loyal friend and to place gifts in his coffin. His girlfriend Millie took along various grooming products, including a pot of hair gel to "make him look nice", after he had been cruelly tampered with by the various professionals involved in handling people period between their death and their funeral. It seemed strange to think that she was more familiar with his body than I, his mother. Did she also harbour a desire to steal a look beneath his clothes, or take one last look at the eyes that had seduced her, not only when they first met, but on the many occasions when he would plead for forgiveness, or persuade her to succumb to his wishes? I didn't know. I don't know now. I've never asked.

Is it the absolute desperation, the disbelief and the inability to accept that our loved one's body is no longer functioning in any way that makes us think such strange thoughts and perform such odd and sometimes morbid actions? Even now, I cannot comprehend the notion that my son, who was always so full of life, no longer exists in the form that I knew him. Each time I visit his grave, I cannot erase the grisly images that creep to the forefront of my mind. I visualise at what stage of decomposition his body has reached; my handsome son with facial features that were far too beautiful for a young man. How could that beauty have just withered and metamorphosed into something so horrific and repugnant? How can people adore someone one minute, but then be almost repelled the moment that person stops breathing? Maybe it's because the soul is released and the body literally is an empty shell that no longer serves a purpose, even though it was the body that we loved and nurtured from the moment of conception.

When someone takes their own life, the horror of such an inconceivable tragedy often prevents those who have access to details of the scene from divulging those details to other members of the family. They want to spare others from further trauma, even though there is usually an inherent desire to know.

Lesley's 25-year-old son Jonathan was found hanging in the bathroom of his fiancée's house in January 2002 following an argument. Computer programmer Jonathan and his fiancée Gemma had been together for four years and had planned on getting married the following year, but the relationship had never been entirely stable. After each falling out with Gemma, Jonathan would often appear at Lesley and her partner's house, but he always acted in a matter-of-fact manner and never seemed unduly concerned that it would be a terminal arrangement.

Inevitably, after a brief cooling off period, Jonathan and Gemma would be back together as though nothing untoward had occurred.

Although Lesley describes Jonathan as a sensitive soul, to her knowledge he had never suffered from depression, nor had he ever expressed any desire to kill himself, even in the most difficult periods of his life.

Lesley continues the story.

"My partner Doug and I had just gone to bed when there was an urgent knocking at our front door. It was a distraught Gemma accompanied by a police officer. So much of that night is a blur; like a weird dream that jumps about from one scene to the next in a random fashion. There are chunks missing, but I presume that was the effect of shock. I remember the words, 'Jonathan', 'dead' and 'hanging'.

"Gemma had found Jonathan and had already given a statement to the police, but she refused to tell us any of the details, saying that we didn't need to know and that she did not want to share it with us. She made out that she was trying to protect us from further pain, but I wanted to know. It was my right as a mother and I knew my son. He was the last person that I ever thought would use suicide as a way out of his problems. I felt that Gemma was keeping something from us.

"I tried to show concern for her by telling her that I didn't feel it was fair for her to have to carry around that burden all by herself and that perhaps it would ease her conscience if she told us. Doug spoke to her alone and tried to persuade her to perhaps just tell him, but she refused. We knew that she was keeping something from us and although she said that there was no suicide note, I began to wonder whether she had destroyed it before she called the police.

"By the time we were informed, Jonathan's body had already been taken away. Gemma had formerly identified him and I felt cheated that I had been denied that privilege as his mother. Even though we were able to visit him at the chapel of rest after his sliced and stitched body had been prepared for viewing, I began to feel extremely angry towards Gemma. I actually found myself feeling envious that she had been the one to find him. She was the one who had seen him closest to the last moments of his life. In the days and months following his death, I spent every day trying to visualise the scene. What did he look like? Was he still warm? Were his eyes bloodshot and bulging from his face? Did he look unhappy? Did he look at peace?

"Each time I went to sleep I would see him hanging everywhere. I would be having a perfectly normal dream and then he would appear dangling in front of me. Sometimes he would still be alive and laughing at me, as though he was play acting and at other times he would look like a zombie, as though he had already been dead for weeks. It was horrific. It got to the point where I was afraid to go to bed.

"About eight months after he died, we received a phone call from Tom, a mutual friend of Jonathan's. Tom told us that two months before Jonathan hung himself, Gemma had had an abortion without Jonathan's consent. He had wanted the baby; she didn't. Jonathan had confided in Tom and told him that it was the worst experience of his life and that he didn't know how he would ever cope with the thought that his baby had been murdered against his will. Tom felt that we ought to know, but he didn't wish to add further to our pain by telling us so soon after the tragedy. Eventually, he felt that he could no longer keep it to himself and since he could not forgive Gemma for triggering his best friend's suicide, he felt no loyalty towards her.

"The news was devastating, but at least we had some sort of an answer to that gnawing question, 'Why?' It was like a double tragedy. We had lost a son and a grandchild, but took very small comfort in knowing that they were united in the afterlife, even though they had never met in this life.

"We never spoke to Gemma again and almost immediately after the revelation, the horrendous nightmares stopped. I still dreamed about Jonathan, but they were more pleasant dreams, which I felt sure were visitations where he had come to put his arms around me and let me know that he was alright. In some dreams he would be accompanied by a baby boy whom I imagined was his son, but rather than feeling sad, I felt an amazing sense of calm whenever I awoke from such dreams.

"When I first discovered what Gemma had done, I cannot even begin to describe the intense wrath that I felt. I was like a crazed psychopath, screaming that I was going to murder her and make her pay for killing two people. At one point I grabbed my largest kitchen knife from the drawer and had to be restrained by Doug. If he hadn't been there, I feel sure that I would have done something that I would have regretted. At that point, I was totally out of control, but did not feel responsible for my actions and I would defy anybody to say that they wouldn't have felt the same if exposed to similar circumstances.

"I had lost my son because of his selfish girlfriend and I will never forgive her for that. Most of those who talk about forgiveness and letting go have never even experienced the loss of a child to suicide, let alone as the direct result of someone else's actions. I know that feeling bitter will not bring my son back, but were it not for his girlfriend, he would still be alive. He should still be alive. He was only 25 for heaven's sake. He had so much life ahead of him. How can I ever forgive her for that?

"Nobody can tell me that what I'm feeling is wrong. It doesn't stop me from moving forward in my life. I am learning to live without Jonathan and I don't feel trapped in my resentment. I just hope that Gemma carries the guilt with her to the grave."

Fourteen months after Kristian's passing, I began to have ghastly dreams about digging up his coffin. Each time, the circumstances would be slightly different, but each time I would notice the lid of the coffin coming away and would experience this terrible fear of looking inside and seeing my son's rotting body. I would catch a glimpse of the shirt in which he had been buried and would be afraid to lift up the lid or look too closely for fear of the smell and the horrific sight of seeing my son's face looking green, collapsed and decomposing like a character from a horror movie. The horrendous part about waking up was the realisation that the images in my dream were true. My son was dead and his body was cold, sodden and decomposing.

In the week leading up to Christmas 2005, I had one of the most disturbing dreams about Kristian's body being exhumed. In this particular dream, I approached Kristian's freshly re-dug grave, which was in a cemetery that was not recognisable to me in my conscious life. However, in my dream this appeared perfectly acceptable. There often appears to be no logic behind the way in which the subconscious mind takes images and events and forms them into scenarios that appear to bear no relation to one's real life.

As I approached the grave, in the knowledge that Kristian's coffin had not yet been removed, I was filled with the same dread that had consumed me in previous dreams, not knowing what harrowing sight would await me. I peered into the lidless coffin, which was filled to the brim with rainwater.

The first thing I noticed was that Kristian's face had hardly decomposed, although his eyes and mouth were now open. I wanted to put my hand into his mouth to lift him up and empty his body and the coffin of water, but the fear of feeling his dead face crumble in my hands was too horrifying to contemplate. As I gazed at his face, his lips regained a pink hue, closed slightly and formed into a smile. I interpreted this vision as a sign that he was communicating with me and letting me know that he was ok, despite the torture and ghastliness of seeing his cold, lifeless body submerged in water.

It was these sickening and distressing dreams that further embedded my belief about the futility of superficial, external beauty, knowing that it doesn't last forever. The dreams and imagined visions of Kristian's decomposing body would have destroyed me had it not been for my spiritual beliefs and realisation that the real person had simply discarded this temporary outer shell to move onto a different vibratory level where physical bodies are no longer needed.

Nevertheless, Kristian's graveside has become the focal point for my grief. I find it easier to connect with him when I am standing on the ground beneath which his physical body lies. The base of his gravestone and all around is adorned with objects of affection from his family and friends, objects that give some insight into his personality. Models of sports' cars show his passion for motor vehicles and speed; cuddly toys and ornaments of bears honour his sensitive, affectionate side and angels represent his heart of gold. His friends have even placed the occasional can of beer by his gravestone to celebrate his love of socialising!

Kristian's headstone

Chapter Twelve

Memory Triggers: Sights, Sounds, Smells and Possessions

It's equivalent to living life through a constant hail of rubber bullets, never knowing when one is going to strike you, or how hard. When it does, it can knock you down and back to the blackest depths of grief.

Jan Andersen

The loss of your child is not something that you experience just once. You constantly re-live it, not only on anniversaries and other special occasions, but each time you encounter something that evokes a memory; a sight, a sound, a smell or your child's possessions. These can be extremely powerful and can reduce you to a state of intense emotional turmoil.

A piece of music with powerful words, an emotional scene in a TV drama, movie or news feature, a smell of aftershave worn by Kristian or a smell that reminds me of a past event in his life, a photo, a drawing, or even a single word like "suicide" or "heroin" can submerge me in an ocean of grief. I can make a quantum leap from a state of effectively managing my emotions to one of drowning in pain.

In the first week after Kristian died, I began desperately searching for anything that he had ever created, touch or owned; his old schoolbooks, a picture of his handprints in a myriad of colours, his baby shoes, old Mother's Day cards and letters that he had sent from the young offenders' institution.

How thankful I was that I had kept so many of these things for sentimental reasons, knowing now that there would be no more opportunities to create more memories with Kristian, to take photos, buy him gifts or receive letters, drawings, Mother's Day, birthday and Christmas cards.

Your child's possessions take on a new significance. Even the most illegible scrawl on a torn piece of paper can seem like the most priceless item, because it was created by your child's hand and is, of course, irreplaceable.

When my daughter Anneliese managed to retrieve some of Kristian's belongings from a friend's flat, I remember the intense pain of removing each item from the black, plastic dustbin liner, one by one, not just holding on to what I had left of him, but searching for the smallest clue about his recent life and perhaps a reason for his death. Even the smallest piece of paper was something that he had touched and something with which I could never part. In addition to a few items of clothing that I would hug tightly, inhaling the scent of my son, there was a battered, brown A4 envelope containing a couple of old payslips, a photo of his little sister Lauren, a worn toothbrush, a small brown bear with "Lover Boy" embroidered on the front and a fluffy, tortoiseshell kitten that purred when you pulled a cord from its body.

Kristian had always loved cuddly toys and his friends would often make fun of the way that he would line up his toys on his shelf. Like a young child with a security blanket, these were his comfort toys. He was still a small boy in a young man's body. I can put my hands on these possessions that Kristian once held and treasured and symbolically we touch. For the briefest of moments, some small comfort intermingles with enormous pain.

Each day when I look at my youngest daughter, I am reminded of Kristian; the animated expressions, the zest for life and insatiable curiosity for everything. The innocence radiating from her face mirrors that of Kristian at the same age and the joy and pain collide violently, both battling for power; joy and pain, pain and joy. I cry and I laugh. I laugh and I cry. My heart aches with love for my daughter and grief for my son.

I cannot leave my house, watch TV or flick through a magazine without seeing young lads of Kristian's age; many dressed in a similar style, adopting the "in" attitude, moving with a certain gait that shouts, "I want to be one of the trendy crowd."

I wondered whether I would have experienced more anguish had Kristian still lived at home and had a vacant room that I would have had to enter after the event, or would I have been grateful for more material mementos of the life that he had led?

Carrie's 16-year-old brother Shaun took his own life in January 2001. Carrie still lives at home, as did Shaun, but it was weeks before she felt able to enter his bedroom, which his parents had left untouched since his suicide.

"Shaun was always very protective of his belongings and hated it if I ever went into his room without asking. I suppose that I believed that entering his room without his permission would be wrong, even though I knew that he was no longer there to ask. By not entering his room, I could also believe that he was still alive and sitting in his room sulking, or playing his music, as he used to do for much of the time. Entering his room would be like acknowledging that he was no longer there and I didn't know whether I could bear the pain.

"We would fight and argue like any normal brother or sister, but we also had a very special connection that could not be severed by anyone or anything – even death. We would share the most ridiculous jokes that no one else could understand and would see humour in the strangest of situations. In order to keep this connection alive, I felt that I had to overcome the fear of entering his room.

"The first time I went into Shaun's room was about seven weeks after he died. I began sobbing as soon as I opened the door. I stood in the middle of the room for ages, just looking around, talking to him and asking him to give me a sign that he was still with me. I then began moving around the room randomly, touching his things and trying to feel his presence. There was a checked, brushed cotton shirt crumpled at the end of his bed, the same shirt that he had worn the night before he died. I sat on the bed and held it to my face. I could still smell him above the smell of stale smoke and ale from the bar he had been to that particular night. I rocked backwards and forwards, shaking and sobbing into his shirt. It smelled of life, not death. I took that shirt and kept it in my wardrobe. Every now and then I take it out and hug it, but there may come a time soon when I'll stop doing that because the aroma has faded and I'm afraid that I'll take it out one day and won't be able to smell Shaun on it anymore.

"I also found some of my CDs in his cupboard that I thought I'd mislaid somewhere, which made me smile, since he always complained if I borrowed any recordings of his without asking.

"There were so many memories in his small room; photos, postcards, birthday cards, letters, football trophies, a collection of baseball caps and many items that I hadn't realised he'd kept. In the top of his bedside drawer was a model of one of his favourite footballers that I'd given to him for his twelfth birthday.

"Beneath it were all the birthday and Christmas cards that I'd given to him since I was old enough to buy my own cards. I think that these made me cry more than anything else. It made me realise how precious our friendship was to him and how important it was to him to be shown that he was loved. Maybe keeping those cards was a way of affirming that love, even when we'd had an argument and weren't speaking to each other. What a shame he never realised the deep anguish and inconceivable pain that his suicide would cause to those who loved him so deeply.

"I don't know why he ended his life. All I do know is that he was a very deep person who would often retreat into his shell without any explanation. If left alone, he would emerge as bright as ever. Clearly he was troubled, but did not wish to share his sorrow with anyone else, not even me. I did feel betrayed, but I also believe that he did not want to inflict his pain on others. I guess he felt that death was the only escape.

"All I have left now are the memories, but I am grateful for those memories and the constant reminders, even though I would give anything to have the opportunity to create more memories with my brother."

At Easter 2003, five months after Kristian's death, my partner, Lauren and I decided to take a short break away over the bank holiday weekend. We secured a fantastic bargain at a hotel in Cambridgeshire, but although the weekend was as wonderful as could be expected so shortly after the tragedy, I experienced a painful shock that has vividly remained with me ever since. Whilst we were checking in at the lobby, my partner turned to me and said, "Did you see that blond lad who just walked past? I had to do a double take. He looked exactly like Kristian did when he was 14."

I was immediately transported back in time. I stood there in a trance, gazing motionless at this clone of my son. I instinctively wanted to run over and hug the lad, but the rational part of my mind kept me rooted to the spot. I wanted to speak to him, to hear his voice and study his mannerisms, but above all I wanted to tell him about Kristian.

This lad possessed the same sadness that penetrated from within through his green eyes, even though his outer façade did not exude an aura of misery. I felt as though I wanted to save him from the same fate as Kristian. Was this an opportunity being presented to me? Maybe I was supposed to speak to him, but I didn't. The intellectual part of my mind reasoned that this lad might think I was some kind of child snatcher. At the least, I might risk upsetting him with comparisons to my dead son and perhaps instil fear into the poor lad that the same fate awaited him.

During our brief stay, we saw this lad and his father on numerous occasions. At one point we all entered the hotel lift at the same time and, in such close proximity, the likeness of this lad to Kristian was even more remarkable. Had he and Kristian stood side by side, one would have had no difficulty in believing that they were identical twins.

My eyes brimmed with tears and I silently wished this lovely boy a happy, pain-free life. Although I never spoke to him, I left hoping that perhaps he had benefited from our brief, silent encounter and the healing thoughts that I was sending to him.

Although such similarities in other people and actual photos of our children are the most heartrending, there are many other triggers that hover near us on a daily basis and can descend upon us without warning; a song on the radio, a certain smell, a voice, a place, a TV programme, something someone says or does and so many other prompts.

It's equivalent to living life through a constant hail of rubber bullets, never knowing when one is going to strike you, or how hard. When it does, it can knock you down and back to the blackest depths of grief. They can also make us smile through our pain, if they elicit fond memories. These triggers cannot be shut out or avoided. One learns to live with their unpredictability and the knowledge that we can be forced from a place of relative equanimity to an abyss of uncontrollable anguish in an instant.

A few months after the tragedy when I thought I was holding up remarkably well and was engaging in many supportive projects to help others, I received a phone call from someone asking to speak to Kristian. After attempting to explain that my son had died, I broke down in tears, I am certain to the extreme embarrassment of the woman at the other end. I felt that I had placed her in a terribly awkward position, not knowing me, not expecting such a response and not really knowing what to say. After mumbling her apologies and vowing not to call me again, the conversation terminated. I then felt awful for this poor woman who must have come off the phone feeling mortified by the reaction provoked by what was initially a perfectly innocent enquiry.

This was not the only time that I had to explain to someone in authority that my son was no longer with us. For a long time following the tragedy, I continually received letters addressed to Kristian, mainly from the local council. Despite numerous requests to remove his name from their database, the letters continued to arrive. I had considered replying to them on Kristian's behalf and heading the paper, "Letter from Heaven", with threats of haunting them if they didn't cease sending him letters, although I imagine that I would have be labelled as mentally unstable and subsequently ignored, which would be indicative of society's general attitude towards those who are not of sound mind.

Seven months after the tragedy, I was invited to a local Chamber of Commerce networking event. Following a presentation given by one of my clients on the importance of good PR, I was introduced to an engagingly interesting gentleman, a professional photographer, who had just returned to the UK after living in the Middle East for 30 years.

My friend who had initiated the introduction began extolling my virtues (bless her) and then added that I had also created several websites that attracted a global audience of hundreds of thousands. When this gentleman asked me what topics the websites covered, I found myself giving a quick description of the first two and then explaining in detail my reasons behind the creation of the (then) most recent site; Child Suicide.

I sensed an immediate empathy with this man. His large, kind brown eyes had seen more atrocities in a week than most of us would experience in a lifetime. He then told me that he had experienced the tragedy of death many times in his life. He talked about losing close friends to the barbaric actions of suicide bombers and other acts of terrorism during his 30 years in the Middle East. He gave the perfect example of a paradox when he told me that death had become a regular part of life in that part of the world. He said that to a certain extent people had become immune to the horror of murder.

A little later, whilst I was embroiled in conversation with a Feng Shui consultant, this gentleman beckoned me over. He said, "It's amazing isn't it, how one word can elicit a vivid memory? When that man over there mentioned the word 'Zurich', it immediately brought to mind an incident that occurred in 1969. A pilot was about to take off from Zurich airport when some Palestinians on the ground shot at the plane. He was hit in the stomach and it took a month for him to die in the Swiss hospital."

He then looked straight at me and said, "When you mentioned your son, I could see that look in your eye. Don't feel guilty. You mustn't feel guilty."

Of course, I always would feel guilty, irrespective of how many people gave me permission not to. At least I understood that these memory triggers affected everyone, even decades after the event.

On the morning of Wednesday 15 October 2003, the clothes that Kristian had been wearing when he died were finally returned to me in a large white plastic sack. Within the sack, each item of clothing had been sealed within large brown envelopes. The police officer apologised for the delay in returning his clothes and warned me that none of the items had been laundered, because of the need to conduct forensic tests on them. I stared at the sack in horror and was instantly consumed by dread and suffocating grief. The final traces of my son's life were in that bag; the clothes that had hugged his body during the last hours of his life, the trainers in which he took his final steps and, worst of all, the drug paraphernalia that he had used to terminate his life.

I wept as I spoke to the police officer and found myself apologising for getting upset, as though I had no permission to do so nearly a year after the event.

This was the same day that I was due to travel to London to appear on a Kilroy discussion show on the topic of male suicide. I needed to be calm and composed in order to make my contribution as eloquently as possible, since there were no re-recordings or practice sessions. We had to get it right first time. The show was screened exactly as it was recorded; no editing or tweaks, as some might believe. Robert Kilroy Silk did not have a producer issuing instructions in his ear; he had a plan beforehand of where every participant was sitting and had to memorise their names in advance.

The police officer departed and I was left with the gruelling choice of either removing my son's possessions from the bag, or waiting for my partner to come home from work and support me in the harrowing process. However, I knew that I needed to be alone as I removed each item and symbolically held my son to me, breathing his aroma and hugging the closest thing to him that I could, imagining my arms around his body rather than around a superficial piece of cloth. His clothes contained his vibrations. Maybe I thought that I would sense what he had been feeling that night and share his pain with him, although I couldn't imagine it being any more agonising than the pain I was in at that moment.

I opened the bag with a sense of foreboding, terrified of finding something distasteful or something that would further intensify my grief. My body began convulsing in sobs from the moment that I opened the first package. I removed his favourite white coat, the one that he had promised to a close friend just a couple of weeks before he died and the one that had been folded up outside his girlfriend's flat on the night that he ended his life. It smelled musty and was covered in spots of black mildew. He would have been devastated.

I pulled out his favourite navy MacKenzie sweatshirt and in that moment wondered whether he had planned his death outfit; whether he wanted to look his best when he was found. These were the last clothes that had embraced his living physical body. These clothes were the closest that I would ever get to experiencing my son's physical rather than spiritual presence.

His jeans and belt were the only items intact. His T-shirt and sweatshirt were in tatters as a result of the emergency team cutting them from his body and were symbolic of the efforts to save his life.

What was most poignant was the one 10 pence piece that had been discovered in the pocket of his jeans, which symbolised the phone call that he should have made, but didn't. Was this all the money he had in the world? I decided to take it with me to London.

Later that morning, prior to leaving for London, I spoke to the gentleman whom I had met at the aforementioned networking event. He said, "It reminds me of the time when I produced a memorial book of the soldier I served with. In addition to discoloured photographs, there was a small box containing a worn passport and identity card, a dog tag, sunglasses, some posthumous military insignia and a bunch of keys. I could not believe that this was all that remained of a person who had made such a positive impact on so many people, be they family or friends."

In September 2009, this gentleman mentioned that he had attended the above soldier's memorial service the previous July and that his parents still hug him when they greet him.

In August 2006, leading up to the fourth year since Kristian's loss, we decided to clear out our attic. I was unaware of how many mementoes of Kristian's childhood there were nestling in the dark, dusty recesses; an old pillowcase across which I'd painted "Kristian, Christmas 1987" and in which "Santa" left all of his presents, a pair of Dennis the Menace braces used to hold up his trousers when he had no waist to support them and, once again, the clothes that he had been wearing on the final day and night of his life in 2002. I buried my face in the lacerated T-shirt that the medical emergency team had cut from him, hoping to smell just a trace of my living, breathing son. For the briefest of moments, I captured his scent and could feel his arms around me, but this was rapidly replaced by the damp, musty aroma that had impregnated the material over time.

All that I could smell then was death, not life. With tears streaming down my face, I replaced the items in the plastic sack and sealed it up to be stored back in the attic once again. They were all that remained of my son in the physical sense and I could not bear to throw them away.

Sometimes it was the most unexpected sights that would send me into flashback mode. At the beginning of October 2006, we took Lauren to an historical museum, which traced life from the Iron Age through to the English Civil War. One section recreated a scene from inside a Roman home and contained four waxwork effigies of a Roman family. Their stiff, inanimate, pallid hands immediately transported me back to the funeral parlour's chapel of rest where we had visited Kristian over the three days prior to his funeral.

It was the sight of his defrosted hands that had disturbed me the most and which were the most shocking indication that the body lying there was just an empty shell and not really my son at all. It was the soul within that had given such dexterity to his hands, the hands that had gripped mine so tightly as a small lad seeking reassurance and security, the hands that had crafted the words, "I love you Mummy" on birthday, Christmas and Mother's Day cards and the hands that had embraced me and patted my back in greeting and departure as a teenager. They were the hands that had gripped me tightly the last time that I saw him alive. Did he know then that he was saying goodbye forever?

I realised that throughout the rest of my life I would be regularly exposed to such memory triggers, all painful and heartrending, but some evoking smiles rather than tears.

Annual school nativity plays move many parents to tears at the best of times, whether their child is a sheep or Mary, has a minor or main role. Just over a month after losing Kristian, my daughter Lauren performed in her nursery nativity play, dressed as an angel.

I still don't know now how I managed to maintain my decorum throughout. It was the combination of cuteness, innocence, Christmas carols, a celebration of new life and memories of Kristian's similar school productions that tore at my heartstrings. I wanted to freeze that moment, to be able to keep my daughter in this place of magical awe and blissful ignorance, safe from the harsh realities of this world. I didn't want her to grow up and be dragged away from her fantasyland where everything was beautiful and had a happy ending. But of course, she would grow up and would have to face both the good and bad situations in life and have her own spiritual lessons to learn.

In the UK every year, the BBC screens Children in Need and Comic Relief, two campaigns aimed at raising funds to help disadvantaged children and families in the UK and around the world. Both programmes show footage of these children and families, many of which are harrowing and have the ability to move the most hardened person to tears. Naturally, when you watch these programmes, you cannot help but think of your own children, not least the child you have lost. In fact, any heartbreaking news story or TV drama involving children is enough to send you spiralling into the depths of grief and remembering.

Wherever you look, there will be memory triggers, even if you shut yourself away from the outside world. When an experience is as painful as losing someone, you don't want to relive it totally and yet escaping from our memories is impossible. We cannot run away from them, so the only way to cope is to face them. By doing so, the reliving of these experiences may not be any less painful, but one becomes more accustomed to dealing with them.

Some psychologists might suggest disassociating that particular trigger with that particular memory and trying to link it to something else more positive, but the part of us that carries guilt may not want to do that, because it would be like erasing a memory of our loved one.

We can try to hide from our pain, or we can choose to face it. It is up to us all to find our own coping mechanisms, but whatever method we choose, our memories can never truly be taken away from us.

Photo compilation and Kristian's baby boots
by Mike Horton

Chapter Thirteen

The Inquest

To endure oneself may be the hardest task in the universe. You cannot hire a wise man or any other intellect to solve it for you. There's not writ of inquest or calling of witness to provide answers.

Frank Herbert

In general and certainly in the UK, an inquest will need to be held following the death of someone via suicide. It is yet another ordeal to be faced by the bereaved families. However, the law does vary in other countries.

An inquest must be held when there is reasonable cause to suspect that the deceased died a violent or unnatural death, or a sudden death of which the cause is unknown or uncertain.

The inquest involves confirming the identity of the deceased and where, when and how the victim came to his or her death. This involves enquiring into more than just the medical cause of death and often involves a wider examination of the circumstances of the death, limited to answering how the death occurred. The inquest is a fact-finding exercise and not a means of apportioning blame for the death. The Coroner's Inquest is neither a civil, nor a criminal trial, even though the hearing is held in an official court of law.

The moment that Kristian died, an inquest was opened, the first part of which involved a post-mortem to ascertain the cause of death. My son no longer felt as though he belonged to me, even though some will say that you never "own" your children, but that they are simply lent to you for a time to nurture and guide until they make their own way in the world.

I was not even allowed to hug my boy. He was no longer regarded as a person, but simply as an object for forensic examination. The inquest also involved piecing together not only the events that led up to Kristian's suicide, but compiling a chronological history of his life to ascertain what sort of a person he was and to highlight any significant events in his past that could have contributed towards his fate. It was the responsibility of the police officer handling the case to write this report, which would be formulated from my answers to his questions. However, in order to avoid any misinterpretation – and to make the officer's life easier – I decided to write Kristian's life history myself. That would give me time to think about past events and ensure that I did not omit any information that may be relevant. What I had written also formed the basis of a memory book that I created as a tribute to him.

The post mortem was not performed until two weeks after Kristian's death. We were only permitted to see him once during that time, four days after his suicide in the hospital's chapel of rest. My dad and stepmum came with me. It was the first time that they had seen him since hearing the awful news. Even then, it was evident that Kristian's body had been tampered with via whatever medical or forensic procedures were necessary. There were spots of blood on his blue gown and there was a trace of brown fluid oozing from the corner of his colourless mouth. It appeared as though his lips were being held together unnaturally, almost as though they had been stapled. They were very different to the softly parted lips that I had seen four days earlier. I didn't ask any questions. Maybe I thought that the answers would be too painful to absorb.

It was the first time that I had ever seen my dad cry and it further splintered my already shattered heart. My stepmum kept remarking on how beautiful and peaceful Kristian looked, which offered some comfort. He was no longer suffering and that is what I had to focus on when the grief threatened to suffocate me.

The coroner told us that because Kristian had used a needle to inject the fatal dose of heroin into his system, his blood would first have to be sent away to a lab to establish whether or not he was carrying any infectious disease such as Hepatitis or HIV. His blood would then have to be sent to another location for toxicology tests to ascertain exactly what substances were in his body and in what quantity. If it had been discovered that he was carrying an airborne virus, then the post mortem would have been performed at another hospital with secure, specialised facilities in order to avoid contamination of the pathology staff. All these processes had to be carried out before it was possible to organise his funeral. In one sense it meant that we could delay saying our final goodbyes to Kristian, but it was distressing in that we did not know to what degree his body would have deteriorated by the time we were able to bury him.

One of the most painful sights was re-visiting him at the funeral parlour the day after family photos and unopened Christmas presents had been laid on him in his coffin, together with a small, cuddly Christmas dog that I had placed in his left hand. To see the presents untouched and the dog resting in exactly the same position beneath his fingers was heartbreaking. His inability to see, to open, or to hold and appreciate these gestures of affection hit me with forceful and excruciating reality. He would never move again, nor laugh, nor hug those dear to him, nor watch his baby daughter grow, nor say to me as he always did when he phoned, "Love you mum". At least he would never cry again.

9 July 2003 was the date set for Kristian's inquest, just over eight months after his death and exactly a year after his release from the young offenders' institution. Until that point, I had felt as though a part of my life was on hold, not just because of the intense grief, but in feeling that until the inquest was heard there were details surrounding the last few days of his life of which I was unaware; his state of mind, his movements and the way in which he had behaved. There was even the smallest of possibilities that a verdict other than suicide might be delivered, although no verdict would have made the loss any easier to bear. I also wanted to be able to hear other witness statements in order to have more insight into the sequence of events on Halloween 2002 prior to his fatal overdose.

My dad and stepmum travelled down for the inquest and my daughter Anneliese and Kristian's girlfriend Millie also accompanied us. The local ITV news had already contacted me the previous day, along with the local newspaper, to ask for my permission to cover the hearing. I gave my consent on the condition that they reported upon the proceedings accurately and did not in any way embellish, sensationalise or fabricate any details.

The TV crew were already waiting outside the court and began filming us as we walked up to the entrance door. It somehow seemed obscene that Kristian had attracted more attention in death than he had in life; that an act of self-harm could create far more media interest than all the wonderful, unsung acts that he had performed in his short life.

As we sat in the reception area of the court, it felt as though we were awaiting the commencement of a criminal trial, where the verdict would subsequently affect our lives in some way. The wait was agonising. The searing heat in the claustrophobic waiting area without air conditioning was suffocating, not helped by the intense emotional atmosphere.

Millie kept saying that Kristian believed she was returning to her flat the night that he took the overdose, as though she had already convinced herself that his intention had not been to succeed in ending his life. Would a verdict of accidental death help to alleviate some of the tremendous guilt that we all felt? If it was a horrible accident, then the "If onlys" would still remain. "If only the neighbour had called an ambulance earlier; If only Millie had returned to her flat instead of staying at her mum's house; If only he had called someone; If only, if only, if only…"

After what seemed to be an eternity, a court usher appeared from a side door to take us up a winding staircase to the circular courtroom. The courtroom contained numerous rows of chairs facing the coroner's table positioned at the front of the room. The same police officer who had delivered the tragic news on 1 November 2002 and who had been in charge of the inquest was present, as were a reporter from the local paper, a broadcast journalist - Derek Tedder - who had accompanied the TV camera crew and the pathologist who had conducted Kristian's post mortem.

I sat next to Millie on the second row, alongside Anneliese, my dad and my stepmum, once more feeling somewhat detached from the situation, like a spectator of a courtroom drama, similar to the sensation I experienced on the day we lost Kristian.

The sequence of events is not entirely clear in my mind. I remember having to stand when the coroner entered the room and I remember Millie beginning to cry as the coroner began to talk about what had happened to Kristian and chronicled the events leading up to the final moments of his life.

Hearing witness statements for the first time was like being held down and tortured. It was clear that his distress was visible to everyone he encountered on that final night.

To hear my son referred to in the past tense was overwhelmingly heartbreaking. "Kristian was this, Kristian was that…"

"He looked as though he had been crying," one person's statement read.

"We heard loud moaning and sobbing noises outside our flat, as though someone was deeply distressed," was the statement from his girlfriend Millie's neighbour.

"Where are you going now?" asked one of Kristian's friends after he had spoken to her in the off licence where she worked.

"I don't know," he replied, "I've got nowhere to go."

That last statement was the most distressing of all; the fact that he felt that he had nowhere to go, that no one cared enough to open their door for him, that his family didn't want him and that he was totally isolated in his misery.

The pathologist was asked to deliver his post mortem report, in which he said that Kristian did not show signs of being a regular heroin user. He said that what Kristian had taken constituted a normal bag of heroin, which in a regular user would not have been enough to kill. He then described what had happened to Kristian's body, which made me realise that when he was found, there was absolutely no chance of saving him. He was already "moribund" (at the point of death) and had bleeding into his brain and lungs. His body temperature was only 22°c and his respiratory rate only three breaths a minute. My son's life had already ebbed away in that inhospitable, lonely stairwell.

The hearing involved the coroner questioning Millie, Anneliese and myself, again trying to establish the life that Kristian had led over the months prior to his death and to ascertain what state of mind he had been in during the weeks leading up to 31 October 2002.

It was apparent that Millie did not believe that Kristian had intended to end his life. She said she felt sure that Kristian was convinced she would be returning to her flat that night and that he was hoping that she would find him and save him. I knew that she did not want the verdict to be one of suicide.

After all witness statements had been read and the questioning was complete, the coroner retired to consider the evidence and deliver a verdict.

When the coroner returned to the room, he read out a summary of events and then explained that a verdict of suicide could only be delivered if there was, what they termed as, "corroborating evidence". If Kristian had not left any suicide notes, then a verdict of "accidental death" would have been recorded. However, the coroner said since Kristian had left two notes that had clearly been written in a coherent fashion when he was not under the influence of alcohol or drugs, his intentions were clear.

He concluded by saying, "I therefore deliver a verdict of suicide."

It was not what anyone wanted to hear, although up to that point we had always talked about him having taken his own life.

A reporter from the local paper approached me immediately after the inquest. I told him about Kristian's final wishes in one of his notes ("....I am not a skag head who od'ed on drugs. This was just the easiest way to kill myself, so make sure it doesn't get printed in the paper, 'Junkie overdoses on heroin....'") and said that in order to respect those and the grief of his family, he needed to report upon events with 100% accuracy. He assured me that this would be done and that if anyone in the editorial department altered his words in any way, they would have him to answer to.

Sadly, sensationalism always takes priority, as proven by the News of the World Hacking scandal in 2011.

Media intrusion is almost inevitable after a suicide and does not cease until the inquest has occurred. One would think that journalist training would include teaching responsible approaches to the reporting of sensitive issues such as suicide, but still the desire for sensationalism and newspaper sales seems to outweigh ethical responsibility.

I owed it to Kristian to ensure that events were reported upon accurately and with the greatest sensitivity to Kristian, Millie, Kayla and the rest of the family. It was for that reason that I contacted them immediately following the tragedy before they had time to contact me. If I told the story first, it would hopefully prevent some apprentice reporter trying to dig around for facts that would then be misreported, misinterpreted or even fabricated. Numerous reports did subsequently appear and still there were points that were completely incorrect, but without my intervention a lot more mistakes would have been made.

The following day, Kristian's photo as a 3-year-old in a wedding suit was emblazoned across the front page of the local paper, along with the headline, "The Scourge". The reporter to whom I had spoken at Kristian's inquest the day before had done an incredible job. Rather than portraying Kristian as a down and out drug addict, he painted a story of a life that had been full of promise and of a fate that could happen to anyone. It was a touching tribute to a lost soul.

The inquest hearing is a gruelling time for families who have lost a child to suicide, or indeed anyone who has lost someone in suspicious circumstances. Shocking information can come to light and one can learn of situations and events that one would rather not have become common knowledge.

Not only is it an emotionally trying time, but it can sometimes feel as though the family are on trial, as in the case of Andrea whose 27-year-old daughter Erika threw herself in front of a train in September 2001.

"If I hadn't been required as a witness, then I would never have attended Erika's inquest. However, I was told that I needed to go in the witness box. I never thought I would stay in there and at one time I refused to go. At that time, I felt so strongly about it that I was prepared to let them arrest me if that's what they wanted. I was told that if the Coroner was having a bad day, this would be the worst thing that could happen.

"As the date of the hearing drew near, I felt a need to know what had happened and in the end we all stayed right through the inquest. When the time came for me to give my statement in the 'box', it felt as if I were looking down on myself, but in hindsight I realise that this was a coping mechanism - as though it were somebody else in the box. It was really awful, but I had to know everything about our darling daughter's last moments. How can something so awful have happened to someone so precious to us? It feels so unreal, so hard to believe.

"Of course, the evil press made our lives even more awful afterwards by the story they wrote; it covered over two pages in our local paper. Our lives were opened up for everyone to see and, as a very private family, what they did was indescribable. Erika was always so very private, so I felt she had been betrayed. I felt extremely angry. Several of our friends and even my husband's boss wrote letters of complaint to the Editor, as they were also disgusted by the graphic detail of the story. I also complained to our local MP, but never got so much as an apology directly from the Editor. Eventually, I wrote to The Press Complaints Commission, but got no joy there either. Needless to say, the local press are not my favourite people.

"This all happened at a time when I felt as though I could very easily have done the same as Erika. I don't recall how long I felt that way, but thankfully something or someone snapped me out of it and now I cope on a day to day basis."

Shona's brother Ethan was found in his home with a fatal shotgun wound to his head in March 2004. However, an inquest was never held, which meant that there were many more unanswered questions than in cases where an inquest is deemed necessary.

"I wish there had been an inquest, because I had – and still have – so many questions that may never now be answered. How for example, could the police assume that he had shot himself when there were no traces of gunpowder on his hands? I know that it sounds as though I am in denial, like so many other families of suicide victims, but I don't know how they can just rule out the possibility that he was murdered. After all, he left no suicide notes, so there is absolutely no evidence that he intended to kill himself.

"Even the autopsy report, which we had to fight to obtain, convinced me that it wasn't suicide, but the police were quite obstructive and even our attorney told us that he did not think there was much point in pursuing the matter.

"The law in this country is crazy. Why is it that some states seem content just to accept the personal opinions of the police or coroner? Does it occur so frequently that they just can't be bothered with all the bureaucracy involved in carrying out an inquest? I was surprised to learn that many coroners also have other jobs or occupations and that it is not necessary for them to be physicians. Their main role is to collect and document information and make decisions based on that information. How can they possibly obtain a full picture without opening an inquest and questioning people who may have crucial information?

"It's not that I can't accept that Ethan took his own life; it's just that I don't believe it. If an inquest had been held and evidence had come to light that proved that it was suicide, then I would accept that.

"The most worrying thing about all this is that there could be a murderer out there somewhere waiting to do the same to someone else. An inquest should be mandatory in all such deaths."

Whilst an inquest is inevitably an emotionally challenging and painful process for the families concerned, it does at least offer the opportunity to piece together some missing pieces of the puzzle surrounding a loved one's suicide. Very rarely will all the pieces be found, or be in place, yet without an inquest this opportunity will be denied, leaving friends and relatives with many more unanswered questions.

The inquest is generally the final chapter in all the practical and legal procedures involved following a suicide. Although everyone feels and reacts differently, for me it was the point at which I felt able to try and move forward with my grief in a positive manner without any outstanding issues hanging over my head. Of course, there were still many unanswered questions and although I would never fully accept what had happened, I could accept that I had received all the answers I was going to get and that dwelling on the parts that remained a mystery was not constructive.

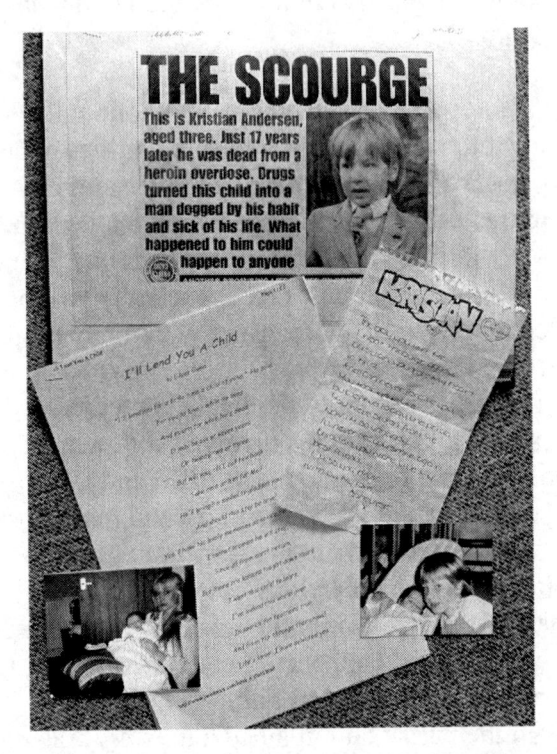

Memories and Newspaper Coverage of Kristian's Inquest

Chapter Fourteen

Handling Insensitivity from Others

"I Expect You're Getting Over It Now"

It's not a cold, it's not the flu.
Would you be "over it," if it were you?

How can you ask so stupidly?
Do you think you'd be "over it," if you were me?

I'm learning to live with it since I'm still here,
But I'll never "get over it," my dear.

It's not the flu, it's not a cold,
It's true my child will never grow old.

How can you ask so insensitively?
Do you think you'd be "getting over it," if you were me?

It's not a cold, it's not the flu.
Do you think you'd be "getting over it by now," if it happened to you?

How could you ask so thoughtlessly?
Honestly,
Do you really expect you'd be "getting over it by now," if you were me?

©Jean Beith

Dedicated to the memory of Jean Beith's very special son Mark who took his own life on 10 August 1993. He was 23-years-old.

In the first few months after Kristian's suicide, I would walk down the street and feel as though those who knew me were staring at me and saying to their companions, "You see that woman over there? Her son committed suicide you know." The truth is that they were probably thinking what an awful tragedy it was and how must I be coping with such unbearable loss. Some of them may also have mistakenly believed that after a few more months, Kristian's suicide was old news and that I would be feeling so much better.

Four months after Kristian's death, I bumped into a gentleman with whom I had ice-skated many years previously. After exchanging polite greetings, he told me that he had seen the coverage of my son's death in the local paper. He then said, "You look well. So, you're over it now then?" I felt like asking him whether he thought I'd just recovered from a cold or some other transient illness, but instead I informed him that I would never "get over it" and that since it had only been four months since my son died, I could not even visualise a time when I might not have a bleeding heart every minute of every day. He appeared not to have even heard what I said and quickly changed the subject before telling me that he had to get on. I thought it strange that someone of this gentleman's mature years should act so thoughtlessly, since it seemed almost inevitable that he would have lost someone in his lifetime, albeit maybe not a child and not to suicide.

Although most people did not voice their opinions to my face, one person had no qualms in talking in a derogatory manner about Kristian, referring to him as "very selfish." She would also frequently contradict herself when attempting to apportion blame for his suicide. In just one conversation with my daughter Anneliese, this person blamed Kristian's biological father, then she blamed my partner and, finally, she blamed Kristian himself because it was a "choice that he made" to take his own life.

When I mentioned this to her in a letter and asked her whom exactly she believed was responsible, she replied, "It is not helpful to blame." Precisely. I think she probably blamed me too, but did not have the courage to say this to my face. The only person she had ever openly blamed in front of me was Kristian's biological father. However, she was the type of person who blamed everyone else for everything that was wrong with her life and her health, never actually wanting to take responsibility for her own situation, which explained why she would wish to point her finger at others for such a tragic event.

Apportioning blame is never beneficial or constructive and it can also tear families apart at a time when they need to rally around and support each other. Similarly, some families may blame the "system", if they feel that it failed their child. Maybe they feel that their child was not receiving appropriate medical treatment for mental illness, or even that the illness was not acknowledged by the medical profession, or by those who might have been in a position to help. If a child was subjected to bullying at school, for example, the family may not only blame the culprits who undertook the bullying, but the education system for not dealing with it effectively. Whatever the reason, blame and anger is the result, which just adds an unbearable burden onto already devastated families.

Another cracking comment that some people feel compelled to offer is, "Suicide is a sin. People who kill themselves go to hell." In fact there are many unspiritual people still living and making people's lives hell on earth, with minds far less pure than those victims whose pain was so great that they saw no solution other than suicide. Those who end their lives often view it as an unselfish act, because they have convinced themselves that they are a burden to others and that they are eliminating that burden from the lives of those they know and love.

One has to view the life that the victim led and the way in which they behaved towards others, rather than judge them on the way in which they chose to die. To talk about heaven and hell in such black and white terms to anyone, let alone those who may not hold the same blinkered beliefs, is extremely spiteful.

My spiritual belief is that we simply learn and make many "mistakes" along the way. Whether we perceive what others do as "good" or "bad" is a personal and human judgement. We were all given the freedom of choice and what happens to us is very much dependant on the choices that we make, both prior to this incarnation and during.

I also believe that you do not have to visit a place of worship to be spiritual. We can talk to our spiritual guides, Angels and God at any time and in any place. They are omnipresent.

Those who are truly spiritually enlightened do not condemn others or judge, irrespective of their beliefs, nor do they try and brainwash others by knocking on their doors and preaching to others in an attempt to "convert" them to their way of thinking. This is something to be remembered whenever any pious individual attempts to preach to you about God, sin or religion.

Sadly, many people are chained within the beliefs and behaviour of others, even though they may query these beliefs in their hearts, afraid that if they dare speak out and question the rules and regulations of their culture, they may attract the wrath of those who are unable to open their minds to any other concept.

Onto the topic of platitudes, following any tragedy the standard line that the majority of people offer is, "I'm sorry." Of course, it is difficult to know what else to say that expresses one's concern to hear such news. However, some bereaved people take exception to this overused expression, as the experience below demonstrates.

Tara's 12-year-old son Anthony took his own life in October 2004. Her thoughts and feelings are highlighted in more detail in Chapter Five, Wearing a Mask, but here she speaks briefly about the seemingly insensitive platitudes offered by others after the tragedy.

"I mentioned to one of my close friends that, 'If one more person says they are sorry, I'm gonna scream.' She looked at me and said, 'Tara, it's not like there is a book out there on suicide etiquette.' She had a valid point. Nobody wants to talk about it, so nobody knows what to say, or better yet, what NOT to say.

"Shortly after Anthony's suicide, (within 48 hours), someone very close to me had the nerve to ask me, 'Do you think it was a sexual thing?' Of course, my response was instantly, 'No, he was only 12!' Then I walked away. I didn't know what else to say and, more honestly than that, I was afraid what they would ask next! That comment still hurts and haunts me. They have no idea how badly that cut. It is probably because of the person it came from. It would have been unacceptable even coming from someone outside the circle, but this person should certainly have known better than to ask something so tacky and tasteless."

Wendy, whose 23-year-old daughter, Claire, took her own life in May 2001 said, "I am not sure how people who think we look so well expect us to look. When people tell me how well I look, I sometimes have to say to them 'Yes, that maybe the case, but you can't see how I'm feeling inside.' Because I chat and smile while talking to them, they think I am so much better.

"The sunshine helps me feel a little better and of course smiling helps, but nothing stops the pain that is going on inside all the time - as you know. I think people hope we are 'getting over it', so that we are not likely to break down or start talking about our child, for that might embarrass them.

"So often in a conversation I end up talking about Claire, for I truly believe she is a huge part of what keeps me going, not the other way around as people seem to think it would be.

"People say to you, 'I don't know how I would cope in the same situation', as though they would never be able to continue living and doing the normal everyday things that people do. Do they really expect us to rush out and do the same as our children, without a thought for the rest of our family, when we have seen how suicide devastates people's lives? What would that achieve? Not coping is not an option. Of course there have been times when we all feel so bad that it must occur to us, (I know it did me), but something thankfully stops us, for our sadness has been caused by one tragic circumstance – our child's death.

"When our children chose to take their own lives, there were probably a number of reasons why they felt that they could no longer tolerate life. Sometimes, maybe there isn't a reason for the hopelessness, such as in some cases of depressive illness when suicide is just an impulsive act committed in a moment of total desperation.

"I tell people that I carry on out of respect for Claire. I tell them that I put on make-up and do my hair, because Claire would want me to look nice. I tell them that everything positive that I do is my way of honouring my daughter.

"Claire had been on the self-destruct path for years, battling with an eating disorder and then self-harming. Our struggle began long before she died and yet so many people fail to see this. Death adds a totally different perspective to how people view you and how they expect you to be coping.

"I have often felt like wearing a sign that says, 'If you don't want me to talk about my late daughter, then don't bother talking to me at all.'

"I have, however, learned to be more tolerant of others' ignorance. I am honest with people I meet. If I am having a particularly bad day I tell them so and if I want to talk about Claire, then I talk about Claire. Those who truly care will stay and listen and those who feel uncomfortable will walk away. At least it has helped me separate the true friends from acquaintances who are only interested in passing the time of day with you when life is rosy."

I soon realised that I would rather people speak to me, in whatever capacity, than have them ignore me completely. Some people whom I had known for many years on a casual basis, such as other mums from the junior school that Kristian had attended, suddenly began avoiding me. Those that had already caught my eye would smile briefly and quicken their pace. I could detect the look of ill-concealed horror on the faces as they realised it was too late to change direction and pretend that they hadn't seen me. I could sense their fear that I may stop them in their path and initiate a conversation that involved the mention of my dead son. I wanted to be able to say to them, "If, for a fleeting moment, you could experience the pain that I'm feeling, you wouldn't ignore me. You'd want to wrap your arms around me and allow me to cry. Your ignorance won't necessarily increase my pain, but speaking to me could possibly make me feel a little better. I might be having a day when I am coping well and can honestly say that I do feel ok, but when you ignore me, I immediately become aware of my open wounds and the pain consumes me once again."

Despite the fact that death is inevitable and that it will touch most people's lives at some point, why are we so incapable of dealing with the bereaved, particularly those who have lost a child or suicide? Is it because child death and suicide goes against the natural order of life?

Is it because the combination of child loss and suicide is just so tragic and unimaginable? Is it because it makes people question the safety of their own children and that by speaking to you, their family might somehow be cursed with the same tragedy? Is it simply because what has happened to you is so unfathomable, that they just don't know what to say?

Agnes's 18-year-old son hung himself in March 2001 and although she admits that she is far from fine, she says that she never tells people how she is really feeling.

"This may sound cynical, but I have come to the conclusion that it's inherent for humans in general to be not just ignorant about issues that don't personally affect them, but largely uninterested. I am afraid I don't bother telling people how I am really feeling anymore, because I sense that they don't really want to know. They only ask me how I'm feeling out of politeness and because they feel they have to.

"Although it's difficult, I keep my feelings locked away and try to forget them when I interact with others. Maybe it's not the healthiest way to deal with the situation, but it's the only way in which I feel able to handle their indifference and lack of understanding to my situation. The only answer that they want to hear is, 'Fine' or 'Ok', so I tell them what I think they want to hear. They don't know how to react to any other answer."

Suzannah's 32-year-old son, James, jumped in front of a lorry in October 1999. She agrees with Agnes. She said, "The only people with whom I am honest about how I am truly feeling are fellow survivors of child suicide. How can anyone else even begin to understand? They treat you as though you have just encountered one of life's everyday hurdles and that you should simply be able to pick yourself up, dust yourself down and carry on.

"And so I do carry on and behave in the way that they expect me to. I know that if I try and explain how I really feel, they won't really understand and probably won't really care.

"That may sound harsh, but it's amazing the number of people who I regarded as good friends who suddenly stopped calling after James died. It's only since I have resurfaced and attempted to resume a normal life that they have appeared again. It does make me want to reassess those friendships and I have to admit that I do feel a degree of animosity towards them. After all, true friends stick by you through thick and thin and more especially during the times when you need them most. Thankfully though, it made me realise who my real friends were and I was lucky enough to have a couple of wonderful friends who were always there in my darkest moments. I shall be grateful to them for as long as I live."

Eight months after Kristian's death, my daughter Anneliese told me that she had heard through a friend that someone had said that Kristian deserved to die. The words this person used were, "All Skag heads *(a term used to describe a heroin addict)* deserve to die". I told her that her friend should have said, "So does that mean that smokers who contract lung cancer or alcoholics who develop liver disease also deserve to die?" There was this mess of a person, staggering around in front of my daughter's friend and probably on his way to death from liver disease telling her that all drug users deserved to die. Was he also talking about himself? After all, alcohol is a drug too and I know for a fact that this guy regularly took ecstasy. More recently, my daughter told me that this lad now sits and watches his own brother shoot heroin into his veins.

Whenever I see a huddle of adolescents awaiting their school bus in the mornings, I wonder how many of them will be lured towards the same grim underworld in which my son circulated. Hopefully none, but almost certainly some. I wonder how many of their parents will experience the same agony and grief that we are currently suffering. I also wonder how many of their parents self-righteously believe that what happened to Kristian will never happen to their children. Unfortunately, my son was not the first victim and will not be the last.

Some blinkered people never look beyond the addiction to analyse why some addicts initially turn to drugs. For some, it is not just juvenile experimentation, but a need to escape from the harsh reality of a very unhappy life.

Our minds operate in a complex manner and we all seek different coping mechanisms for stress. Some people smoke, some people drink alcohol and others develop an addiction to shopping or coffee or chocolate. There is no doubt that some addictions are more harmful than others, but they are still creating dependence, nonetheless. Who can judge whether someone is a better person because they have chosen one vice over another? Thankfully, some people have the strength and maturity to seek more constructive solutions to their problems, but this is when you are dealing with a rational mind and not one that is being controlled by depression.

Thankfully, I am self-employed and work from home and so did not have to face the awkwardness of returning to a mainstream job where I would encounter colleagues for the first time since the tragedy.

With friends and acquaintances that you meet on the street, you have the option of walking away from those who are insensitive to your plight, but how do you handle the same insensitivity in the workplace? You cannot walk away unless you resign from your job and ignoring those who upset you may only heighten your grief through self-induced isolation.

Nevertheless, even in the safe haven of my home office, the internet opened up other avenues for inviting personal attacks. On the anniversary of Kristian's funeral one year, one of the disagreeable individuals mentioned in Chapter One left a particularly offensive message in the guestbook on my suicide support website. For the benefit of the reader, I have corrected the appalling spelling and punctuation of the culprit. It read as follows: "I hate you, you ugly bitch. Why don't you just crawl back into the hole you came out of and die." The perpetrator was foolish enough to sign with his name and location, which ultimately backfired on him. After the message was reported to the appropriate establishments, I temporarily removed the guestbook, along with all the wonderfully supportive messages that all the other visitors had posted. However, not wishing to be controlled by a bully, I reinstated the guestbook, but with greater security controls and a pre-posting approval system to prevent the same thing from happening again.

One of my spiritual friends said: "Your light shines too brightly for his darkness. It's like symbolically shining a light on a vampire or showing a cross to a demon."

Until someone reported him, this person advertised his religious affiliation on Facebook as "Nazi", which simply reinforces other people's views of his distorted psyche.

I feel it important to mention that if, at any point in the future, I should be found physically harmed in any way, the above person will be the prime suspect.

There are a few people who are aware of the identity of this person, but I feel that by documenting this, it may be used as an additional backup for the relevant authorities.

Jenny went back to work just two months after her 18-year-old daughter Sophie hung herself in December 1997.

"I work in a relatively small, friendly office, which is part of a larger company in town and although I was apprehensive about returning to work, everyone was very supportive initially. The moment I walked through the door, several of my colleagues came up to me and asked me whether they thought I ought to be returning so soon, but did everything that they could to ease me back in whilst being aware of my raw grief.

"I had only been back a few weeks when my boss asked me why I had not applied for a position for which I was qualified in the main branch. Although it would have effectively been a promotion and I would have received a salary increase, I explained that I was not emotionally or physically ready for such a role at that time. I also explained that I did not wish to leave the supportive colleagues with whom I worked and move to a place where no one understood my personal circumstances.

"He told me that I ought to be moving forward in my life because I couldn't dwell on something that I couldn't change. He then had the nerve to tell me, 'When my mother died, there was nothing I could do about it, so I just had to get on and make the most of my life. You should do the same.' Tragic as it is to lose your mother, how could it even compare it to my loss? Would he still say the same if he lost a child? Mind you, he and his wife don't yet have any children, so I don't suppose he could even try and imagine how it feels to lose a child under any circumstances, let alone to suicide.

"I was so incensed that I said to him, 'I am sorry for the loss of your mother and I know that it must be difficult for you to imagine how it feels to lose a child, but how would you have felt if your mother had felt so unhappy that she taken her own life?

"'You couldn't prevent what happened to your mother, but with suicide you cannot just move on with your life, because you are trapped in a vicious circle of whys and what ifs?'

"I was almost certain that I would be asked to leave, but instead my boss blushed furiously and mumbled an apology. He hasn't broached the subject since. His comments made me seriously consider resigning. Were it not for the continued support of my colleagues, I am certain that I would now be unemployed."

Heidi works in a busy customer service department, which comprises of a mostly young, female workforce. When her brother Lars shot himself in February 2002, she found that taking six months' compassionate leave made the return to work far more difficult.

"Although six months is not a great deal of time in the general sense, in terms of changes within our office and my rustiness after several months of inactivity, it was a very long time. We work within an extremely demanding environment, taking hundreds of telephone calls daily, many of which are often from irate customers. Not surprisingly, the staff turnaround is very high and many new employees do not stay longer than a few weeks. Although I did not feel that I could have handled dissatisfied customers in the early days of my loss, particularly those whose order problems would have seemed trivial compared to my brother's suicide, taking such a long break did not benefit me long-term.

"The first day that I returned, I could not even remember how to log onto the system, let alone start recording details of phone calls, amending orders and handling a never ending stream of customer queries. Dealing with the basics of the job was bad enough, without even taking into consideration how others were going to react to my loss.

"There were so many new faces; people who weren't aware of what had happened or what I was going through.

"My supervisor and a couple of others whom I knew fairly well before Lars died asked me how I was doing and to take it easy. That made me laugh, because in this role you don't have the option of taking it easy. As soon as you have finished one phone call, there are fifty others waiting. The futility of the sentiment became brutally apparent about a week after I had returned. I had just dealt with a particularly difficult phone call with a customer who seemed only able to communicate with me using a string of four-letter words. I managed to remain controlled throughout the conversation, but when I put the phone down, it became all too much and I burst into tears.

"Later that day, a colleague whom I didn't know too well came up to me and asked, 'How are you really doing Heidi? I can see that you are putting on this false face most of the time and the reason I can see that is because when I look at you I can see myself.' She then confided how she had lost her father to suicide eight years previously. As soon as she said that, I could feel this enormous burden of suppressed thoughts fall from my shoulders. At last somebody understood! What I wasn't prepared for though was learning about other colleagues' reactions to my earlier emotional breakdown.

"My compassionate colleague told me that she felt compelled to come and speak to me after she heard a couple of the other girls say, 'It's been over six months since her brother died. Surely she should be over it now!' and 'I suppose she's going to use her brother's death as an excuse for job incompetence.'

"I was so angry and upset at these insults that I burst into tears again. The only reason I didn't confront these girls was because my newfound friend explained that ignorance creates insensitivity and that one day she believed that people who made comments like that would have the tables turned on them.

"From that moment on, I vowed never to talk to them about my brother, nor break down in front of them, and confined my communication with them to work issues. I accepted that my pain was something that they could not understand unless they too had been forced to live with a similar tragedy.

"The payback came sooner than expected when, around ten months later, one of these girls lost her mother in a car accident. It might not have been the same as suicide, but it was a sudden and unexpected death all the same. This girl did not return to work. I heard on the grapevine that because of the stress caused by the loss of her mother, she did not feel able to resume her job. I sent her a sympathy card with the appropriate words, but I can't tell you how tempted I was to write, 'Never mind, after six months you'll be over it.'"

Unfortunately, there are some uninformed people in this world, which of course is often not their fault, but some of the worst comments have come from those who have allowed their narrow-minded religious beliefs to control their opinions on suicide.

As mentioned earlier in this chapter, some people relish in throwing the "God does not approve" line at those bereaved by suicide. Someone told me that God did not allow people like Kristian in heaven because suicide was a sin. He told me that Kristian would now be spending his time with the devil.

It was one of the rare moments when I was provoked to offer an immediate response without even taking the time to consider what I was saying. I snapped, "That just shows that you understand nothing about depression and even less about God." Obviously a little taken aback by my response, he then said, "I didn't mean to upset you."

I then asked him whether he thought his first comment was supposed to make me feel better about losing my son. He didn't know what to say. Did he think that by making out Kristian to be some sort of sinner that I would feel he deserved his fate? I told him that if his assumption about suicide victims was correct then no one would go to heaven, since we are all sinners and who are we to judge whether suicide is a worse crime than any other?

I tend to distance myself from negative people like that and choose to surround myself with positive souls. I know that Kristian always forgave everyone, but I am afraid that I have limited tolerance towards those who seem to want to provoke a reaction at the expense of my loss. My spiritual side tells me to "let go", but my human side knows how difficult this is. Kristian made mistakes, but he wasn't a bad person. He was kind, loving and caring and I would gladly shoulder his problems if only I were given the chance to have him back again.

There are so many people who feel duty bound to act as messengers of God, deciding what is and isn't a sin and who will go to heaven and who won't. In actual fact, in the spiritual world, there is no right or wrong as such and no sin or Divine judgement (because that is a contradiction to "Love").

There is simply karma, where every thought, word and deed that you send out is recorded. I believe that if people don't have anything positive to say, then they shouldn't say anything at all. Until they have walked in my son's shoes, they cannot possibly criticise. My son should be judged by the kind, caring, compassionate and forgiving boy that he was during the 20 years of his life and not on the few seconds that it took to exit this world.

It is tragic that in addition to our already intense grief, we are subjected to further torment through ignorant remarks of those who really have no clue what it is like to lose someone to suicide.

Although most insensitivity comes from those who are somewhat detached from the tragedy, the suicide of a loved one can also create conflict within the immediate family unit.

Helen's 17-year-old son Aaron died from a heroin overdose in February 2000. Although he did not leave a note, Helen says that he had been very depressed for some months and had said on more than one occasion that he felt he would be better off dead. Helen had spent the previous four years trying to help Aaron in his battle with drug addiction, even to the point of giving up a lucrative career to devote herself to caring for him.

"Although no one dared utter the sentiment before he died, I always felt that Aaron was a burden to everybody except me. I loved him so much and would have done anything, everything, to help him to recover. That's not to say that I never complained. There were many times when I felt frustrated and angry at what Aaron was doing to himself and his family, so I suppose I can understand why others wouldn't have had as much patience, but then again there is nothing stronger than the love of a devoted mother.

"When Aaron died, I couldn't believe that some people had the audacity to say, 'It must be a relief for you and your family.' A relief? My son was dead, for goodness sake. Despite all that he put us through, I would gladly endure the frustration and the exhaustion for the rest of my life, if I could have him back today. If I had the chance again, I might be able to save him. When he was alive, there was always hope, but that hope has been taken away forever.

"The insensitivity of others didn't just extend to the sentiments that they voiced, but their behaviour. Within a few days of Aaron's death, friends and relatives began fighting over his belongings and telling me what they wanted and why they felt they were entitled to it!

"I have never before seen such an outrageous display of selfishness and lack of consideration. This, from people who had practically disowned the poor boy when he became involved with drugs. I could have just given them what they wanted, so that they would go away and leave me to grieve for my son in peace, but I felt that it would be an insult to Aaron's memory to farm out his belongings to people who turned their backs on him when he needed them most.

"I said to them, 'Do you want these things to remind you of the boy you ostracised, or do you want these things out of greed? Either way, it's not your decision. I am not ready to part with any of his belongings at the moment and if and when I decide to do so, I will also decide who has what. Now please respect my grief and leave me alone. You weren't there when we needed you, so I can survive without you now.'"

Shelley's brother Nathan jumped to his death in May 1994. He had just become a father for the first time and his daughter, Ciara, was only 5-weeks-old when he died.

Shelley says that although her niece reminds her of Nathan when he was younger, there is another more dominant side to her that she finds difficult to handle.

"Ciara is rude, spoilt and has no manners. If she can't have her own way, she goes into a sulk and refuses to speak for days to the person who has denied her certain privileges. My sister-in-law, Alex, does discipline her, but even she has a hard time dealing with her a lot of the time, especially since she is a single parent and feels responsible for giving her the love of two parents. She has never been able to maintain a relationship with anyone else since Nathan died and I don't really think she is that interested.

"She loved my brother so much that I think it will be a long time before she is ready to become involved with anyone else. To be honest, I think they would have to have endless patience to cope with a stepdaughter like Ciara.

"We can't even blame her father's death for her behaviour because of course she doesn't remember him, even though Alex talks about him to her all the time. She feels it is important for her to know who her father was and what a wonderful person he was in order to make her feel valued. She also kept a lot of Nathan's belongings to give to her when she is older, even though she just doesn't seem concerned that her father ever existed. Items of sentimental value just don't seem to interest her.

"Ciara has almost reached puberty now and really should be behaving in a more adult manner, but she just seems to get worse.

"I confess that I really don't know how to handle her when she is having one of her spoilt brat tantrums and obviously I cannot discipline her in the same manner that I would my own children, because I am not her mother.

"I have told her that if she doesn't wish to live by our rules when she comes across to stay, then she will have to go home, but she just shrugs her shoulders and I know that I could never actually send her home because Alex needs the break.

"It's not fair of me to say that she is all bad, because she's not. There have been many times when she has snuggled up to me on the sofa and told me how much she loves me. When she says things like that and gazes up at me with her huge blue eyes, I just want to cry because she reminds me so much of Nathan. Unfortunately, the rest of my family aren't as forgiving and tend to ignore her most of the time, even when she is being sweet. I think that is very damaging, personally, and will only make Ciara feel rejected and perhaps even more badly behaved, but I can't tell other people how to feel and act.

"I know that my parents still have a hard time dealing with the fact that Nathan had become addicted to drugs. He was their blue-eyed boy and even when I told them that I thought he had a problem with drugs, they didn't want to believe me and thought that I was trying to cause trouble and diminish their opinion of their 'perfect' son. Even now I think they believe that someone else was responsible for his death and that he would never have consciously chosen to leave us like this. I, on the other hand, believe that he had a problem living up to their high expectations of him and turned to drugs to escape from the pressure. There is a lot of anger within the family and my relationship with my parents has been under enormous strain since Nathan's death.

"I actually believe that they partly blame Ciara for his suicide and the pressure of being a new dad, even though she was only a tiny baby at the time. Maybe they just find it hard seeing her because she looks so much like Nathan.

"It's so sad, because at a time when the family should be brought closer together, a rift has formed and it is becoming wider with each passing day. One expects a level of insensitivity and lack of understanding from those outside the family who have been unaffected by such a tragedy, but you really don't expect it from your loved ones.

"I've never expressed my opinions to my parents, because although they have not given any consideration to anyone else's feelings, I know that they are grieving deeply and I would not wish to add to their grief."

Not only is blame a cause of discord, but family disputes can arise when dealing with the practicalities and processes involved after the death of a loved one. The choices involved in organising the funeral, or the distribution of the deceased person's possessions are just a couple of examples of fuel for disagreements.

Stella's 33-year-old son, Tim, had only been married to his new wife Ally for eight months when he shot himself in July 1998. Tim had a history of depression and had previously tried to take his own life on a couple of occasions when he had been married to his ex-wife Jenny. However, after his divorce five years prior to his death, he seemed to "recover" and after meeting Ally, he returned to the good-spirited, outgoing person that his family had known prior to the onset of his depression.

"The night that Tim shot himself was a complete shock. Of course, all sudden death is a shock, but suicide adds the element of total disbelief, particularly when no one could see it coming. Yes, he had a history of depression and yes, we were painfully aware that he'd attempted suicide on two previous occasions, but he had seemed so well and happy since he had met Ally that this act seemed completely irrational and unexpected.

"And of course, the two previous attempts didn't seem intentional, but just his way of screaming to everyone about how desperate he was feeling at the time. We all assumed that his depression was linked to his unhappy marriage, because it was only when he was with his ex-wife that his depression was diagnosed and after they divorced he didn't appear to have any further episodes.

"It was Ally who found him when she arrived home from work. He was on the kitchen floor, across which ran a river of blood. Ally was hysterical; I was hysterical. I think we were all hysterical. My memories of that day are somewhat vague. Maybe I just don't want to remember, because it is too painful. I recall the horrific howling and screaming that seemed to go on for hours, as though someone was being viciously tortured, but in actual fact, that's what it felt like. It was far worse that any physical pain I'd suffered. I'd give birth without pain relief a hundred times over just to be spared even a minute of that awful emotional agony after Tim died.

"What I do clearly remember, however, is the way in which Jenny behaved. I did not want my ex-daughter-in-law to come to the funeral, not least because of the way in which she had treated Tim when they were married and the fact that she had cast him off when he was at his lowest ebb. However, as someone who likes to see the good side of everyone, I also felt that she had a right to attend should she feel the need. Maybe somewhere, deep down she did have a compassionate, caring side and maybe she did feel some remorse about her previous behaviour. I was in no state to become embroiled in a battle with anyone and, to be honest, I didn't even think that I would even notice who was there and who wasn't. I didn't think for one moment that Jenny would attend purely to cause trouble.

"It was only when I saw her near the front of the church, smirking at me as she draped herself over her new partner that I realised that she was not attending out of respect. I am not an aggressive person, but at that moment I felt like grabbing her by the throat and telling her that she was responsible for my son's death. How poor Ally must have felt, I don't know, but she seemed a lot calmer about the situation. I guess she never really knew the full story, because Tim was not the sort to discuss his previous relationships with anyone, least of all a new partner.

"Even more unbelievably, Jenny and her partner turned up at our house for the wake. I saw it as an intrusion into our lives and our grief. Had she truly wanted to pay her respects, she could have done so at the funeral and then gone home. However, she hovered around asking the most insensitive questions, which were obviously fuelled by greed. She had the audacity to ask my husband about Tim's finances and possessions as though she had a legal or emotional right to something.

"She and Tim did not have any children, so he did not have any heirs and by law, as his ex-wife, she was entitled to nothing. Did she think that we were going to take pity on her and offer her something? She'd already taken his sanity and, indirectly I believe, his life.

"My husband said to her, 'Have you forgotten that Tim was married to Ally and not you?' Her response was a cool, 'They've only been married for eight months. I was married to him for four years.' My husband told her that any legal entitlement that she had was severed the moment the divorce papers were signed. He asked her politely to leave and we haven't seen or heard from her since.

"I still find it hard to believe that people like Jenny exist; people who are so consumed by their own greed that they do not seem to have the capacity to show compassion or respect for others.

"As time has passed, my rage towards Jenny has grown. I was so overwhelmed by grief at Tim's funeral that I wasn't really in a position to confront her. However, I keep hoping that one day I will bump into her again so that I have the opportunity to tell her exactly what I think of her. I am an old lady now and perhaps it's not constructive or healthy, but I feel that it is unfinished business and that until I have done so, I will be tormented by these thoughts and feelings of immense rage and resentment."

Tragedy either brings out the best or worst in people. Sometimes people can surprise you with their generosity and you see a side of them that was invisible before. On the other hand, others whom you previously respected may suddenly turn their backs on you in times of crisis. In Jenny's case though, she fully lived up to Stella's expectations of her and probably even surpassed them with her selfish greed and total lack of compassion. I am certain that at some point in the future Jenny will face her own crisis, but will have no one to turn to for support.

As a result of my son's suicide, I have learned to distance myself from anyone who makes me feel bad, choosing to surround myself with people who are caring and supportive and that is the advice that I would give to anyone who is grieving the loss of a loved one. Of course, there will always be occasions when one has to face negative people, but where possible one should make the choice to avoid such confrontations.

In today's society, blended families are becoming just as common as traditional families. The high rate of divorce means that many people with children from a previous marriage embark on new relationships and the stepparent situation arises. This often brings with it inherent complications, even in families who have not experienced the loss of child, so what happens when a stepchild dies by suicide?

The fabric that makes up stepfamilies is complex and the combinations are endless, which is why the death of a stepchild can create highly sensitive and complicated situations, often causing great pain and evoking unpleasant emotions. There are many factors that come into play, such as the relationship that the stepparent had with the deceased stepchild, how the stepparent is viewed by the stepchild's biological family and with which parent the stepchild lived at the time of the tragedy. Often the stepparent feels that there is no social recognition of the relationship that he or she had with the deceased child, nor that of the great loss that the stepparent is also enduring, irrespective of how much time and love has been invested in the relationship.

Moira and her husband Ron had been together for nine years when Ron's 24-year-old daughter Esmé (from his previous marriage) took an overdose of sleeping pills. Although Ron's ex-wife initially had custody of Esmé, she chose to live with her dad and Moira between the ages of 17 and 19.

When she was 19, she obtained a place at university and had to move 50 miles away, yet still kept in regular touch.

Moira said that she had a built a particularly close relationship with Esmé and thought of her as her own daughter. Moira said that she was aware that Esmé was suffering some financial difficulties, which is always common amongst students, but had no idea of the extent of her debt until after her suicide. Although Moira and Ron helped Esmé out by sending her money, they were unaware that she owed as much as she did. In her suicide note, she wrote that she did not wish to be a financial burden on anyone, but that she could no longer cope with the fear of debt collectors on her back with no immediate way of paying back what she owed.

Moira said that following Esmé's suicide, her friends said that they were all in a similar situation, but that Esmé spent all her time worrying about it and could see no light at the end of the tunnel. She said that Esmé was never frivolous and her debts accrued purely through the extortionate cost of basic living expenses. They all urged her to seek advice, but she was very proud and they believe that she was determined to try and handle the situation herself. It obviously all became too much for her.

Moira said that her anger was manifold. She felt enraged by the "system" with regard to lack of assistance for students who are working towards becoming valuable and productive members of society and she was infuriated by the lack of controls regarding harassment from the debt collection industry. In addition to dealing with these feelings of anger and her deep grief at the loss of Esmé, she had the additional burden of insensitivity from other family members, who totally disregarded her feelings as a stepparent.

"Although Esmé's contact with her biological mother over the past few years of her life had been minimal, other family members gave absolutely no consideration to this after Esmé died. I felt as though I had suddenly become invisible. The entire focus was on Ron (naturally) and Esmé's mother. The only time when I felt included was when someone else was ordering me to do something, as though I was immune to the pain and hence had to be the one who would rally around and do things at other people's command.

"Despite being expected to be the 'strong' one, I had no clout when it came to organising the funeral. I was totally excluded from any discussions regarding arrangements and Ron was too emotionally exhausted to fight my corner. Whenever Ron's sister phoned, she would always ask to speak to Ron and was never prepared to discuss anything with me.

"It wasn't just an insult to me, but to Esmé. I loved her so much. I had never been fortunate enough to have any children of my own, so she was like the daughter I'd always longed for. To me the word 'mother' isn't defined by the fact that you have carried a child in your womb, but more by your actions, your love and the relationship that you build with that child in life. There are many stepparents, foster parents and adoptive parents who invest more time, effort and love into the children in their care than some biological parents, yet this is something that is often overlooked when a child dies.

"Immediately following Esmé's suicide, sympathy cards would arrive at our home addressed to Ron only. Some were even addressed to Ron and his ex-wife, which hurt me deeply. It was actually my own family and friends who were the most sensitive to my grief. They helped me immensely and, were it not for their support, I think I would have had a complete emotional breakdown.

"I am privileged to have had nine years with Esmé in my life and yet my grief was still overlooked by so many. What must it be like for stepparents who have had less time with their stepchildren? Do people assume that there is a set period of time for bonding to occur? What utter nonsense!

"I knew Esmé so well. She told me that our relationship was more like a mother-daughter relationship than that with her biological mother. I was the one she would call if she needed to talk to someone in confidence and she told me things that she hadn't even told her father.

"The most upsetting incident of all was on the day of Esmé's funeral when Ron's family had reserved the front row of the church and told me that there was a place for me further back. Ron immediately intervened and told them that I had been a greater part of Esmé's life than they ever had and that he wanted me by his side in the front row. It's the first time I have ever seen Ron's sister speechless!

"Things were very frosty after that, which is terribly sad. It just shows that tragedies such as this can either unite or separate people. I feel more sorry for Ron than for myself, because it is his family and they should have supported him.

"Essentially, I lost my only daughter, as did Ron. Following the funeral, we pretty much distanced ourselves from all the negative, selfish people in our lives and only chose to associate with our true friends. It was no great loss to me, but I know that Ron was deeply hurt, even though he has not really said much about it. We have continued to support each other and have only just reached a point where we feel that we are beginning to live again, rather than just existing. We know that Esmé would never have wanted us to be miserable, but we do make sure that we visit her grave most days, because we feel that's our way of honouring her.

"What I would say to anyone in a similar family situation who experiences such a tragedy is to acknowledge and respect the grief of the stepparent. To those who are stepparents, I would advise you not to sit back and suffer in silence. Difficult as it may be, it is important to convey your feelings to other members of the family, so that they realise that you also have a right to grieve and to be involved in the funeral arrangements."

Libby's only son Harry took his own life in October 2006 at the age of 15. Libby's husband, Clive, also has two sons from his previous marriage who lived with their mother in a neighbouring town.

Libby said that one of the hardest things she has had to come to terms with is the fact that Clive still has children, even though his devastation at losing Harry was just as severe as hers. Nevertheless, she feels that Clive still has two good reasons to carry on living, whereas her life came to a halt when they lost Harry.

"Harry was the biological bond between us. I'd like to say that I feel the same way about Clive's children as I did Harry, but I don't. They have never really accepted me and several years ago when they were still coming to stay with us every other weekend, they made my life hell. I remember the time when I was expecting Harry as being particularly horrendous. I feel sure that they did everything in their power to make life so stressful for me in the hope that I would lose the baby. Well, I did lose him eventually, although I am grateful for the fifteen years that we were blessed with him in our lives.

"Harry was such a gentle, sensitive young man. I remember how Clive's boys taunted him when Harry was younger and how he just stood there and took all the (excuse my English) crap that they dealt out. Harry did his best to discipline them, but they seemed to have no respect for him either and, for that, I blame their mother.

"Eventually, their behaviour became so intolerable that Clive told them that they were no longer welcome in our home. He told them that he was prepared to go and see them when and if they learned to treat people with respect. I can't tell you how relieved I was and, for almost the first time since Clive and I had been together, Harry and I could enjoy every weekend instead of every other weekend. The selfish part of me didn't want their behavior to change, so that Clive would sever contact with them completely.

"It would be easy for me to partially blame Clive's kids for what happened to Harry and in some ways I do. I know that it was a very tragic and irreversible choice that Harry made, but I know that the bullying from Clive's kids did nothing to boost Harry's self-esteem. He found it difficult to cope with any disharmony in his life and was too much of a gentle soul to ever fight back.

"I don't believe for one moment that any of them are sorry about what happened to Harry and I have never heard any feedback to the contrary. They were not welcome at Harry's funeral. I think I would probably have flattened them had they been there and would have said many things that I may or may not have regretted later. I feel bitter that they are still cheating their way through life, even though I feel sure that their misdemeanors will backfire on them eventually. I just hope that I am still around to witness it. I may sound bitter, but it would give me great pleasure to know that there had been some retribution for the way they treated me and my son.

"Although Clive's relatives were supportive towards him, I still felt like an outcast and my grief was almost overlooked because I wasn't one of their blood relatives, even though Harry was my son too. Whenever his mother or sisters called they would ask how Clive was bearing up, but never thought to ask the same of me.

"On one occasion, his mother must have phoned when I was having a particularly bad day and I remember saying to her, 'At least Clive has his other children to focus on. I've lost my only child.' Instead of acknowledging my grief, she simply replied, 'But Clive has still lost a child too.'

"Eventually, without Clive's knowledge, I sat down and wrote a letter to his family telling them exactly how hurt I felt. I also mentioned the way in which my stepsons had treated Harry, but did not go as far as to say that I lay some of the blame for his suicide at their feet. However, it was implied. Amazingly, I received an apologetic letter from Clive's sister, which was also signed by his mother. Even if the response had not been positive, I would still not have regretted sending it. Sometimes, people act without thinking and if you are honest with them about your feelings, then maybe it will help them to be more sensitive towards others in the future.

"I do feel such empathy for anyone in this situation. Thanks to the internet and Jan's website, I have been able to communicate with other mothers who have sadly endured similar experiences. It is such a relief to know that what I am thinking and feeling is not unusual and that by sharing experiences with those who understand, I have been able to carry on."

As any parent who has lost a child to suicide will tell you, the tears we have shed could fill an ocean and yet we could carry on weeping until eternity. Nevertheless, we will still encounter those who will say, "It's been xx years now. Isn't it time you let go?" There's another worn out phrase, "let go". What do they mean by that? Do they mean that we should stop feeling sad, or stop missing our child, or stop loving him or her? Our tears show that we still feel all of the aforementioned and more.

"Of course, you can always have more children" is another classic statement that I have heard uttered on many occasions to those who are still of childbearing age. It's as though our lost son or daughter was some sort of worn out commodity that could be replaced by a newer version.

Just a couple of weeks after Kristian died, someone asked me whether I was considering having another baby to "replace Kristian". Replace him? I responded by saying that nothing and no one could ever replace Kristian; that he wasn't some inanimate object of limited value. I could have another child, yes, but that child would never be a replacement for Kristian. Another child would be a very much loved individual in his or her own right, not some substitute that I would attempt to mould into a clone of Kristian. In fact, I did become pregnant again – though not planned – in December 2004. Very sadly, I experienced a miscarriage on 13 March 2005, but even then, the pain of losing a child I had never seen did not compare to the pain of losing my son to suicide.

I tell people that the healing process after losing a child can be compared to the healing journey after having an essential part of your body amputated. You have to learn to live without that element in your life. The emotional and physical scars will always serve as a reminder of what once was and what will never be again. A part of you will always be missing. I even believe that "healing" is the wrong word to use. We adjust, but we can never heal. The wound might not always be visible to others, but we can still feel the pain.

Instead of making unqualified judgements, those who know someone who is bereaved, or suffering from depression, or struggling with drug dependence or encountering any other problem should be asking, "How can I help those in need?"

They shouldn't give the bereaved a deadline for "getting over it" because they will grieve for their children until the day they die. They shouldn't tell them that they should be "getting back to normal", because life will never be normal again. They shouldn't tell them that they "have to get on with their lives", because that is not a concept that they can possibly imagine when they have lost someone so precious. You have to grieve to your timetable and not someone else's. Burying your grief to suit someone else's schedule will only cause more damage in the long-term, both emotionally and possibly physically.

People make casual, jocular comments about dying or killing themselves if something in their lives does or doesn't happen. Although not intended to hurt, people throw around comments like that without realising the impact it has on anyone who has lost someone to suicide. It's a comment that is generally made with regard to some highly insignificant occurrence e.g. "If I have to listen to her going on about her ex-boyfriend once more, I'll kill myself" or "She's got a figure to die for."

Is it this frequency of use that causes people to ignore the real threats from those who are genuinely feeling desperate enough to want to end their lives?

There are so many forms of insensitivity, some of which we bereaved parents may even have been guilty of ourselves before the tragedy. Although we have to exercise understanding, because few people intend to be thoughtless, we also have to educate.

The media are also to blame for gross insensitivity towards the bereaved. They are excited by the prospect of an attention-grabbing headline, particularly when there is a death via suicide or murder, for example. Misreporting of some facts and total fabrication of others can cause great distress to grieving families. More on this topic has been covered in the previous chapter, The Inquest.

There are many books for the bereaved, but few that deal with the issue of how to behave in the presence of the bereaved. After all, who would buy a book like that in advance so that one could prepare for such a tragic eventuality? Not many. People want to focus on life, not death. The topic of death, naturally, makes people feel uncomfortable and to start preparing oneself in advance of a tragedy that hasn't yet occurred is somehow macabre.

I hope that, in some small way, this chapter in particular may help some readers to think more carefully about what they say and how they conduct themselves when communicating with anyone who has experienced such an unspeakable loss.

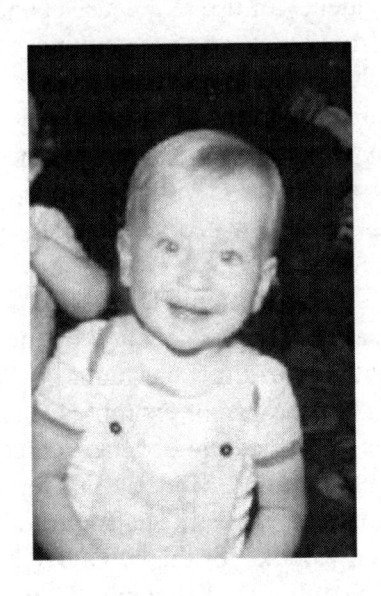

Kristian, aged 15 months

Chapter Fifteen

Firsts of Everything

I think he wants you to use the anniversary of his death to celebrate his release into happiness. It's like he got to go to Disneyland.

I began writing this chapter on 14 February 2003, the first Valentine's Day since Kristian's suicide. On the night of 13 February 2003, I lay awake silently crying, feeling not only my own pain, but also that of Kristian's girlfriend, Millie. How empty her arms must feel on a day when families and loved ones exchange tokens of affection and openly demonstrate their feelings for one another. Although it is traditionally a day when our hearts are open, both to giving and receiving affection, newly bereaved parents may only be able to focus on their shattered hearts and images of their lost child.

Whilst Kristian's death highlighted the importance of cherishing close family and friends and demonstrating my love on a daily basis, I still felt this emotional detachment. I wanted so much to hug and love my partner and yet each time I felt his arms around me, I was overwhelmed by feelings of guilt. I felt that I was unworthy of such affection when my son was the one who had needed warm, caring arms around him at the moment when his desperation caused him to end his life prematurely. Perhaps I was punishing myself, but it was what I felt I deserved.

As I entered the cemetery on Valentine's Day, I was greeted by an almost surreal array of helium balloons that danced in the breeze above the graves. They were like an empty invitation to a party that would never be; at least not on the earth plane.

An ethereal aroma of fresh flowers saturated the air and a sense of peace engulfed me. Was it Kristian's presence that I sensed, or was I being comforted by all the souls surrounding me in this place of rest?

Kristian's daughter Kayla's first birthday on 10 November 2002 was the first of all firsts, just 9 days after her daddy's tragic departure from this world. Millie still held a first birthday party for her at her mother's house where she lived following the tragedy. I don't know how everyone managed not to fall apart on a day that should have been shared and celebrated with Kristian.

When I arrived to a house full of Millie's family and some of Kristian's closest friends, Kayla was sleeping in her pushchair, completely oblivious to everything that was happening, or had happened. My heart broke for her, knowing that she would probably grow up with no real memories of her daddy, only photos and anecdotes from her family. I gazed at her with my back to everyone else in the room to hide the tears brimming in my eyes, afraid that should I start crying, I would never stop. I could sense Kristian's presence everywhere, because Millie's mum's house was one of the last places Kristian had visited before he decided to take the fatal overdose on Halloween. Maintaining my decorum whilst engulfed in a dark cloud of grief was inexplicably tough.

When I sat down, Millie's cousin Amanda introduced herself to me. She told me that Kristian had been her best friend. She was so warm and friendly and I was desperate to learn more about the life of my son from those who had spent far more time with him than I had over the past four years of his life. I learned how popular he was and how everyone described him as "such a happy lad", something that I would hear on many more occasions over the following weeks.

Amanda told me that on a few occasions she had noticed that he had suddenly gone quiet and was deep in thought, but as soon as she asked him whether he was ok, he would always smile and say, "Yes, yes, I'm fine."

She told me how she looked after Kristian for two weeks when he decided to go "cold turkey". There was this young mum with three children of her own taking on what would be an enormous responsibility even for a professional. I felt ashamed and useless as a mother for not being the one who should have been there to help him, yet I knew that he would never have wanted me to know about his secret life. In asking me for help, he would have had to admit to succumbing to something that, as a parent, I had been so against and had fought so hard to warn my children about. I could see his reasoning. If he could conquer his addiction without my help, he might never have to tell me about it.

How excruciating it was to hear from Amanda, Millie's family and Kristian's other friends about how kind-hearted and caring he was. It also hurt to hear about how depressed he had seemed in the two weeks leading up to his suicide. In my agony, I convinced myself that it would have been easier to bear if everyone had slated his character.

Millie's mum told me how, on the evening of Halloween following Kristian's visit, she had gone into the bathroom and cursed Kristian because he had left two fish stick wrappers in there instead of putting them in the bin. Although such an insignificant incident, it made me smile, reminding me of the times when I would discover chocolate wrappers and worse stuffed underneath his mattress, because he couldn't be bothered to take them downstairs and put them in the bin. She also told me about the time when Kristian had gone out and left a cigarette for her on the arm of the sofa with a little note underneath. One absent-minded action would be balanced by a thoughtful gesture.

When I finally left, I felt as though I had had the briefest glimpse into Kristian's world and realised that there was so much about his life that was alien to me and also alien to the life that he had led when he was still living at home. It reinforced my belief about how little control one has over their children once they begin to lead independent lives. It also made me incredibly fearful for the wellbeing of my other three children.

Christmas 2002 was Kristian's first in heaven and our first in hell. At the time of Kristian's death, the irrepressible greed of the retail businesses was already evident from the premature garish displays of sparkling baubles, tinsel and often tacky Christmas characters adorning many stores. Worst of all were the heartrending Christmas carols and songs about loneliness that the stores seemed intent on blasting out continually over the PA system. Silent Night had always been one of those carols that brought tears to my eyes, but now I could not even listen to it without sobbing.

The retail sector seems to forget to cater for people who are grieving. That first year that I remember thinking how wonderful it would be to have a Christmas-free zone where I could shop without having constant reminders of a time of year that should be joyous, when one spends time with their families, but that for me, that would mean the presence of one less person and one more empty chair. Walking around the supermarket, or any store for that matter, was unbearable. I remember wanting to run out and cry, but instead felt as though an invisible hand, the coping hand, was slowly pushing me through this torture chamber, forcing me to experience this pain and to show me all the things that Kristian would never again be able to enjoy.

I can't even remember now whether I bought Christmas presents and cards for everyone, but I am certain that I did. I was functioning on autopilot at that time. My body performed the actions it was supposed to do, even though my mind was elsewhere. It was like two people living in the same body. One part of my mind was still able to make rational decisions that enabled me to keep living and take care of my family, but there was this other part could concentrate on nothing except the tragedy and my grief. It is a state of being that I still feel now, yet find difficult to put into words because it seems such an impossible concept in the physical sense, but not the spiritual.

That first Christmas was horrendous. However, I had to do my best to make the day as magical as possible for Lauren. I didn't think I could bear to put up the tree, but I did it for Lauren. I also strung up the "Thinking of you" cards, although was amazed by the tactlessness of people who still sent cards saying, "Have a wonderful Christmas" and similar. I am sure that people did not mean to be so careless, but probably got caught up in the robotic mindlessness of Christmas preparations and automatically wrote out cards to people on their list. How indicative that is of our world today, when no one has time to stop and give much thought to what they are doing, nor to consider those for whom Christmas is a tremendously difficult and poignant time.

Nevertheless, I still bought Kristian a card wishing him a happy Christmas wherever he was. I also bought him a bear, which I gave to Lauren to "look after" for him. It now sits on her bed during the daytime and under the duvet with her when she sleeps. He is called, simply, "Kristian Bear."

On Christmas morning I did not want to get out of bed. I wanted to sleep until the day had passed by to spare at least some pain, however insignificant. Again, I thought of Lauren. This was her day. I wrapped myself up in a grey dressing gown that I had never really liked, but its colour accurately represented my mood. The only thing I liked about it was its blanket-like softness, which provided me with some physical comfort, if not emotional.

I do not even remember what I received that Christmas, but I do remember weeping as I gazed at the pile of unwrapped gifts illuminated by the twinkling tree lights. To me the lights represented birth and death. As one startled twinkling, another stopped. I tried to view it the other way around. The ones that stopped twinkling represented our life here on earth; the darkness, the sadness, the hardship. The lights that twinkled represented the pure love and light of the spirit world. That was where my son was. I had to try and find the smallest comfort wherever and however I could. Of course, it was a joy to see Lauren open her gifts, as she was always appreciative of everything that she received and I visualised Kristian there with us sharing his sister's delight.

As soon as we had finished eating breakfast, my partner took Lauren to see his family 25 miles away, leaving me on my own. This was something that he did every year, although in my ignorance I assumed that this year would be different, given that I was in the depths of grief. When I mentioned the fact that I thought he would be with me all day, his response to me was, "Well, you're not going to enjoy Christmas anyway, so it doesn't matter."

That is one of the most insensitive statements he has ever made in the history of our relationship, although I am sure he didn't intend it to be hurtful. I think I was too shocked and distressed to even bother replying.

My partner and daughter did not return until 3pm that afternoon, by which time I did not think I had any more tears left in me. I sat and thought about the Christmas that Kristian had spent on his own, believing that no one wanted him. I told myself that it was my penance to suffer in the same way. For that reason, I was grateful to have been left alone.

I do not remember a great deal more about that first Christmas, with much of each day passing in a fog. My mind was still trapped at 1 November 2002, the day on which the normal routine of my life came to an abrupt halt, when everything was thrown into a disorganised, broken mess like the aftermath of a hurricane. Nothing made sense any more.

In the week leading up to what would have been Kristian's 21st birthday on 22 March 2003, I was engulfed in a huge cloud of incredible sadness and despair. The joy of the new life about to emerge from within me 21 years earlier contrasted violently with the sorrow that I felt. Everything I saw, heard or thought about made me want to sob uncontrollably. Even the sunshine and beautiful spring flowers beginning to blossom made me aware of the simple joys that Kristian would never again experience with me. Just a few minutes after his birth on 22 March 1982, as he gazed with alert eyes from his Perspex cot, little did any of us know that 21 years later we would be honouring his coming of age at his graveside.

Two days before his birthday, my mum sent through a Happy 21st Birthday card to place on his grave. Just seeing the name "Kristian" on the envelope pierced my already splintered heart. I cried out loud. The pain was so intense, I wanted to scream, but Lauren was already alarmed by my sobs, so as always, I shut down the part of me that allowed me to feel.

I thought about Kristian whilst keeping the lid on the box of pain and anguish firmly locked. It was the only way that I knew how to prevent myself being suffocated by the grief and the only way that I knew how to protect my daughter from the sorrow. I was so conscious about not wanting her to feel that she had done something to make me unhappy. However, for a 3-year-old, she had amazing powers of understanding. Whenever she saw me crying, she would ask, "Are you sad about Kristian?" She would then smile her most beautiful and sweetest smile that pushed her cheeks up towards her huge blue eyes, making them fold into shiny half moons.

In some respects, Kristian's birthday was one of the worst firsts, because his birthday was something that was individual to him. Everyone was aware of my sadness at Christmas, a time that is difficult for many people, but it was only close friends and family who were aware of the date of Kristian's birthday. It would also have been his "coming of age" birthday, although I feel sure that it was a happier birthday on the other side than it would have been had he survived.

As I stood at his graveside, I cast my mind back to the same day 21 years earlier when he had been born; what an exciting and happy day that was. Had I known back then that I was only going to have him for 20 years, I feel sure that I would have done some things very differently. Clichés such as "Live for today, because you never know what might happen tomorrow" and "Never part on an argument" suddenly became so much more significant. They are also philosophies that I have attempted to live by since losing Kristian. There are so many things in our lives that we take for granted, such as waking up each morning and expecting our loved ones to do the same.

Unfortunately, on the morning of 1 November 2002, Kristian never woke up and I would never have another opportunity to tell him all the things I had failed to tell him, or had not told him enough, when he was alive.

Mother's Day fell on 30 March 2003, just 8 days after Kristian's birthday; another first. Despite cards and gifts from my other children, the absence of a card from Kristian pierced my heart once more. I searched through the filing cabinet and pulled out an enormous Mother's Day card that Kristian had sent me a couple of years previously. In it he wrote, "I love you lots and lots and lots, Kristian xxxxxxx" So much love. I wondered whether he had ever felt that he was loved as much in return. I traced my fingers across the letters, which were a sign that he had once been so full of life and love and tried to feel what he had been feeling when he wrote them. Was he seeking acceptance or confirmation of my love for him, or was he simply expressing his unconditional love for his mum? Whatever, I was so thankful for being a hoarder and keeping items whose sentimental value far outweighed the monetary value of the most luxurious items in the world. There was nothing on earth more precious than something that had been created by hand with a child's love.

I thought about all the mothers who had lost children, especially those who had lost their only child and all the children who had lost mothers. It was on a day like this that suicide was such a hard word. Suicide seemed like a total disregard of love, yet I knew that those who were victims would never have viewed it that way. It is a sickness that swamps rational thought and actions. For some, the logic comes in the belief that what they are doing is for the good of all and that they are doing it out of love, not in spite of it.

Easter came and went that year. It was the one event that held no real significance to me in terms of my memories of Kristian, apart from the giving of Easter eggs and so was probably the least harsh of all the firsts.

My birthday on 6 June was another heartrending time. It was also a day on which my grief was shared with the general public, because the local BBC news' team had chosen that day to come and film me talking about the tragedy of losing a child to suicide and the issue of drug use. I felt that I was channelling my grief into something positive and using the poignancy of the day to raise awareness of drug abuse and suicide, in the small hope that it may just prevent one more tragedy.

The cameraman and broadcast journalist took me to the block of flats where Kristian had been found on the morning of 1 November 2002 and filmed me laying a bunch of flowers outside the door to the building, which was locked. They briefly interviewed me there, before conducting a lengthier interview in a café in town. I provided the team with a list of statistics, which they used in the programme as a prelude to Kristian's story. They also took away a copy of a photo of Kristian holding Lauren when she was a year old, which they magnified on screen and used to wrap up the item.

In giving a TV interview, I had the advantage of presenting the facts and my feelings firsthand, rather than relying on some second-rate newspaper reporter misquoting me and fabricating details to try and over dramatise the story. As always when attempting to articulate Kristian's story in a composed manner, I kept the lid on my emotions firmly shut, but in such a way that I was still able to convey my thoughts with feeling.

That same evening, the story was broadcast on the local news. At the end, when Kristian's photo filled the screen, I wept. If only he could have commanded as much attention in life as he had in death.

Father's Day 2003 fell on 15 June. This was another of those days where I felt for Millie and Kayla. This would have been the first Father's Day that Kayla would have shared with her daddy, because on his first Father's Day the previous June, he was still a few weeks away from being released from the young offenders' institution. I don't think the rest of the family even considered that this was another particularly difficult time. Had they all forgotten that Kristian was a dad himself, even though it had been for such a short time? Of course, I never mentioned anything to anyone. Perhaps they did all think of him, but just didn't feel it was necessary to phone me.

Anneliese, Millie, Kayla and I met up at the cemetery. It tore at my heart to watch Kayla toddle over to Kristian's grave and place down a card and a glass heart that was inscribed with the words, "I Love my Daddy."

It would be unrealistic of me to believe that Kayla would ever have any real memories of Kristian, only those memories that others relayed to her. Although she would have no memories of giving her dad a card and gift in person, would she still find it difficult having to endure that gut-wrenching scenario of watching other children making cards for their dads at school? Although I hoped that Millie would meet someone lovely whom Kayla would regard as her daddy, I wondered whether she would ever experience regret at never having had the opportunity to get to know her biological father. Would she ever feel angry with him for never giving her the chance to know him? These are only questions that will be answered in time.

Kayla's christening on 7 September 2003 was another incredibly emotional first. The christening was arranged at the last minute by Kristian's girlfriend Millie and her mother. In fact, as a result of my daughter Anneliese forgetting to tell me about the christening the week before the event, I was only informed two days beforehand. For that I am strangely thankful.

I had less time to dwell on the pain of Kristian's absence at this very special day in his daughter's life.

Kayla looked like an angel. She wore a beautiful white christening dress, with a photograph of Kristian pinned to her underskirt. Her fine blonde hair had been gathered into two tiny ponytails on the top of her head and she wore a silver christening bracelet on her right wrist. Kristian would have been so proud of her. No, Kristian *was* proud of her.

My mum, Anneliese, Carsten and I sat behind Millie and Kayla in the second row of the church. I tried so hard not to weep, but it was impossible. The most painful parts were where any references to "father" had been removed from the clergyman's speech, although he did mention Kristian during the service, which brought some comfort.

Shortly after Kayla's christening, when the air began to chill and fallen leaves in mingling hues of rust, yellow, orange and red signalled the end of the summer, I began to experience anxiety and dread. The season of my son's passing had arrived. Each time I thought about the anniversary, I experienced a sickening and tightening feeling in my chest, as though I were about to have a panic attack. Total fear engulfed me. Until the anniversary, I could still say, "This time last year Kristian was alive." I dreaded no longer being able to say that.

One of my virtual friends, who lost her only son to suicide in October 2000, sent me these comforting words immediately prior to the first anniversary of Kristian's departure:

"I think he wants you to use the anniversary of his death to celebrate his release into happiness. It's like he got to go to Disneyland. That's where he wants you to picture him when you think of him; riding the rides and laughing with joy and freedom with no cares.

"After mourning him deeply on October 31st, on November 1st Kristian wants you to take time to be by yourself; light a candle in his favourite colour, close your eyes and walk through Disney's gates where he is waiting with open arms and a big smile. After a long hug and looking into each other's eyes, picture yourself getting onto a ride together. He will have his arm around you...and the joy you feel is the joy he feels every day now. And your joy will add to his. And whenever you feel down at any time after that, and you will many times, just close your eyes and take another ride. I can feel how much Kristian loved you. The two of you had a special bond. Love is the only thing that survives when you die. Everything else is not of God, so it falls away as we leave the earth plane. Kristian only feels love and he wishes the same for you."

A week before the day that I had been terrified of facing all year, I ordered some helium balloons from a local party store. Not considering any environmental impacts, I had planned to release them at Kristian's graveside on 1 November 2003 attached to little notecards containing his photo and instructions to return the cards to me, saying when and where they had been found. None of them were ever returned and I wondered whether anyone had actually read any of them, whether they had landed in some obscure location, or had simply been ignored as another piece of discarded litter stuck in a hedge.

Some people may wonder how anyone could benefit from releasing tagged balloons and littering the countryside, but bereaved people don't always think rationally. At the time, they want to do anything to honour their child and anything that may offer the smallest degree of comfort. In some, there is also a desire to let the world know how special their child was, because no one will ever again have the opportunity to discover this for themselves.

All the people that their child may have encountered during their lifetime will never know that he or she existed. Until one has the strength to put effort into something positive like establishing a charity or website, or organising a fundraising event, it is important to take small steps each day and do whatever one needs to do in order to cope, even if that means being environmentally irresponsible just once in your lifetime.

Late morning on 1 November 2003, my partner, Lauren and I loaded up the car with the yellow and blue balloons and went down to the cemetery. At 12 noon, I released the balloons one at a time, because it must have been around that time that the medical team who tried to save Kristian's life realised that there was no hope. I watched the wind grab each balloon and carry it upwards, equating it to the life quickly ebbing from my son's body. I watched until the balloons became mere specks in the atmosphere and were no longer visible to the naked eye.

We were in the car on our way back from the cemetery when the clock struck 12.20pm; the official time of Kristian's passing. As I often did, I gazed up into the clear sky at some birds spiralling gently upwards and my spirit was up there with them, feeling the freedom that my son felt in the moment that he found peace and was released from a body and mind that had become too great a burden for his soul.

At the end of that first anniversary, I felt somewhat relieved that I had managed to get through what I imagined would be one of the worst "firsts." It was only in subsequent years that I realised that the second, third, fourth and so on, ad infinitum, are just as painful.

Of course, the "firsts" don't end after the first Christmas, Easter and birthday. There will be many more firsts in the years that follow; perhaps the first trip back to a holiday destination that you last visited when your child was alive, the first time you venture back into the church or building where your child's funeral was held, or indeed any activity that you undertake or place that you visit for the first time following the tragedy.

When we took our daughter Lauren to Legoland for the first time, it was also the first time that we had been there since the tragedy. The last time we had visited, a couple of years before Lauren was born, Kristian had been with us. Although he was 15 at the time, he still possessed the enthusiasm of a small child when presented with the vastness of such an adventure playground and all its endless possibilities for exploration and enjoyment. In fact, he was far more enthralled by the toddler play areas than he was by the more stomach-churning rides for older children. The most outstanding memory I have of him that day is contained within a single photo of him attempting to squeeze his body into a small, wooden horse attached to the ground by a large spring, allowing it to move with ease when an excited toddler was sat in it rocking to and fro. I recall my partner and I chuckling in amusement as we watched him from a distance.

Returning to Legoland with those memories was both heartwarming and heartbreaking. There had been few changes and the children's playground remained as it was when we were last there, including the same rocking horse that had previously captivated Kristian's curiosity. I spoke to him in my head and visualised his spirit walking beside us and enjoying the rides with Lauren, in an effort to find some comfort on what could very easily have been a difficult and harrowing day.

There have been countless other "firsts" since that trip, all of which bring different memories and stir a gamut of emotions. I am sure that there will be many more. As bereaved parents, we have to try and use these memories in a positive way, as a celebration of our children's lives rather than just a time to grieve.

Kristian, aged 16

Chapter Sixteen

The Domino Effect – Is Suicide Contagious?

It is better to fail in originality than to succeed in imitation.

Herman Melville

Most people have heard of mass hysteria, a phenomenon where a large group of people exhibit the same state of violent mental agitation. It can cause large groups of people to fall sick at the same time, with no apparent underlying medical reason for their symptoms. There has been much debate about a similar phenomenon called Suicide Contagion, whereby suicides appear in clusters within the same community or families. An example of this is the spate of suicides - the majority by hanging - of young people in Bridgend, South Wales, beginning in 2006. All of the victims were linked in some way, whether via friendship or family. According to some reports, suicide has become a fashionable trend that has somehow been glorified via social networking sites. Several of the victims had pages on Bebo and had posted messages in each other's virtual books of condolence.

There is no denying that there are incidences of suicide that occur in clusters, but not everyone who comes into contact with suicidal behaviour "catches" the desire to do the same thing themselves. There are many factors that one has to take into consideration. When more than one family member, for example, dies by suicide, it could simply because the pain of losing a loved one was too much to bear, or there could be a family history of depression. This is completely different to "copycat" suicides.

Some studies suggest that there is a correlation between reporting of suicide in the media and subsequent suicide attempts. At the Suicide Prevention 2000 symposium, Dr. Madelyn S. Gould, professor of psychiatry and public health at Columbia University's College of Physicians and Surgeons in New York said: "New studies show that the incidence of 'copycat' and clusters of suicides, which occur most often with adolescents, increases after extensive newspaper or television coverage. Suicide contagion does not occur in individuals without other risk factors, which include pre-existing mood disorders such as depression or bipolar disorder, a family history of suicide, aggressive behaviour, substance abuse and impulsivity. Imitating a suicide appears to be more likely if a news story provides details on methods, minimises the influence of mental illnesses, and portrays the victim in heroic or romantic terms."[2]

Without doubt - and from personal experience - other people's thoughts and emotions can affect how you feel. If you do not have healthy emotional boundaries with someone else, whether it is a friend, relative or work colleague, your emotional energies will often become enmeshed. As a result, you could end up feeling emotions that do not even belong to you and which actually come from the person with whom you are interacting. If someone else's emotions are entering your aura, you will probably be emotionally unstable and irritable. Similarly, if your emotions are going into someone else's aura, they would experience these emotions. Therefore, if you do not have healthy emotional boundaries with someone who is feeling suicidal, then you too could take on these feelings. This could be another explanation for suicide contagion.

Naturally, this is one of those topics where debate will rage on, with different conclusions being drawn from year to year based on new studies by various research bodies on different segments of the population, on people of different ages of different psyches, from different social circumstances and exposed to different types of stimuli. I am not professionally qualified to pass judgement on this issue, nor do I wish any part of this book to be an academic study of suicide. The most rational comment that I can make is that it is very difficult to reach a definitive answer, because everyone is an individual and the circumstances surrounding every suicide – whether occurring singly or with others – are also very different. What I can do, however, is to present personal stories and opinions of others.

Stefanie's 27-year-old brother Michel killed himself in April 1996 after suffering from, what Stefanie believes was, undiagnosed depression. He drove his car over the side of a cliff bordering a mountain pass in Switzerland.

"In September 1985 I had attempted suicide myself, so I have an understanding of the hopelessness a person feels when they see death as the only way out. I won't go into the full reasons why I was depressed, but I took an overdose of antidepressants and it was my brother who discovered me before I lapsed into a coma. I still remember Michel alternately hugging me and shaking me to keep me conscious whilst we waited for the ambulance. He kept saying, "You idiot, you idiot. Don't you know how much I need you?"

"He never left my side. My parents and other family members came and went, but Michel was there the whole time. He was only 17 at the time and yet he saved my life and was far more supportive than either of my parents.

"I now feel as though I failed him, because I could not return the favour. Why couldn't I see he was depressed? Why couldn't I prevent him from dying?

"I blame myself totally for Michel's death, despite other people telling me that there was nothing I could have done. When I left hospital following my suicide attempt and for a long time afterwards, the focus was on me. I think that my family were so afraid that I would do the same thing again that they watched me like a hawk. As a result, I now believe that Michel was suffering in silence. There were times when he didn't appear to be himself, but when I asked him if he was ok, he would always say that he was fine. I suppose he didn't want me to worry when he believed that I was so fragile myself.

"Some people might ask why he then killed himself if he was telling me what an idiot I was. The thing is that depression is not something that you can control. No one chooses to be depressed after all. If it were that easy to control, suicide would not exist.

"I still ask myself though whether I planted the idea into Michel's head. I have also considered whether suicidal tendencies run in families, or is it just personality traits and someone's inability to deal with stressful situations that are inherited and so predisposes them towards suicide?

"I know that my mother had a nervous breakdown when she was in her early twenties, but it was just a one-off episode from which she fully recovered. As far as I am aware, she hasn't suffered from depression since and I have always known her to be a very strong woman who seems to be able to cope with anything that life throws at her. My father, on the other hand, seems to be terminally gloomy, although I wouldn't say that he was depressed. He just has what he calls a 'realistic outlook on life', whereas I just regard him as an eternal pessimist.

"He is the only person who will not accept that Michel's death was self-inflicted, even though we found an unfinished suicide note in his flat. I don't call that being realistic. I call that being in denial.

"I don't believe that suicide is contagious, even though I had a few friends who avoided me after Michel's death. I think that was more because they didn't know what to say to me rather than feeling that I was a bad omen. I'm sure that suicide may appear to run in some families, but then again you could say that about a lot of other things such as murder, or divorce, or even illnesses that aren't known to be hereditary.

"My belief is that we all create our own fate, but because we are all unique, each of us will make choices and face situations in a different manner. What one person views as an insignificant problem that can be easily overcome, will be regarded as a huge obstacle to someone else. It all depends on the value that we place on everything in our lives and where our priorities lie.

"The end of a rather significant relationship triggered my depression back in 1985, amongst other things, and yet I have witnessed much more traumatic relationship breakdowns amongst some friends that did not cause the same reaction. They just picked themselves up and carried on with life. Human nature is so complex and who knows what havoc the environment, chemicals, drugs and other exposure to unnatural substances has on our fragile brains. I don't think we are even close to understanding how our minds truly function. Perhaps if we did, we could do more to prevent the tragic loss of life to suicide and perhaps Michel would still be with us."

The power of suggestion is enormous and is a factor that comes into play when people visit pro-suicide websites, some of which provide details of various suicide methods. Some of these sites include discussion forums or chat rooms, where people can actually discuss suicide methods and ask for information on how to implement these. Young people who are feeling suicidal are often very impulsive, so having instant access to this type of information means that they are more likely to act on it before they give themselves time to consider their actions.

It is important to mention, however, that there is a clear difference between online support groups and discussion forums that help the depressed or suicidal people and those that promote or encourage suicide. Help groups do not allow the posting of any messages that discuss suicide methods, or which may influence someone to take their own life. Most genuine support groups and discussion forums are heavily moderated and would immediately ban anyone who attempted to promote suicide in any way.

Sadly, it appears that the number of pro-suicide websites outnumber those that are designed to help prevent suicide.[3] In 2008, researchers from the universities of Bristol, Manchester and Oxford discovered that people are more likely to find websites that offer advice on how to end life than sites offering help and support.

In July 2005, Sarah's 17-year-old-daughter Harriet (Harri) ended her own life by cutting her wrists. Afterwards, Sarah discovered that Harriet had spent weeks visiting pro-suicide websites and suicide discussion forums on the internet. Sarah believes that Harriet was brainwashed into believing that suicide was a fashionable way to die and the evidence that she has for this are the nature of the messages that she read on some of these forums.

"Firstly, I think it is important to mention that as far as I am aware, Harri had never suffered from depression. We had always had such a close relationship and she never hesitated in coming to me to talk about anything and everything. I never had any reason whatsoever to suspect that she might be visiting such hideous websites, so I never even thought to check her computer. Of course, I wish now that I had. After all, I have always prided myself in being such a responsible parent, so part of that should have been regularly checking her pc, or at least ensuring that certain permissions were set up so that such sites would be inaccessible to her. However, she was always so mature for her age that I did not expect to have to treat her like a small child. She had gained my respect, so in turn I widened her boundaries and trusted her to make wise decisions.

"After the tragedy, my friends and family told me that surely I should have noticed some sort of sign that Harri was feeling suicidal, yet even in hindsight I cannot think of a single way in which she was different. She behaved as she had always done and I don't even know now what was troubling her, because she left no suicide note. I have spoken to many of her friends and even they told me that they had not noticed anything different about her behaviour. As far as everyone is aware, her life was going well, she was excelling at school and she had a close network of loyal friends.

"Why she began looking at pro-suicide sites, I will never know. Sometimes, young people have a macabre interest in such things – for whatever reason – so maybe someone suggested as a joke that she look at the sites. There was, for instance, another site that she looked at that showed the most horrific photographs taken of people whose bodies had been mutilated in various types of accidents.

"Harri was always so squeamish that I feel sure that she would not have searched out this type of site herself. I am also sure that if someone she knew did encourage her to visit such sites, then the person concerned would never admit it. That would be like admitting that they had contributed to what happened.

"People might try to convince me that Harri was responsible for what she did, not these websites, but I cannot accept that. Suicide is a choice, yes, but I don't believe that Harri would have made that choice had she not been influenced by what others had said. I have read many of the posts and can see how a young, vulnerable person could be hi-jacked by these thoughts. The most luring words I read were those that talked about all the media attention that one's suicide would arouse and all the love that would pour from the hearts of victims' friends and families; in effect, how a suicide victim would be in some way revered, because ending one's own life was a courageous and currently 'fashionable' thing to do. They mentioned how everyone would focus on their positive aspects rather than mention any faults they possessed. They were trying to convey the idea that ending one's life was tantamount to being placed on a pedestal.

"I never considered Harri to be an impressionable sort of person. She was not easily persuaded by others' opinions and would prefer to make her own judgements rather than be guided by anyone else's views. However, what happened to her just proves that none of us can ever truly know what someone else is thinking and feeling. It may seem obvious now that there was something that was troubling her. Why otherwise would she allow herself to be influenced by these websites?

"Despite this, I still believe that Harri would still be here now, had she not been under the spell of suggestion. I could have helped her. She could have found some other way. My belief is that suicide contagion does exist and is being spread via these pro-suicide websites and forums."

The other form of contagion that rears its ugly head following a suicide is the reaction of some people towards the grieving family. They believe that if they associate with the family concerned, or visit their house – particularly if it was the house in which the loved one ended their life – that their family will somehow be inviting the same tragedy into their own family. In a way, it's a little like cancer. Although everyone knows that you cannot catch cancer from someone else, there are many who give a wide berth to cancer sufferers as though they are somehow attracting the sickness vibes into their own personal space.

For a while after Kristian's suicide, there were some people who seemed reluctant to allow their children to enter our home, where before they had been more than willing to offload their small charges onto me. In fairness to these families, it could be that they did not feel that I was up to coping with a houseful of little people, even though Carsten and Lauren delighted in their company. Of course, without ever daring to ask, I would never know and I am certain that no one would ever admit the "contagious" element.

There is no definitive conclusion regarding suicide contagion, suffice to say that most people are open to suggestion and how they react to that suggestion very much depends on their frame of mind at the time.

When you consider that just one suicide intimately affects many people within one's family and social circle and can impact hundreds if the suicide victim was at school or college, then it is understandable that at least one of these affected people may be driven to consider suicide themselves.

The solution, as far as I see it, is more responsible reporting of suicide in the media, the policing of pro-suicide websites and the involvement of doctors, counsellors, youth workers and school staff in the aftermath of every teenage suicide.

[2] Brower, Vicki. Media may play role in copycat suicides. Reuters Health, New York, May 12. http://www.yspp.org/media/copycat.html

[3] Pro suicide websites outnumber counselling ones. Sifynews, Washington, April 11, 2008. http://sify.com/news/fullstory.php?a=jegqpEcheaj&title=Pro_suicide_websites_outnumber_counselling_ones&tag=internet

Chapter Seventeen

Refocusing Your Energies on the Living

Each person comes into this world with a specific destiny; he has something to fulfil, some message has to be delivered, some work has to be completed. You are not here accidentally; you are here meaningfully. There is a purpose behind you. The whole intends to do something through you.

Osho

It's amazing how life has a way of making you refocus your efforts, by throwing new crises at you whilst you are still in the depths of trying to deal with another. In particular, when you have suffered bereavement and another difficult situation presents itself, you may feel that you cannot possibly endure any more stress. You may be thinking, "How much more can one person take?" or "It's just one thing after another" and yet maybe there is some unknown force at work helping to shift your focus onto those who are still living. Whatever the reason, rather than feeling that you have already had more than your fair share of trauma, try to view it as a blessing and a sign that you are still very much needed in this world.

A good friend of mine said to me, "Maybe Kristian was placed on this earth to show how drugs destroy lives and he chose you as his mum to help him on his chosen path." I found those words incredibly comforting, but they made me realise how I did have to focus on nurturing, guiding and helping those who were still alive.

Kristian's suicide fell in the middle of a testing phase that we were enduring with my eldest daughter, Anneliese. Her problems began in late 1999 when she was 13 and developed an eating disorder and, looking back now, I clearly remember feeling afraid that she was the child I was most likely to lose. She was totally in control of what she ate and how much she allowed her body to absorb, by deciding when to purge and how many laxatives to take. In contrast, I felt totally out of control and experienced a similar helplessness to that which I suffered following Kristian's death.

Anneliese became very much influenced by the freedom that Kristian appeared to have in his life and despite the fact that his life was visibly far from perfect, in Anneliese's eyes it was far preferable to living within the guidelines set at home. At the point when she seemed to be "recovering" from the eating disorder, she entered an uncharacteristically rebellious phase, during which time she decided to go and live with her father and stepmother. Although she got on very well with her stepmum, who was also a friend of mine, she had never had a close relationship with her dad, so when he began enforcing law and order, her lack of respect for him caused this arrangement to fail.

She started dividing her time between various friends' houses, exploiting their goodwill and also missing a great deal of school as a result. The organisations that existed, such as the local social services, were totally inadequate, if not useless. They claimed not to be able to help out until Anneliese reached the age of 16, until which time she was regarded as a minor. I thought that was the whole point. She was a vulnerable minor who, in theory, was not regarded as mature enough to lead a lifestyle that was independent from an environment ruled by a legal guardian. At that point, I lost all faith in an establishment that is supposed to protect children. They had previously failed Kristian and now they had failed his sister.

Anneliese progressed from staying with friends to circulating with Kristian's acquaintances. I use the word "acquaintances" loosely, since the parasitic lifestyle that they were leading meant that they only ever considered their own needs. They had no aspirations, no jobs and lived their lives in the imaginary cocoon created by heroin use, although at the time I was not aware that Kristian had also fallen victim to its demonically powerful effects. I can't deny that I felt dreadfully sorry for them, but it was not a way of life to which Anneliese should have been exposed. Kristian constantly lectured her and begged her to return home, but since he had been such a poor role model, she dismissed his pleas.

Whilst Kristian was in the young offenders' institution between January and July 2002, Anneliese began a relationship with a 26-year-old lad, ten years her senior, as mentioned earlier in the book. As a naïve 16-year-old, she believed that she was in love, a feeling that clouded her rationality and caused her to endure circumstances that would test the sanity and the patience of the most wise and virtuous adult.

When Kristian died, I believed that this would be the event that would force her to re-think her lifestyle and make her realise that her boyfriend was like a walking time bomb, for whom she had become responsible in a nurturing capacity, rather than being the vulnerable child who herself should have been supported. Anneliese was fully aware that if her boyfriend did not die from an accidental heroin overdose, his liver and kidneys would shortly cease to function. He had been warned by his doctor that he would die if he refused to stop bombarding his body with poisons and yet rather than be deterred by the fact that she may one day wake up with a dead boyfriend next to her, Anneliese gushed the usual, "Oh, but I love him", or "I can't live without him".

I reminded her that soon she may have to live without him, because he was killing himself, albeit not in the suicidal sense.

After Kristian's death, Anneliese seemed to cling even more closely to her boyfriend, or at least as close as his erratic lifestyle would allow. It seemed that every time I spoke to her on the phone, she was playing the waiting game, never exactly certain of where her boyfriend was, but knowing that he was probably out blowing his social security handouts on a bottle of cheap sherry and his next heroin fix. It was an incredibly worrying time for all the family, not least because we feared that Anneliese may end up following in the footsteps of her brother. More worryingly, we wondered what she would do if she were to lose her boyfriend, even though we secretly hoped that he would disappear from her life for good.

A few months after Kristian's suicide, I discovered a letter on his grave that had been written by Anneliese. The envelope had disintegrated in the rain and the letter was there for all to see. Normally I would not read someone else's personal mail, but for some reason felt compelled to read Anneliese's words to her brother. In her letter, she talked about how depressed she felt and how she had often thought about joining him. Fear sliced through my heart until I read the next bit that said, "But I couldn't do that to mum, not after what she's been through". Nevertheless, I knew that she too had contemplated suicide. I gazed at the empty plot next to Kristian, which we had also purchased and wondered whether I would be visiting two of my children in the near future.

Over the following year there was much disharmony in Anneliese's life. I felt as though I was also grieving for the loss of my daughter's life; the life that could have been, had she not been lured into the negative world in which my son had been ensnared.

Although she was not a drug user herself, she was being affected by those who were, but in particular her boyfriend. Not only did she contract Hepatitis A, which resulted in a stay in hospital, but on two occasions he beat her up. Although I was horrified, I felt some comfort in believing that this would be what would finally force her to leave him. She did, but only temporarily. However, shortly after they were reunited, Anneliese somehow found the strength to terminate the relationship on the proviso that they remain friends.

Despite my feeling of compassion towards most people, irrespective of their circumstances or conduct, I could not comprehend how she could contemplate remaining friendly with someone who had physically assaulted her and who had told her that he was "going to kill her".

Anneliese's contact with her ex-boyfriend thereafter was minimal. She would only pass the time of day with him if she happened to bump into him in town, but I was never totally convinced that she was not going to be charmed back into his needle-punctured arms. I was not judging him because he was a drug addict, but because of the way in which he treated my daughter.

Still determined not to have to return home to an existence of rules and curfews, Anneliese began staying with another of Kristian's friends. Since he was 19 years her senior, I did not imagine that she would enter into a relationship with him, but again I was wrong. Although at the time I did not view it as an ideal union, her new boyfriend was at least not a drug addict.

It was another volatile relationship, not because of the age difference, but because both Anneliese and her boyfriend were unhealthily possessive and there was no calming influence within the relationship.

Despite several very temporary separations, the relationship continued and culminated in the birth of a beautiful baby boy, Bailey Kristian, in October 2004. Prior to this, Anneliese had decided that she could not live with her boyfriend and did not want her baby raised in an unsettled environment. As a result, she was housed in a complex of flats for people in a similar situation and began to make a real home for herself.

Although she was only 18, I was thankful that the baby had given her a focus in life. Before the conception, she had been diagnosed with depression and put on medication, but the news of the pregnancy seemed to change all that. She began taking care of herself and was constantly asking for advice on what she could or couldn't do. At one point she told me that she suddenly realised that she had been so focused on the baby that she hadn't thought about Kristian for some time. Of course, she then experienced terrible guilt, but I told her that this was something positive and that Kristian would be happy that she was moving forward with her life at last.

In July 2006, Anneliese's second son Ashton Rhys was born. Kayla, Bailey and Ashton have brought love and light into our lives, as babies and small children always do and although Kristian is not here in the physical sense, I do believe that he is sharing the joy with us from his new world.

Anneliese and I have an amazing relationship and we can now reminisce about those difficult years and laugh about some of the incidents that occurred and the challenging situations we both faced. We accept that there were harsh lessons to be learned, but we muddled through and emerged with much wisdom and a greater zest for life.

Margaret, a retired nurse, whose 23-year-old daughter Gemma took a fatal concoction of painkillers in 1997 after a fight with her boyfriend, said that after her daughter's death she felt that no other crisis would come close to the devastation she felt at losing her youngest child.

"As a nurse, I saw death practically every working day of my life, including that of children. I didn't become immune to it and I was always affected by the loss of a child, but no amount of training could have prepared me for the devastation of losing my own child. I had comforted so many bereaved parents and spouted the usual platitudes, but it was only when Gemma died that I realised how inadequate those words of consolation were to someone whose entire life had just crumbled.

"Shortly, before Gemma died, I remember being astounded and equally impressed by one mother's reaction to her son's death from leukaemia. It was almost as though she were playing the part of a friend or family member coming out with some ill-timed cliché when she said to me, 'Ah well, life goes on. I have my other two children to think about now.' I remember not only envying her for being so strong, but also for having the benefit of knowing that she was going to lose her son and having time to adjust to that dreadful moment in advance. I know that if you speak to many parents who have lost children to terminal illnesses, they will say that knowing their child was going to die didn't make the loss any easier to bear, but at least they were not burdened with guilt. At least they had the chance to spend the final moments of their child's life with them, telling them that they loved them, hugging them and allowing them to go peacefully.

"Although it was some time before I could understand how this mother could be so strong immediately after being told that her son had died, I experienced similar feelings just four months after Gemma's death.

"My father suffered a massive stroke and died after five days in hospital. Whether or not this was precipitated by the shock of Gemma's death, we will never know, but he had always been particularly fond of her and seemed to lose his enthusiasm for life after she died.

"Of course I was heartbroken, but awful as this may sound, I just accepted it in the same way that the mother mentioned previously appeared to accept her son's death. I know that this was a different situation and I suppose that the sadness was somehow cushioned by the knowledge that my father had had a decent life, lived to the full and I also derived comfort in believing that he had joined Gemma. My family and I also had the opportunity to sit with him in hospital and chat to him. Even though he was in a coma, I believe that he could hear every word that we were saying and I am convinced that he responded. For that I am thankful. I felt that I was doing something positive for him, an opportunity that had been denied when Gemma took her own life.

"Although I have now lost two people who meant the world to me, I still have a purpose here. If I didn't, then I too would be dead. I strongly believe that I have to focus on those who are still here and who I am able to help, rather than shrouding myself in misery and mourning those who cannot return."

Mari's 23-year-old son Eric shot himself with a friend's handgun in January 1999. Mari believed that her life was over when Eric died, but then realised how her love for her family and friends and their need for her would carry her through

"When Eric died, I thought I'd lost everything, but then I looked at my beautiful daughter, my partner, my friends and my family and realised that I still had so much in my life.

"I hadn't lost everything, even though the pain I am still experiencing is impossible to describe. I then felt incredibly guilty for acting as though they were not as important as Eric.

"Grief makes you do strange things. When someone dies, suddenly that person becomes the entire focus of your life, when in reality you should be focusing on those who are still alive. No amount of grieving or removing yourself from everyday life is going to restore life to your child. It is inexplicably agonising trying to move forward, but I figured that if I were to suddenly lose the rest of my family, I would regret not having taken the opportunity to spend every possible moment with them. I won't have a second chance with Eric, but I do have a chance with my daughter, my wonderful partner, my brothers and my parents."

Joan's 22-year-old son Cameron shot himself after a mission to find the stepfather who had bullied him and his mother for seven years. Joan believes that it was sheer frustration and pent up anger that made him kill himself on impulse when he was unable to find his stepfather.

"My son Cameron was bullied by his stepfather for seven years and I know he couldn't understand why I stayed with him. In truth, I was scared to leave him. He was such an obsessive, controlling sort of man that I was terrified about what he might do to me if I were to end the relationship. I feel such a coward now and I can't believe that I considered my own fear over the feelings and safety of my son. Maybe I thought that the damage my husband would do would be far greater if we left. I suppose I feared for our lives, but thought that we were more likely to live if we stayed with him, although it wasn't much of a life.

"Understandably, Cameron never could forgive his stepfather for the years of mental abuse, although he was never physically abusive towards him. However, he did make physical threats, but thankfully never carried them out on Cameron.

"Cameron left home at the age of 18 after he had completed his education, but would have left sooner had he had the opportunity. When I realised that it was just my abusive husband and I alone in that house, I knew that I had to do something. One night, whilst he was at work, I packed my bags and left. I moved in with my mother, so it wasn't difficult for him to find me. He knew that I had nowhere else to go and very soon afterwards the phone calls and visits began. He came across as being a super charmer, as he was when we first met. No threats, no put-downs, just a calm, remorseful man who was declaring his undying love for me. It made no difference. I didn't love him anymore and I knew that as soon as I went back, the abuse would begin again.

"I finally thought that I was rid of him when the visits stopped and it seemed as though he had resigned himself to the fact that the relationship was over. In fact, shortly afterwards I heard that he'd been seen out with another woman. My instant reaction was one of pity for her.

"I began to move on with my life, found my own place, a new job, new friends and, three years later, a new relationship. I had only been with my new partner Will for two months when I received an unexpected visitor one evening. Since Will and I did not see each other every day because of work commitments, I was alone that particular evening. When I opened the door, I was shocked to see my ex-husband standing there with an expression that I can only describe as pure evil.

"My instant reaction was to try and shut the door in his face, but he barged his way in and slammed the door behind him. He then launched into a tirade of abuse, calling me a slag and asking me how many times I had cheated on him during our marriage. He accused me of having an affair with Will whilst we were still married and blamed that for the breakup of our relationship.

"It was impossible for me to defend myself, because he wouldn't allow me to get a word in edgeways. Every time I started to speak, he yelled at me with such rage that I knew that something horrible was coming.

"When I attempted to pick up the phone to call the police, the punches started. I don't remember how many times he hit me, but all I can recall is blow after blow and the awful pain. I thought he was going to kill me and I do remember thinking that at least it was me and not Cameron. Eventually, a neighbour must have heard my screams, because there was a loud banging at the front door and I could hear shouting outside. At that point my ex-husband stopped hitting me and left the room. I heard the back door slam and knew that he must have left.

"The neighbour called the police, but by the time they arrived, my ex must have been some way away. I did not even know where he was living at the time, so I could only give the police limited information. I telephoned Cameron from the hospital where I was taken for a check up and treatment for the multitude of cuts and bruises, but instead of coming up to see me, he went out searching for his stepfather. I was absolutely terrified that he was going to end up being badly hurt – if not killed, but never did I believe that he would kill himself.

"I don't know the exact chain of events after that phone call, but from what the police said, he was seen driving all over town, covering the same ground over and over again.

"He never did find his stepfather, but at some point the frustration and anger must have been too much for him to bear and the revolver that he was carrying with him with the aim of shooting his stepfather was turned on himself. My injuries from my ex-husband that night were nothing compared to the pain of losing my son.

"There was part of me that wished that my ex-husband had succeeded in killing me that night, because at least I wouldn't have to live with the unbearable pain of not just life without my son, but of living with the knowledge that I allowed him to be bullied by his stepfather for so long. However, from deep within I felt this insatiable urge to help other victims of bullying and domestic abuse and, hopefully, prevent another family from enduring the same torture. I undertook voluntary work for a local woman's refuge and became heavily involved in a national anti-bullying campaign. Some good had to come out of my devastating experiences.

"Bullying in any form should be taken seriously. It's not just physical, but mental and emotional. I am not afraid to become involved where others walk by and ignore situations. On one occasion, I actually stopped my car in the middle of the road when I saw a young lad being punched and kicked by two other boys of about 12 or 13 years of age. The two boys who were doing the bullying told me that it was none of my business, so I told them that when I see someone being abused then I make it my business to intervene. I told them that the law would see it as their business too and that if they preferred, I would call the police and let them deal with the situation. With that, they ran off.

"I asked the bullied lad which school they all attended and what the names of these lads were. Without hesitation, I contacted the head of the school and made an appointment to go and see him. He assured me that the boys responsible would be dealt with appropriately.

"The reason why these things are allowed to happen is because so many people turn a blind eye, not wishing to become involved. I can't bring Cameron back, but I can do my best now to help others who are being treated unfairly and perhaps, hopefully, save someone else from the same tragic fate as my son.

"My energy has been refocused on doing something positive rather than spending the rest of my days pining for the loss of my son."

Nine months after Kristian died, I received a heartrending email from a young man called Nathan who had known Kristian for a short period of time. He had written to me after reading an article in the local paper about the child suicide website I had created and was looking for emotional support and understanding from someone whom he felt would listen. He too was suffering from phases of deep depression and admitted to lying awake at night contemplating suicide. He had a lovely wife and a young son, but not only didn't he want to burden his wife with his problems, but he felt that she wouldn't understand and would view it as a sign that he was unhappy in the relationship.

After spending some time communicating with Nathan and establishing a good friendship with his family, he found a renewed vigour for life and began opening up to his wife.

His email was just one amongst the many that I had received from young, depressed people and bereaved parents. These people had given me another purpose in life and made me feel as though Kristian was responsible for helping them. Had it not been for his suicide, I would not be doing what I am doing now and potentially helping to save lives. I was unable to rescue my son, but I can do something to help bring some positive meaning into the lives of others who are suffering in a similar way.

'It's no wonder so many young people suffer from depression'

Jan in local paper feature about depression in young people

Chapter Eighteen

Dispelling Suicide Myths

Myths and creeds are heroic struggles to comprehend the truth in the world.

Ansel Adams

The moment that my son decided to take his own life was the moment when the claws of depression grabbed hold of any remaining hope and tore it mercilessly from him. This hopelessness took my son from me. This hopelessness is rarely understood and is something that is often condemned by others who, in their limited knowledge, utter insensitive comments about suicide being a selfish or cowardly act. Many of those tortured souls who end their lives are very sensitive and caring and would do anything for anybody. Although they value others, they don't always value themselves and don't always realise the positive impact that they have had on others' lives. They certainly never intended to cause pain and heartache to their families and friends.

Many families chastise themselves for not noticing signs that their loved one might be considering suicide, but people who attempt suicide will often hide their feelings from people for many reasons. They may fear being told to "pull themselves together" or feel that others will view it as an attention-seeking threat and will criticise them rather than offering the support and understanding they need. They may also have been made to feel by society that suicidal behaviour is sinful and feel ashamed to admit to their true feelings, but when suicide and suicidal behaviour is now almost as prevalent as other major diseases, then it is an illness that requires serious attention and far more understanding.

It is an issue about which everyone should be educated, because the probability is that at some point it will touch most people's lives, whether within their own family or that of a friend, acquaintance or work colleague.

Few people who end their lives do so because they truly want to die. What they want is for their pain to end, but in the moment that they take the fatal action, whether on impulse or carefully planned, the pain has become too much to bear and ending it quickly seems the only solution. That little ray of light that we all seek has disappeared. The darkness engulfs them and all hope is lost. In choosing death, they only wanted to end their pain. They could not see a future. They felt unworthy of this life.

I am not just speaking from the perspective of a mother who has lost a child to suicide, but from the viewpoint of someone who has also suffered from those same feelings of hopelessness in the past. I would be lying if I said that I hadn't thought about ending it all myself on more than one occasion since losing Kristian, but that was directly linked to the horror of what happened to my son. However, in addition to the circumstantial depression mentioned in Chapter One, the depression that I experienced as a teenager was totally different. I couldn't pinpoint any one particular reason; all I knew was that I felt wretched enough to want to die. At that time, however, there was no one in whom I felt I could confide.

Many families believe that their loved ones chose suicide to escape from their families, but I contemplated it to escape from my pain. I never told anyone and certainly not my parents. I didn't think that they would understand, but above all I would not be able to explain to them why I felt the way I did. I knew that I was sensitive and I was aware that I was a magnet for other people's pain, but I did not consciously link this to my own feelings of despair.

Thankfully, though, I didn't complete the act of suicide, primarily because I felt that however unbearable life seemed, I still had a purpose to fulfill and that I would not pass over until it was my predestined time. I feel grateful to be spiritually attuned enough to be aware of greater forces too complex to be totally understood by the limitations of the conscious mind.

Some people talk about wanting to die beforehand and others say nothing. Some have a recognised depressive or mental illness, whereas others have not been clinically diagnosed with any form of mental disorder. Some may come across to the ill-informed as being dramatic and attention-seeking when they make open claims about wanting to die. Others may hide their unhappiness extremely well and some may seem a bit down, but not enough to make friends, family or other close acquaintances worry that they may be feeling suicidal. None of these may be perceived by others to be risk factors and, sometimes, even qualified medical professionals fail to detect the true danger that a patient might be to him or herself. Many patients have been discharged from mental hospitals when they are no longer regarded as "high risk" or a danger to themselves, only to subsequently succeed in completing the act of suicide.

A person who has been noticeably depressed may suddenly perk up, thereby conning others into believing that they are feeling better. Often, the cheerfulness is the relief that they are feeling because they have found a permanent solution to their problems; death. Others may feign wellness to prevent others from keeping too close an eye on them. After all, if their intention is to kill themselves, they do not want to be saved.

Delaney was 15 when she relayed her experience to me. Her shocking and heartrending story clearly shows that attempting suicide is not a selfish, attention-seeking act, but one of total desperation, often borne from mental illness that appears to be inescapable.

"Last year I suffered from severe depression and thought about taking my own life many times. My parents are social workers and know all the signs, but I was different. My grades stayed high and I didn't' withdraw, except at home. I stayed pretty much the same for months and months. But I grew worse and worse. I cut my arms and still have scars that will remind me of what I have done.

"I was too afraid to go ask for help. I kept it all bottled in until one day right before Thanksgiving I snapped and cried and spilled everything. My mom was also depressed and she left for a week to go to a crisis centre right after she said, 'I'll be here for you and help you.' I didn't understand how she could help me if she went away and I was really mad. I even hated her. She would call and I'd have her in tears before I slammed down the phone. I told her I hated her, that she was a horrible mom and that I never wanted to see her again. She came back the next week, but it was awful and she drove me into Winnipeg to a Crisis Centre. However, they wouldn't take me because I was only 14. No other places would even talk to me. I was fighting a losing battle against a government and family that didn't seem to want to, or know how to, help me.

"After another week of crying, screaming and doing nothing except sleeping, my parents took me to a children's hospital in Winnipeg. It took a whole day and at least a million gallons of tears before I explained what was happening to me to half a dozen nurses, doctors, admittance staff and a mumbo jumbo of people I wanted to see dead.

"They decided I should be admitted to Psy1-North, a section of the hospital for suicidal, depressed, paranoid and other 'freaks' as I viewed myself, aged 11-18. I was the youngest and surrounded by three 18-year-olds and one 16-year-old.

"Psy1-South was for the little kids and sometimes I could hear a 5-year-old banging his head against the wall crying, or an 8-year-old shouting to get rid of the ghosts, or screaming that his butter would hurt him. I saw so many things that I never want anyone else to have to see. My friend Sam tried to hang himself in his room with his bed sheet, but was caught a second early, or four minutes too late, whichever way you look at it. I've seen many things I want to shelter others from seeing and things I never want to see again.

"Every now and then I have bad days where I think about killing myself and can't stop crying. But that passes and the longest it usually lasts is two days. My friends say that committing suicide is selfish. How can they say that, unless they have suffered from depression themselves?

"I've been there, done that, but am not entirely sure what stopped me from ending it all. Every day is still a battle and every now and then I have horrible recurring dreams about what I've seen at the hospital. The thoughts that hound me and the scars I bear prove that I was troubled. But aren't we all a little troubled? I'm sorry to all those 'survivors' of suicide i.e. those who are left behind after losing someone to suicide, but I feel I bring more meaning to it because I am a true survivor of suicide."

Suicidal thoughts are not confined to the minority. At least one third of all people will contemplate thoughts of suicide at some point during their lives.

These thoughts may indicate mental illness, or they may simply be as the result of an exceptionally unfortunate event or set of circumstances e.g. the death of a loved one, divorce, job loss, bullying, financial worries etc.

Suicidal thoughts are not entertained only by those who aren't intellectually developed enough to evaluate one's situation and find a solution. On the contrary, the highest rate of suicide occurs amongst highly gifted and talented individuals. Intelligent people are often more aware of, and affected by, social and personal issues and may philosophise a great deal about the grim aspects of the world and their own lives. They often have high expectations, or feel that others have high expectations of them and fear that they are not living up to the standards that they have set for themselves, or that others have set for them. Sometimes, therefore, being less sensitive and less aware can be a blessing.

Depressed people can often be consumed by feelings of guilt, however undeserved this may seem to family and friends, whereas others may feel guilt as a result of accusations and abuse from family, friends, work colleagues or neighbours.

Drug and alcohol abuse can also play a part in suicidal behaviour and interestingly 50% of people who kill themselves have a recent history of substance abuse.[4] Some depressed individuals begin drinking heavily or taking drugs as a suppressor for their pain, whereas others may become depressed as a result of their addiction.

Paradoxically, the person who uses drugs as an escape will often end up creating greater problems caused by dependence. Financial problems, the destruction of relationships, a decline in health, an inability to obtain or sustain employment and an increasing sense of hopelessness can lead one to the point where suicide seems the only immediate solution to the misery.

Lynn's 25-year-old son Joe hung himself in August 2000, after suffering from bipolar disorder for six years. Lynn says that none of his friends ever knew about his disorder because he hid it so well.

"Although Joe had been diagnosed with bipolar disorder at the age of 19, his friends viewed him as the life and soul of the party; always laughing and joking in the presence of others. No one would ever have guessed that he had a depressive illness. I think he kept it to himself, not because he was ashamed or that it was a sign of weakness, but because he was such a kind, loving young man and didn't want anyone worrying about him. Of course, his father and I knew about it, but he made me swear that I wouldn't tell anyone else about it.

"I think that he needed to be in company the whole time and needed attention from his friends. It was always when he was alone that he would enter into his phases of morbid depression, down on himself and life and nothing that I said to him would convince him that he was loved. He would believe that his friends just used him as and when they wanted, which of course wasn't the case. They adored him – something that was clear after his death.

"Despite our knowledge of his disease and the fact that he knew he didn't have to hide anything from us, he never once mentioned the word 'suicide'. I guess he didn't want to add to our worries, but I wish that he had told us. Maybe we could have done something to help; maybe we couldn't. We'll never know. However, what I regret is never having that chance. I guess that's a common feeling amongst those who have lost a loved one to suicide.

"Joe was suffering from a chemical imbalance in his brain. It obviously became so unbearable to the point that ending his pain took priority over the pain that would be caused to those he loved. Maybe he thought that we'd be better off without him. Maybe at that point he didn't believe that he was loved by anyone.

"The point is that there are so many myths surrounding suicide and everyone seems to have an opinion on the topic. Unfortunately, many of these opinions are unqualified and unless someone had the ability to totally see inside Joe's mind, then they are in no position to pass judgement or condemn or say why it happened. Sometimes it might be possible to say why someone has taken their own life, particularly if they are doing it to escape the ignominy of a crime they have committed, but often it is just not possible to say why some people self-destruct and others don't, irrespective of their circumstances."

So many people believe that the person who decides to end his or her own life gave no thought to those who would be left behind to gather up the remains of their shattered lives. Evidence from those who have contemplated or attempted suicide show that this is not the case and that these troubled individuals are very much aware of those they would be leaving behind.

Taisha is 22-years-old. Her family originates from Jamaica and Taisha lives in an area that is predominantly white. She feels that her skin colour is the root of her depression and suicidal behaviour.

"As a person who has been on the verge of taking my own life on many occasions, I can say that many suicidal people reach a point where they feel that no one around them can help. This may be why so few people actively seek help, or admit to those they love how they are feeling.

"I know that those around me love me tremendously, I am sure. But sometimes, love isn't enough. Sometimes there are circumstances, feelings and thoughts in our lives that just cannot be changed and which become unbearable. Children who take their own lives will have thought about it over and over again; they would have no doubt thought about the pain it would cause their loved ones and the consequences. But unfortunately, their pain seems stronger.

"Sometimes, when I think about those around me, I feel guilty of the hurt that would happen to my family, but then I realise that I will also have to continue living in this turmoil just for their benefit. I carry on just to protect them, but this pain I feel is too great, especially to continue living only to ensure everyone else is happy. Maybe suicide is a very selfish way to think, but I am not strong enough to become a martyr and sacrifice my sanity and carry on living forever with these thoughts and feelings just so that everyone around me will be ok.

"Parents must never ever beat themselves up and think that they could have done something, or wonder whether their child knew how much they loved him or her, or fret about why they didn't they come to them when they were feeling so desperate. Once that pain consumes someone and they are determined to end it all, there is often not really much that can change that. I realise that this is just my personal opinion, so maybe for others, it is not too late.

"It is too painful living a life as fraught as mine. I no longer wish to have to pay and suffer for not being born as a white person. The dreams I would never be allowed to dream, the opportunities that I can yearn for only in my heart, the beauty that I shall never possess. I could go on. Yes, there are many people who are not white who manage to cope, but at what cost? I simply cannot cope with it all. I want to be proud of who I am, but I have been made to feel ashamed because I live in a predominantly white area and am viewed by many as different. I see that as different in a disadvantaged way, not different in a favourable way. It is a cross I have to bear and will have to bear for the rest of my life, like a crucifix permanently nailed to my back.

"I can understand the fury that my account will almost certainly provoke amongst sectors of society who despise racism. It is evil and it comes from within people's own minds.

"I do not understand how the amount of pigment that someone has in their skin can influence another person's opinion of them. If black is so unappealing, then I'd like someone to tell me why so many white people are damaging their skin in pursuit of a tan? The ridiculous thing is that some of the people who have taunted me spend all summer frying themselves to a shade of dark brown.

"There is no amount of counselling that will help me, because at the end of the day life around me will still be the same; the lack of opportunities, hopes and dreams etc. There is no hope for me whatsoever. The only way out of this eternal misery is death.

"If someone has cancer or another terminal illness and is consumed by pain and they go to a euthanasia clinic in Switzerland, or someone in their family helps them to end their life, then many people condone this and see it as an act of kindness, relieving someone's suffering. Well, to me this is my cancer, my lifelong illness, so why should I be condemned for wanting to relieve my pain?

"It angers me that I live in a country where my skin colour still determines what I do or achieve with my life. There is no one around me that is not white so, yes, I know they love me and care for me, but they do not understand my pain. They do not know what it is like to walk about not being white. I am tired of the disgusted looks I get when I venture out, tired of people moving if I sit next to them on a bus, tired of it affecting my employment chances and tired of the race hate crimes I see happening around me. I'm tired of people looking down at me, tired of the name calling and tired of that feeling of insignificance.

"I'm tired of the beautiful, perfect white women I see on the TV and covers of magazines, feeling I will never be as good as they are. I can almost hear people saying as they read this, 'But there are many beautiful, intelligent and successful black people out there.'

"However, they are lucky enough to live in a part of the world where racism is less rife.

"I am lucky in certain ways. The worst I have had happen to me is being chased down the street by a group of youths - male and female - who were throwing stones at me and calling me offensive names. There are many people who have endured far worse.

"Yes, I know things improve with time and in 50 years' time, the situation may be better, but I cannot endure 50 more years of this. Having a positive attitude, or being proud of what I am, or getting all the counselling in the world would never change my life around me. I will still be classed as ugly, still have a lack of opportunities career wise and still be held back in all walks of life. Who would want an existence like that? Some may ask me why I don't move to a different place, but it's not that easy. If it were, I would go tomorrow, but I would still carry the burden of my past around with me. It would take years for me to build any sort of trust and restore any sort of faith in human nature.

"My question is this: Will my death hurt the others around me? Will they feel guilt about not being able to do anything to help me? I don't believe there is anything anyone can do, but will they know that? I believe they will be a bit sad, but in time, they will understand and move on. I don't know whether I am right."

Some people may feel that suicide is more likely to occur in dysfunctional families and that if a child takes his or her own life, it is a sign that there must have been something horribly wrong at home. Professionals can spend endless amounts of time and money researching reasons why this dreadful tragedy hits certain families and not others.

They may look for errors in the way in which their family life was run, or for circumstances such as divorce and other areas of potential disharmony that may have contributed. However, the frightening truth is that suicide can strike any family, anywhere and at any time.

Choosing suicide is not an expression that I like, although one that I have used, since I am certain that most of those who end their own lives would desperately have liked to have lived, but without the pain that eventually became too great to endure. They therefore felt that suicide was the only option available to them at the time.

Another aspect that has received more notice over the past few years (aside from websites that promote suicide, which was covered in Chapter Sixteen), is the influence of songs with dark and depressing lyrics. Unfortunately, for a lot of young people, music is a heavy influence and they are often looking for a role model, someone famous to emulate. Of course, not everyone will be influenced by lyrics and websites, unless they already have a propensity towards depression, or become obsessed with a particular pop band and idolise them to the extent that they feel compelled to follow everything that they say or do. Sadly, there will always be those that do.

Some sceptics might say that people use music's influence as a poor excuse for bad parenting, but this is simply not the case. Unfortunately, those with limited understanding of the psyche will often blame bad parenting for all the misdemeanors in this world, when the majority of the time there are numerous other reasons. Many suicidal people are well-educated individuals from loving, caring homes where reasonable levels of discipline have been exercised. This has been backed up via communication that I have had with hundreds of depressed people.

It is the "bad parenting" attitude that sadly leads so many bereaved parents to remain silent and isolated in their grief through fear of having their sorrow compounded by such narrow-minded and ignorant opinions. Most parents are already chastising themselves horribly for things that they feel they did or didn't do and to have their feelings of incompetence, failure and parental inadequacy endorsed by others is deeply distressing.

Suicide is far more common than most people believe, so why are these statistics not reported accurately? Some suicide deaths are not reported as such, because there is no corroborating evidence to confirm that it was suicide as opposed to accidental death or death by misadventure. If, for example, my son had not left two suicide notes, then the verdict at his inquest would almost certainly have been one of accidental death as a result of a heroin overdose.

When you consider all the intentional suicides where the victim does not leave a note, or where there are no witnesses, it's clear to see why it is difficult to compile an accurate set of statistics. Where the deaths don't involve what would be regarded as more intentional methods such as hanging, carbon monoxide poisoning or shotgun injuries, it is easy to assume that the victim wanted to be saved, or that it was an accident rather than a suicide attempt.

The social stigma and embarrassment that is still associated with suicide could also account for this under-reporting, as could issues such as insurance claims, unwanted publicity, the psychological trauma to the surviving family members and certain religious beliefs against suicide in certain sectors. However, these skewed statistics undoubtedly add to the stigma. More accurate reporting would raise greater awareness of this issue and cause it to be treated with the same concern, sympathy and understanding as other illnesses, which in turn may help to reduce the incidence of suicide.

I see suicide as a major public health challenge, but one that is not currently being addressed as well as it should be, especially since the horrifying fact is that children as young as five are experiencing suicidal thoughts. It is an increasing phenomenon that transcends age, race and socio-economic conditions and can affect anyone, anywhere and at any time. By dispelling all of the myths associated with suicide and suicidal behaviour, we will be more able to identify those at risk and provide necessary assistance, which of course begins with listening, understanding and never preaching.

Remember, everyone has the potential for suicide.

[4] Suicide and Substance Abuse. Encyclopedia.com.
http://www.encyclopedia.com/doc/1G2-3403100435.html

Chapter Nineteen

Professional Views

I personally believe that we bring fears, traumas and unresolved issues into this life from previous incarnations, which is not a factor that would generally be considered by a traditional psychologist.

Jan Andersen

Suicide is an issue that has preoccupied professionals from diverse disciplines for decades. Some of the experiences in this book show that it is difficult to pinpoint exactly why someone chooses to end his or her own life, but whilst many show that there was a circumstantial reason, professionals tend to examine the psychological, sociological, biological, environmental and genetic and risk factors.

One of the world's most influential sociologists, Frenchman Emile Durkheim (1858-1917) published numerous sociological studies on suicide. First published in 1897, his book *Suicide: A Study in Sociology* addresses the phenomenon of suicide and its social causes. Durkheim's definition of suicide is such: "The term suicide is applied to all cases of death resulting directly or indirectly from a positive or negative act of the victim himself, which he knows will produce this result." [5]

Durkheim argues that suicide primarily results from too little or too much integration of the individual into society. In his book, he argued that individuals with too little integration (Egoistic suicide) who were not sufficiently bound to social groups (and therefore not connected to social "norms") were left with little support or guidance, resulting in an increased propensity towards taking their own lives.

On the other hand, those who were too integrated into social groups (Altruistic suicide) lost sight of their individuality and became willing to sacrifice themselves to the group's interests, suicide being the ultimate sacrifice. Military suicides are an example of the latter.

Durkheim identified two other forms of suicide: Anomic suicide, where a victim's means are unable to fulfil their needs and Fatalistic suicide, which Durkheim only describes briefly and relates it to overregulated and unrewarding lives.

However great one's knowledge of psychology, human behaviour and suicide, and however often one deals with death in his or her profession, nothing can prepare one for the aftermath of a child's suicide.

Sue Scott (was Neill), the nurse who supported me on the day that Kristian died and who has remained in touch since had this to say:

"Although I have been nursing now for over twenty years, I have tended never to be complacent. I have yet to become used to some of the sights, traumas and suffering I have witnessed. Despite people who believe one must get used to it, believe me, you do not. It was the events of 1 November 2002, which changed so many lives; it gave me personally an almighty kick up the backside. I realised that despite all medical intervention and modern technology, the human body and mind are so fragile.

"That night as a nurse, I felt inadequate, both practically and emotionally. I was a mere bystander. Kristian's death was thought provoking and a wake-up call for me as a mum.

"My heart broke for Jan that day, especially when she collapsed and sobbed, asking 'Why?' I never had the answer. I know that I gave my three children an extra hug that day and to this day have thought, 'There but for the grace of God!'

"My children are still young enough that I have control of their whereabouts, their purse and, to some extent, the company they keep.

"Over the years, I have often asked questions about drug addiction. How does it start? Who succumbs? Why? Three questions yet left unanswered. How do we as parents warn our children? Do we educate, discuss drugs with them when they become teenagers, or must we approach the subject before they can speak? Whom do we warn them to avoid? Some scruffy down and out in the street, a 'suit and tuckered' businessperson, or a friend whom they have known since playgroup? Where do we stop them visiting, in order that they are not exposed? Discotheques, public houses, clubs, wine bars, department stores, school or even the local library? Everyone's guess is as good as mine.

"What we must all know as parents and something that I now appreciate is that our children will be offered drugs at some point in their lives, guaranteed. It can only be, must be, they themselves who make the conscious decision that it is a road to nowhere. They must learn that to say 'Yes' to drugs will allow them to be possessed and controlled by another; the pusher, the drug or the needle. They must be able to refuse and then have the courage to inform their parents and the police. Many parents are shocked to the core at the discovery that it was even possible that their well-educated, deeply loved child would contemplate the use of drugs, let alone die from their use.

"Illicit drugs are wicked, leading to a painful trail. It is so much harder, I believe, for those who have to pick up the pieces after a drug related death, to continue to live, than the victim of a drug overdose or misuse.

"We of course, as Jan so rightly said, have no control when the child leaves home. You cannot, nor would they tolerate your interference or attempts at monitoring their every move.

"I would love to know if there are accurate documented figures of successful rehabilitation and what these statistics are. I imagine this to be a very small proportion of the population. I have heard it said that once a smoker always a smoker, once an alcoholic always an alcoholic, so once addicted to drugs always addicted, often after just one 'fix'.

"To legalise Cannabis or decriminalise illicit drugs is mindless; it will lead to tolerance. Easier access to Class 'A' drugs on our streets and increased availability will, ultimately, lead to many more deaths. It must never happen. Drug pushers are people for which no prison term, however long, will suffice. Nor will it repair the damage they have caused up until capture, to those already caught in their deceitful webs.

"I know that with my busy schedule; work, family, study, mortgage and everything that makes up the rat race of life, I have often neglected to ask people, 'Are you alright?' I refer in particular with regard to my children. I have taken it for granted that they will talk to me, if, or when, the going gets tough. What might happen if they do not talk to me? Could it be that they see a 'mum' who works, runs a home, provides a taxi service, juggles finances and, more often than not, is exhausted and too old to understand. They could think then that they will not worry mum! I will, and have made a concerted effort, because of Kristian and Jan, to ask regularly the simple question, 'Are you ok?' Whether or not it will change the course of the future, I do not know.

"Sometimes it is life itself that leads to drug use. We must not forget the vulnerable few who live a life of abuse, with no love. For them it is to escape reality, to hide from their inability to cope. Still at fault are the providers of the substances abused, who prey on that vulnerability. A person's involvement in illicit drugs in any capacity cannot and must never be tolerated or excused.

"As a society, we must adopt a zero tolerance for 'dealing in drugs'. The NHS (National Health Service) finances the process in part, to repair the damage of drug and alcohol misuse, at enormous cost."

"To see me must be very hard for Jan. It will always be a stark reminder of the very day Kristian died, the very acute pain his loss causes every day, now and always.

"Nearly seven years after Kristian's death and Jan has finally finished what must have been a terribly painful process; (writing her book). Well done Jan, you have my utmost respect. My children are much older now and so far have chosen to say 'No' to drugs, including tobacco. I am proud of them.

"Jan and I would not have met but for Kristian's premature death and I believe this changed my outlook. I have never forgotten that night; it had a profound effect on me. I vowed to talk to my children more and opened the channels of communication; we discussed the consequences of drug misuse. It is because of November 1 2002 that we reached this place.

"Illicit drugs are still a huge problem and I will never stop worrying about my children, nieces, nephews, friends' children - and in years to come, grandchildren - being exposed or tempted in the future, so talking about it with all of them is so important to me."

I shall be eternally grateful to Sue for the support that she gave me on the day of Kristian's passing and since. I remember seeing tears in her eyes as she spoke to me while I was holding Kristian's lifeless hand. It showed that she had been deeply touched by the tragedy and, that as a mother herself, she could feel my pain. She wasn't just going through the motions of offering platitudes and a listening ear, as so many believe that nursing staff do, because it is what they have been trained to do.

She spoke to me as an individual, as a mother and as someone who was enduring the worst pain that a parent can ever imagine.

I can't imagine that one ever becomes hardened to seeing the death of someone so young and of course it must continually make those in the caring profession question the mortality of their own loved ones.

Ex-Social Worker and Founder of Safeconcerts.com, Deborah Rees says, "What so many people forget is the intensity of feeling and lack of experience that all young people have. The here and now is so strong and they don't see the bigger picture or a longer future; those emotions and hormones are so powerful and strong. Some are just such sensitive and gentle souls that they are unable to cope in this greedy, intolerant and violent world. Sometimes these souls just cannot be reached, even by those they love and those who love them the most. Parents are usually the last people that the young think are capable of giving advice and support. Even if they know deep down that parent knows best, they won't usually accept it at that age.

"I suspect that your intellect tells you all you need to know and puts things into some sort of perspective, then wham, along comes the emotions, which tell you a completely different story.

"The loss of a child is the hardest thing in the world for a parent to bear because your child will always be your baby - even if they were 50. You don't plan for your child to die before you, but your child did make his or her own choices and you must remember that, even though it is impossible to understand it. Sometimes we can't influence what and who we want to; sometimes people seek escape in ways that are difficult to understand. Sometimes there is just no understanding. The problem is that we all want answers and when we can't find them we still keep looking and hoping.

"I know that suicide grievers will go on torturing themselves, so I wouldn't even presume to say 'don't', but my advice would be to try and do some little things that lift you a little - even if it is momentary. Jan has done something very special with her website for grieving families and depressed youngsters and with that she is achieving something that many of us just wouldn't be able to do. I hope that she draws some strength from that.

"I guess that if Kristian left notes then he did mean to do what he did, even though that's almost impossible to accept. It's just that this world is really a very hard place and some souls are just not equipped to cope. It doesn't matter what their nearest and dearest do; they just can't influence it. I don't think it's a reflection on friends and relatives; there's a much bigger picture and there are places that only some go to. The horrible bit is that those left behind want answers and sometimes there just aren't any. I also don't think that those who do this understand what it does to those they leave behind. I think that maybe what drives them is different and beyond what we can understand, none of which helps.

"Just know that you probably couldn't have done anything more. I think that had he made contact with you, it would have happened some other time and some other place. Some souls are tortured and delicate and have a different agenda. Inevitably, they go to a better place, but of course you won't want to believe that there a better place than with you.

"Your work will help many to cope with what is essentially an intolerable, inexplicable and painful situation. Grab what you can from that because you are making a difference and it matters."

From speaking to many health professionals and psychologists, it appears that there is a strong link between abuse and suicide, but it is important to stress that in no way does this imply that all suicides are the result of abuse or bullying.

A 2008 review of studies from 13 countries, published in the International Journal of Adolescent Medicine and Health, said that there was a likely association between bullying and subsequent suicide in children.[6]

Young-Shin Kim, M.D., assistant professor at Yale School of Medicine's Child Study Centre and her colleague Bennett Leventhal, M.D. analysed 37 studies, which took place in various countries around the world. Almost all of the studies showed a link between bullying and suicidal thoughts in children. More surprisingly, the studies showed that the bullies themselves also had a greater disposition towards suicide.

There are, of course, numerous factors that may predispose someone towards suicidal behaviour, including undiagnosed depression, mental illness, physical illness, bereavement, financial problems and many more. Comprehensive information about suicide risk factors, studies and statistics can be found at the Mental Health Foundation website (UK) and the National Institute of Mental Health website (US).

[5] Durkheim, Emile. Suicide: A Study in Sociology. Originally published in 1897. Routledge; 2 edition (21 Feb 2002)

[6] Int J Adolesc Med Health 20 (2), 2008

Chapter Twenty

Life after Death

What happens after death is so unspeakably glorious that our imagination and feelings do not suffice to form even an approximate conception of it.

Carl Jung (Psychologist)

A rose once grew where all could see,
Sheltered beside a garden wall,
And, as the days passed swiftly by,
It spread its branches straight and tall.

One day, a beam of light shone through
A crevice that had opened wide;
The rose bent gently toward its warmth
And then passed to the other side.

Now you who deeply feel its loss,
Be comforted; the rose blooms there,
Its beauty even greater now,
Nurtured by God's own loving care.

Author unknown

  I cannot begin this chapter without imparting my own personal beliefs, although I would never try to persuade others to subscribe to my beliefs, because it is up to everyone to discern his or her own truth. I am a spiritualist and do not follow any orthodox religion, but that is my choice. Everyone has to follow what they believe in their hearts. I love spirituality, because it does not seek to control, nor does it revolve around man-made doctrines.

My religion is simply kindness, compassion, tolerance and acceptance. Nevertheless, I respect everyone's beliefs and would never criticise someone because of race or religion. I have some beautiful friends of many different religious denominations, from many different cultures and of many different nationalities. As far as I am concerned, we are all part of the same consciousness, all brothers and sisters. I do not believe in violence or war, some of which have their roots in religion. I see it as a Neanderthal reaction from people who want power over others. War is like multiplying bacteria; war creates more violence, which in turn creates more war and so on. War never has its roots in Love and is *never* the answer, although that is another topic entirely.

I have never doubted the existence of the afterlife, or what I would prefer to term as "real life". I see the earth plane as the illusion; a place where we incarnate many times to gain knowledge and learn tough lessons. I believe we all choose our life lessons and the paths we will follow before each incarnation. However, we are also born with the power of choice and these choices also affect what happens to us. I previously believed that suicide is one of those unfortunate choices. My next book, Kristian's Heaven, puts a slightly different perspective on this belief through some beautiful words channelled directly from Source.

Although I have to respect others' feelings, I still cannot help but feel irritated when I hear some people say, "Where was God in all this?" or "Why would a loving God allow this to happen?" My belief is that God is not responsible for all the bad things that happen in this world. We often have difficult lessons to learn, because in order to develop spiritually, we have to encounter challenges. Many people fail to see the value in struggle and pain. In fact, it is during the most difficult times that we are most supported by the angels, our direct messengers from God.

We just need to ask for their help and be open to the responses they give. They cannot intervene with choices that we make – and that includes suicide.

How strange that when everything is going right in some people's lives, they are more accepting of God and the angels. Do they not ask the same question when things go wrong in other people's lives, or are they so self-righteous that they only believe that bad things happen to non-believers? It is the difficult times that afford us the greatest spiritual development, yet sadly it is during these testing times when some people feel that they have been deserted.

Before Kristian's tragic loss I believed, without any doubt whatsoever, in life after death, karma and reincarnation. I have "seen" ghosts and communicated with the spirit world throughout my life, always regarding intuition or gut feelings and coincidences as messages passed on from our "helpers" or spirit guides and angels. I tried to think of death as simply a move to another world - a gentler place where one is free from the burden of a physical body, although a place where one still has lessons to learn and preparations to make for the next incarnation on the earth plane. Nevertheless, although one would assume that my beliefs should better equip me for dealing with loss, from the moment that Kristian died, I began questioning everything that I believed in. I was afraid that death of the body really was death of the spirit and soul too.

I began torturing myself with all those awful questions that I imagine many in a similar situation might also ask: What if there is no afterlife? What if all the spirit communication I have had has just been my imagination, or aliens feeding me information, even though their advice has always been correct?

What if he never knew how much I loved him? What if I will never be able to say sorry? What if he is never able to see what an impact he had on others' lives? What if he can't see how much everyone cared about him? What if he never sees his beautiful daughter grow up?

The reason why even the most spiritual of people find the death of a loved one as hard to bear as anyone else is because, as souls within an earthly body, we are still subjected to the physical emotions associated with separation and loss.

Some parents take comfort in believing that it was their child's time to go. With any other type of death, this is true. However, although our death clock begins ticking the moment we are born and is pre-programmed to stop at a destined point, we are all born with the power of choice. Suicide, I believed, was a choice to exit this life prematurely before one's life purpose had been fulfilled. I felt that Kristian had so much more to do and so many more lessons to learn and I felt that I had also been deprived of many more years of his physical presence. Having said this, however, a chapter in my next book, Kristian's Heaven, puts a completely different perspective on this in words channelled by my dear friend Angela. This suggests that even suicide may be destined to occur as a victim's life purpose of giving more lessons that he or she is set to receive in this incarnation.

In communicating with hundreds of bereaved families, I discovered that even those who were previously sceptical about the afterlife now spend much of their time desperately searching for proof that the spirit of their loved ones lives on. The death of their child, grandchild, sibling, relative or friend is inconceivable. They don't want to believe that the death of the body is the end of that person, because it's far too painful to accept.

Many bereaved families will begin to experience "signs" that their loved one is still around. Smells, sounds, electrical anomalies, vivid dreams and uncanny coincidences are commonly reported occurrences. They want to believe that their loved one is letting them know that they are still with them in spirit. Many families find these signs comforting, whereas others may find them a little frightening, particularly if they were previously non-believers.

I have experienced many of these signs, with smells, electrical anomalies, visitation dreams and actual visions of my son being the most common. Some sceptics might have more rational explanations and will dismiss paranormal occurrences, but my beliefs have helped to keep me sane and have certainly helped me to get through each day that has passed since losing Kristian. Logical explanations are given because of the limitations of our brains that have been damaged through the centuries, making it more difficult to access the areas responsible for the divine consciousness that we were all able to experience thousands of years ago. This logic limits our ability to perceive and experience anything outside that which can be explained rationally. The sceptics could never find a logical explanation for all the premonitions I've experienced in dreams, including the 9/11 disaster, natural disasters, deaths, pregnancies, a partner's online affair and many more.

At one of the services at the spiritual church I used to attend on a Sunday evening, a visiting medium described the earthly body as just "wrapping paper for the soul". This is a perfect metaphor. We don't see the soul of a person; we see the external wrapping paper and we think of that wrapping paper as being that person. We miss the "wrapping paper" because it is through this that the spirit of the person shines.

That is why it is so difficult to accept when someone dies and the wrapping paper no longer serves a purpose and disintegrates. I find great comfort in believing that the real person, the soul within, continues to live. This same medium said that she preferred to use the term "life after life", because death didn't exist and this is something that I have heard so many times.

Ruth's 24-year-old son Samuel died by suicide in March 2003. Ruth would previously have described herself as an "open-minded sceptic" with regard to her beliefs in the afterlife. However, since Samuel's death, she has had many experiences that have convinced her that life continues after the earthly body dies.

"I have had many unusual experiences since Sam died that I refuse to pass off as pure coincidence. One of the first was the day of his funeral in April 2003, three and a half weeks after his suicide. It was the most glorious sunny day, which seemed to brighten an otherwise desperately sad occasion. The forecast for the entire day was good.

"We chose one of Sam's favourite songs to be played at his funeral; 'The Show Must Go on' by Queen. A friend of mine read out a touching piece that had been written by a dying man, pleading with his family and friends not to grieve for him, but to know that he would still be around because life was eternal. Just as she had finished reading the piece and Sam's song began to play, there was a terrifying rattling of the church door and the sound of a hurricane force wind howling around outside. The door, which was incredibly heavy, swung open and a fierce blizzard was raging outside. Only a few minutes earlier it had been calm and sunny and the curious thing is that the temperature was not even cold enough for snow. In fact, snow in April was rarely heard of in our area.

"Even more bizarrely, the moment that the song stopped, so did the blizzard and it was once more sunny and calm outside. In listening to news reports later that day, it seemed that nowhere else in our area had suffered the same freak blizzard. It was one of those inexplicable occurrences that began to make me question my cynical outlook on the paranormal, particularly since Sam loved snow.

"There have been many times since when I have been thinking about Sam, or having a particularly bad day and I switch on the radio to hear 'The Show Must Go On' being played. It's happened on so many occasions now that I truly believe that he is trying to connect with me, which is why I instinctively turn on the radio when his song was playing.

"There has been more than one occasion when I have seen a young man who looks so much like Sam that it could have been his identical twin brother. It first happened about three months after his suicide. I was driving along and a truck drew up beside me at the traffic lights. I'm not normally one of those people who stare into other people's vehicles, but for some reason I turned my head to look at the person driving the truck, which was exactly the colour and make of truck that Sam used to drive. My heart skipped a beat, because I could have sworn that it was Sam driving the truck. He looked at me and smiled, before lifting his hand to wave in the way that Sam always used to do. Was he doing this to reassure me that he was fine? I like to think so.

"What is even spookier is that when I switched on the radio a few minutes later, 'The Show Must Go On' was playing. I felt strangely elated after that experience and for a long time afterwards could feel Sam's presence around me constantly.

"I am not the only one in the family who has felt Sam's presence. My mother told me that she awoke to find him sitting in a chair in the corner of her bedroom. She could see him so clearly that she was able to describe what he was wearing and note that he was sitting cross-legged, which is very unusual for a guy, but is something that Sam used to do. He was wearing the same sweatshirt and jogging pants that he had left at their house on a previous visit. She could see his face clearly, even though it was dark and said that it was as though there was a spotlight on him. She turned to wake up my father, but when she turned back, he was gone."

"My mother is very spiritual, so this vision seemed perfectly natural to her. She told me that those who pass over will rarely reveal themselves to those who might be scared, but instead let us know that they around via other means, such as smells, sounds, white feathers and butterflies appearing from nowhere and other 'coincidences'. How thankful I am to have her to reinforce my newfound beliefs. I don't think that I would ever be able to carry on if I thought that death was final."

Lynne's 22-year-old brother, Gary, took his own life in May 2001. On the day that he died, Lynne believes that either he, or someone else on the other side, communicated with her in an unusual way.

"I had an appointment with a tattoo parlour to have the Chinese symbol for love tattooed on the base of my back. Strangely enough, I had been trying to get an appointment for about two months, but they were always fully booked and this was the earliest available appointment that fitted in with my schedule. I was absolutely certain about the tattoo that I wanted and did not think for one moment that I might change my mind.

"Whilst I was waiting for my appointment, I picked up a book of designs that was on the table. The book fell open at a page containing a picture of a dove. In that instant, I knew that that was what I wanted. Whilst the tattoo was being done, I suddenly thought about Gary and his love of flight. He had always wanted to be a pilot and had just signed up for a course of flying lessons. He was fascinated by birds and often said that if he were any other animal, he would choose to be a bird because of the freedom and peace of flight.

"Later that day, I received a hysterical phone call from my father. The police had just turned up on the doorstep informing my parents that Gary had taken his own life. His flatmate had found him in his bedroom. He had taken an overdose of heroin and had left a suicide note by the side of the bed. At the bottom of the note next to his signature, he had drawn a picture of a dove and written, 'Free at last'.

"I truly believe that someone was communicating with me that day in the tattoo parlour. I don't believe in coincidence. Everything happens for a reason. Maybe others will disagree with me, but I believe that my tattoo was a message and is a part of my brother that will always be with me."

There will be many people who have very inflexible views on karma, reincarnation and spirituality. Instead of recognising the incredible opportunity in this current age for spiritual growth and liberation, most people concern themselves with the material aspects of life; money, luxurious homes, expensive cars, the latest mod cons and other luxuries that are wanted, rather than needed. Instead of giving unconditional help to others, they are instead focused on their own personal comfort and seem to judge success by the salary that one earns, or the material possessions that one has accrued, rather than their service to humanity.

Some parents have turned away from traditional religions after losing a child, whilst others have discovered a level of spirituality that they didn't have prior to the tragedy.

Beverley's 25-year-old daughter Annabel took her own life in February 2005 after being bullied at work. Whilst Beverley has always believed in life after death, she says that she only found true spirituality after losing Annabel and has since turned away from the narrow-minded preachings of her local church.

"Developing spiritually has helped me tremendously. My beliefs have altered somewhat over the past year and I now believe that I have found true spirituality. It is something that I discovered after Annabel died, despite the fact that I had been attending our church since a child. I quickly realised that much of what was preached to us in that church was prejudiced and was not what I now know to be spiritual.

"Looking back, I don't believe that I ever came away from a service feeling uplifted. In fact, if anything, I used to come away feeling guilty about certain things and believing that if I didn't abide by the preachings, then I would be punished. However, it was something that my parents did and something that I did as a matter of routine each week. I suppose that one could call it the misguided brainwashing the vulnerable.

"The point at which I realised I had to stop attending our local church was when some of the parishioners told me that my daughter had sinned and would be punished. Punished? How could they use the word 'punished' when my daughter's depression was as a result of being bullied?

"Those who deserve the punishment are those who drove her to suicide and yet my local church would have condemned me for saying something like that. They would have felt that I should have shown compassion and forgiveness to those who bullied my daughter, but that my daughter should not have been forgiven for finding a way to end her misery.

"I now view most religion as a form of brainwashing, practised by those who wish to impose their inflexible views and way of living onto the impressionable, or onto those who are afraid to question what they are being taught. Look at all the conflict, greed, hate and violence in the world, the majority of it to do with religion and control. What has that to do with love, compassion and peace?

"In my mind, the only law that matters is true spiritual law and the only currency that counts is spiritual currency. I believe that everything that you do or think is logged and that everything one does will eventually be returned, if not in this lifetime, in a future lifetime. Some people might take exception to my views, but I have a right to an opinion in the same way that they feel they have the right to bombard others with their religious beliefs. What's the difference?

"Although Annabel chose to end her life prematurely, she will continue learning on the other side and hopefully will better prepare herself for her next life.

"I'm not saying that I don't miss her, nor that I wouldn't give anything to have her back again, but I feel thankful that she is no longer suffering and that I can still communicate with her. I may not be able to hug her physically, but I feel her presence around me constantly. She appears to me in dreams and always gives me advice when I need it. I would love for everyone who has lost a child to have the beliefs that I now have and to experience the peace that I have felt through spirituality and the knowledge that there is definitely an afterlife."

Roger is a retired clergyman who openly admits his disillusionment with the church. He feels that he was pushed into the profession by his father, who was also a clergyman. Being raised in a strict Christian household, Roger feels that he was never able to question his parents' beliefs, despite having many doubts about the attitude of the church. He was, however, extremely popular in his parish because of his slightly unorthodox approach. He became renowned for his service to the community and for his work with minority sectors, particularly the gay community. Through his belief in life after death, he had an enviable ability to offer enormous comfort to the bereaved as a result.

When Roger's 21-year-old son took his own life in 1997 whilst at university, Roger decided to take early retirement from the church.

"Personally, I have always had a huge problem with those who live by the Bible word-for-word and try to continually quote its verses to others, especially those who claim that the Bible cites suicide as a sin. What some people fail to realise is that the Bible is 66 separate books, written over more than 1,500 years by vastly different writers, each with their own diverse views, needs and values to promote. Who knows how much of it is true and who knows how much of it was written by those who wanted to control humanity by forcing them to live by their personal values?

"The Bible is, after all, just man's interpretation of events, not always written at the time of the occurrence. This is no different to the way in which news is reported today. You take one event and ask several different journalists to report on it and each of them will produce a different spin on the story. Some of what is reported will be fact, whereas some parts will be skewed, misinterpreted, embellished or even made up.

"I think that a number of people believed that someone in my profession should be immune to the tragedy of suicide, so when my son took his own life, I felt as though I was somehow viewed as a failure and know for certain that a minority of parishioners lost faith in me as a man of the cloth. Sadly, suicide can strike anyone's family at any time and is not just confined to certain sectors of society, certain professions, or within difficult family situations.

"I have had many communications with my son since he passed over and although I may still not fully comprehend the reasons why he did what he did, I am thankful that his pain has ended. I am certain that all parents who have lost a child to suicide will say that. Of course, his soul lives on and he will eventually reincarnate into a new body, but for now I know that he is still around me.

"I feel that our roles have been reversed. He is the one who is now watching over me, although I also feel that maybe I didn't watch over him as much as I should have. However, unless one's child is clinically diagnosed with depression, I suppose that one never considers that they might choose suicide as a solution to their problems.

"My profession has brought me into contact with death on a weekly basis and I have seen and felt many things that I can only describe as overwhelming evidence of the afterlife. I wish that I could convince everyone that life definitely continues after the physical body ceases to function. I am certain that it would offer so much more comfort to the bereaved. I hope that one day everyone will have the benefit of this knowledge and will no longer be afraid of death."

With a single thought, one can instantly be transported back to the early years of our child's existence, to happier times or to more painful times, such as reliving the events on the day of the tragedy, the funeral, or the very early days of grief. When one is taken back to an early vision of their child's existence, it is as though all the years in between then and now have temporarily been erased.

The past, present and future can merge through memories and yet on the other side, parallel time zones are reality. There is no such thing as time. As earthlings living a physical existence, we can only comprehend the concept of time in the physical realm. Time is what we experience as a sequence of events, which create the past, present and future, so we don't have to experience everything at once. In actual fact, in the physical world where time never stands still, there is no such thing as the present. By the time you have finished saying, "At the present time", time has moved on from the moment you began saying the sentence to the moment you finished saying it. At no point did time stop. However, spiritual time has no beginning and no end, hence the meaning of the phrase "eternal life". St Augustine of Hippo said, "God created the world with time, not in time".

The purpose of most afterlife exploration is not just curiosity, but a real attempt to be able to offer comfort to those who fear death and, more importantly, to those who are bereaved.

The problem we have is that when we talk about life after death and spirituality, many people assume we are talking about religion. People have difficulty separating God from organised religion. They don't realise that God and religion are separate entities. As Mahatma Gandhi once said, "God has no religion."

When I posted the above view on a social networking website, one friend who often quoted passages from the Bible on her profile took exception to this, because she totally misinterpreted the message. She perceived the criticism of organised religion as a criticism of God.

Naturally, I corrected her and also told her that God was not responsible for everything that happened in the world; people were. It is people who have created division, hate, violence, greed, control and all the other negative aspects of our world. She gracefully accepted this explanation.

All of the above is, of course, not directly relevant to this book, but it is important to mention because of the many insensitive comments that suicide survivors may be subjected to by some people who have rigid beliefs and whose minds are closed to any other possibilities.

Most bereaved people would love to have evidence of the afterlife, yet the greatest evidence we have as individuals is our own experience. However, it is still uplifting to hear about the spiritual encounters of others and, even more so, the link between science and spirituality. Consequently, I have included some links below that I feel may be of interest to readers.

My next book, Kristian's Heaven, provides an explanation of the soul, the reasons for our existence and what really happens to the souls of those who end their lives by their own hand through words channelled from Kristian, the angels and other children who have passed over. The book will offer words of comfort and answers to the many questions that plague people's minds following such a tragedy.

Scientific Evidence of Life after Death

http://www.victorzammit.com/
http://news.bbc.co.uk/1/hi/health/986177.stm
http://www.leaderu.com/truth/1truth28.html
http://www.near-death.com/evidence.html
http://www.reincarnation2002.com/photos.htm
http://www.mellen-thomas.com/

Chapter Twenty-One

Coping Strategies

> *You gain strength, courage and confidence by every experience in which you really stop to look fear in the face. You are able to say to yourself, 'I have lived through this horror. I can take the next thing that comes along.' You must do the thing you think you cannot do.*
>
> Eleanor Roosevelt

A child you loved has ended his or her life. How can you possibly cope? How can you ever live with the pain of realising how much agony and mental trauma your child must have suffered? As mentioned in Chapter Two and Chapter Seven, you may be so overwhelmed by negative emotions, not least of all guilt, you may even believe that you don't deserve to enjoy life again, or even continue living.

Many families who have lost a child to suicide have initially felt that they too wanted to die and yet they haven't. The legacy of their child's suicide has been a renewed strength to create something positive, to help others and build a life that that their child would wish for them.

In the beginning, I found myself vacillating between wanting to reach out to try to give comfort to other parents and families in the same miserable position and wanting to contract emotionally into a little ball in an irrational effort to try to stop the pain from spreading. In the end, I did both.

Immediately after Kristian's suicide, I had to find something that would make me put my feet on the floor everyday; a new purpose in life. That purpose seemed obvious.

I could not allow my son's suicide to cause me to give up on everyone; those I knew and those I didn't know who needed help, comfort and hope. My son bequeathed to me the love, compassion and forgiveness that he showed to so many when he was alive. This was a gift that I had to use to the best of my ability; a gift that could not be wasted. It would be an insult to my son's memory to give up on life and fail all the others who were dear to my heart. My suffering would be channelled constructively and would help to make sense of such a senseless tragedy.

The one comforting thought that I try to dwell on is the knowledge that my son is at peace. He is happy at last, but I also know that he feels regret for what he did. All I ever wanted for my children was for them to be happy. I desperately wish that my son had not chosen death as a vehicle to happiness, but I know that he is no longer tortured.

I very quickly learned to re-frame the way that I viewed situations, believing in a reason for everything and learning to recognise each setback as a learning curve and an opportunity to do something productive. The overriding driving force behind my ability to cope has been my determination not to allow Kristian to have died in vain.

Coping is a much misused word. Coping is not the same as healing. One needs to be able to cry and release the pain in order to be able to heal and yet when one cries others perceive us not to be coping. When we mask the grief and go through the motions of daily living, others believe that we are feeling better and on the road to healing when the opposite is true. When we allow the tears to flow, others don't see this as healing; they see it as quite the opposite.

It seems that in whatever manner we conduct ourselves, we are always being watched and judged. We are either viewed as being "strong" or "not coping very well"; with no middle ground.

I viewed all the grieving families around the world as being trapped in individual whirlpools of grief in a gigantic ocean. Some of these whirlpools would occasionally merge when grieving parties interacted with each other. Some would remain merged, forming strong bonds and friendships, whereas others would separate again and merge with other whirlpools.

Sometimes, you are in a situation where it's impossible to keep the mask in place and you know that with all the will in the world, you are not going to be able to prevent yourself from crying. When all that pent up emotion comes flooding forth, it makes one realise how we just cope on a daily basis, but don't really heal. We just muddle through, going through the motions of existing, trying not to "feel" at times, because if we allowed ourselves to experience that pain continually, we would never survive.

The day that Kristian died, I began writing the poem that was read out at his funeral three weeks later. How did I manage to form those words and channel such intense grief into such eloquence? What fuelled this creativity was an overpowering compulsion to honour my son and let the world know what a special young man he was, despite his faults, of which we all have many. What was the point in being a writer if I could not use my talents to pay tribute to Kristian in a personal way that no other ready-written verse could do? This was the very least that I could do for him.

A few weeks later, in addition to starting on this book, I began creating a website to support both families who have lost a child, grandchild, sibling, friend or relative to suicide and people who may be feeling suicidal. Just being able to offer comfort to one family, or to prevent one person from ending their life would mean that Kristian had achieved something amazing.

Establishing the child suicide website was one of the most positive and constructive things I could have done. From small beginnings, the site grew into an incredible support network around the world, linking people with others in a similar situation and with organisations who are equipped to help both the suicidal and those who have experienced suicide within their family.

The weekly email communication that I have with other families who have experienced a similar tragedy is helpful from both sides. In addition, as time has moved forward, I can speak to newly bereaved families from the perspective of someone who is several years further on in the grieving process.

As a result of establishing the website and connecting with other families, I linked up with a lovely lady in the US who had established several online support groups for suicide survivors and also a support group for people who are experiencing suicidal feelings. These groups are a fantastic resource for anyone who wishes to express their innermost feelings in a non-judgemental environment. They are particularly helpful for those who find face-to-face communication difficult, those who do not have access to a local support group and those who wish to remain anonymous. At the same time, the groups are heavily moderated and do not allow any offensive messages to be posted, nor do they support any pro-suicide discussions.

Everyone copes in different ways and what works for one person may not be suitable for another. Following is a list of suggestions, some of which I hope will be helpful to all those who are desperately seeking ways to move forward in a positive way. This is not an exhaustive list, but just a guide. You may find many other constructive ways of managing your grief.

- **Be gentle with yourself.** Take one small step at a time. Don't force yourself to do too much too early. If you feel like wrapping yourself up in the duvet and doing nothing, don't let anyone persuade you differently. Do things when you feel ready to do them, not when someone else feels you ought to be ready. Take control over the aspects of your life that you can and accept those that you can't.

- **Seek the company of supportive people.** Spend time with people who offer you support and comfort and try to avoid those who don't. You don't need anyone's permission to grieve, or to talk about your child. If you encounter people who make you feel like this, then limit the time you spend with them where possible. You need to be with people who make you feel better, not worse. If you don't feel that you have a supportive network of family or friends, then try to find a local support group. Alternatively, if you have internet access, there are many excellent support groups online where you can connect with other bereaved parents and voice your innermost thoughts, feelings and grievances without being judged.

- **Do something positive.** Create a memory book of your child. You can chronicle your thoughts about him or her, write down happy or amusing memories that you have, add drawings, schoolwork, certificates of achievement, letters, poems, photos or any other memento that you would connect with your child. Set up a support group or initiate a suicide awareness campaign in your area. Raise money for a mental health organisation, or establish a charity in your child's name.

- **Laugh.** Yes, it really is ok to laugh. You don't need anyone's permission to laugh in the same way that you don't need anyone's permission to grieve. In the beginning, you may feel that you will never laugh again, but you will and when you do, you should not feel guilty. Laughter is healthy and it releases feel-good chemicals into your body. Laughter offers a temporary relief from the intense pain of grief. Rent out a hilarious movie, seek the company of someone who has a fantastic sense of humour, or simply reminisce about some amusing moments that you shared with your child in the past.

- **"Talk" to your child.** Just because your child's physical body has died does not mean that you should stop talking to him or her. Talking to your child can be extremely therapeutic and is also a way of acknowledging that they still exist in your mind, your heart and in spirit. Tell them things that you never had the opportunity to say when they were alive. Don't be afraid to talk about your fears, your sadness and how much you miss them, but also talk about happy memories that you have of them and positive things that you plan to do. Sometimes you may feel that your child has answered you, or has visited you in a dream after you have spoken to them. You are not crazy. These things happen and they offer great comfort to those who already believe in the afterlife and those who have, until now, been more sceptical.

- **Do something new.** You may feel that you are not even capable of dealing with the process of just functioning on a daily basis, let alone taking up something new, but when your mind is occupied, you will find temporary relief from the unbearable pain of grief.

Learning something new means that you have to focus and concentrate and when you do this, you will find that for a short period of time you have not been totally consumed by your loss. You should not feel guilty about this. You have a right to carry on living, even though you may feel that you do not deserve a life. Don't view this as doing something for yourself, but as doing something for those who are still in your life - your family and friends. If you do something constructive and derive even the smallest satisfaction from achieving something new, then you will be in a better position to make others around you feel good. It's easier to give your best to others when you feel better about your own life.

- **Treat Yourself.** Think about the things you used to enjoy before you lost your child. There is no reason why you should not enjoy these things again, whether it is a meal in a restaurant, a countryside walk, a massage or a shopping spree. Anything that gives you a "lift" is important and should be savoured without guilt. If it makes you feel better, you can also "treat" your child; buy a special ornament to place on their grave, order a memorial plaque that you can place on a bench in the garden, or plant a tree in memory of them.

- **Write a grief journal.** Chronicle your thoughts, feelings and actions on a daily or weekly basis. Not only can this be extremely cathartic, but it can help you to gauge how you are moving through the grieving process. Although you may not feel that you have moved forward at all, by re-reading where you were in the beginning and where you are now, you will see that certain things will have changed.

You may find that you are achieving more, enjoying more and coping better. This in itself can give you a much-needed boost. You may also learn a great deal about yourself, which you can use to your advantage in the future.

Below are some personal experiences highlighting coping strategies that other suicide grievers have found helpful.

"I found that going to a local support group and speaking to people in person was more helpful than an online support group. It made other grievers seem more real somehow, rather than communicating in a virtual manner with a faceless name. I actually found it easier to open up because you could see people's emotions and reactions. I guess it is because I am a visual person and feel a lot more comfortable conveying my thoughts and feelings when I can see someone's face."

"I tried attending a support group that was based 15 miles from my home, but it just wasn't for me. The distance wasn't a problem at all. I would have been prepared to drive a 100 miles if I felt that I would gain some benefit. I just didn't feel comfortable in a face-to-face situation. Eventually, I made excuses for missing sessions, until I stopped going completely. What does work for me is the anonymous nature of online support groups for people who have experienced the loss of someone close to suicide. I am able to reveal far more about what happened to my daughter and the pain I am enduring than I ever did in the in-person group."

"After my son's suicide, I tried various support groups initially and whilst these were great as an outlet for my grief, there were many issues that I needed to resolve and I eventually felt this required the involvement of a professional. I enlisted the help of a grief specialist and this has helped me to view so many things differently. Although these things are not related to what happened to my son, I can see how they have impacted my grief and my reactions to what happened. Whilst nothing can ever cure the grief, I feel that my sessions with the therapist have helped me to cope more effectively."

"Despite all the various methods I employed to cope with my sister's suicide, nothing would remove the image that I had of finding her hanging in our room. I did not want her asphyxiated features to be the last memory I had of her and yet her face kept haunting me. I wanted to remember her as she was before that horrific day. A friend of mine suggested a psychiatrist she knew and whilst I did not believe that this would help, I took her up on her advice and made an appointment. I am now glad that I did. He told me to place happy photographs of my sister around the house and focus on these. It was not an instant cure and the memory of her suicide will never disappear, but now the happy images are uppermost in my mind and the horrific image has faded."

"When my son's 18th birthday came around just three months following his suicide, we decided to throw a party in his memory. We had always held parties for him, even as a teenager, so we decided to continue the tradition, even though he could not be with us in the physical sense. My husband and I did not want it to be a sombre occasion, but one of celebration and happy memories.

"I would be lying if I said that we didn't all shed a lot of tears, but we also laughed a lot and decided to honour him by holding a party every year on his birthday."

"When my mind starts replaying the events of my daughter's death, I make a conscious effort to say 'Stop!' and focus on the beautiful events in our lives together, such as the day she was born, her first smile, first word, first steps, her hilarious toddler tantrums, picking her up after her first day at school and so many other wonderful, charming memories throughout her short life. I acknowledge that she had problems, but I choose not to focus on these, because it is not healthy and does nothing to promote any degree of healing. I also created a separate photo album that chronicled many of these special events in her life, so that if I am having difficulty switching off from the negative thoughts, I can open up the album and smile again."

"In order to cope, I realised that I had to let go of all the superficial crap in my life, including worn out, difficult relationships that drained me of what little energy I had. My brother's suicide altered the way in which I viewed everything, but most of all the insignificant, materialistic attitude of some people within my immediate social circle. I did not realise how draining these relationships were until my brother's suicide; a time when I was at my lowest point and temporarily looked to other people for emotional support and upliftment. I found that I was less tolerant of self-absorbed, superficial people, yet more tolerant of others who had genuine problems."

"A few weeks following my adult daughter's suicide, I had an amazing spiritual awakening. Deep down, I never really believed that God truly had anything to do with religion, because there are so many different - and sometimes obscure - rules and beliefs associated with them and they can't all be right. For that reason, I rebelled against anything that had any religious connections. It did not mean that I did not believe in some sort of God, just that I did not believe in all the pious preachings of some people. It also did not mean that I did not associate with people who had these religious beliefs. I have friends who call themselves Christians, friends who are Muslims, a friend who practices Hinduism and another who is a Buddhist.

"I never understood the expression, 'God fearing' either, because it seemed like a contradiction to love and forgiveness. I did, however, research everything that I could about spirituality and life after death and began 'talking' to my daughter and asking her to show me a sign that she was still with me.

"I suddenly began experiencing signs and communications from the other side. At first I dismissed them as being 'just coincidence' or 'just my imagination', but they occurred with such increasing regularity that I began to have faith. The more I took notice of these signs, the more often they occurred. For example, it seemed that each time I spoke to my daughter, a white feather would appear from nowhere, or a butterfly would land by my side, or every time I switched on the radio, her favourite song would be playing. I then experienced this huge sense of elation and enormous comfort in receiving confirmation that death of the physical body is not death of the soul, the real 'person'.

"It is these signs and this belief that has enabled me to cope more than anything else."

I would like to conclude this chapter with some words from my late friend Louise, whose son James passed over in December 2002 following a heroin overdose. We communicated regularly via email, with our thoughts and feelings often mirroring one another. We were also at a similar stage in our grieving process, since there was only a month between the passing of our sons. Four years following James' death, Louise found herself fighting another battle; that of cancer. She sadly lost her fight for life a few months later, but I will always remember how, prior to her diagnosis, she told me that she no longer feared old age, but almost welcomed it because it would be one step closer to being reunited with her son.

"I'm not entirely sure what my beliefs on the afterlife were before losing James. I have always tried to find rational explanations for everything and yet clearly there are happenings that defy all logic.

"For a long time after James passed over, I couldn't bear to touch anything in his room; I couldn't even bring myself to clean it. I was so afraid of erasing memories, of erasing his personality, of erasing him. I would stand in the middle of his room just staring at everything, but I didn't want to disturb anything. My husband, James' stepfather, refused to even enter the room and kept telling me that I had to clear it out sooner or later. I have nobody with whom to share the extreme loss as one would if one were married to your dead child's father. He tried to understand at first, but now I don't think he has any comprehension of the ongoing pain.

"Two months after James passed, I was frenetically searching through boxes of old photographs, looking for one in particular that my ex-husband had taken of us just after James' birth. Despite searching through every packet several times over, I could not find this particular photo. I berated myself for not having put them into albums.

"At the point where I had given up hope of ever finding it, assuming that at some point during various house moves it had been lost, I am absolutely certain that I head James' voice say, 'You'll find it'. For a moment, I began to question my sanity, wondering whether the grief was causing me to hear imaginary voices in my head. I was alone in the house at the time and upon looking out of the window, thinking that perhaps there was someone outside having a conversation, there was no one in sight. I must add that we live in a small, isolated village, so it is extremely unusual to see or hear anyone other than the occasional neighbour, of which there are very few.

"That same evening, I walked into James' room and, for the first time since the tragedy, sat on his bed. As I put my hand down on the duvet, it rested upon what felt like a piece of card. I looked down and a shiver ran through me from the base of my spine to the top of my head. There, in a generic cardboard frame, was the photo I had been seeking for so many hours!

"It is absolutely impossible for me to explain how that photo had got there. I had been into James' room so many times before and his bed had been totally clear; it had definitely not been there before. I thought about the words I had heard and for the first time in my life I felt I had had indisputable evidence of some inexplicable force outside the realms of physics.

"From that point on, I no longer feared old age or death. In fact I welcomed it, because I realised that I would, indeed, see my son again."

Although I was saddened by her loss, I felt a strange comfort in knowing that Louise had finally been reunited with James and so much sooner than she ever expected. Bless you Louise and thank you.

Chapter Twenty-Two

The Years Ahead

When the young bury the old, time heals the pain and sorrow. But when the process is reversed, the sorrow remains forever.

Joseph P. Kennedy

There is always the assumption that the pain of losing a child, grandchild or sibling to suicide will lessen with time, that the second year will be easier than the first, the third easier than the second and so on. It doesn't always happen in such a predictable fashion. When one loses a child, emotional triggers can bring an intense grief to the surface that is as raw and powerful as it was in the beginning, even years after the tragedy. When dealing with such a devastating loss, time is immaterial. In an instant, the mind can bring the past to the present, when it appears as though no time has elapsed between a tragic event and the current moment. Few people comprehend that, usually only those who have experienced it themselves.

When one has a permanent physical or visible disability, it elicits far more sympathy than an emotional disorder. If grief appeared hand-in-hand with some form of physical impairment, then perhaps others would have more sympathy and we would have permission to continue to cry years after the cause.

At no point does one ever return to the "normal" that was familiar to us before. The "normal" that follows the loss of a child or loved one to suicide will be very different to the past "normal".

It is a normal that still entertains joy and does not have to be a normal of perpetual misery, but it will never again be the same normal that we knew when our child was alive. It encompasses an acceptance of life with a valuable part missing and where phases of intense, resurfacing grief have become customary. There will be periods when you feel that you are coping well and then something will send you spiraling downwards again.

I began writing this chapter on 1 November 2004, the second anniversary of Kristian's passing. This same time the previous year, I was dreading the moment when I was no longer able to say, "This time last year Kristian was alive". I relived his final steps on the night of October 31 2002, piecing together his perceived movements from the information that had been collated by the coroner at the inquest. I put myself in his position, trying to feel the absolute desperation and hopelessness that led to his premature exit from this world. The emotional agony and overpowering sadness consumed my entire body. I curled into a foetal position to try and ease the physical pain that had manifested within. I could not have felt more pain had I been nailed to a wall and beaten relentlessly, with no form of defence.

Knowing how much my son must have been suffering was intolerable, but I believed that I deserved to feel his pain, to share his anguish and to be punished for not being able to save him. I hoped that I would eventually be able to accept my loss in a healthier way, rather than one based on guilt, self-flagellation and wanting to suffer now as my son had, because not only had I been unable to take away his pain then, but I felt largely responsible for it.

Everyone told me that time would heal and that eventually the intense pain would subside and lead to a bearable pain with which one could live. As time passed, I found this to be somewhat of a fallacy in the physical sense.

As the day of Kristian's passing moved to the back of everyone's memory, there was a pain that grew deeper; the pain of moving further away from my son's life and the fear that I would forget. I was afraid that I would forget what he looked like, forget the sound of his voice and forget his expressions, his mannerisms and all of the quirks that shaped his personality. I was afraid that I would reach a point where I would have difficulty in believing that he had ever existed; that he would simply become a dream.

Birthdays have always been particularly painful. I begin writing this paragraph on 22 March 2006, on what should have been Kristian's 24th birthday. Once again, I cannot help but compare the contrast between the sadness and emptiness that envelops me now and the elation that I felt on this same day 24 years ago when my first baby entered the world. I experienced a sense of disbelief when he was born, as do so many mothers. I spent hours staring at this perfectly formed little person, finding it impossible to believe that here was the bump that had been growing inside me for nine months and that he was really mine. Today, I am experiencing a different sort of disbelief; the continuing disbelief that my son is no longer alive. Would I have done things differently had I known what was going to happen? Some things, no, but other things, definitely. I know that I would certainly have told Kristian more often how much I loved him.

My youngest daughter Lauren began school in September 2004, a day that I had dreaded for so long. I wanted to hold onto her forever. I wanted keep her as an angelic, white-haired, rosebud-lipped four-year-old; the age of innocence, of a rose-coloured fairy story world of happy endings and good prevailing over evil. I didn't want her to see the magic gradually disappearing with each passing year, as she was increasingly exposed to the harsh realities of life.

I didn't want her to witness violence, greed and hate or to experience heartache and pain, but most of all, I didn't ever want her to experience the same loss of hope and absolute desperation that her brother had suffered.

Losing a child brought such a sense of distrust with it. I feared the capabilities of others into whose care I entrusted my daughter, even qualified schoolteachers. Would she be safe at playtime? Would she be bullied out of jealousy, because of her beautiful, long white-blonde hair and angelic features? Would she feel lost and alone? Would she experience kindness or cruelty? Would her numerous talents be recognised? Would her natural creativity be nurtured or suppressed? Of course, one might suggest that all these fears are natural parental concerns under any circumstances, but losing a child brings with it a level of paranoia that surpasses any natural parental worry that one might have experienced before the tragedy.

Of course, when Lauren began school it brought back memories of Kristian's first day at school, still looking far too small to be trussed up in a smart uniform and removed from my maternal cloak for six hours a day.

It was several months before I could hear the phone ring and not immediately imagine that it was the school calling to inform me that some awful accident had befallen Lauren. In fact, I did receive one such phone call after a heavy door had swung into her head. As I raced up to the school, I was imagining the worst case scenarios of a cerebral haemorrhage or fractured skull and, at the very least, concussion. She had sustained a small scratch and bruise and was clearly unfazed by the incident, but nevertheless I feared that this was just the beginning. I wanted to keep her at home with me, to protect her and never have to lose control over her destiny as I had done with Kristian.

The paranoia remains and often manifests itself in the most horrific nightmares. Knowing that my daughter would be going swimming with the school when she entered Year 2 in September 2006 brought with it shocking dreams of her drowning. And when I finally allowed her to play outside our house with her friends, it generated fears about abduction and resultant nightmares of a stranger taking her whilst my back was turned for just a second.

My fears aren't just confined to Lauren. I am still unable to see a police car turn into our cul-de-sac without imagining that they are coming to relay some tragic news about my daughter Anneliese or son Carsten. Previously, I would probably have wondered what the other neighbours had done to warrant such a visit, but rarely considered that they might be the bearers of life-changing news. Now, the assumption always is that the doorbell is going to ring and that I am going to be confronted by uniformed officers who are about to send the already unstable foundations of my hastily rebuilt world crashing around me once again.

The flashbacks were, and still are, horrendous. Although it is natural to experience these following such a tragic event, they began to occur with frightening and excruciating regularity during the fourth year after Kristian's suicide. Not only did I experience flashbacks of seeing Kristian after he had died, but also of various traumatic incidents throughout his life in which I had either been involved, or had witnessed. Some of these are too painful to relay, but they crucify me with guilt to the point where I don't feel that I can survive the agony. However, I will and I must, for giving up on my own life would be to give up on my other children and to unjustly punish them. I would also be doing an enormous disservice, not only to my son, but to all those traumatised individuals I hope I have helped and all those I hope I shall help in the future.

The simplest way to describe the flashbacks is to say that it is as though I have been transported back in time. For the briefest of moments, my surroundings change and I am there with my son, seeing in vivid detail what I saw at the time that these events occurred, feeling the same feelings, smelling the same aromas and hearing the same sounds; I am in a trance, no longer in the present. As I return to the present reality, I am once again consumed by grief and guilt, where the tears flow relentlessly and I repeat over and over again, "I'm so sorry Kristian; I'm so, so sorry." Kristian then responds with, "My dear mum; you did what you felt was right at the time."

When you have lost someone under such devastating circumstances, particularly a child, time doesn't heal. Time provides an acceptance that one has to live one's life without the physical presence of the person who has died, and time simply increases the distance between periods of overwhelming and incapacitating grief. I imagine that the bereaved are only ever able to say that they are healed when they can think about the person they have lost without feeling any fragment of pain, sadness or guilt. However, I have never spoken to a suicide survivor who has been able to say that they are healed, even twenty, thirty or forty years after the event.

Vera's 19-year-old son Peter hung himself in 1971. She says that the four decades that have passed have never eased the pain.

"Time? What is time? It's irrelevant. Time may change the appearance of physical things, but it doesn't always alter the emotions. It may distort mental images and memories, erasing some of the parts we would rather forget, but the mind is an amazing piece of machinery. Even the scenes you want to forget can suddenly re-emerge at the forefront of your mind and when you least expect it.

"I can remember the day of Peter's suicide with such clarity that it could have happened yesterday. In that sense, I am trapped in a moment in time from which there is no moving back, or moving forward.

"That doesn't mean that my life stopped the moment that Peter's did. I have continued to live my life to the max and have achieved many more things than I think I would have done, had he survived. I am sure that some people find it hard to understand the concept of leading a fulfilling life and grieving simultaneously, but I am certain that most bereaved people do the same. If they are continuing to eat, work and find time for leisure pursuits, then they too are proving that when one carries on functioning after loss, it does not mean that they are not grieving, or that they are over it. Similarly, there are others who cannot believe that I am still crying for my son after all this time. It makes me laugh when some of them view this as a sign that I haven't moved on. I look at my life and know that I have achieved more than the majority of them have, so if that's not moving on, then I don't know what is."

Time can also bring with it a host of other fears that may seem absurd to someone who has not been bereaved. However, to a survivor these fears are not unfounded, even when the person experiencing them feels that they are illogical.

Janine lost her only brother to suicide in May 1996 when he was just 15-years-old. Janine explains her fears of dying herself or losing others close to her leading up to the 10th anniversary.

"When the 10th anniversary of my brother's death approached, I didn't think it would be as much of an issue as it was, but I suddenly found myself worrying that I might die.

"I felt that others would believe that it was so irrational that I didn't feel able to discuss it with anyone, not even my husband. Although I desperately wanted to share my fears, perhaps in the hope that I would be offered reassurance that it wouldn't happen, I felt too embarrassed to say anything to anyone. Besides, how could anyone honestly say that it wouldn't happen? There are no guarantees in life. Any one of us could be run over by a bus tomorrow.

"Now, several years on, not only am I worried that I might die, but that I might lose my only son. Although he is seven-years-old, I still compulsively check him several times a night and when my husband is away on business, I allow him to sleep in my bed, more for my comfort and security than his. When you lose someone close at such a young age, you realise that death isn't confined to the physically sick or elderly."

Although living alongside grief can be a terminal struggle, our continuing existence keeps the memory of our precious children alive by enabling us to share aspects of their lives with family, friends and strangers. Time also allows us to offer support or comfort to newly bereaved parents.

In the beginning, I realised that if I could live through the first week, then I could make it through another week, then a month, then six months, then the first anniversary and so on. By reviewing my life since the event, I have been able to see where I was in the beginning and where I am now. Time has not healed the deep wounds, but it has allowed me to manage the pain in a constructive manner. With many ailments, we have the option of a taking pill to quickly and effectively relieve a physical pain, but there are no instant fixes or fast resolutions for grief, which is a chronic condition.

Everyone will encounter different obstacles at different times along the grief road. Whilst we can foresee the obviously difficult times, such as anniversaries and Christmas for example, most cannot be predetermined. We cannot always predict when we are going to encounter an intense grief trigger, as mentioned in Chapter Twelve. In these situations, the time that has elapsed bears no significance.

Time has caused me to reassess even more my abilities as a parent. I accept that I was not a perfect parent, although I did my best with the physical and emotional tools that I possessed at the time. I hope that the mistakes I made when raising Kristian have helped me to be a better parent to my surviving children. In the past, I would have said on many occasions, "Not now, I'm busy" or "I'll do that with you later", but I realise now that there may not be a "later" and that I have to cherish every moment possible with my children, family and friends. We cannot control our children's destiny, but we can teach them certain values and equip them with the knowledge and discipline that they require to make the best possible attempt at building strong foundations for a successful life.

What still shocks me is how little sensitivity and understanding some people have, not only about depression and suicidal behaviour, but about grief in relation to time. There is so much scope for education on this uncomfortable topic, but it is not something that can be achieved by the minority. Those survivors who have the courage to speak out may help to dispel the myths in some small capacity, but in order to reach the masses and achieve a greater level of understanding and tolerance, there needs to be relentless global campaigning and education.

Mel's story begins in 2000, when her son David took his own life following a disagreement with his father and brother.

"David was 22-years-old and he had some problems, drugs being one of them. He thought he needed these because of his shyness. I spoke to our doctor and got someone from the drug squad to come to my home to speak to him. He tried; he really did. I sent him away to be with his brother and away from his old crowd of friends. Wow, he came back great feeling good and I had my son back.

"He then met a girl and fell in love. After a while of going out with her, the girl told me how much she loved my son, so I told her not to hurt him, as he was vulnerable. She knew about the drugs and I explained to her that my son had depression and felt suicidal and to please go slowly as I had just got my boy back.

"Two months later, she was two-timing him and did it in his face. He cried hard to me. We were very close. I tried to keep him strong and she kept trying to get him back.

"On 8 October 2000, he had the run in with his dad and brother. On 9 October 2000, he hung himself in an old shed up the lane from where we lived. That was a morning I will never forget. I am sure that all families who have lost a child in the same way know the devastation that comes. The police were very good. They were the ones who found him.

"I have left out bits and pieces of my story, which are too painful to think about. On that morning of 9 October 2000, I was in the kitchen making a cup of tea thinking I would drink it and watch a TV chat show. David came downstairs. I asked him what he had up his jumper and he said it was rubbish he wanted rid of and he went out the back door. The sign was there; I knew something was wrong. I felt it. I kick myself now for not acting on my instincts. Maybe I could have stopped him, maybe I couldn't; but now I'll never know and constantly torture myself over the 'What ifs'.

"He came back in and went back upstairs. I don't know what made me go and call him about 15 minutes later, but when I did, I got no answer. I went upstairs. He was not there. I looked everywhere. I felt scared and so I phoned a friend in the police. I told her what I feared. She told me to put the kettle on and that they would be there soon.

"It was lashing down with rain. I went up and down the lane, passing the shed and calling his name. Then Susan, the police friend, arrived with another police officer. Susan got me to make tea while the police officer went looking everywhere. A while later, Susan got a call on her phone. I knew it was about David. She looked at me and said she would be back shortly, as she had to speak to the police officer. I sat there. I knew, but I sat praying; not even praying - I was talking to God, 'Please make this be ok.'

"There were no tears, just fear. I must have sat there an hour until I had to know where they went, so I went looking. I found them at the old shed.

"People think because it happened 10 years ago that I have 'got over it' and that I should be over it. Well yes, after 10 years of living in limbo I have learnt how to cope. I had to, like everyone else. Have I got over it? No. Neither a mother nor a father can ever get over this. I must have written two thousand letters to my son about how I was feeling; like my anger, the pain of missing him and the guilt. It did help to a degree, but then I wanted to talk to a mother that had gone through a loss like I had. No one else would do and it did help. We all reach out for help, or we would go insane.

"I miss my son so very much. It will always feel like yesterday and I have lived on for my four other children now and grandchildren.

"I always read and keep my son's picture in Romans Chapter 8, verse 27 to 31. I am not a good Christian woman. I wish I was and I don't know why we go through what we do. I hope in some way my letter can help someone out there."

Louisa lost her 21-year-old brother Terry in January 1994, but as with all bereaved families, the passing of time means nothing in terms of how the grief can still affect you.

"Today marked 15 years since Terry took his last breath. 15 years!!!! I can't believe I just typed that. How can it be possible that I have lived for a decade and a half without my precious brother? It's amazing how time doesn't stop for anything or anyone, but how 15 years ago could be yesterday in terms of the clarity of memories. I can still remember everything about that day, but the most painful part is how I never got to say goodbye.

"Terry died from a gunshot wound to his chest. Amazingly, the bullet didn't penetrate any of his major organs, but he bled to death before the paramedics could reach him. It wasn't their fault. By the time my father discovered him in the barn on his land, it was probably too late to save him, but I guess that it was his intention not to be found in time. I don't know whether I derive any comfort from that or not. If it had just been a cry for help and he'd really wanted to live, then it would have been even more devastating, if that doesn't sound insensitive.

"If he really was in such emotional distress, at least I know that his pain has ended. Of course, if we could have helped him to find a less fatal solution to his problems, then we would have done so, but the truth is that none of his family or friends had any inkling what was going through his mind. He was always such a cheerful person, but he was also never very good at discussing his personal feelings. I just think now that he hid his misery from people exceptionally well.

"The night that Terry died I was staying over at a friend's house. I remember the phone ringing in the middle of the night, but my friend Suzie told me that they'd had a lot of silent calls lately from a withheld number, which they assumed was a prankster. She told me that they always had the answer machine on, so that the caller would leave a message if it was important. It was only after I returned home the following day that I discovered that it was my aunt who was trying to call me to tell me the news. She didn't want to leave such a tragic message on someone else's answer machine.

"The only words I remember hearing were, 'Terry's gone.' I remember thinking, 'Gone where?' but when I saw the look on the faces of my parents and other family members, neighbours and friends, I realised what they meant and collapsed onto my knees. I remember someone picking me up and holding me tightly whilst I screamed and sobbed hysterically.

"There are no words to describe the pain, guilt and anger that I still feel. It has got to the point where I feel unable to discuss my feelings with anyone outside of the family, because they believe that I should have got over it a long time ago. The only 'strangers' with whom I can divulge my true feelings are those I have met on suicide bereavement forums on the internet. It's funny how they all say the same thing; that you never get over it, that the pain is just as real and strong as it was in the beginning and that other people who haven't experienced the loss of someone in such a way just don't get it.

"I am sure that some people believe my brother's suicide is a trump card that I play as an excuse for times when I am feeling irritable, miserable or bad-tempered, in an attempt to gain some attention or sympathy. I can't deny that his suicide has affected my emotional health, but I certainly do not play on it. On the contrary, I always use some other excuse.

"To say that it is because of Terry would be a horrible thing to do and it would mean that I was blaming him for my moods.

"I can't talk about why he did what he did, because no one knows. Terry didn't leave a note, so of course there is a little part in the minds of all his family that believes that what happened was just a horrible accident, although the police and the pathologist believe that it was an intentional act.

"Will I always feel like this? I don't know. I have learned to live hand-in-hand with my grief, but as far as I see it at the moment, it will follow me to my own grave."

Bethany's little sister Dani was only 14 when she took a fatal overdose in August 1988 after enduring relentless bullying at school.

"On 16 August 2008, the 20th anniversary of Dani's tragic passing, I went through a really bad period of mourning and also guilt that here I was experiencing all these things in life that she should have enjoyed. She would have been 34-years-old, perhaps with a wonderful career, or even with a husband and children, cousins to my three children. I couldn't help thinking what might and should have been. I suppose that's normal for any family who's been through this, but it may not seem normal to those who haven't. I just hope that some of those people who haven't will also read this book to help them have a little more empathy and understanding.

"I remember the day of Dani's suicide with alarming clarity and I know that dozens of other bereaved families to whom I have spoken have said the same thing. I also remember wishing that I could jump forward ten or twenty years so that perhaps the pain would have lessened and I had learned to live without her in my life. Now I am here, over twenty years on and although I have learnt to live without her, the pain has not diminished.

"What shocked me most was how she knew what to do. I would not know the first thing about how to hang myself successfully without permanently disabling myself. Did she read about it somewhere? How did she go about finding out such nauseating information? Did she do it in ignorance, assuming it was easy? She hung herself from the bedpost of our bunk beds, which I would never have thought was high enough, but evidently it was. It was like a horrific nightmare, especially realising that people so young - and people you love so much - know how to kill themselves in such a sickening way.

"People think that I have a settled, happy life and that Dani is just a small piece of my past that no longer affects me. However, part of me died that day and now, over two decades later, I am still living with that part missing. It will never be replaced. I don't talk to anyone about it, not even my family. Parents, grandparents and friends experience a different pain to that of siblings. I'm not saying that it's any better or worse than parental grief; of course it's not. In addition to not wishing to add to their own grief, I know that my relationship to Dani was different to theirs, so I miss her in different ways.

"I don't know that I would really want this hole in my heart to mend. That would be like admitting that I was over it, or that she had never existed. This void is a sign of how much I loved my sister and how much I miss her - and always will. Time means nothing."

Trudy lost all of her family over a period of 20 months. Her 17-year-old brother Josh died when he was hit by a train in February 1995. Her parents never recovered from the shock and nine months later in November 1995, her father died, followed by her mother in 1996.

"My dad was in his early fifties when Josh came along and my mother was in her mid-forties. Josh was an unexpected, but very welcome surprise. My parents really cherished him because he was their baby and their last. And so did I. My parents had also had me later in life and I was only three-years-old when Josh was born.

"In reality, three years is such a small age gap, yet I always thought of Josh as my baby brother, even when he reached his teens. We were very close and he also had a brilliant relationship with my father. I suppose he could do all the "boy" things with him that I was never interested in doing; football, rugby, carpentry and tinkering around on old cars, which was my dad's passion.

"Josh was incredibly bright, but he also set himself high standards and worried terribly about not achieving top grades at school and then at college. If ever he felt he hadn't done as well as he should have in any subject, he would reprimand himself and sink into a black mood for a few days. Despite being told that he was brilliant and that what he regarded as a poor result was still better than most pupils' best result, nothing would console him. We just had to leave him alone and allow him to emerge from his mood in his own time. In retrospect, we now all see that this was probably a sign of undiagnosed depression.

"Josh and I had a very happy, loving childhood. I cannot pinpoint any particular circumstance or event that would have contributed to Josh suffering from depression, other than the pressure that he placed upon himself to be the best at everything. This was something that came from within him and was certainly not put upon him by our parents. All they wanted was for us to be happy and to try our best, but at no time was there ever any pressure to be better than everyone else.

"The strange thing is that just before Josh died, he had achieved particularly good results in his mock exams and appeared really happy. He did have a fairly unsettled relationship with his girlfriend, but their disagreements never seemed to worry him in the same way as any sort of perceived failure in his college work. Maybe we all missed something and maybe other things did bother him more than we realised, but how could we help him if he never admitted was he was feeling? Maybe it's because he viewed that as a weakness, or failure.

"I still feel sick whenever I think about the night it happened. Even now, it still seems like some horrendous nightmare. In fact, 'horrendous' is not a strong enough word to describe it. It was a Friday and Josh had told my parents that he was going to his girlfriend's house straight after college and that from there they were going to a party. He often did this, so none of us had any reason to feel concerned.

"It was 1.30am when we were awoken by the police at our door. I stayed in bed, but could hear several voices downstairs. Suddenly, I heard this awful wailing sound and it was a moment before I realised it was my mother. I then heard my father saying, "Oh my God no, not our baby, not our baby!" I knew then that something awful had happened and all I could do was to lay there frozen in terror. I knew it was something to do with Josh. I think I knew then that he was dead.

"After what seemed like an eternity, my father came up and sat on my bed. His face was grey and his eyes were red and swollen. He put his hand on my arm and opened his mouth to say something, but no words came out. I said to him, "Josh is dead isn't he?" He bowed his head and nodded, before lifting me up into his arms and sobbing like a baby. In the background, I could still hear my mother howling whilst a police officer comforted her.

"No one really knows why he did it. He did go to his girlfriend's house and they did go to the party together, but later in the evening without anyone's knowledge, he left. His girlfriend and a few of his other friends thought that he was playing a prank and was hiding in the house or garden somewhere. The house where the party was being held backed onto a railway line. It was while a couple of his friends were searching the garden that they heard the screeching of the train wheels against the tracks and a sickening thud, as though the train had hit an animal or a tree had fallen across the line. Of course, you already know that it wasn't an animal or a tree. It was my baby brother Josh.

"At the inquest, the train driver said that there was no doubt in his mind that Josh stepped in front of the train deliberately. Josh was on his own, so it wasn't a dare and he wasn't running. He just stepped slowly and deliberately into the middle of the track and stood there facing the oncoming train. At this stage, it was too late for the driver to stop in time.

"Prior to the inquest hearing, the police had to interview everyone present at the party. The strange thing is that Josh was only drinking coke and the pathologist who conducted his post mortem said that there were no traces of alcohol in his bloodstream. His actions could therefore not be blamed on inebriation or lack of co-ordination. It was clear that he knew exactly what he was doing.

"I know that all suicide survivors ask the question 'Why?' In Josh's case, however, it is a huge 'Why?' There was absolutely no sign at all that he was feeling depressed or suicidal. If we had known, would we have been able to prevent what happened? I can't answer that and I don't like to dwell on it, because it is still too painful.

"Nine months after Josh's suicide, my father suffered a fatal stroke. My mother's physical and mental health really deteriorated after that and she totally lost the will to live. The following year, she also suffered a stroke. She died in hospital 9 days later. I had only just turned 22 and I had lost almost my entire family.

"I often think that I haven't grieved for my parents like I should have, because at the time of their deaths, I was still in shock from Josh's suicide. It has also affected other people's opinions of me, I am sure. I think they expected me to fall apart after losing both of my parents in such a short space of time. Because the loss of a parent is something to which more people can relate, the empathy appeared to be far greater towards me than when Josh died. I wasn't an emotional wreck because I still hadn't accepted the loss of my brother, so they must have thought I was hard. In fact, I felt completely numb, as though it were not physically or mentally possible for me to suffer any more grief.

"I don't like to compare different types of grief, but having suffered the loss of both parents to natural causes and that of my brother to suicide, I can say without a doubt that one of the worst types of grief is that after a suicide. It must be the case for any death that you feel could have been preventable.

"Even when my parents were alive, I found it very difficult to talk to them about Josh, but I think that was partly because I did not want to make them suffer any more. Although I think we all needed to talk about him, it was also too painful at that time. I thought that maybe a time would come when we would be able to laugh about the good memories rather than just focus on his loss, but sadly that was never to be.

"I have struggled through the past 17 years without ever really being able to speak to anyone about Josh. Other people are ok with me talking about my parents, because more people are able to relate to that loss, but I can sense the discomfort whenever I try to talk about Josh. Whenever I have tried to bring up the conversation of Josh's suicide with friends or my husband, they just don't seem able to handle it.

"Just recently, I have been experiencing terrible flashbacks and the grief has completely overwhelmed me. It may sound ridiculous to some, but in many ways I feel worse now than I did when it happened. How can I explain this to people I know though? After all, in other people's minds it happened so long ago, so why would they understand? I feel a real need to talk about what happened and maybe this is why I am suffering now, because I have never really had an outlet for my feelings.

"I am just thankful for the internet and for being able to connect with people like Jan, the author of this book. I can't explain what a relief it is to know that my feelings are completely normal and that there are (albeit sadly) many other people who have experienced the loss of someone close to suicide. I am not happy that they have also suffered such a terrible tragedy, but I do feel better knowing that I am not alone on this painful journey."

Pamela's daughter, Marie, was 24 when she took an overdose of painkillers and alcohol in July 1992 after separating from her adulterous husband. She left behind a two-year old son Ben, whom Pamela and her husband took custody of following the tragedy.

"My daughter has been gone for nearly 20 years now and yet on occasions I still find myself picking up the phone to call her and tell her how well Ben is doing and how he has just been offered a place at his chosen university. How absurd does that sound?

"If she were still here, she would know how well he was doing. However, I think it's still impossible for my mind to process what happened. It still seems like the most awful dream that one could imagine. Her dad won't even talk about it and thinks that I should have moved on long ago. The reality is that I don't think he has moved on either. He has just chosen to push his grief under the carpet and leave it there, believing that he has dealt with it. One day that carpet will move and the grief will hit him with full force.

"We have had several bereavements in the family since; grandparents, parents and other relatives, but these were all natural deaths that were of course sad, but which we accepted. In my mind, nothing can ever come close to losing a child to suicide, except perhaps murder. I've never been able to say this to anyone who hasn't also experienced the loss of someone to suicide, because I am sure that my belief would offend some. I agree that you cannot put different types of grief into separate little boxes, but at the same time you cannot say that grief following a death by natural causes is the same as grief following a suicide.

"Marie was not meant to die when she was 24. She had her whole life ahead of her. She was intelligent, beautiful and adored her son. She was also very trusting and I think that the betrayal she felt when her husband Paul had an affair destroyed her faith in people. Paul and Ben were her life. I know that she began questioning her worth as a mother after Paul left and I am wondering whether she believed he would be better off without her. That's the part that I find most difficult to understand - the fact that she did this to Ben. She loved him so much, but maybe she did it out of love. Marie was such a caring person and I truly believe that if she realised how much pain she would cause to everyone who knew her, maybe she would have found another way.

"Every day I think about what might have been. I try to picture how Marie would look now and what she would be doing. Would she be happily married to someone else and would she have had more children? I do talk to Ben about his mother, but only focus on the good things. I don't ever want him to feel that he was in any way responsible for what happened, or that his mother didn't love him. Ben doesn't have any contact with his father, but I feel secretly glad about that. I could not look at Paul without blaming him for what happened.

"What I would like to get across to people is that regardless of whether it has been 16 days or 16 years, the grief doesn't necessarily diminish. There are many things in life that I have forgotten, but the memories of the day we lost Marie will always remain crystal clear. The pain, the loss, the shock, the disbelief and all those other horrid emotions that go hand in hand with losing someone to suicide are just as sharp now as in the beginning. I don't see myself feeling any differently in another 16 years' time."

Melvin's only son Gary was 21 when he hung himself in April 2003. Melvin and Gary's mother had separated when Gary was 15, but Gary had chosen to live with Melvin, although he still saw his mother regularly. Gary's suicide was a total shock to everyone who knew him. There were no signs that he was feeling depressed or suicidal and, as many other parents have said about their own children, Gary had no history of depression and his life appeared to be good. He also did not leave a suicide note, so he left absolutely no clues as to why he ended his life.

In addition to grieving for his son, Melvin has had to endure blame thrown at him by his ex-wife, who believes that he must have noticed that something was not right and that Gary needed help.

"It's over five years on and yet I don't know if the intensity of my pain and grief will ever decrease. I felt like the entire reason for my existence was wiped out the moment Gary passed away. As far as everyone who knew him was aware, he was his usual fun-loving self leading up to the tragedy. I don't know whether I would have felt better if he had left a note, but not having any clue at all is so frustrating. I have even felt angry with Gary for not providing us with any possible reasons.

"My ex-wife refuses to believe that there were no signs. She just believes that I was failing in my duty as a father to pick up on whatever it was that was troubling Gary. It doesn't matter how much I retrace those last few days and weeks in my mind, there is nothing at all that was unusual about his behaviour. The blame doesn't help anyone. When something so awful happens, friends, family and acquaintances need to support each other, but I suppose that it is natural to want to blame someone when a life has ended so unnaturally.

"In the first year, I was living in a state of numbness, oblivious to everything around me, because all I could focus on was my desperate and overwhelming need to be with Gary. I had a sense of being all alone in this battle. In some ways, I found the years that followed much harder. The first year passed in a blur, but when the fog began to lift and the realisation of what had happened truly hit me, it was almost too much to bear. Carrying on with my own life knowing that my only son had ended his seemed like an impossible task. I felt that there was no hope of ever enjoying anything in my life again. I felt as though I was just biding my time until the end of my life so that I could be with Gary again. I still have days when I feel like that and days when it feels as though no time has passed at all since that dreadful day.

"My parents had very old-fashioned values, where the man was expected to be strong and not display any emotion. Being brought up in such a household obviously had an effect on me and, as a result, I have never felt entirely comfortable talking about my feelings, even though it is something that I desperately need to do to help me cope with the pain.

"I used to wonder whether my inability to open up emotionally had prolonged the pain, but having finally had the opportunity to communicate with other parents who have suffered the loss of a child to suicide, I realise that this is not the case. Even those parents who have spoken openly about their loss from the beginning, parents who are many years further on in the grieving process, all say the same thing; that the pain doesn't necessarily subside with time.

"Speaking about my grief has not reduced the pain, but it has offered some modicum of comfort in knowing that there are others who are travelling with me on the same road; a road peppered with deep potholes and obstacles. When one of us falls, there is someone else there to pick us up and help us continue, because they understand what you are going through. It is far better than travelling the road alone."

When you are several years along the grieving path, it becomes more difficult to know how to conduct yourself when the bad moments strike and you are in the company of those who have difficulty relating to your feelings. If you become upset or start crying, you may find yourself blaming your emotional state on anything other than the loss of your child. If you do admit the truth, you fear that others may believe that they are crocodile tears used to gain attention by blaming an "old tragedy."

Naturally, many of these fears could be products of our own minds and lack of faith in human nature, but in my experience and that of so many other bereaved parents to whom I have spoken, these fears have proved to be true in some, but not all, cases. Perhaps it's not just people's disbelief that you could still be so deeply affected by something that happened years ago, but rather their own discomfort and inability to handle such emotional breakdowns.

Norma lost her 23-year-old son Dominic to a deliberate drugs' overdose in December 2000. At the time that it occurred, Norma feels that she was in such a state of shock that she did not really grieve in the way that most people expected her to. She carried on going to work and performing everyday functions in a trance-like fashion, something to which I can totally relate. I believe it is the mind and body's way of coping with what has happened to enable you to continue living. That does not mean that you never grieve, or breakdown or feel that you can't carry on, but in public you are able to shut off your emotions and communicate with others without dissolving into a sobbing heap every two minutes. That can lead people to believe that you are "bearing up well" and not suffering too much. Others may view you as strong, hard or even without feeling.

At some point, the shock subsides and you are faced with reality, but this can occur many years after the tragedy. Any sudden outpouring of grief can appear totally unexpected to those who have never witnessed it before. Even if you did grieve outwardly in the beginning, some may still find it difficult to comprehend how you can still suffer just as deeply when you have become used to living for so long without the presence of your child in your life.

Norma said, "I've recently been having problems controlling the grief in 'inappropriate' moments; and what a stupid word to use in this context, as how the hell do you define a moment as 'inappropriate' when you are grieving for your lost child? I seem to have been transported back to emotions somehow similar in their unexpectedness to how they were in the early days and just as overwhelming in their strength, so much so that I have ended up in great floods of tears, missing Dominic so much that I don't know what to do.

"Because these moments are so unexpected and not always related to any particular trigger, such as something I have seen or heard, it is almost impossible to prevent the release of my emotions. I remember one particularly embarrassing time when my partner Tim and I were lunching in a rather upmarket restaurant with his parents. For no particular reason, or at least not one of which I was consciously aware, I had a flashback of Dominic lying in his coffin. The emotion welled up with such force that I could not prevent myself from bursting into tears in front of everyone. I apologised and excused myself to go to the bathroom, but as I walked off I heard Tim's mother say, "Is it the menopause?"

"The thought never occurs to anyone these days that I might possibly be having a 'Dominic moment', however unfeasible that may seem to them after this length of time. Sometimes I can prepare myself, such as occasions when I know that I am going to encounter something that will remind me of Dominic, or times spent with him. I can try and shut down emotionally in advance (although this doesn't always work), but the worst times are those when the grief hits me without warning.

"I just live my life now expecting the unexpected in terms of my grief. I have toughened up with regard to other people's responses. If they are not very tolerant towards my grief, then I regard that as their problem, not mine.

"It's hard enough trying to live with the loss of my son to suicide, let alone have to worry about hiding my feelings from others and considering their discomfort before my own. Does that sound selfish? Maybe it does, but I have spent too many years being unselfish and it has not helped the grieving process at all.

"My advice to anyone going through the same thing is to give in to your grief; cry when you want to cry, shut yourself away when you want to be alone and never allow other people to tell you how you should feel and when. Unless they too have lost a child to suicide, then they cannot possibly be in a position to hand you advice. They only want you to stop grieving to make them feel better, but you cannot be responsible for how they feel or for their ignorance. Think of yourself. Sod everyone else."

As all the above experiences show, you simply learn to live with the grief, but the pain that you feel during the rough times does not necessarily diminish in intensity. In fact, as you will have read above, the pain can increase once the initial shock has worn off.

There will always be definite periods in every year ahead when you know that you will be grieving heavily; periods such as birthdays, the anniversary of the tragedy, Mother's Day, Christmas and other occasions that you associate with your son, daughter, brother, sister, grandchild and so on. The other times can strike without warning.

There is a fear of alienating people at times when you need them most, but it can also be a good filtering process; determining your true friends from fairweather acquaintances. True friends will allow you to be yourself and will stick by your side during the tough times. They will allow you to cry on their shoulder and just be there for you, even though they cannot remove your pain.

Over the years, I have learned who my true friends are and have distanced myself from those who have been unsupportive or indifferent to my pain. There are those to whom I can comfortably talk about Kristian and those with whom I avoid the subject entirely. I am civil and friendly to the latter, but I have no interest in spending extended periods of time with them, except in a purely superficial capacity. Strangely, it is often these friends who come to me with their problems and, despite listening to their woes and offering comfort and advice when necessary, they are the first to make themselves conveniently unavailable if I am going through an emotionally trying period. I am sure that most readers will have encountered the "Me-me-me" person in their lives at some point.

I do feel a need to educate those who have limited understanding of suicide and the grief that follows, in the hope that they never have to discover firsthand how debilitating that grief can be, even years after the event. Some are more open to learning than others, but it is those with closed minds who often end up finding out the hard way, the ones who then need the support that they were unable to provide when they were not the victims.

Finally, I would like to conclude this chapter with a few words from my daughter Lauren, aged 9 at the time of writing:

"I do not remember the day that my brother died, because Mummy removed me from the scene and took me across to our neighbour Kerry's house, so to me it was probably like any other day. Because Mummy and Daddy did not want to upset me, they tried to make life as normal as possible for me. People don't remember "normal"; they are more likely to remember "unusual", so I do not have any striking memories about the ordinary days.

"There are, however, memories of that time that are very clear, but I think that is because they were extraordinary.

"What I do remember is going to the Chapel of Rest to see Kristian with Mummy and my sister Anneliese. I did not understand that Kristian had died, so when I saw him in his coffin, I remember asking, "Why is Kristian asleep in a big box?" I thought he was trying out a new type of bed or something. I then remember trying to climb up into the box with him, so that he could cuddle me like he always did when he came 'round to see us.

"I also remember the first time that Mummy told me why Kristian had died. We were in the kitchen and she was taking the medicine box out of a high cupboard. When I asked her why it was up so high, she told me that it was for safety reasons because the box contained a lot of medicines that would be poisonous to me if I swallowed them by mistake, thinking they were sweets. She then explained that Kristian died because he was very silly and took some poison. Many times after that, I would say, "Kristian was very silly because he took some poison."

"The only memories that I have of Kristian are happy ones. I remember pushing my niece Kayla in her pushchair, I remember the cuddles and I remember Kristian's laugh. He was always so cheerful and kind.

"When I understood that Kristian wasn't coming back, I began to cry and miss him. I also began seeing him walk past and standing at the end of my bed, but I was never afraid. I used to look up at the stars and imagine him there; free and happy.

"One day, I asked Mummy to explain exactly what had happened to Kristian. I can't remember my reaction when she told me, although I know that I accepted it. I'm sad he was only in my life for three years and that he couldn't find any other way at the time to solve his problems.

"I often ask myself why he did it near my birthday and Kayla's birthday, but I don't believe that thought even occurred to him.

"I sense him walking with me on my left-hand side and I am happy that he is not suffering anymore and although I know that he is with us in spirit, I still miss being able to hug him. Mummy said he loved his hugs and so do I.

"I love you Kristian."

Chapter Twenty-Three

Inspirational Thoughts

In order to develop spiritually, you need to stop thinking about your own needs and desires and concentrate on what you can do to help humanity.

Jan Andersen

This chapter contains a random selection of inspirational quotations, poems and articles that have touched me in one way or another. I hope that they will also comfort others in some way, however small.

When Someone Takes His Own Life

by Dr Norman Vincent Peale
31 May 1898 – 24 December 1993

In many ways, this seems the most tragic form of death. Certainly it can entail more shock and grief for those who are left behind than any other. And often the stigma of suicide is what rests most heavily on those left behind; and my heart goes out to those who are left behind, because I know that they suffer terribly. Children in particular are left under a cloud of differentness all the more terrifying because it can never be fully explained or lifted. The immediate family of the victim is left wide open to tidal waves of guilt. "What did I fail to do that I should have done? What did I do that was wrong?"
 To such grieving persons I can only say, "Lift up your heads and your hearts. Surely you did your best. And surely the loved one who is gone did his best, for as long as he could.

Remember now that his battles and torments are over. Do not judge him and do not presume to fathom the mind of God where one of His children is concerned."

A few years ago, when a young man died by his own hand, a service for him was conducted by his pastor, the Reverend Weston Stevens. What he said that day expresses far more eloquently than I can, the message that I'm trying to convey. Here are some of his words:

"Our friend died on his own battlefield. He was killed in action fighting a civil war. He fought against adversaries that were as real to him as his casket is real to us. They were powerful adversaries. They took toll of his energies and endurance. They exhausted the last vestiges of his courage and his strength. At last these adversaries overwhelmed him. And it appeared that he had lost the war.

"But did he?

"I see a host of victories that he has won! For one thing, he has won our admiration, because even if he lost the war, we give him credit for his bravery on the battlefield. And we give him credit for the courage and pride and hope that he used as his weapons as long as he could.

"We shall remember not his death, but his daily victories gained through his kindness and thoughtfulness, through his love for family and friends, for animals and books and music, for all things beautiful, lovely and honourable.

"We shall remember not his last day of defeat, but we shall remember the many days that he was victorious over overwhelming odds. We shall remember not the years we thought he had left, but the intensity with which he lived the years that he had. Only God knows what this child of His suffered in the silent skirmishes that took place in his soul. But our consolation is that God does know, and understands."

Norman Vincent Peale is regarded by some as one of the greatest spiritual leaders of the 20th century. Ordained in the Methodist Episcopal Church in 1922, Peale served as pastor at a succession of churches before changing his affiliation to the Dutch Reformed Church so that he could become pastor of the Marble Collegiate Church in New York City (1932–84). Peale's simple, optimistic and dynamic sermons, which were regularly broadcast on radio and later on television, brought Peale increasing fame. Peale was also the best-selling author of books such as The Power of Positive Thought (1952), The Art of Living (1937), Confident Living (1948) and This Incredible Century (1991).

"Each person comes into this world with a specific destiny; he has something to fulfil, some message has to be delivered, some work has to be completed. You are not here accidentally - you are here meaningfully. There is a purpose behind you. The whole intends to do something through you."

Osho

"Every person, all the events of your life are there because you have drawn them there. What you choose to do with them is up to you."

Richard Bach

A Day, a Week, a Lifetime

When I wake up in the morning,
I ask myself,
How will I get through this day
Without You?

As I dress and prepare to start my day,
I wonder,
How will I go on
Without You?

As the day slowly slips away,
I remember how you made me laugh
And I smile
Without You.

At the end of the day,
As I prepare to close my eyes,
I know in my heart
I couldn't have gotten through the day
Without You.

Author Unknown

"Just like a sunbeam can't separate itself from the sun, and a wave can't separate itself from the ocean, we can't separate ourselves from one another. We are all part of a vast sea of love, one indivisible divine mind."
Marianne Williamson

Dear Mum and Dad,

I know this is a rough time for you. So I will be as gentle as I can be.

First of all, thank you for so many tears, particularly those shared with another that you love. They are a gift to me, a precious tribute to your investment in me.

As you do your mourning, do it at your pace only. Don't let anybody suggest that you do your grief work on their timetable. Do whatever it takes to face directly the reality of what has happened, even though you may need to pause frequently and yearn for my return. Do this with courage and my blessings. Know that sometimes inertia is the only movement possible.

Give your best to keeping a balance between remembering me and renewing your commitments to life. It's ok with me if you go through minutes, hours and even days not thinking about me. I know that you'll never forget. Loosening me and grabbing hold of a new meaning is a delicate art. I'm not sure if one comes before the other or not; maybe it's a combination.

Be with people who accept you as you are. Mention my name out loud and if they don't make a hasty retreat, they're probably excellent candidates for friendship.

If, by a remote possibility, you think that there is anything that you could have done for me and didn't, I forgive you, as my Lord does. Resentment does not abide here, only love.

You know how people sometimes ask you how many children you have? Well, I'm still yours and you are still my parents. Always acknowledge that with tenderness, unless to do so would fall on insensitive ears or would be painful to you. I know how you feel inside. To be included as your child honours me.

Read, even though your tears anoint the page. There is an immense library here and I have a card. In Henri Nowens' "Out of Solitude", he writes, "The friend who can be silent with us in a moment of despair and confusion, who can stay with us in an hour of grief and bereavement, who can tolerate not healing and face with us the reality of our powerlessness, that is a friend who cares."

Mum and Dad, I don't know where you are spiritually now, but rest assured that our God is not gone. The still small voice you hear in your heart is His voice. The warmth that sometimes enfolds you is Him. The tears that tremble just beneath your heartbeat are Him. He is in you, as I am.

I want you both to know that I am ok. I have sent you messages to ease your pain; they come in the form of flowers that bloom out of season, birds singing, voices and visions and sometimes through your friends and even strangers who volunteer as angels. Stay open but don't expect the overly dramatic. You will get what you need and it may be simply an internal peace. You are not crazy. You have been comforted.

Please seek out people bereaved longer than you. They are tellers of truth and, if they have done their work, are an inspiration and a beacon of hope.

One more wisdom before I close. There are still funny happenings in our world. It delights me to no end when I hear your spontaneous, uncontrolled laughter. That, too, will come in due time.

Today, I light a candle for you. Joined with your candle, let their light shine above the darkness.

Affectionately,
Your Angel child.
PS: I'll see you later!

Author Unknown

Keep Your Fork

There was a woman who had been diagnosed with a terminal illness and had been given three months to live.

So, as she was getting her things "in order", she contacted her pastor and asked him to come to her house to discuss certain aspects of her final wishes.

She told him which songs she wanted sung at the service, what scriptures she would like read and in what outfit she would like to be buried.

The woman also requested to be buried with her favourite book. Everything was in order and the pastor was preparing to leave when the woman suddenly remembered something very important to her.

"There's one more thing," she said excitedly.

"What's that?" asked the pastor.

"This is very important," the woman continued. "I want to be buried with a fork in my right hand."

The pastor stood looking at the woman, not knowing quite what to say.

"That surprises you, doesn't it?" the woman asked.

"Well, to be honest, I'm puzzled by the request," said the pastor.

The woman explained. "In all my years of attending church socials and potluck dinners, I always remember that when the dishes of the main course were being cleared, someone would inevitably lean over and say, 'Keep your fork.' It was my favorite part because I knew that something better was coming...like velvety chocolate cake or deep-dish apple pie. Something wonderful and with substance!"

"So, I just want people to see me there in the casket with a fork in my hand and I want them to wonder, 'What's with the fork?'

Then, I want you to tell them: 'Keep your fork....The best is yet to come.'"

The pastor's eyes welled up with tears of joy as he hugged the woman goodbye.

He knew this would be one of the last times he would see her before her death. But he also knew that the woman had a better grasp of heaven than he did.

She KNEW that something better was coming. At the funeral people were walking by the woman's casket and they saw the pretty dress she was wearing and her favorite book and the fork placed in her right hand.

Over and over, the pastor heard the question, "What's with the fork?"

And over and over he smiled.

During his message, the pastor told the people of the conversation he had with the woman shortly before she died.

He also told them about the fork and about what it symbolised to her. The pastor told the people how he could not stop thinking about the fork and told them that they probably would not be able to stop thinking about it either.

He was right.

So the next time you reach down for your fork, let it remind you, oh so gently, that the best is yet to come.

Author Unknown

"The intent with which you give everything out, whether in thought, word or deed, is recorded and returns to you in one way or another."

Jan Andersen

Chapter Twenty-Four

Recommended Books and Resources

Good advice is always certain to be ignored, but that's no reason not to give it.

Agatha Christie

    At the time of going to print, all the resources listed on this page are current and valid. This does not mean, however, that at some point the details will not change, or the listed organisations discontinued.

    Additionally, I make no representation whatsoever regarding the content of any other resources that you may access as a result of following the suggestions and links in this book. Please understand that any other website or organisation you visit or contact, or any other book that you read as a result of a recommendation in this book, is independent from this book and its author. I have no control over the content on any website other than my own.

    Although I have tried to include resources that I feel may be of use to readers, it does not mean that I am responsible for monitoring the conduct of any such resources. Therefore, a recommendation does not mean that I endorse or accept any responsibility for the content or conduct of the resources listed.

    There are many wonderful websites and support groups available - and new ones being established all the time - so this is just a handful.

Grief Resources and Support

General List of Support Resources
http://childsuicide.org/GriefResources.html
http://childsuicide.org/SurvivorLinks.html

The Compassionate Friends
http://www.tcf.org.uk/ (UK)
http://www.compassionatefriends.org/ (US)
http://www.thecompassionatefriends.org.au/TCFAustralia.htm (Australia)
http://www.tcf.org.uk/tcflinks.html (TCF links around the world)

The Compassionate Friends (TCF) is an organisation of bereaved parents and their families offering understanding, support and encouragement to others after the death of a child or children. They also offer support, advice and information to other relatives, friends and professionals who are helping the family.

Adult Sibling Grief
http://www.adultsiblinggrief.com/

This site is dedicated to the formation of a support community for those who have suffered the devastating loss of an adult sibling.

KIDSAID
http://kidsaid.com/

KIDSAID is a safe place for kids to share and to help each other deal with grief about any of their losses. It's a place to share and deal with feelings, to show artwork and stories, to talk about pets and to meet with one's peers.

The Drowning Support Network
http://health.groups.yahoo.com/group/DrowningSupportNetwork/

The Drowning Support Network is a peer grief support group for people who have lost loved ones in drownings or other aquatic accidents, including when no physical remains have been recovered, or the recovery process has been lengthy and difficult.

Books

All of the books listed below are also available at Amazon and in most good book stores.

Karma and Reincarnation: The Key to Spiritual Evolution and Enlightenment by Hiroshi Motoyama
ISBN: 978-0749919160

Children Who Have Lived Before by Trutz Hardo
ISBN: 978-0852073520

Angels in My Hair by Lorna Byrne
ISBN: 978-0099551461

How to Hear Your Angels by Doreen Virtue
ISBN: 978-1401915414

Healing with the Angels by Doreen Virtue
ISBN: 978-1561706402

Angel Medicine by Doreen Virtue
ISBN: 978-1401902353

Suicide Survivor Support

SMHAI – Parents
http://health.groups.yahoo.com/group/SMHAI-Parents/

A wonderful online support group from the Suicide and Mental Health Association International for parents who have lost a child to suicide. Highly recommended.

SMHAI – Families and Friends
http://health.groups.yahoo.com/group/SMHAI-FF/

A support group from the Suicide and Mental Health Association International for friends and family members of suicide victims.

Child Suicide
http://www.childsuicide.org

The author's website site for anyone who has experienced the tragedy of child suicide. Link up with other parents, grandparents, brothers and sisters who have suffered the indescribable loss of a loved one to suicide. The site also offers support to anyone who is suffering from depression or experiencing suicidal thoughts.

Memory Tree of Lights
http://www.memorytrees.org/index.html

The "Memory Tree of Lights" is a ministry that focuses on the Christmas holiday season and provides comfort, education, intervention and hope to people whose lives have been impacted by the loss of someone to suicide and who are overwhelmed by this loss during the Christmas season.

Mental Health

YoungMinds
http://www.youngminds.org.uk/

YoungMinds is the UK's leading charity committed to improving the emotional well being and mental health of children and young people and empowering their parents and carers. Parents' Helpline on 0808 802 5544.

Befrienders Worldwide
http://www.befrienders.org/

Befrienders listen to people who are lonely, despairing or considering suicide. They don't judge them and don't tell them what to do. They listen. That may not sound much, but it can make the difference between life and death.

Depression Alliance works to relieve and to prevent this treatable condition by providing information and support services to those who are affected by it.

Mental Health Foundation (UK)
http://www.mentalhealth.org.uk

National Institute of Mental Health (US)
http://www.nimh.nih.gov

Maytree – A sanctuary for the suicidal
http://www.maytree.org.uk

Maytree offers a short stay in a safe residential setting in London where you can talk, reflect and rest - and restore hope.; a place where you will be heard, respected and accepted, without judgement and in confidence.

Anti-Bullying

Kidscape
http://www.kidscape.org.uk/

The UK charity committed to keeping children safe from bullying and abuse. £1 from every copy sold of this book will be donated to Kidscape.

Beat Bullying
http://www.beatbullying.org

Empowers young people to lead anti-bullying campaigns in their schools and local communities and assists and supports young people who are being bullied.

Bully Police USA
http://www.bullypolice.org/

Bully Police USA posts current anti bullying laws, research, news and support information for parents and/or anti bullying activists who are dealing with bullying in schools.

Bullying. No Way!
http://www.bullyingnoway.com.au/

Created by Australia's educational communities, this website aims to provide a nationwide resource of State and Territory approaches to minimising bullying, harassment and violence in schools.

Conclusion

In the immediate aftermath of a suicide or the loss of a child in any way, those left behind cannot see further than the next hour, let alone the next day, month or year. This is how I felt.

So, where am I today? What difference does 9 years make in the life of a bereaved parent? The difference is not in the way I feel, but in the progress that has been made in terms of channelling the grief into something positive. With just one word, sight or sound, I can be transported into the depths of sorrow, guilt and excruciating emotional torture. In most of my interactions with other people, I still wear "the mask" and it is only with those who are closest to me in the spiritual and emotional sense with whom I feel comfortable removing this mask. However, the grief has also enabled me to write this book, to establish and maintain the child suicide website and to offer support to other bereaved families and young people suffering from depression or suicidal thoughts.

I have not changed as a person. I have just become more aware. I still hate conflict, war, cruelty, prejudice and greed. I do not judge people based on image, race, social status or personal circumstances; actions, compassion and altruism speak greater volumes. I dislike crowds even more than I did before Kristian's suicide, because the more sensitive I have become, the more difficult I have found it to process the diverse lower-vibrating energies emanating from egos within a crowd. For this reason, I try to distance myself from these energies as far as possible and choose to surround myself with positive people, even though I accept that everyone comes into our lives for a reason, a season or a lifetime for a learning exchange.

My grief has not changed with time, but time has enabled me to accept this grief as a permanent part of my remaining life.

My Brother Kristian

An acrostic poem

©September 2009, Lauren Erica Baker, aged 9

Kristian, I feel your spiritual embrace,

Remembering your heart of gold and smiling face.

I sometimes lie in bed and cry,

Sobbing to myself, "Why Kristian why?"

Then I realise that you are still there;

Inside my heart there is a place for you, which helps me to care and share

And helps me to forgive and show compassion like you.

Never stop loving me and we will be one, not two!

A Million Miles Away

©*Lauren Erica, 9 November 2011, Age 11*

A million miles away,
Through another day,
We are far apart,
But close in our heart.

The tears that I shed,
Are of love, not of dread;
Although you hated your existence,
You are still living to me, despite your distance.

You are my brother;
You can't be replaced by another.
You are unique - can't be sold,
You are special, no matter what you were told.

People seem to not care,
They just stop and stare,
But inside they feel my pain
And secretly want to pull the plug for it to drain.

They don't know what to say,
Apart from "Are you ok?"
No words seem quite right,
To acknowledge our plight.

You are my other half,
You are my father; I am the calf.
Without you here my heart is incomplete,
But I know you live inside me - from my head to my feet.

I have written this poem in a variety of views from different people in my family. People grieve differently and have individual views and ultimately you can't tell someone how they are feeling. This poem is just from my perspective of how I think people feel. Some try to block the pain out, but when people say the right words, the plug is pulled. Some try to act tough, but inside they have a heavy scar of pain. Some just need a friend's shoulder to cry on and that's when you realise how much the people around you love and care for you. No matter how you deal with grieving, the pain will never stop. But if you look at your experience with the right attitude, you can turn your grief into something on the other side of the leaf. My mum has written a book about my brother and I have written this poem. Together we can help reduce the amount of suicide by using our experiences to show people the damage and pain it will cause. We can't tell people what they can and can't do, but we can still say that at least we tried.

Lauren Erica

The White Dove Project

http://whitedoveproject.com
http://www.childsuicide.org/whitedoveproject.html

The White Dove Project was created to convey the stories of a group of young people in spirit, in their own words, channelled via my dear friend Angela Jane Grace. Each carries a message reaching out to anyone in any kind of emotional pain, but especially to young people who have thought that suicide might be their only option.

The website is one of hope embedded in the words of young people who speak through a mediumship connection from the other side. Most ended their lives through suicide. They give their words in a series of books and messages with the following purpose: To educate, inspire and empower and to breathe the oxygen of love into the flame of hope that burns within everyone.

These are the suicide notes never written and the words never spoken whilst these children were alive. They are given in the hope that they bring some comfort and understanding to the bereaved, awareness to bring suicide out of the shadows of society's taboos and hope to those who feel they have none and believe no one understands.

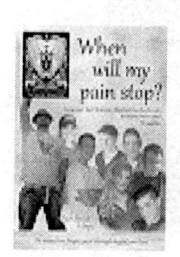

On 1 November 2011, to coincide with the publication of the second version of Chasing Death, the first book from the project, "When Will My Pain Stop" was also published. In the book, young people who took their own lives share their stories from the other side.

In Remembrance of Kristian Mikhail Andersen, my "special little boy"

22 March 1982 – 1 November 2002

With us always in our hearts, minds and in spirit

He had a heart of gold